ISBN 978-1-332-12707-8
PIBN 10288330

1 MONTH OF
FREE
READING

at

www.ForgottenBooks.com

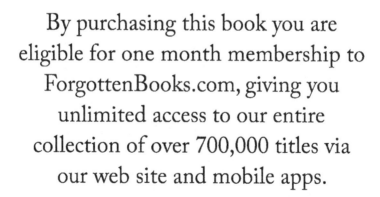

By purchasing this book you are eligible for one month membership to ForgottenBooks.com, giving you unlimited access to our entire collection of over 700,000 titles via our web site and mobile apps.

To claim your free month visit:
www.forgottenbooks.com/free288330

Similar Books Are Available from
www.forgottenbooks.com

"They have done for me at last."—*Page* 261.

FARRAGUT

AND OTHER

GREAT COMMANDERS

A Series of Naval Biographies

BY

W. H. DAVENPORT ADAMS

AUTHOR OF "WASHINGTON AND OTHER GREAT COMMANDERS," "FAMOUS SHIPS
OF THE BRITISH NAVY," "WELLINGTON'S VICTORIES," ETC.

GEORGE ROUTLEDGE AND SONS
LONDON: BROADWAY, LUDGATE HILL
NEW YORK: 9 LAFAYETTE PLACE

CONTENTS.

698

GREAT COMMANDERS.

SIR FRANCIS DRAKE.

A.D. 1541—1596.

I.

To omit from a record of Eminent Sailors the story of Sir Francis Drake would be as grievous an error as to omit from the play of Hamlet the moody prince himself; yet we feel some difficulty in re-telling a story that has been so often told, and told by such competent tellers.

There has ever been a wonderful consensus of opinion concerning Drake. The main lineaments of his character were so bold that it was impossible to mistake them; just as the principal actions of his life were of such high importance that it is impossible to over-estimate them. Hence, from Stow and Fuller to Froude and J. R. Green, our historians have described him in almost exactly similar terms.

This is what Thomas Fuller says, in his customary quaint fashion :—*

"If any should be desirous to know something," he says, "of Sir Francis Drake's person, he was of stature low, but set and strong grown. A very religious man towards God and His

* FULLER, *Worthies of England*, art. *Devon.*

houses, generally sparing the churches wherever he came; chaste in his life, just in his dealings, true of his word, merciful to those that were under him, and hating nothing so much as idleness; in matters (especially) of moment he was never wont to rely on other men's care, how trusty or skilful soever they might seem to be, but always contemning danger and refusing no toyl; he was wont himself to be one (who ever was a second) at every time, where danger, skill, or industry was to be employed."

This is what John Stow says :—

" He was more skilful in all points of navigation than any that ever was before his time, in his time, or since his death ; he was also of a perfect memory, great observation, eloquent by nature, skilful in artillery, expert and apt to let blood, and give physic unto his people, according to the climate; he was low of stature, of strong limbs, broad-breasted, round-headed, brown hair, full bearded, his eyes round, large, and clear, well-favoured, fair, and of a cheerful countenance. His name was a terror to the French, Spaniard, Portugal, and Indians; many princes of Italy, Germany, and others, as well enemies as fiends, in his lifetime desired his picture. He was the second that ever went through the Straits of Magellan, and the first that ever went round about the world. He was lawfully married unto two wives, both young; yet he himself, and ten of his brethren, died without issue. He made his younger brother, Thomas, his heir, who was with him in most and chiefest of his employments. In brief, he was as famous in Europe and America as Tamerlane [surely an unlucky comparison!] in Asia and Africa.

" In his imperfections he was $\begin{cases} \text{Ambitious for honour.} \\ \text{Inconstant in amity.} \\ \text{Greatly affected to popularity."} \end{cases}$

Of this man, who played so large a part in the struggle

between England and Spain for the sovereignty of the ocean, Mr. Froude also draws a portrait as he was in the prime of his strength :—

" Of middle height, with crisp brown hair, a broad, high forehead; grey, steady eyes, unusually long; small ears, tight to the head; the mouth and chin slightly concealed by the moustache and beard, but hard, inflexible, and fierce. His dress, as he appears in his portrait, is a loose, dark seaman's shirt, belted at the waist. About his neck is a plaited cord, with a ring attached to it, in which, as if the attitude was familiar, one of his fingers is slung, displaying a small, delicate, but long and sinewy hand. When at sea, he wore a scarlet cap with a gold band, and was exacting in the respect with which he required to be treated by his crew."

Francis Drake was born near Tavistock, in Devonshire, in 1541. His father, Edmund Drake, was a tenant of the House of Bedford, and by marriage was connected with those famous seamen, the Hawkinses of Plymouth. That he was esteemed by the Russells, we infer from the fact that Francis was godson of the second Earl, and named after him. Embracing the Protestant doctrine, Edmund Drake fell into trouble under the Six Articles Act, was forced to fly from his Devonshire home, and found an asylum at Chatham, where he lived for awhile, it is said, in the hull of a stranded ship. On the accession of Edward VI., he began to preach the new creed to the sailors of the King's fleet, and afterwards, taking orders, was made vicar of Upnor, on the Medway.

Young Drake's early years were spent in an atmosphere that smacked of the sea, and while yet a boy he was apprenticed in a Channel coaster. Being " painful and diligent," he so won upon his master's affection and esteem, that at his death he bequeathed to him the vessel which constituted his sole fortune. He was then about twenty-three. At this time,

John Hawkins, a man of bold and enterprising character, who had previously made two voyages to the Spanish Main in connection with the slave trade—not then stamped with the infamy that afterwards was so justly attached to it—undertook a third expedition, and persuaded Drake to join him in it. For this purpose he sold his vessel, and accompanied by some of his Kentish friends, repaired to Plymouth.

The little squadron collected by Hawkins consisted of one large ship of 700 tons, the *Jesus of Lubeck*, lent to him by the Queen, in which was hoisted his own flag; the *Minion*, Captain John Hampton; the *William and John*, Captain Thomas Bolton; and the *Judith*, Captain Francis Drake.

They sailed from Plymouth on the 2nd of October, 1567; and reaching the Cape de Verde, landed a body of 150 men in the hope of securing a supply of unfortunate negroes. They obtained but few, however, and those few at heavy cost; for many of the kidnappers were wounded by the poisoned arms of the natives; and, two days afterwards, died of their wounds. The poison seems to have produced a kind of tetanus or lock-jaw. Cruising along the Guinea coast, they succeeded, at a further cost of life, in obtaining about 200 negroes in all, after which they made for St. George da Mina. There a negro chief came to solicit their aid against the neighbouring potentate, offering them in reward all the negroes that should be taken. Hawkins was tempted by the prospect of so much booty, and sent a contingent of 150 men, who assaulted a palisaded town or village of some 8,000 inhabitants, but met with so stout an opposition that they were compelled to solicit additional support. " Whereupon," says Hawkins, " considering that the good success of this enterprise might highly further the commodity of our voyage, I went myself; and with the help of the king of our side, assaulted the town both by land and sea." After a hard struggle it was set on fire, and the inhabitants fled in dismay, leaving 250 men, women, and children in Hawkins's hands, besides 600 whom his negro ally had captured, but, when the victory was won, refused to give up in fulfilment of his promise.

Lingering no more upon the African coast, Hawkins and his comrades stretched away to Dominica, and stopping at various points on its coast, proceeded to exchange their negroes for gold and silver. In voyaging towards Florida the little squadron was buffeted by a succession of gales, and put into the harbour of San Juan d'Ulloa. Thence Hawkins sent a message to the Viceroy of Mexico, to the effect that stress of weather had driven him into that port, that he was in want of provisions, and that his ships needed repair; and that as Englishmen and friends of Spain he and his comrades desired permission to purchase what they wanted. On the morrow they saw in the offing thirteen great ships of Spain; and Hawkins immediately apprised their admiral that he would not suffer them to enter the harbour until conditions of peace had been decided upon between them—a message of sublime audacity when sent by the captain of five small weather-beaten craft to the commander of a noble fleet.

" And here," says Hawkins, " I begun to bewail that which after followed, for now, said I, I am in two dangers, and forced to receive the one of them. That was, either I must have kept out the fleet from entering the port, the which with God's help I was able to do, or else suffer them to enter in with their accustomed treason, which they never fail to execute, where they may have opportunity to compass it by any means; if I had kept them out, then had there been present shipwreck of all the fleet, which amounted in value to 6,000.000 pieces of eight, which was in value of our money £1,800,000, which I considered I was not able to answer, fearing the Queen's Majesty's indigna-tion in so weighty a matter. Thus with myself revolving these doubts, I thought rather better to avoid the jutt of the un-certainty than the certainty; the uncertain doubt, I account, was their treason, which by good policy I hoped might be prevented; and therefore, as choosing the least mischief, I proceeded to conditions."

These conditions were : assurance of security for himself, his people, and his ships; liberty to trade and purchase provisions; and temporary occupation of the island, with possession of the eleven pieces of brass cannon planted upon it. The Spaniards accepted them, and their fleet then passed into the harbour amidst mutual salutations ; after which the English ships ranged up on one side, and the Spanish on the other, "the captains and inferior persons of either part offering and showing great courtesy to one another, and promising great amity on all sides." The good-will and courtesy of the Spaniards were simply intended to lull the suspicion and disarm the vigilance of the English ; and, watching their opportunity, they suddenly attacked Hawkins's little fleet, capturing and burning three of the ships, making their crews prisoners, and compelling the smaller vessels to escape as best they might, without provisions, after a desperately heroic struggle.

One of the survivors* has left on record a plain, unvarnished description of the slaughter of St. Jean d'Ulloa. The *Minion*, he says, which was in a tolerable state of defence, "hauled away, and abode the first brunt of the three hundred men" on board the largest Spanish galleon. Then they (the Spaniards) sought to fall on board the *Jesus;* a cruel fight ensued, and many of the defenders were slain. The *Jesus* by this time had slipped her moorings, and came to the support of the *Minion;* the fight waxed hot, but the Spaniards had got possession of the island, and the English suffered heavily from the fire of the battery of brass cannon. So that before long the *Jesus* was

* Miles Philips, whose narrative is preserved in Hakluyt's Collection.

"very sore spoiled ;" and the discomfiture was complete when the Spaniards sent against her a couple of fire-ships. "How-beit the *Minion*, which had made her sails ready, shifted for herself, without consent of the general, captain, or master, so that very hardly our general could be received into the *Minion*, and those which the small boat was not able to receive were most cruelly slain by the Spaniards." None of Hawkins's ships escaped except the *Minion* and the *Judith*—Drake's vessel, which he seems to have handled with wariness and courage ; and all such of their crews as were not on board them "were inforced to abide the tyrannous cruelty of the Spaniards. For it is a certain truth, that whenever they had taken certain of our men ashore, they took and hung them up by the arms, upon high posts, until the blood burst out of their fingers' ends, of which men so used there is one Copston and certain others yet alive, who by the merciful providence of the Almighty were long since arrived here in England, carrying still about with them (and shall go to their graves) the marks and tokens of those their inhuman and more than barbarous cruel deal-ings."

In the contest the Spaniards lost three ships, two being sunk and one burnt.

Drake, in the *Judith*, made the best of his way back to England, much the poorer for his venture, and animated with an intense desire to be revenged upon the Spaniards. And with Drake where there was a will a way was sure to be found. By some means or other he contrived to equip two small ships, the *Dragon* and the *Swan*, with which he made a voyage to the West Indies in 1570; in the following year he under took a second voyage in the *Swan* alone. These were recon-noitring expeditions, "to gain such intelligence as might further him to get some amends for his loss." And having acquired full and satisfactory information of the condition of the Spanish settlements, he prepared for a longer voyage and a bolder enterprise with the prudence and forethought that distinguished him beyond all other Elizabethan navigators. No doubt one prominent thought in his mind was the acquisition of a great booty; but this was not his only, perhaps not his chief motive. Drake was at bottom a Puritan, and inspired by the true Puritanic hatred of the "superstitions" of Rome. He was also a thorough Englishman, and resolute to break down the monopoly of the seas which Spain arrogated to herself. Thus a twofold feeling, patriotic and religious, inspired him against the Spaniard, and led him to regard his projected buccaneering expedition in the light in which one of the early Crusaders regarded the march into the Holy Land, or the Swiss heroes their war with Charles the Bold of Burgundy. Moreover, English seamen had been done to death in Mexican prisons and on the Cadiz galleys; others had been burnt as heretics at Seville. Drake aspired to be their avenger. He would exact a terrible retribution for the innocent blood that had been treacherously shed. All these motives combined to strengthen the fibre of his purpose; and in them was enough of the heroic to elevate and dignify his character, and fit him for the work he was appointed to do.

On the 29th of May, 1572, he set sail for the Spanish Main, having under his command the *Pasha*, of 70 tons, and the *Swan*, of 25 tons, the latter bearing the flag of his brother John. On board these two small craft went some seventy-three men and boys, of whom the eldest man was fifty, and all the rest under thirty years of age, so divided that there were forty-seven in one ship and twenty-six in the other. Both vessels were "richly furnished with victuals and apparel for a whole year; and no less heedfully provided of all manner of munition, artillery, stuff, and tools that were requisite for such a man-of-war in such an attempt, but especially having three dainty pinnaces, taken asunder all in pieces, and stowed aboard, to be set up as occasion served."

Occasion so served at Port Pheasant, in the island of Santa Martha, where Drake rested his men from the 2nd to the 22nd of July. With his usual wariness, Drake fortified himself on a plot of three-quarters of an acre of ground, enclosing it within a stout palisade, and having only one gate to issue at, near the waterside, which every night was shut up, with a great tree drawn athwart it. He was joined here by an English barque of the Isle of Wight, belonging to Sir Edward Horsey, wherein James Rouse was captain and John Overy master. On the 22nd Drake took his three pinnaces and Captain Rouse's shallop, with fifty picked men, well armed, and set out for Nombre de Dios. There he met with some friendly natives, the Symerons, who had been ill-treated by the Spaniards, and guessing that they might in the future be of some assistance to him, he carried them to the mainland. His descent upon Nombre de Dios had all the advantage of a surprise; and it was not until he reached the market-place that he met with any opposition. The Spaniards encountered him there with a volley of shot, which he returned with a deadly flight of arrows that overcame their resolution. They fled precipitately; but Drake himself received a dangerous wound, which he was careful to conceal, knowing that if the general's heart stoops the men's will fail, and that if so bright an opportunity once setteth it seldom riseth again. Leaving twelve men in charge of the pinnaces, he divided his little company into two sections, which, parading through different parts of the town, with drums rolling and trumpets blaring, effectually terrified the enemy.

Drake then made his Spanish prisoners lead him to the governor's house, where, in a lower chamber, lay a glittering heap of bars of silver, each of which they computed to weigh between thirty-five and forty pounds ; and afterwards **he** strode away to the royal treasure-house, telling his followers that he had brought them to the mouth of the treasury of the world, and that if they did not gain it none but themselves were to be blamed.   He ordered his brother, with John Oxenham and eighteen men, to break it open, while **he** with the rest mounted guard in the market-place.   But **as** he stepped forward strength and sight and speech suddenly failed, and he fainted from loss of blood.   Great was the alarm of his men, who felt that their success and safety depended wholly on Drake's genius and courage.   They gave him a stimulating drink, bound up his wound with his scarf, and when he re-covered conveyed him, much against his will, to his pinnace. Several of his men were wounded, but only one, a trumpeter, was slain.   Many of them loaded themselves with booty before they left the place.   The wines in a Spanish ship which they found in the harbour they took along with them for the relief of their captain and their own enjoyment, and conveyed their prize to an island named for the nonce the "Island of Victuals."   There they sojourned two days to cure their wounded men, and refresh themselves in its prolific "gardens," which abounded in all sorts of roots, fruits, poultry, and " other fowls no less strange than delicate."   An officer from the gar-rison of Nombre de Dios paid them a visit, ostensibly out of wonder and curiosity, and to see the heroes of so incredible an enterprise, but really, it was believed, at the instigation of the governor.   He asked whether the commander was the same Captain Drake who had been on their coast the **two** preced-ing years, and whether their arrows were poisoned, and what cure might be found for the wounds they inflicted.

Yes, quoth Drake, he was the man they meant ; but it **was** no custom of his to poison arrows, and the wounds given by English weapons might be healed by ordinary remedies. As **for** himself, he wanted nothing more than some of that excellent commodity, gold and silver, which the country yielded, for himself and his company ; and, by the help of God, he was resolved to reap of the golden harvest which they got out of the earth, and then sent into Spain to trouble all the world.

To this bold answer the Spaniard replied : "If he might without offence put such a question, what then was the cause of their departure from the town at that time, when it contained above 360 tons of silver ready for the fleet, and much more gold in value resting in iron chests in the King's treasure. house ?"

But when Drake had explained the true cause of his reluctant retreat, he acknowledged that the Englishmen had no less reason in departing than courage in attempting.

Thus, with great freedom and courteous entertainment, besides such gifts from the captain as most contented him, he was dismissed after dinner to make report of what he had seen, protesting he had never been honoured so much of any in his life.

Returning to the Isle of Pines, Drake parted with Captain Rouse, who showed no disposition to pursue the adventure, and with his two ships and three pinnaces set sail for Cartagena. From information furnished by a prisoner, he learned that his presence on the coast was known and prepared for, and that an attack upon Cartagena had become an impossibility. His future enterprises, he saw, would depend mainly on the use he could make of his pinnaces, and as he had not seamen to man them if he kept up the complement of his two vessels, he resolved on destroying one of them. So desperate a project could not be carried out openly ; and therefore he instructed the carpenter of the *Swan*, in the middle of the second watch, to steal down into the hold, and bore three holes as near the keel as he could, taking precautions to deaden the sound of the inrushing water.

On the following morning, August 13th, Drake went out with his brother in his pinnace, fishing; and at the proper time said to him carelessly : "Why is your ship so deep in the water?" An alarm was raised, and one of the men hastening below, found himself waist-deep in water. Immediately he cried out that "the ship was sinking!" The pumps were set going; but as the depth of water increased instead of diminishing, the crew gladly accepted Drake's proposal that they should abandon their sinking craft, and go on board one of the pinnaces.

On the 15th Drake steered for the Sound of Darien in search of a sequestered cove where he might lay up his ship, and so delude the Spaniards into a belief that he had quitted the coast. He discovered what he wanted, landed his men, cleaned his vessels, and collected supplies of fresh provisions. Then, on the 5th of September, leaving his brother in charge of the ship and one of the pinnaces, with the other two pinnaces he cruised about, and made several prizes. In the middle of October he took the three pinnaces and anchored in sight of Cartagena, for he knew it would not be safe to land. On the 20th the Spaniards sent out a couple of frigates without any cargo in them, in the hope, it is supposed, that Drake would take and man them, and thus weaken his force by dividing it. But he was too wary, and contented himself with burning one and sinking the other, in sight of the full-manned frigates, which sailed out of the harbour only to sail back again. He then landed alone, in defiance of all the Spanish soldiers collected on the hillside or concealed within the woods—an act of daring which finds its sole excuse in the profound admiration it excited in the breasts both of his enemies and his followers.

On the 27th of November he returned to his ship, where he was apprised of the deaths of his brother John, and of a young man called Richard Allen, both of whom were killed in an attempt to board a Spanish frigate. In January, Drake's little company was smitten with a calculus, which carried off eight-and-twenty victims; but, nothing daunted, that resolute leader completed his arrangements for crossing the isthmus to Panama, and set out on Shrove Tuesday, February 3rd, with sixteen Englishmen and fifty Symerons. In eight days the little party arrived near the summit of a lofty hill, on the very crest of which flourished a great tree, commanding a view of the vast Pacific. One of the Symeron chiefs, taking our sea-captain by the hand, desired him to ascend some steps which had been fashioned in the trunk of "that goodly and great high tree," into an arbour constructed amidst its branches; and there he sat, and gazed with profound emotion on the shining waters that spread away on either hand to the farthest horizon. And, as he gazed, he solemnly besought God to give him life and leave once to sail an English ship upon them. As we know, to the prayers of men such as Drake Providence usually vouchsafes the desired answer. "From that time forward," says Camden, " his mind was pricked on continually night and day to perform his vow."

The incident is sufficiently picturesque; but it has escaped commemoration by our English poets, except by one of the minor order, Sir William Davenant, the author of "Goudibert," who has made "the History of Sir Francis Drake" the subject of a kind of opera, masque, or musical drama of no great merit. In the fourth scene or tableau, the hill and tree associated with the hero's first view of the Pacific are duly represented, and the following dialogue occurs between Drake and Pedro, the Symeron chief :—

> "*Drake.*   Is this that most renowned of Western trees,
>   On whose main-top
>   Thou gav'st me hope
>   To view the North and South Atlantic seas ?
>
> *Pedro.*   It is. Therefore, with speed,
>   Thither, my chief, proceed :
>   And when you, climbing, have attained the height,
>   Report will grow authentic, by your sight.
>
> *Drake.*   When from those lofty branches, I
>   The South Atlantic spy,
>   My vows shall higher fly,
>   Till they with highest heav'n prevail,
>   That, as I see it, I may on it sail.
>
> *Drake, jun.* No English keel hath yet that ocean plow'd.
>
> *Pedro.*   If prophecy from me may be allow'd,
>   Renownèd Drake, Heaven does decree
>   That happy enterprise to thee :
>   For thou of all the Britons art the first
>   That boldly durst
>   This Western World invade :
>   And as thou now art made
>   The first to whom that ocean will be shown,
>   So to thy isle thou first shalt make it known."

On approaching Panama, the little band of adventurers
sought concealment in a thick wood bordering on the road
from Panama to Nombre de Dios, while one of the Symerons,
disguised as a native of Panama, went out to inquire when one
of the *recoes*, or convoys of mules laden with treasure for
Europe, would pass that way. He ascertained that the
treasurer of Lima would start that very night with nine mules,
eight carrying gold and one jewels, and Drake immediately
took measures to intercept him. At a convenient point near
Vera Cruz he made his men lie down among the thick high
grass, half on one side of the road and half on the other, but
with the one party mounted in advance to insure that the
whole string of mules should be simultaneously attacked. In

about an hour the welcome sound of the mules' bells tinkled in the ears of the expectant adventurers, but unfortunately a varlet, heated with liquor, was so excited by the prospect of a great booty, that he rushed from his line before Drake's signal was given, and being seen by one of the Spaniards in the van of the convoy, enabled him to give the alarm. The mules were hastily sent back, and all through the country-side arose a call to arms.

In a position of so much danger, Drake judged the boldest course to be the safest; and instead of retreating, ordered his men to advance against the Spanish position. There was something in his dauntless demeanour which cowed the Spaniards. After a feeble resistance they retreated hastily into the city, with Drake's fighting-men at their heels. Thus one of the chief European settlements on the American coast fell into the hands of a small company of adventurers as swiftly as Jericho at the sound of Joshua's trumpet! Drake's prudence was not inferior to his daring; and he forbore to raise the inhabitants to resistance by any act of high-handed power. He behaved with courtesy and forbearance, exacted a moderate ransom, and then, utterly unopposed, began the return march to his ship, which he reached on the 23rd of February.

Continuing his predatory career, he captured between Rio Francisco and Nombre de Dios three recoes of 49 mules in all, carrying 300 lbs. weight of silver. The plunder was too heavy to be removed all at once, and a portion was hidden in holes and pools, where the Spaniards afterwards discovered it; with the rest Drake marched to the Rio Francisco (April 3rd). His pinnaces, however, were not there to meet him, but instead, he descried some Spanish shallops, well armed and equipped, which were evidently prepared to attack. Recognising the urgent necessity of reaching the pinnaces before the Spaniards, he drew upon his inventive resources, and ordered a raft to be swiftly made, upon which, with a biscuit-sack for sail, and a young sapling for rudder, accompanied by three volunteers, he boldly put to sea. For six hours he continued his laborious voyage, he and his companions sitting waist-deep in water, and at every rolling wave sinking to their armpits. Then, to his high delight, the pinnaces were seen approaching them ; but at dusk, not perceiving the water-logged raft, they altered their course, and ran with the wind to take shelter under a point of land. Drake immediately steered for the shore, and walking across the little promontory had the satisfaction of regaining his ships, in which he embarked at once for the Rio Francisco. It was then time to turn their faces homeward ; but first he rewarded the Symerons liberally for their faithful assistance, and to Pedro, the Symeron chief, presented a richly wrought scimitar. The gift so delighted Pedro that he pressed upon Drake in return five wedges of gold, which the politic sea-captain threw into the common stock, remarking, " It was only just that those who bore part of the charge with him in setting him to sea, should likewise enjoy their full proportion of the advantage at his return."

With a good wind Drake covered the distance between Cape Florida and the Scilly Isles in twenty-three days, and arrived in Plymouth on Sunday morning, the 9th of August, 1573. At the news of his return the congregation turned their backs on the preacher, as the congregations in some of the smuggling villages on the south coast were wont to do when a contraband cargo was " run " on a Sunday, and hastened to welcome the bold seaman. The welcome spread from town to town, and was taken up by Elizabeth and her court, for all England instinctively came to the conclusion that in Drake they had a man upon whom firm reliance might safely be put in the hour of the national need.

The interest of Drake's career necessarily centres in his

wonderful voyages, and over the five years that he spent in comparative inaction, from 1572 to 1577, the biographer may pass at a bound. That they were well utilised by Drake we have good evidence to show. It is clear that he worked his way into the confidence of the Queen and of many of the leading nobles, for in the last-named year he was able to organize an expedition—inconsiderable from our modern point of view, but quite a splendid fleet in the judgment of his contemporaries— to carry out his heart's special desire, the navigation of the great South Sea, and an attack upon the Spanish monopoly of the treasures of Peru. This expedition consisted of his own ship, the *Pelican*, of 120 tons ; the *Elizabeth*, 80 tons, Captain John Winter ; the *Marigold*, 30 tons, Captain John Thomas ; the *Swan*, a flyboat, 50 tons, Captain John Chester ; and the *Christopher*, a pinnace of 15 tons, Captain Thomas Clevon.

The *Pelican*, the largest vessel of the little squadron, was no larger than "the smallest class of our modern Channel schooners," but she was splendidly fitted up. Drake, like all the great Elizabethans, like Elizabeth herself, was fond of pomp and bravery ; they were congenial to his taste ; but he also knew their influence on the minds of men, and their value as the accompaniments and evidence of authority. He "did not omit," says Prince, "to make provision for ornament and delight ; carrying to this purpose with him expert musicians, rich furniture (all the vessels for his tables, yea, many belonging to the workroom, being of pure silver), with divers stores of all sorts of curious workmanship, whereby the civility and magnificence of his native country might, among all nations whither he should come, be the more admired."

Besides rich furniture and all sorts of curious workmanship, the *Pelican* carried twenty brass and iron guns, with others as ballast in her hold, heavy stores of cartridges, wild-fire, chain-shot, guns, pistols, bores, and other weapons in great abun-

dance. Her consorts were not less completely equipped. The
total complement of men on board the squadron was 164.
Such great preparations aroused the suspicions of the Spanish
ambassador, who, through traitors at Elizabeth's court, ascertained that the expedition was bound for the coast of Peru, and
wrote to the Madrid Government to warn the Viceroy, and
direct him " to sink every vessel that he could meet, with every
living thing on board." If any mercy were shown, there would
be no more peace for the Indies. Fortunately for Drake, no
heed was given to Mendoza's counsel, and the Spanish officers
in the New World were left to be taken by surprise.

On the 15th of November, 1577, Drake set sail, but encountering a violent gale, was compelled to put into Falmouth, and
thence to return to Plymouth to refit and repair. The weather
moderating, he set sail a second time on the 13th of December.
His ships were well-found and swift sailers, and they ran to
Mogador in twelve days. On his way to Cape Blanco he
captured a caravel of forty tons, which he substituted for the
Christopher. At the Cape de Verde Islands he stayed for five
weeks—in Elizabeth's time men did everything leisurely, even
great deeds!—trading with the natives, and capturing and
rifling several Spanish and Portuguese vessels. Stretching
across the Atlantic, they passed the equator on the 19th of
February, 1578, and reached the coast of America, in lat.
33° S., on the 5th of April. Skirting the coast, Drake looked
into the vast river-estuary of La Plata, where to his astonishment he found fresh water in $5\frac{1}{2}$ fathoms. Several seals were
killed and salted for future use.

Putting to sea again, Drake lost sight of the *Swan* and the
Portuguese prize, which had been re-christened the *Mary*. Captain Winter was sent in search of them; he brought in the
former, but the latter was seen no more. On the Patagonian coast
they trafficked with the natives, who painted themselves, we

are told, all over their body, some with one shoulder white and the other black, some with white moons and others with black suns. They wore no other covering than a skin. " Magelhaens," says the chronicler of the voyage,* " was not altogether deceived in naming them giants, for they generally differ from the common sort of men, both in stature, bigness, and strength of body, as also in the hideousness of their voice ; but yet they are nothing so monstrous or giant-like as they were reported, there being some Englishmen as tall as the highest of any that we could see ; but, peradventure, the Spaniards did not think that ever any Englishman could come thither to reprove them, and thereupon might presume the more boldly to lie ; the name Pentagones, five cubits, nearing 7½ feet, describing the full height (if not somewhat more) of the highest of them." There are no grounds for believing that, in reality, they exceeded the ordinary stature of Europeans.

On the 20th of June Drake dropped anchor in Port St. Julian, which was fated to become the scene of a lamentable tragedy. Drake's second in command was a Mr. Thomas Doughty, a gentleman belonging to an old Catholic family. For some unknown cause he showed a mutinous disposition, and Drake deemed it necessary to bring him before a court-martial consisting of all the seamen of the squadron, lest his ill example should be followed by others, and imperil the expedition. Partly by Doughty's own confession, and partly by independent evidence, his disloyalty was established ; " which, when our General saw, although his private affection to Mr. Doughty (as he then in presence of all sacredly protested) was great, yet the care he had of the state of the voyage, of the expectation of her Majesty, and of the honour of his country, did more touch him (as indeed it ought) than the

* " The World Encompassed," edited by Drake's nephew, also a Sir Francis. See, too, Francis Pretty's narrative (Hakluyt).

private respect of one man ; so that the cause being thoroughly heard, and all things done in good order, as near as might be to the course of our laws in England, it was concluded that Mr. Doughty should receive punishment according to the quality of the offence. And he, seeing no remedy but patience for himself, desired before his death to receive the communion, which he did at the hands of Mr. Fletcher, our minister, and our General himself accompanied him in that holy action. Which being done, and the place of execution made ready, he, having embraced our General, and taken his leave of all the company, with prayer for the Queen's Majestie and our realm, in quiet sort laid his head to the block, where he ended his life."

Some authorities have suggested that in this matter Drake was the agent of the Earl of Leicester, who had his special cause for dreading and suspecting Doughty ; but then Drake's men must also be regarded as accomplices, and there is no reason to charge them with such wholesale subserviency. Nor does it seem probable that Drake would have postponed the blow for so many months. Mr. Froude, on the other hand, looks upon Doughty as an agent of the priests, employed to thwart and baffle Drake in his enterprise. The true explana-tion we take to be that which lies on the surface : Doughty was an ambitious and discontented man, who endeavoured to excite a mutiny against Drake, and his sharp and swift punishment was absolutely essential to the success of the expedition.

At Port St. Julian the Portuguese prize, the *Mary*, being no longer seaworthy, was broken up ; and Drake's fleet was reduced to three ships, the *Pelican*, the *Elizabeth*, and the *Marigold*.

" The fruits of the voyage were now about to commence. No Englishman had as yet passed Magellan's Straits—Cape

Horn was unknown. Tierra del Fuego was supposed to be part of a solid continent which stretched unbroken to the Antarctic Pole. A single narrow channel was the only access to the Pacific then believed to exist. There were no charts, no records of past experiences. It was known that Magellan had gone through, but that was all. It was the wildest and worst season of the year, and the vessels in which the attempt was to be made were cockshells." But no difficulties or dangers could daunt our great sea-captain when there was work to be done. Moreover, what had been possible to a Catholic Spaniard was surely possible to a Protestant English-man. On the 20th of August he entered the Straits, and care-fully steered through their winding and irregular passage, with walls of mountain frowning on either hand, so drawing together at certain points as apparently to present no outlet. When near the western extremity, Drake allowed his men to land on " a large and fruitful island," which he christened Elizabetha, in honour of the Queen, and they amused themselves with a massacre of penguins, killing three thousand in one day. They found there " many fruitful valleys, full of grass, and herds of very strange creatures feeding. The trees were green, and the air temperate, the water pleasant, and the soil agreeable for any of our country grain ; and nothing wanting to make a happy region, but the people's knowing and worshipping the true God."

After a voyage extending over three weeks, Drake's ships passed out into the Pacific (September 6th), to find that never was name more inappositely bestowed ! A tremendous gale arose, which carried them a hundred leagues or more to the south-west, and for six weeks buffeted them about most sorely. The cutter went down with her living freight, and perished. The *Pelican* and the *Elizabeth*, after driving to the south of Cape Horn, and discovering that Tierra del Fuego was an island, were separated ; and the latter re-entered the Straits, and was navigated back to England by her faint-hearted captain. The more resolute Drake found shelter for the *Pelican*, or the *Golden Hind*, as he had renamed her, among the Tierra del Fuego archipelago, where he re-freshed his crew with good water and wholesome herbs, and waited until returning spring brought with it more genial weather.

The storm subsided on the 30th of October, and Drake then ran to the northward to the rendezvous which he had appointed for his squadron in the latitude of Valparaiso. None of his consorts, however, appeared ; and after a short delay he con-tinned his exploration of the coast. On the 30th of November he landed in St. Philip's Bay, and opened up a friendly intercourse with the Indians, one of whom piloted him to a place called by the Spaniards Volpaieja, where he obtained supplies of every kind, and plundered a Spanish ship of gold and other valuables. We find him afterwards at Tarapaca, in about 20° S. lat., where they found the Spaniards asleep, with a heap of thirteen silver bars, worth about 4,000 ducats, by their side. Drake would not allow his men to do the sleepers any injury, but carried off their treasure.*

---

* Silver bullion brought down from the mountains was shipped here. "It was as when men set foot for the first time on some shore where the forms of their race have never before been seen, and the animals come fearlessly round them, and the birds feed upon their hands, ignorant as yet of the deadly nature of the beings in whom they trust so rashly. The colonists of the New World, when they saw a sail approaching, knew no misgiving, and never dreamt that it could be other than a friend. The silver bars lay piled at the Tarapaca pier ; by their side the weary labourers who had brought them from the mines were peacefully sleeping, or if they heard the clash of the moving metal supposed that their comrades had arrived for their lading. There was no gratuitous cruelty in Drake ; he was come for the treasure of Peru, and beyond seizing his plunder he did not care to injure the people. As the last bars were being stowed away in his boats a train of llamas appeared bringing from the hills a second freight as rich

On the 13th of February, 1579, Drake arrived at Callao, the port of Lima, and boldly entering the harbour, rifled seventeen Spanish merchant vessels which he found lying there of all that they had of value and easy of removal. To secure himself from pursuit, he cut the cables of these ships, and let them drive. Then he was informed that a vessel named the *Cacafuego*, and known as "the great glory of the South Sea," had sailed for Panama but a few days before, laden with jewels and precious stones, and carrying also several precious boxes of gold and silver. Crowding on all his canvas, Drake sped northward in pursuit of her, promising a gold chain to the man who first sighted the coveted argosy. On the second day he fell in with and boarded a brigantine, from which he took eighty pounds of purest gold in wedges, and a large crucifix studded with emeralds of the size of pigeons' eggs. He would also have carried off the ship, but by this time two half-armed Spanish cruisers which the Viceroy of Callao had dispatched came up with him, and allowed his prize to join its friends. Smitten with fear of the redoubtable Drake, the cruisers went back to Lima for more men and more guns, while Drake sailed swiftly onward.

At length, one degree north of the equator, off Quito, and close to the shore, the look-out man, John Drake, our hero's nephew, claimed the promised gold chain because he had descried the chase. From the peculiar size and shape of her canvas she was known to be the *Cacafuego*, and a prize the capture of which would enrich every man on board the *Golden Hind*. She was several miles ahead; and it was necessary not to alarm her suspicion, lest she should run in under the wind and escape them. There were several hours of daylight, and Drake did not wish to

as the first. This, too, was transferred to the *Pelican*. Four hundred thousand ducats' worth of silver were taken in one afternoon."—FROUDE, *History of England*, xi. 130, 131.

come up with her until dusk. The *Pelican* sailed two feet to the *Cacafuego's* one, and to equalise their speed, lest the Spaniards should take alarm, he filled his empty wine-casks with water, and towed them astern. Meanwhile, the unsuspicious chase, " glad of company on a lonely voyage," slackened sail, and waited for the approaching vessel. At sunset, when both ships were invisible from the land, the casks were hoisted in ; the *Pelican* recovered her usual sailing trim, and coming up within a cable's length of the *Cacafuego*, hailed to her to run into the wind. The Spanish commander, unable to comprehend the order, took no heed of it; whereupon Drake opened his ports, and with his first broadside brought down the galleon's main-mast. Her decks were swept by a shower of arrows, with one of which the Don himself was wounded. Then the English-men rushed on board, and in a few minutes drove the Spaniards below deck, and took possession of the ship. " The wreck was cut away, the ship cleared, and her head turned to the sea ; by daybreak even the line of the Andes had become invisible ; and at leisure, in the open ocean, the work of rifling began. The full value of the plunder taken in this ship was never accurately confessed. It remained a secret between Drake and the Queen. In a schedule afterwards published, he acknowledged to have found in the *Cacafuego* above twenty-six tons of silver bullion, thirteen chests of coined silver, and almost a hundredweight of gold. This was only so much as the Spaniards could prove to have been on board. There was a further mass, the amount of which it is impossible to guess, of which no account was ever rendered, and a great store besides of pearls, emeralds, and diamonds, supposed to have been of enormous richness. The Spanish Government roughly estimated their loss afterwards at a million and a half of ducats (about £700,000, as money was then valued), which Elizabeth did not pretend to be exaggerated. The total treasure appropriated was perhaps therefore considerably greater."

Placing a prize crew on board, and removing the captain of the *Cacafuego* to the *Golden Hind*, Drake being greatly satisfied, as well he might be, proceeded to sail to the westward, to avoid Panama. San Juan de Centin, the Spanish captain, remained with Drake until he had recovered from his wound, and was hospitably treated. ·He was conducted over the ship by Drake and his Protestant chaplain, who spoke Spanish fluently, and with both he conversed at his ease. He records that it was well equipped, fully seaworthy, notwithstanding its long voyage, provided with all kinds of arms, and not only with arms, but with tools of every kind. The crew were reduced to eighty-five, all told; some had been drowned, some had gone back with Winter, some had died; of those remaining, fifty were "men of war," the rest, "young fellows, ship's boys, and such like." He observed that Drake "was greatly feared and reverenced by all on board." A sentinel stood always at his cabin door. He "was served with sound of trumpets and other instruments at his meals."

There was no attempt made to conceal the extent and character of his cargo. The chaplain showed San Juan the great emerald-set cross, and asked him if he could sincerely believe it was God; for if it were God, why had it not offered resistance to its captors? "God," he said solemnly, "was a spirit in heaven, and images and ceremonies were idle mockeries." Drake spoke frequently of his wanderings and adventures; and when San Juan asked him how he proposed to go to England, pointed to a map of the globe, and said, There was the way he had come, the way by China and the Cape of Good Hope, and a third way, but that he kept a secret.

San Juan wished to know whether there was war between

Spain and England. To this question was returned an evasive answer. He had the Queen's commission, he said, for what he had done, and the booty he had acquired was intended for her, not for himself. But he added that the King of Spain had robbed him and his kinsman Hawkins, and that he was but repaying himself what he had lost. "I know," he continued, "the Viceroy will send for you to inform himself of my proceeding. Thou mayest tell him he shall do well to put no Englishmen to death, and to spare those four that he has in his hands, for if he do execute them they will cost the lives of two thousand Spaniards, whom I will hang and send him their heads."

When cured of his wound San Juan was allowed to go on board the *Cacafuego*, and, a wiser and a sadder man, to return to Callao. On his way he fell in with the two Spanish cruisers from Lima, which had been ordered to take charge of the galleon if they could not find Drake. They were now armed to the teeth, with two hundred picked seamen on board, and had been joined by a ship from Panama. They started in chase, and, the *Golden Hind* being under easy sail, overtook her; but, though three to one, their courage oozed away when they remarked the cool indifference with which Drake suffered them to approach. A second time they put about and returned for more aid.

The Viceroy, in his rage at their cowardice, put the captains under arrest, appointed new officers, and sent the ships once more in pursuit, with peremptory orders to fight. He also dispatched a special messenger across the Atlantic to King Philip, and couriers to spread the alarm along the coast of the Isthmus. The assumption was, that Drake's "third way" was not a sea-way, but across the mountains; where, it was thought, having abandoned his ship, he would transport his treasure, and build a vessel in Honduras to carry him to

England, or find a consort which had been sent out to meet him.*

This, however, was not Drake's intention; he had resolved on attempting to discover a route home by the north-east; a route which Cook afterwards attempted to discover without success, as well as many of our later Arctic navigators; and a route which has recently been achieved by the Swedish physicist, Professor Nordenskiold. At the southern extremity of America the oceans were united: why should they not be at the northern? Filled with this ambition, Drake set sail from Agua-pulco, where he had refitted and reprovisioned his ship; and, with his prow to the northward, followed up the coast of Mexico. From a China ship, loaded with silks and porcelain, he took the best of the cargo, with a golden falcon and another precious emerald. Being in want of fresh water, he put in at the Spanish settlement of Guatulco. The alcaldes at the time were trying " a batch of negroes." Drake's men swooped down upon them, bound them hand and foot, and carried them on board the *Golden Hind*, where they were detained as hostages until the water-casks were filled and the houses of the principal inhabitants had been plundered, after which they were dismissed with grave courtesy.

Sailing northward and still northward, Drake fell in with a Spanish grandee, who was going out as governor to the Philip-pines, and considerately relieved him of all superfluity of cargo. At this time and place, says Francis Pretty, our General, think-ing himself, both in respect of his private injuries received from the Spaniards, and also their contempts and indignities offered to our country and prince in general, sufficiently satisfied and revenged, and supposing that her Majesty would rest contented with his service, began to consider and consult of the best way for his country.

* The foregoing narrative is founded on Froude, who has consulted the MSS. in the Spanish archives.

As a preliminary, Drake set his men to work at repairing the *Pelican's* hull. He had put into the Bay of Carrow in Lower California, and there he erected forge and workshop, and after a month's labour refitted his ships from stem to stern. On the 16th of April he resumed his northward course, and sailed 600 leagues in longitude to secure a wind; and between that and June 3rd, 1,400 leagues in all, until he reached 62° north latitude. On the following night he and his men experienced a sudden and most grievous change of temperature, the heat of the tropics being succeeded by Arctic cold. " Neither did this happen for the time only, or by some sudden accident, but rather seemed indeed to proceed from some ordinary cause, against the which the heat of the sun prevails not; for it came to that extremity, in sailing but two degrees further to the northward in our course, that though seamen lack not good stomachs, yet it seemed a question to many amongst us, whether their hands should feed their mouths, or rather keep themselves within coverts from the pinching cold that did benumb them.

" Neither," continues the historian of the voyage, " neither could we impute it to the tenderness of our bodies, though we came lately from the extremity of heat, by reason whereof we might be more sensible of the present cold, insomuch that the dead and senseless creatures were as well affected with it as ourselves. Our meat, as soon as it was removed from the fire, would presently in a manner be frozen up; and our ropes and tacklings in a few days were grown to that stiffness that what three men before were able with them to perform, now six men, with their best strength and utmost endeavours, were hardly able to accomplish; whereby a sudden and great discouragement seized upon the minds of our men, and they were possessed with a great mislike and doubting of any good to be done that way; yet would not our General be discouraged;

but as well by comfortable speeches of the Divine Providence, and of God's loving care over his children, out of the Scriptures, as also by other good and profitable persuasions, adding thereto his own cheerful example, he so stirred them up to put on a good courage, and to acquit themselves like men, to endure some short extremity to have the speedier comfort, and a little trouble to obtain the greater glory ; that every man was thoroughly armed with willingness, and resolved to see the uttermost, if it were possible, of what good was to be done that way.

"The land in that part of America bearing farther out into the west than we before imagined, we were nearer on it than we were aware, and yet the nearer still we came unto it, the more extremity of cold did seize upon us. The 5th day of June we were forced by contrary winds to run in with the shore, which we then first descried, and to cast anchor in a bad bay, the best road we could for the present meet with, where we were not without some danger by reason of the many extreme gusts and flows that beat upon us ; which if they ceased and were still at any time, immediately upon their intermission there followed most vile, thick, and stinking fogs, against which the sea prevailed nothing, till the gusts of wind again removed them, which brought with them such extremity and violence when they came, that there was no dealing or resisting against them."

Drake, not caring to risk the loss of his precious cargo, now abandoned his northerly course, perceiving that if a passage by the north of America existed it must be of immense length. He was resolved, however, not to return by Magellan's Straits, feeling assured—as, indeed, was the case—that the Spaniards would be lying there in wait for him ; but he started across the ocean to the "islands of the Moluccas," and thence to "sail the course of the Portuguese by the Cape of Buena Esperanza."

Falling back southward to latitude 38° 30′ N., he put into an ample and well-sheltered harbour, now known as San Francisco, or "the Golden Gate," where he once more refitted his ship and refreshed his war-worn crew. With the natives of this part of California he quickly opened a friendly intercourse; and they regarded him with as much wonder as Caliban exhibits in his contemplation of Stephano and Trinculo. A grand entertainment took place, at which they danced and sang after their fashion, and amid the noise placed a feathered cap of network on Drake's head, and a chain around his neck, hailing him as " Hioh," or king. Drake put into this ceremony a meaning of his own, and chose to understand it as a formal surrender of California, with all its treasures, to the Crown of England.*

In commemoration of this event, Drake caused a post to be set up on shore, " a monument of our being there; as also of her Majesty's and successor's right and title to that kingdom, namely, a plate of brass, fast nailed to a great and pine post, whereon is engraven her Grace's name, and the day and year of our arrival there, and of the free giving up of the province

---

* " After they (the natives) had satisfied or rather tired themselves in this manner (singing and dancing, and the women tearing themselves, till the face, breasts, and other parts were bespattered with blood), they made signs to our General to have him sit down. Both the King and divers others made several orations, or rather indeed, if we had understood them, supplications that he would take that province and kingdom into his care, and become their king and patron; making signs that they would resign unto him their right and title in the whole land, and become his vassals in themselves and their posterities ; which, that they might make us indeed believe that it was their true meaning and intent, the King himself, with all the rest, with one consent, and with great reverence, joyfully singing a song, set the crown upon his head, enriched his neck with all their chains, and offered unto him many other things, honouring him with the name of Hioh ; adding thereto, as it might seem, a song and dance of triumph, because they were not only visited of the gods (for so they still judged us to be), but that the great and chief god was now become their God, their king and patron, and themselves were become the only happy and blessed people in the world."—*The World Encompassed.*

and kingdom, both by the King and people, into her Majesty's hands, together with her Highness's picture and arms in a piece of sixpence current English money, showing itself by a hole made of purpose through the plate." To this part of the coast Drake gave, in allusion to its white cliffs, the name of New Albion.

On the 23rd of July the *Golden Hind* sailed from this hospitable coast—the natives, until she sailed below the horizon, keeping up blazing fires upon the hills. Across the vast expanse of shining sea she made her way for sixty-eight days, and on the 30th of September fell in with certain islands about 8° to the northward of the equator. The natives quickly swarmed around the ship, with their canoes full of cocoa-nuts, fruits, and fish. The intercourse was friendly enough at first; but the visitors showing a desire to appropriate whatever articles caught their fancy, Drake dismissed them with a volley of small shot, and stigmatized their archipelago as the " Islands of Thieves," which Admiral Burney identifies with the Pelew Islands.

Continuing a westward course, Drake reached the Philippine Islands ; and on the 21st of October took in a supply of fresh water at Mindanao, the largest. Thence he steered for the Mcluccas, and halting at Ternate, the capital of the group, he landed one of his suite with a velvet cloak for the King, and a request to be permitted to purchase provisions and spiceries. The King himself came off on a visit to the ship, preceded by four large and richly decorated canoes, and carrying eighty rowers, who paddled to the clash of brass cymbals. On each side of these canoes was a row of soldiers, armed with sword, dagger, and target; each canoe carried a small piece of ordnance, mounted on a stock. Drake gave the King a splendid reception ; the trumpets blared, the great guns roared, and he himself and his officers were attired in all their bravery. Afterwards some of the English officers visited the King. On arriving at his palace, they did not at first see the august presence of this barbaric potentate; but in the audience chamber sat sixty grave personages, distinguished as the royal councillors. Four grave persons, apparelled all in red, with robes that touched the ground, and turbaned heads, were said to be Romans, and "ligiers," or agents, to keep continual traffic with the people of Ternate. There were also two Turkish "ligiers" and one Italian. After awhile the King entered, guarded by twelve spearmen, and walking under a rich canopy embossed with gold. The Englishmen rose as he approached, whereupon he did graciously welcome and entertain them. He was attired after the manner of the country, but much more sumptuously than the rest. From his waist down to the ground he shone in cloth of gold; his legs were bare, but on his feet were a pair of shoes made of Cordovan skin. In his head-gear glistened finely wreathed hooped rings of gold, and from his neck depended a chain of perfect gold, the links whereof were great and one fold double. On his fingers were six very fine jewels. As he sat in his chair of state, a page stood on his right hand and fanned him delicately. The fan was two feet in length and one foot in breadth, set with eight sapphires, richly embroidered, and attached to a staff twelve inches in length, by which the page did hold and move it.

When the English seamen had delivered Drake's message to this magnificent potentate, and had received a satisfactory reply, they were allowed to depart, and safely conducted back again by one of the royal councillors.

Drake, by his tact and courtesy, made a very favourable impression on the minds of the King and his court, and his name and memory were cherished at Ternate for many years.

Having furnished his ship with provisions, and procured a

large supply of cloves, our sea-captain sailed from Ternate on the 9th, and ten days after anchored off a small island near the eastern extremity of Celebes, where he sheltered his men in tents, and erecting a forge, employed them in repairing their ship. The island was overgrown with a dense luxuriant forest of large and lofty trees, among which by night gleamed "an infinite swarm of fiery worms flying through the air"—fiery worms, with bodies no bigger than those of our common English flies, but making such a show and light as if every twig and tree had been a burning candle—while at dusk bats as big as large hens fluttered to and fro. On the shore was found an abundant supply of crayfish of exceeding bigness, one being sufficient for four hungry stomachs at a dinner, and very good and sustaining meat. These crayfish burrowed in the earth like coneys.

On the 10th of December Drake took leave of this island of plenty, and with infinite skill and caution began to thread his way among the rocks and shoals of the most dangerous waters in the world. He crept round Celebes slowly, winding through low islets and reefs of coral invisible at high water. In the Portuguese "sea-card," by which he directed his course, no other route was marked than that of the Malacca Straits, between which and Drake spread the Java Sea and the channel between Borneo and Sumatra. But it seemed possible to our mariner that some other opening might exist, and in search of this he steered his small bark along the Java coast. On one occasion she was almost lost, and a sudden and disastrous end threatened to her wonderful voyage. On the 9th of January, while running through the darkness of the clear tropical night, with a fair wind filling her sails, the *Golden Hind* stuck hard and fast upon an unseen reef. Well was it for ship and crew that the sea was smooth and the breeze light! All night she lay immovable. On each side of the shoal the depth of water

was so great that it was impossible to heave her off by getting
out an anchor. The crew were grievously depressed by this
calamity ; but Drake then as always showed himself most
courageous, and of a good confidence in the mercy and protection of God. Rightly believing that nothing would so compose
their disordered minds as an appeal to the religious sentiment,
he summoned them to devotions; and "presently they fell pros-
trate, and with joined prayers sent up to the Throne of Grace,
himself besought Almighty God to extend His mercy unto us
in His son Christ Jesus, and so preparing as it were our works
unto the Rock, we every minute expected the final stroke to
be given unto us."

In the morning Drake determined to lighten the ship by
throwing overboard a portion of her cargo, and for this purpose three tons of cloves were sacrificed, eight of the guns,
and a quantity of meal and beans. And about four o'clock
in the afternoon, the lightened craft heeling over on one side,
slipped off the rocky ledge, and under full sale glided safely
into deep water.*

* Thomas Fuller's quaint account of this incident, derived, apparently,
from one of Drake's companions, must not be omitted : "The ship struck
twice on a dangerous shoal, knocking twice at the door of death, which
no doubt had opened the third time. Here they struck, having ground
too much, and yet too little to land on; and water too much, and yet too
little to sail in. Had God, who, as the wise man saith, holdeth the winds
in His fist, but opened His finger and let out the smallest blast, they had
undoubtedly been cast away : but there was not any wind all the while.
Then they, conceiving aright that the best way to lighten the ship was
first to ease it of the burden of their sins by true repentance, humbled themselves by fasting under the hand of God ; afterwards they received the
communion, dining on Christ in the sacrament, expecting no other than to
sup with Him in Heaven. Then they cast out of their ship six great
pieces of ordnance : threw overboard as much wealth as would break the
heart of a miser to think on't ; with much sugar and packs of spices, making
a caudle of the sea round about. Then they b⋅   ⋅k themselves to their
prayers, the best lever at such a dead lift indeed ; and it pleased God that
the wind, formerly their mortal enemy, became their friend."—*Holy State*,
p. 127.

The behaviour of the crew throughout this painful experience had, on the whole, been admirable. The sole exception was Mr. Fletcher, the chaplain, who, with death before his eyes, found his conscience pricked by the recollection of Doughty's death at Port St. Julian, and ·hinted that their present sufferings were God's punishment for their complicity in an act of so much severity. ·As soon as they had got into deep water, and, skirting the Java coast, had found in the Straits of Sunda the opening on which Drake had calculated, they proceeded to castigate the offending chaplain after the roughly humorous fashion of the men of the sea. Mr. Fletcher was brought to the forecastle, where sat Drake on a sea-chest, "with a pair of pantoufles in his hand," and having been declared excommunicate, "cut off from the Church of God, and given over to the devil," was duly chastised with the pantoufles, and chained by the ankle to a ring-bolt in the deck until he made confession of his craven-heartedness. Drake, however, was not a man to bear malice, and in a day or two he set the unruly chaplain free.

From Java the voyage was unmarked by any unpleasing incident. In fair weather they passed the Cape of Good Hope, once ominously known as the Cape of Storms, and on the 22nd of July reached Sierra Leone, where Drake stopped to take in water, and obtained a welcome supply of oysters and fruit.

It was on the 26th of September that the *Golden Hind* sailed merrily into Plymouth Harbour, and happily completed her extraordinary voyage, after "marking a furrow with her keel round the globe."

"On the 26th, which was Monday," says the historian, "in the just and ordinary reckoning of those who had stayed at home in one place or country, but in our computation was the Lord's Day or Sunday, we safely with joyful minds and thank·

ful hearts to God, arrived at Plymouth, the place of our first
setting foot, after we had spent two years, ten months, and
some odd days besides, in seeing the wonders of the Lord in
the deep, in discovering so many admirable things, in going
through with so many strange adventures, in escaping out of so
many dangers, and overcoming so many difficulties, in this our
encompassing of this nether globe, and passing round about
the world, which we have related."

> " Soli rerum maximarum Effectori,
> Soli totius mundi Gubernatori,
> Soli sacrum Conservatori,
> Soli Deo sit semper gloria."

In this devout strain does the old chronicler of the expedition
conclude his quaintly interesting narrative.

On Drake's arrival at Plymouth the townsmen crowded to
the shore to bid him welcome. When he landed he was received
in state by the mayor and corporation, while the bells of St.
Andrew's Church rang out a merry peal. Next day he paid a
visit to his native village and parental home ; and after a week or
two of festivity rejoined his wave-beaten bark, and set sail for
Deptford. Everywhere his countrymen hailed him with the pride
that his exploits had naturally excited, and sought every means
of doing him honour. He had circumnavigated the world—a
great achievement ; and he had beaten and rifled the Spaniards
—an even more popular action ; and from one end of England to the other he commanded the admiration and sympathy
of her sons. The eulogy embodied in the Latin verse written
(it is reported) by some of the scholars of Winchester did not
seem a whit too extravagant :—

> "Plus ultra, Herculeis inscribas, Drace, columnis,
> Et magno dicas Hercule major ero.
> Drace, pererrati novit quem terminus orbis,
> Quemque semel mundi vidit uterque Polus,

Si taceant homines, facient te sidera notum;
Sol nescit Comitis non memor esse sui.
Digna ratis quæ stet radiantibus inclyta stellis;
Supremo cœli vertice digna ratis."

Fervent as was the popular recognition, it did not wholly satisfy Drake; he desired, as all Englishmen then desired, the praise and approval of his Queen. At first, however, Elizabeth affected to regard him with displeasure. She was not prepared to go to war with Spain; and hostilities might be expected if she openly expressed her sympathy with Drake's buccaneering exploits. That they were in violation of the law of nations, though not unjustified from another point of view by the cruelties of the Spaniards and their attempt to secure a monopoly of the world's commerce, she was well aware. At the same time she was secretly sharing the spoil with Drake, and had no intention of restoring it. After awhile she grew more reconciled to the idea of war, from the prospect war seemed to open up of a diversion of the wealth of the Indies into her own channel, and she no longer withheld her countenance from her daring subject. She invited him to court, made him rare presents, admitted him to frequent audiences, and honoured him with her presence at a banquet on board the *Golden Hind*,* when she conferred upon him the dignity of knighthood.

* The *Golden Hind* was long preserved *in memoriam* in Deptford Dockyard. When it could no longer be kept in repair, a chair was wrought out of its mast, and presented to the University of Oxford, a circumstance commemorated by the poet Cowley :—

> "To this great ship which round the globe has run,
> And match'd in race the chariot of the sun;
> This Pythagoréan ship (for it may claim,
> Without presumption, so deserved a name),
> By knowledge over, and transformation now,
> In her own shape, this sacred fact allow.
> Drake and his ship could not have wish'd from fate
> An happier station, or more blest estate,
> For lo! a seat of endless rest is given
> To her in Oxford, and to him in Heaven."

II.

For four or five years Drake rested tranquilly in his Devonshire home; nor was it until 1585 that he again drew his sword against the hated Spaniards. Elizabeth having determined on sending an expedition against the Spanish colonies in the West Indies, to deal a blow at the commerce which furnished Philip with his main revenue, she called Drake from his retirement, advanced him to the rank of Admiral, and placed him at the head of a fleet of five-and-twenty vessels. With her usual policy, however, she disclaimed all open connection with the expedition, and treated it as a private adventure, though half the cost was defrayed by herself. Drake held her royal commission as far as Spain, with license to effect the release of certain English merchant vessels which had been arrested and detained in Spanish ports. Volunteers rapidly rallied to the flag of the seaman who had ploughed a furrow round the globe. Martin Frobisher and Christopher Carlile, two seamen inferior only to himself in repute, accepted commands under him. For his officers he chose the survivors of his old crew, and young gentlemen of rank eagerly competed for the honour of accompanying him.

Drake was ready for sea in the middle of September, and lest Elizabeth's shifting policy should suddenly countermand the expedition, he set sail hastily on the 14th. Capturing on his way some ships returning with fish from the Newfoundland banks, he carried his fleet in among the islands that shelter the Bay of Vigo. As the tall ships swung to anchor, "it was a great matter and a royal sight to see them." Surprised and alarmed, Don Pedro Benvadero, the Governor, sent messengers to inquire their errand, to offer them hospitality if they were merchants, and if they were of a doubtful calling, to promise them "what they did lack," and to entreat them to depart peacefully. Drake sternly replied that he had come to inquire after his imprisoned countrymen, and must make bold to land his men and refresh them. Don Pedro durst offer no opposition, and endeavoured to conciliate his formidable visitors with liberal presents of wine and fruit. They remained on shore for two or three days, lounging among the churches and chapels, and playing tricks with the images of the saints to provoke them into a show of life. One of their freaks was to relieve " Our Lady" of her clothes, and, after stripping her, to overwhelm her with contumely.

The weather proving unfavourable, and the anchorage among the islands being insecure, Drake removed his fleet into the bay. By this time all Vigo was distraught with fear, and the harbour was covered with boatloads of panic-stricken people hastening up the country with their property. Drake sent his pinnaces in chase, and several prizes were captured ; one of which contained the furniture of the High Church of Vigo, altar cloths, chasubles, copes, chalices, patens, and a great cross of pure silver, exquisitely wrought. The Governor of Galicia arrived with a body of soldiers to the rescue, but when he saw Drake's well-appointed ships and truculent sea-dogs he contented himself, like Don Pedro, with devising the ways and means of persuading them to retire. Meeting Drake upon the water, he promised freely that every English prisoner in the province should immediately be released. Having secured all the booty that was accessible, and being unable to tarry the release of the prisoners, Sir Francis accepted his promise and set sail.

" All Spain," says Froude,* " was in agitation at the news that the world-famed corsair was on the coast. The Council of State sat three days discussing it. That the English could dare to beard the first monarch in Europe in his own dominions

* FROUDE, *History of England*, xii, 34.

seemed like a dream. " Had the Queen of England," it was asked, " no way to employ Sir Francis Drake but to send him to inquire after Englishmen's ships and goods? Did the Queen of England know the King of Spain's force? Did not she and her people quake? Little England, to the King of half the world, was but a morsel to be swallowed at his pleasure. The Marquis of Santa Cruz, however, observed that ' England had many teeth,' and that with Drake upon the ocean, the first object was to save the Indian fleet." What might not be expected from the daring adventurer who, with a ship of one hundred tons, and a crew of seventy or eighty men, could navigate the vast Pacific and plunder one of the great Panama argosies under the eyes of the Viceroy of Peru? What might he not attempt—in what might he not succeed? He might capture the Canaries, or the West Indies, or Lima itself. While the timid courtiers of Elizabeth stood aghast at Philip's naval and military preparations, and every Jesuit's heart was exulting over the growth of the great fleet at Lisbon, intended for the conquest of England, Santa Cruz was urging the Council of State to send every available ship at once to sea, to save the American colonies and the gold ports and the Indian galleons from the desperate sea-rover who made a mock of the Spanish power.

From Vigo, Drake proceeded to the Cape de Verde Islands, where he burned the town of St. Jago; but delaying too long in an unhealthy climate, had the mortification of losing up- wards of two hundred of his men by an epidemic which some- what resembled the plague. Thence he sailed for Dominica, and favoured by the trade winds, reached it in eighteen days. The capital of San Domingo he took by assault; but the entire town being too large for his men to garrison, he quartered them in the central square, occupying castle, palace, and town- hall, where King Philip's scutcheon, a horse leaping upon a

globe, with the boastful motto, *Non sufficit orbis*, " preached
a sermon to conquerors and conquered on the pride of fools.'
Carefully foitifying his position, Drake held it for the space of
a month. One day he sent a flag of truce by a negro boy.
A Spanish officer meeting him, cruelly run him through the
body with his pike, and the victim, crawling back to the
Admiral, told him what had happened, and died at his feet.
In a storm of rage—one of those terrible excesses to which
men of strong deep minds, who habitually keep a stern control
over themselves, are sometimes liable—Drake ordered his provost-marshal to carry a couple of Spanish friars, who had been
taken prisoners, to the spot where the boy received his mortal
wound, and hang them forthwith, while he dispatched another
Spanish prisoner to explain wherefore this execution was done,
adding that until the murderer had been given up to receive the
punishment he deserved he would hang two prisoners daily.
Next day the officer was surrendered, and Drake compelled
the Spaniards to become his executioners. This severe lesson
was not lost upon the Spaniards, who thenceforward understood
that Drake was not a man with whom it was safe to take liberties.

Drake was by no means partial to useless destruction
and he offered to spare the city on receiving a fair ransom.
But when its authorities showed a great reluctance to come to
terms, he tried the effect of a little pressure, and told off 200
sailors to burn and pillage until the money should be forthcoming. The work was by no means easy, the city being very
magnificently built of stone. At length the Spaniards offered
25,000 ducats, which Drake agreed to accept. And having
loaded his ships with wine, sweet oil, olives, vinegar, and
other provisions, together with woollen, linen, and silk
stuffs, he again put to sea and steered for Cartagena.
Landing his troops about three miles west of the town, he sent
them along a narrow isthmus not more than fifty paces broad,

with the sea on one side and the harbour on the other, and at the extremity a solid stone barrier, with an opening only wide enough to admit of the passage of two horsemen or a carriage. This was further strengthened by wine-butts filled with earth and placed on end. But Drake sent his men against it. " Down went the butts of earth, and pell-mell came our swords and pikes together after our shot had first given their volley, even at the enemy's nose. Our pikes were somewhat longer than theirs, and our bodies better armed, with which advantage our swords and pikes grew too loud for them, and they were driven to give place. In this furious action, the LieutenantGeneral (Carlile) slew, with his own hands, the chief ensignbearer of the Spaniards, who fought very manfully to his life's end."

Cartagena was held for six weeks, and finally ransomed for 160,000 ducats, after Drake had applied the same process to its inhabitants which he had found successful at St. Domingo. But yellow fever now broke out on board the fleet, compelling Drake to abandon his meditated enterprise against Panama. He stood across, however, to the Florida coast, and burnt and laid waste the settlement of St. Augustine. Afterwards he sailed northward to Virginia, and at Roanoke supplied the governor with provisions and a reinforcement of arms. In a three days' storm, which broke out immediately afterwards, some ships were separated from the fleet and blown out to sea; all, however, reached England in safety. But various circumstances had so depressed the spirits of the colonists and their governor, that they entreated Sir Francis to convey them home, declaring with earnest protestations that Providence was evidently unfavourable to their design of settling on the American shore. Sir Francis consented to their request, and took them on board to the number of 105.

Drake arrived at Portsmouth on the 21st of July, 1586.

His expedition had lacked the romantic interest of the memorable circumnavigation, and was far inferior in profit, the booty brought home not exceeding £60,000 in value. The loss of life was very great; about 750 seamen and soldiers perished. Yet it had not been a failure. The plunder of Vigo, the assault upon St. Jago, the capture of St. Domingo and Cartagena, and the stern composure and collectedness with which all this work was done, dealt a heavy blow to the confidence which the Spaniards had had in their fortune and themselves, and to the world's belief in their invincibility.*

Stung to the quick by this defiant enterprise, Philip pushed forward with increased energy the preparation of that Armada which was to transform free England into a dependency of Spain, and Protestant England into an appanage of the Roman Church. It was not only as a scheme of conquest that he now devised it, but as a measure of preservation, for he saw that England was making ready to dispute with him the sovereignty of the seas, and that her rising maritime power threatened the security of the Spanish dominion in the New World. He waited only until he could guard himself against a counter-attack from France; and of this there would be no fear if, as seemed probable, the League of the Guises obtained the supreme power. While he thus waited, England's seamen aimed at him another and a more crushing blow, again under the leadership of the indomitable Drake.

In the spring of 1587, Elizabeth consented to fit out a fleet to ravage the coasts of Spain, and do what damage it could

* "Authentic tidings were now coming in of Francis Drake. All that he and others had said before of the vulnerability of Spain was more than confirmed, and the English, already vain of their hero, were raised to enthusiasm at the splendour of his successes. The effect in Europe was almost as considerable. The aggressive power of England had passed hitherto for nothing. The strength of its arm, if once raised to strike, became more earnestly appreciated."—FROUDE, *History of England,* xii. 68.

to the Armada which was being equipped in its various ports.

There were thirty vessels in all: "galleys, galliasses, long ships, great ships, and coys." Six belonged to the Crown—the *Bonaventura*, of 600 tons, carrying Drake's flag; the *Lion*, of 500 tons, Vice-Admiral Burroughs; the *Rainbow*, of 500 tons; the *Dreadnought*, of 400 tons; and two pinnaces. The others were "adventurers," fitted out by London merchants.

On the 12th of April (New Style) they sailed from Plymouth Sound—just in time to anticipate a change in Elizabeth's policy beat down the Channel in the teeth of a strong wind, and on the morning of the 19th were off Cadiz Harbour. The mouth was narrow, both sides were lined with batteries, and Vice-Admiral Burroughs loudly protested against running into danger. Drake and his captains, laughingly disregarding the protest, with a fair breeze stood in between the batteries. A shot struck the *Lion;* and immediately Burroughs, apprehensive of destruction, dropped his anchor, warped out of range, and when the tide ebbed drifted seaward. The rest pressed forward gallantly, attacked and sunk a galleon, dispersed a number of galleys with a single broadside, and brought-to out of shot from the shore, with entire command of the harbour and all that it contained. Scores of store-ships, laden with corn, biscuits, dried fruits, and wines, for the use of the Armada, were plundered of everything that could be easily removed; then set on fire; and, with cables cut, left to drive to and fro under the walls of Cadiz, "an entangled mass of blazing ruin."

The Spaniards of those days could admire a gallant deed, though done in their own despite, and greatly as he had injured them Drake became one of their most popular heroes. "So praised was Drake for his valour of them, that were it not that he was a Lutheran, they said, there was not the like man in the world." King Philip one day invited a court lady to

accompany him in his barge on the Lake of Segovia.* The
lady replied, "She dared not trust herself on the water even
with his Majesty, lest Sir Francis Drake should have her."

Passing out of Cadiz Bay on May 1st, he sailed for Cape St.
Vincent—how all this Spanish coast is alive with memories of
English heroism ! †—capturing and burning as he went fresh
convoys of store-vessels—all loaded with supplies for the Armada
which was to conquer heretic England—until the horizon was
studded with jets of flame. Desirous of engaging a division of
the Armada which was understood to be coming round from the
Mediterranean, Drake made for the watering-place of Faro, and,
as the batteries molested his boat crews, prepared to land and
destroy them. Again Burroughs interfered with his old
counsels of caution; Drake ignored him, landed his men,
stormed the forts, and gained command of the river and
roadstead. And when Burroughs sent complaints to England
of his leader's wilfulness, he was deposed and confined a
prisoner in his own cabin; until, dreading a severer punishment,
he contrived to steal away from the fleet and make all sail for
home.

No Spaniards appearing, Drake abandoned Faro, and sailed
for the mouth of the Tagus, with the bold-resolve of carrying
his ships straight up to Lisbon and attacking the Armada where
it lay. He knew that as his "light low" frigates hovered
round the ponderous galleons, like dragon-flies round an ox, he

---

* FROUDE, xii. 293.
† So Browning reminds us in his *Home Thoughts from the Sea* :—
" Nobly, nobly Cape St. Vincent to the North-West, died away ;
  Sunset sun, one glorious blood-red, reeking into Cadiz Bay ;
  Bluish 'mid the burning water, full in face Trafalgar lay ;
  In the dimmest North-East distance dawned Gibraltar grave and gray ;
  ' Here and here did England help me : how can I help England !"—say,
  Whoso turns as I, this evening, turn to God to praise and pray,
  While Jove's planet rises yonder, silent over Africa."

could outsail them at pleasure, and escape at any time if the battle went against him. Moreover, he had reason to believe that the Spanish Admiral would be taken by surprise, the sides of his ships being probably encumbered with lighters and barges, the ships themselves half-manned, and unable either to make sail or fire a gun. That he would have succeeded in his enterprise is very probable, yet one can hardly regret that English history was not deprived of a chapter so glorious as that which records the defeat and dispersion of the Invincible Armada. As it was, orders from England forbade his intended attack, and he was obliged to be content with burning more store-ships at Cintra and Coruña. Thus, in ten months, he had defied the united navies of Spain and Portugal, and destroyed half the stores which had been accumulated for the Armada. Before he returned home, however, he had to do something for the merchant-adventurers who had supplied him with ships and arms, and his usual good fortune—or his skill, shall we call it? in seizing and profiting by opportunities—attending him, he captured, in the neighbourhood of the Azores, a gloriously rich carack from the East Indies, the *San Felipe*. Triumphant, he returned to England in the midsummer, having effectually accomplished his design of "singeing the King of Spain's beard."

The remainder of the year and the early part of 1588 were occupied in negotiations which everybody knew to be insincere. A revolution in France, which placed Henry III. in the hands of Philip's confederates, the Guises, assured him that from France he had nothing to apprehend. He determined, therefore, on launching the thunderbolt which he had so long held ready. At Dunkirk was encamped an army of 17,000 Spanish veterans, under the command of the Duke of Parma, the greatest general of his time; and a fleet of flat-bottomed transports lay in readiness to carry them across the Channel.

To protect their passage, Philip had assembled in the Tagus, at first under the Marquis of Santa Cruz, but eventually under a less competent chief, the Duke of Medina Sidonia, a fleet of 129 ships, of which 65 were large galleons, "built high like castles," and 4 were colossal galeasses, each armed with 50 guns, besides 4 large galleys, 56 armed merchant vessels, tne best that Spain could produce, and 20 caravels or pinnaces. In all they carried 2,430 cannons, brass and iron ; 22,000 soldiers, 1,000 gentlemen volunteers, 8,000 seamen, and 1,600 men of various ranks and occupations.

It is no part of my province here to dwell on the vacillations of Elizabeth's policy, or on the extent to which they delayed England's preparations to receive her foe. Thanks to Drake, a brief breathing-time had been gained, and this was made the most of by the captains and statesmen who saw more plainly than their Queen did, or owned that she did, the extent and imminency of the peril. The early summer of 1588 saw England armed to the teeth ; and saw Protestant and Catholic putting aside their differences to meet, shoulder to shoulder, the Spanish invader. An army, under the Earl of Leicester, was en- camped at Tilbury Fort to guard the approach to London. The levies of the southern and eastern counties were prepared to resist a descent on either shore ; and the militia of the midland shires was hurrying towards the capital. The chief hope of resistance, however, lay in the fleet, England's first and best line of defence, which was mustered in the Channel. Inferior in number and strength to the Armada, it was ready to do its duty. It consisted of only 82 vessels, and these could not cope in size with the Spanish galleons and galliasses, only 5 of them being equal to the largest, while 50 were of no greater tonnage than our ordinary yachts. They were manned, however, by 9,000 splendid seamen, all active and nimble and accustomed to the great deep, full of confidence in themselves and their leaders. As well they might be, for the admiral-in-chief was Lord Howard of Effingham, a man gifted with a fine chivalry of spirit and a ready courage, and under him were such veteran sea-lions as Francis Drake, Martin Frobisher, and John Hawkins.

On the 29th of May the Armada sailed from Lisbon, but after buffeting about for three weeks was driven by a gale into the Bay of Ferrol. There it remained, refitting and repairing, until the 22nd, when it took leave of Spain for the last time,* and begun its voyage to Dunkirk, where it was to take charge of Parma's army and convey it across the Straits. Losing on the way, in a south-west gale, four galleys and a great galleon, it entered the mouth of the Channel on the 29th, and on the morning of the 30th was under the lee of the Lizard.

All along the English coast the beacons flashed the news of its coming. The Queen's ships and some of the volunteers had got out of Plymouth Sound during the night, and dropped anchor behind the cliffs of Ram Head. By the morning, forty Englishmen were drawn up under the headland, ready for action. But the look-out men, perched on the mastheads, strained their eyes in vain to discover the hostile array. It was late in the afternoon when a cloud-bank gathered slowly on the western

---

* "The scene as the fleet passed out of the harbour must have been singularly beautiful. It was a treacherous interval of real summer. The early sunrise was lighting the long chain of the Galician mountains, marking with shadows the cleft defiles, and shining softly on the white walls and vineyards of Coruña. The wind was light, and falling towards a calm; the great galleons drifted slowly with the tide on the purple water, the long streamers trailing from the trucks, the red crosses, the emblem of the crusade, showing bright upon the hanging sails. The fruit-boats were bringing off the last fresh supplies, and the pinnaces hastening to the ships with the last loiterers on shore. Out of thirty thousand men who that morning stood upon the decks of the proud Armada, twenty thousand and more were never again to see the hills of Spain. Of the remnant who in two short months crept back ragged and torn, all but a few hundreds returned only to die."—FROUDE, xii. 388, 389.

horizon, to be resolved after awhile into a semicircular line of
stately vessels, the centre making its appearance first, and then
the two wings spreading slowly along the blue line of waters.
Ocean, says an old chronicler quaintly, s.eme l to groan beneath
their burden. They came onward, before a light wind, with a
slow and stately movement, which greatly impressed the spectators on the English ships. .

Meanwhile, on board every vessel that carried the red cross
of St. George all was activity and joy. Men rejoiced that the
long suspense was ended, and that the issue between England
and Spain was on the point of being brought to a final decision.
Anchors were weighed, and sails spread to the winds ; but
Howard had no intention of bringing on a general engagement,
and still kept under cover of the shore. Towards dusk the
Armada arrived off Plymouth, and its commander then perceived that he would not be allowed to enter the Sound unopposed. He was not inclined to fight in the darkness ; and
relying on his immense strength, he signalled to his galleons to
lie-to for the night, and prepare for action at daybreak. About
two o'clock the moon rose, and its light disclosed to the
Spaniards that sixty or seventy ships had glided out of the
Sound behind them, and were hanging on their rear, though
not within range of shot.

Bright and warm was the morning of July the 31st, though a
fresh westerly breeze cooled and purified the atmosphere. It
was a fit day for a grand aquatic spectacle, for some such
maritime pageant as the Venetians were wont to display on the
waters of the Adriatic. And spectacle or pageant it might have
been taken for at the outset, when the Spaniards were throwing
out their heavy canvas, to catch every gentle air, and like
" moving castles " bore down upon the English. It assumed a
more serious character when the English frigates, darting hither
and thither at their pleasure, poured their fire into the " high-

towered, broad-bowed " galleons and galliasses, and before
the latter could return the salute nimbly sailed away. It was
a repetition of the tactics by which Themistocles had baffled
the Persians in the days of Greece's need. To the onlooker
there was something curious and suggestive in the scene. A
herd of elephants might as well have essayed to close with a
pack of swift-footed greyhounds. Lord Howard, in his ship
the *Ark Raleigh*, boldly swept along the entire rear of the
Spanish array, and delivered his broadside into each galleon as
he passed, knocking spars and rigging about the heads of the
puzzled " Dons," and then wearing round and skilfully retracing
his course. The hesitation of the Spaniards was extreme. I
think they must have felt that they had met with the men who
would wrest from them the empire of the seas—men their
superiors in seamanship, in steadfast courage, and in patience.
They saw the English ships manœuvring with an ease that
seemed almost magical, the English guns firing with a rapidity
that surprised and confused them. A bull might as well try to
overtake and pin with its horns the terrier that hangs audaciously at its heels or flank, as one of those heavy galleons
to run alongside any of the light frigates which moved over
the waters like things of life. Don Alonzo da Leyva, in
the high-towered *Rata*, attempted to cross the bows of the
Ark. Howard hauled to the wind as if to wait for him, then
swept by with a cheer of defiance, fired into the *San Matteo*,
which lay on the waters like a log, and blithely careered on his
way.

The battle continued all through the afternoon, the Spaniards
fighting bravely whenever they had the chance, and bearing as
best they might the pitiless fire of their antagonists. " So far
as we see," said Drake, " they mean to sell their lives with
blows." Their shot flew over the English ships, while the latter
battered and riddled their antagonists. So the Spanish

Admiral signalled to his fleet to make sail up Channel, ordering Martinez de Recalde, with the Biscay squadron, which contained his finest ships and most experienced seamen, to protect his rear.

Fast as the Spaniards fled, the English followed faster. The blood-red sun went down in a stormy sky, and the sea rolled in heavily from the west. Our light English frigates rode the billows buoyantly, but the great galleons wallowed in the trough of the waves, and as they huddled close together lest their active foe should cut off any stragglers, they fell into dire disorder. The *Capitana* ran foul of the *Santa Cantalina,* and shattered her bowsprit. Immediately afterwards her foremast fell, and the wreck impeding her progress, she fell behind, firing a distress gun for assistance. The Admiral sent two of the galliasses, which would have taken her in tow, but owing to the strong sea the cable broke. Boats were dispatched to bring off her captain, Don Pedro de Valdez, and his men, but the former refused to desert his vessel. Until midnight a London privateer kept close by her side, occasionally firing a shot, and sometimes hearing voices, though, owing to the wind and sea, what they said could not be understood. In the morning Drake overtook her, and she immediately hauled down her flag. Drake carried her into Torbay, and gave her in charge of the Brixham fishermen, while he himself, with Don Pedro and his officers on board, rejoined Lord Howard. He had made a valuable prize, for the *Capitana* had several casks of "red Spanish gold" in her hold, as well as some tons of gunpowder.

This was not the sole disaster experienced by the Armada on its first day in English waters. On board one of the larger galleons, a flag-ship, the officers quarrelled hotly among themselves in their mortification at the inglorious results of the opening scene in the great drama. Words led to blows, and

the captain struck the master-gunner, a German, with his stick—
an insult which so kindled the latter's blood that he flung a burning
brand into an open powder-cask, and then leaped into the sea.
The explosion shattered the deck from stem to stern. Two
hundred seamen and soldiers were hurled aloft, of whom some
dropped into the water, and so perished ; while others, scorched
or mutilated, dead or dying, fell back upon the wreck. But
the stout ship was so strongly built that, with her tall masts
standing, she continued still to float. The Admiral sent boats
to save the officers and men, and the few who had escaped
unhurt were taken off. It was not found possible to remove
the wounded. and they clung to the wreck till morning, when
they were rescued by the English and conveyed ashore. This
humanity did not go unrewarded, for much booty in money
and gunpowder was discovered; the latter was specially acceptable, as, owing to the parsimony of the Queen's Government, the English ships were scantily supplied with ammunition.

The morning of the 1st of August was calm and fair; a light
easterly breeze scarce woke a ripple on the tranquil waters.
The Armada was by this time off the chalk cliffs of Portland,
with the English fleet a league or so to the westward, drifting
with the tide. What little wind there was gave the advantage
to the Spaniards, but Medina Sidonia had no desire to bring
on an engagement, and rested his crews, while he wrote to the
Prince of Parma an account of his mishaps, and entreated that
pilots might be sent to him, as he knew nothing of the English
waters.

On the 2nd, the wind still blowing from the east, he bore
down upon the English to offer battle ; but Howard knew his
inability to come to close quarters, and straightway put to sea.
A throb of joy shot through every Spanish heart ; the heretics
were flying ; and straightway galleon and galliass gave chase.

Among these the swiftest sailer was the *San Marcos,* and she soon got ahead, so that about noon she was at some distance from her comrades ; whereupon Howard, in pursuance of his policy of "plucking the feathers of the Spaniards one by one," ordered an attack. She was gallantly defended, and in an hour and a half received five hundred shots while returning only fifty. At last another galleon came to her assistance ; and Howard. having expended his stock of powder, was forced to withdraw.

The news of the Armada's coming had by this time spread over all England, and to the scene of action volunteers thronged from every quarter. Catholics were not less zealous than Protestants, placing the freedom of their country above the extension of the power of Rome.* Philip of Spain was in their eyes the enemy of England rather than the favoured son and servant of the Pope. "Cliffords and Veres and Percies," representing the old aristocracy, "took their places beside the Raleighs and Cecils of the new era; and from Lyme, and Weymouth, and Poole, and the Isle of Wight, young lords and gentlemen came streaming out in every smack or sloop that they could lay hold of, to snatch their share of danger and glory at Howard's side.

Little of note occurred on the 3rd of August, the English lying about two leagues to the westward, in some strait for ammunition. Medina Sidonia rashly concluded that they had grown afraid of his galleons, and sent them against Howard's fleet; they were easily beaten off. During the night a single day's supply of powder and shot was received; so that next day, Thursday, the 4th, the Spanish Admiral was quickly convinced of the fallacy of his estimate of English courage. Sir George Carew, who had come up in his pinnace, found him-

---

* It should be remembered that English Catholicism had always shown itself jealous of the pretensions of the Holy See.

self, at five in the morning, "in the midst of round shot, flying
as thick as musket-balls in a skirmish on land." For, perceiving that the Armada had fallen into much looseness of array,
Howard delivered a general attack, led by himself in the *Ark
Raleigh*, with Lord Thomas Howard in the *Lion*, Sir R. South-
well in the *Elizabeth Jonas*, Lord Sheffield in the *Bear*, and
Captain Barber in the *Victory*. Exchanging broadsides with
any great ships he passed, Howard made for the Spanish
Admiral, who had taken his place in the centre; but his design
was detected by Don Oquendo, and the latter interposed his
huge galleon, receiving a blow from Howard's ship of such
violence that two soldiers in the forecastle were killed by the
shock. Nor did the *Ark Raleigh* escape scot-free; her rudder
was unshipped, so that her pilot lost command of her, and,
drifting to leeward, she was quickly surrounded by a swarm of
galleons, all eager to overwhelm her. Howard, however,
ordered his boats to take her in tow; as she wore round
her sails filled; and when the Spaniards were rejoicing in the
thoughts of the English flag-ship as their prize, she glided
past them with such swiftness that, though the nimblest ships
in the whole Armada pursued her, " they seemed in comparison
to be still at anchor."

The fight was prolonged for hours, the English losing not
a man, and having but few wounded; while the Spaniards
suffered severely both in killed and wounded, and had much
damage done to their masts, yards, and rigging. Sore was their
discouragement; they had counted upon an easy victory over
the English heretics, and defeat already stared them in the
face "The enemy pursue me," wrote Medina Sidonia; "they
fire upon me most days from morning till nightfall, but they
will not close and grapple. I have purposely left ships exposed
to tempt them to board, but they decline to do it; and there is
no remedy, for they are swift and we are slow." The smart

English ships rattled about their ears a storm of shot which knocked their huge castled poops into splinters, while their own guns, slowly as they aimed and fired, seemed never to hit the mark.

On the 5th Howard was compelled to make sail for Dover, to obtain a supply of ammunition from the castle, and thus Medina Sidonia got a chance of running up to Calais. In the evening both fleets dropped anchor in the Calais Roads, Howard having resumed his position in the rear of the Spaniards; and there they lay watching each other, almost within cannon-shot of the shore. But it was now clear to the English captains that if a junction between Parma and Medina Sidonia were to be prevented, some decisive blow must be struck; a general engagement must be hazarded; and for this purpose the enemy must be driven or beguiled out of the secure position he had taken. The credit of the expedient that was adopted seems to belong to Howard,* to whom it may have been suggested by a recent incident in the war in the Low Countries. Eight of his smaller ships he filled with all kinds of inflammable material, while their rigging was thickly coated with pitch. At midnight they dropped down with the tide, and, like so many blazing engines of destruction, approached the Armada. The panic-stricken Spaniards, remembering the terrible effect of the fire-ships at the siege of Antwerp, hurriedly cut or slipped their cables and ran out to sea. Next morning, the 6th, Howard started in pursuit, keeping towards Calais with the bulk of his fleet, while Drake, with some 50 ships, harassed their rear. His keen eye detected the signs of a coming storm, and he felt assured that

---

* "On Sunday, at midnight, the Admiral, having the wind, sent certain ships on fire amongst the enemy, who in great confusion slipped their cables, ran foul of each other, and ran out to sea, pursued by the English. Out of 124 that anchored off Calais only 86 can be found." —*Letter to Walsingham, in State Papers, Domestic,* July 30 (O.S.), 1588.

if it overtook King Philip's heavy galleons in the eddying currents of the North Sea they would suffer severely.

All through the long summer day the English maintained the unequal fight, and when at dusk they ceased, because shot and powder were almost spent, they had good reason to be satisfied with the result of their work.   Protestant England had encountered Catholic Spain, with the odds against her, and had won—had shown a greater energy, a stauncher resolution, a loftier courage.   Three galleons had been sunk, three driven ashore, many rolled on the water dismasted and with shot-torn sides ; 4,000 men had fallen.   Far worse, indeed, was the condition of the Armada than Howard and his captains knew. Scarce a ship but had been pitifully maltreated.   Their guns were dismounted and knocked to pieces, their sails fluttered in shreds and tatters, and many were so torn by shot that, as they heeled over and brought their sides below the surface, some were with difficulty kept from sinking.   "We are lost," said Medina Sidonia to Don Oquendo, the ablest of his lieutenants ; "what are we to do ? "   " Let others talk of being lost," was the brave reply, "your Excellency has only to order up fresh cartridge "   But Oquendo stood almost alone in intrepidity of spirit, and a council of war having been hastily summoned, it was resolved that the Armada should return to Spain by the only open route—that is, by way of the North Sea. And so the great ships were lightened of all superfluous cargo and put before the wind, steering for the Orkneys. England drew breath; the danger was past.   "Never anything pleased me better," wrote Drake to Walsingham,* " than seeing the enemy fly with a southerly wind to the northwards.   I have a good eye to the Prince of Parma, for, with the grace of God, if we like, I doubt not ere it be long so to handle the matter

* *State Papers, Domestic,* August 7, 1588.   The dates, it must be remembered, are Old Style.

with the Duke of Sidonia as he shall wish himself at St. Mary Port among his orange-trees."

Lord Henry Seymour, with a squadron of 30 ships, was left to guard the narrow seas, and keep watch and ward upon Dunkirk, while Howard and Drake, having on board only five days' rations and a scanty supply of shot and powder, pursued the flying foe. At first they seem to have expected that the Spaniards might turn at bay, but by degrees their beaten and desperate condition they began to understand. Past them floated the dead bodies of mules and horses which had been thrown overboard for want of fresh water. "More than one poor crippled ship dropped behind as her spars snapped, and as the water made its way through the wounded seams in the straining sides." The Spaniards, stricken, it was very plain, "with a wonderful fear, made no attempt to succour their consorts, but passed on leaving them to founder." It must not be thought that the victors were in very good case. The men suffered from disease, and their rations were poor in quality and small in quantity. So at last, when only three days' scanty provisions were left, Howard abandoned the chase: with the largest of his ships he reached Margate safely, while the others put into Harwich.

The following extract from a journal of the ten days' contest with the Armada, written by Lord Howard, the reader, I think, will find full of interest :—*

"July 19 (29 N.S.), Friday. Upon Friday, being the 19th of the present month, part of the Spanish navy, to the number of 50 sail, were discovered about the isles of Scilly, hovering in the wind, as it seemed, to attend the rest of the fleet; and the next day, at three of the clock in the afternoon, the Lord Admiral got forth with our navy out of Plymouth, though with

* *State Papers, Domestic,* August 7, 1588. The dates, it must be remembered, are Old Style.

some difficulty, the wind being at south-west. **Notwith-**
standing, through the great travail used by our men, they not
only cleared the harbour, but also, the next day being Sunday,
about nine of the clock in the morning, recovered the wind of
the whole fleet, which being thoroughly descried, was found to
consist of 120 sail, great and small.

"At the same instant the Lord Admiral gave them fight
within the view of Plymouth, from whence the Mayor with others
sent them continually supplies of men till they were past their
coast. This fight continued till one of the clock the same day,
wherein the enemy was made to bear room with some of his
ships to stop their leaks. The same day, by an accident of
fire happening in one of their great ships of the burden of
tons, they were blown up with powder, about 120 men, the
rest being compelled to leave her, and so she was by the Lord
Admiral sent into the west part of England.

"July 22, Monday.—Upon Monday, the 22nd, one of the
chief galleons, wherein was Don Pedro de Valdez with 450
men, was taken by reason of his mast that was spent with the
breaking of his bowsprit, so as he presently yielded with sundry
gentlemen of good quality.

"July 23, Tuesday.—On Tuesday, the 23rd, the Lord
Admiral charging the enemy, who had then gotten some
advantage of the wind, and therefore seemed more desirous to
abide our force than before, fell in fight with them over
against St. Alban's, about five of the clock in the morning, the
wind being at north-east, and so continued with great force on
both sides till late in the evening, when the wind coming again
to be south-west and somewhat large, they began to go homeward

"July 24, Wednesday.—The same night and all Wednesday
the Lord Admiral kept very near unto the Spanish fleet."

And so the unpretending chronicle runs on, the writer

apparently unconscious of the greatness of the work he so simply records.

Writing to King Philip of the English victory, the Duke of Parma said, " Todo la gloria se da á Drake " (All the glory belonged to Drake). And this, the verdict of Drake's contemporaries, has been confirmed by posterity. He it was who conceived the plan of battle. He it was who encouraged the despondent, lent strength to the feeble, infused courage into the timid. He it was whose presence inspired the seamen with confidence. He it was who, when the Admiral grew faint of heart, nerved and supported him with his bolder resolution. And therefore it was fitting that with his own pen he should sum up the grand results of the contest in which he had played the leading part, and should tell how—

" It was happily manifested in very deed to all nations, that their navy, which they termed invincible, consisting of one hundred and fifty sail of ships, not only of their own kingdom, but strengthened with the greatest argosies, Portugal carracks, Florentines, and large hulks of other countries, were, by thirty of her Majesty's own ships of war, and a few of our merchants, by the wise, valiant, and advantageous conduct of the Lord Charles Howard, High Admiral of England, beaten and shuffled together even from the Lizard in Cornwall, first to Portland, where they shamefully left Don Pedro de Valdez, with his mighty ship; from Portland to Calais, where they lost Hugh de Moncado, with the galleys of which he was captain ; and from Calais, driven with squibs from their anchors, were chased out of the sight of England round about Scotland and Ireland ; where, for the sympathy of their religion, hoping to find succour and assistance, a great part of them were crushed against the rocks, and those other that landed, being very many in number, were, notwithstanding, broken, slain, and taken ; and so sent from village to village, coupled in halters to be shipped into England, where her Majesty, of her princely and invincible disposition, disdaining to put them to death, and scorning either to retain or maintain them, they were all sent back again to their countries to witness and recount the worthy achievement of their invincible and dreadful navy—of which the number of sailors, the fearful burthen of their ships, the commanders' names of every squadron, with all other their magazines of provisions, were put in print, as an army and navy irresistible and disdaining prevention ; with all which their great terrible ostentation they did not, in all their sailing round about England, so much as sink or take one ship, bark, pinnace, or cock-boat of ours, or even have so much as one sheepcote on this land."

" I sent my ships against men," said Philip, "not against the seas"—unwilling to do that honour to his brave enemies which all civilised Europe proclaimed to be their due.   On the other hand, England did not claim the victory as wholly the work of her Drakes and Howards, her Frobishers and Seymours ; she recognised the hand of Providence in the storm that drove the defeated Armada on the rocks of England and Scotland.   On the medal struck in commemoration of this great event were engraved the words, " The Lord sent his wind, and scattered them."   A solemn public thanksgiving was held at St. Paul's, and praise and prayer went up from every altar as from every heart.   For, as a modern writer graphically puts it, " The victory over the Armada, the deliverance from Spain, the rolling away of the Catholic terror, which had hung like a cloud over the hopes of the new people, was like a passing from death unto life.   Within as without, the dark sky suddenly cleared.   The national unity proved stronger than the religious strife. . . . . Nor were the results of the victory," adds the historian,* " less momentous to

* J. R. Green, *History of the English People*, iii. 447, 448.

Europe at large. What Wolsey and Henry had struggled for, Elizabeth had done. At her accession England was scarcely reckoned among European powers. The wisest statesmen looked on her as doomed to fall into the hands of France, or to escape that fate by remaining a dependency of Spain. But the national independence had grown with the national life. France was no longer a danger. Scotland was no longer a foe. Instead of hanging on the will of Spain, England had fronted Spain, and conquered her. She now stood on a footing of equality with the greatest powers of the world. Her military might, indeed, was drawn from the discord which rent the peoples about her, and would pass away with its close. But a new and lasting greatness opened on the sea. She had sprung at a bound into a great sea-power."

In this great work Drake had been the prime mover. It was he who had taught English statesmen the important lesson that the way to conquer Spain was to attack the New World colonies from which she drew her wealth. It was he who, by his voyage round the world, had roused the maritime ardour of the people. It was he who by his surprising victories had inspired them with confidence in their prowess, and a belief that they were entitled to the supremacy of the seas. His name was the rallying-cry of all the bolder spirits of the country. The naval enterprise of England owes its origin to the impulse given by the seamanship, courage, and good fortune of Francis Drake.

Philip thanked God that he could easily, if he chose, "place another fleet upon the seas," and with the sullen persistency of his character prepared to make good his boast. Early in 1589 the western ports of Spain were once more crowded with men and ships, and a second armada, it was announced, would shortly issue forth to chastise and subjugate the presumptuous islanders. Drake, in pursuance of his old policy, that it was safer to attack the enemy than to wait his assault, offered to lead an expedition against Spain; and the Queen, accepting the offer, furnished six of the largest ships, with a body of troops under the veteran Sir John Norris. The London merchants and other adventurers came forward with their usual readiness, and in the course of a few weeks a fleet of 80 sail, including transports, was collected, manned by 1,500 sailors, and carrying 11,000 troops. But the Queen, as usual, stinted her supplies of money and provisions, and the departure of the fleet was disastrously delayed by contrary winds. At this juncture the Portuguese showed a keen desire to release themselves from the bonds of Spanish domination; and a certain Don Antonio, who laid claim to the throne of Portugal, promised that if an English fleet appeared at Lisbon, the whole country would rise in arms. Drake and Norris were therefore instructed to sail to Lisbon.

The fleet weighed anchor on the 21st of April, but was still baffled by adverse winds, and many of the ships put back to England, or even into French ports, weakening the expedition by nearly 3,000 men. The rest proceeded to Corunna, then called the Groyne, which was captured without much resistance, and yielded a large booty of wine and oil. About 500 Spaniards lost their lives in the sack, and a large quantity of ammunition and stores was destroyed. The upper town was afterwards besieged, and a breach having been effected, an assault was ordered; but the enemy mustered in such force and displayed so much courageous obstinacy that it completely failed. Sir John Norris then resolved to re-embark his troops, but to protect them from annoyance it was necessary, in the first place, to disperse an army of 15,000 men, under the command of the Conde de Antrade, which had advanced to within some five or six miles of the English position. What followed is thus described by Drake and

Norris in their dispatch to the Queen's Council, dated May 7th (17th) :—

"Even as this letter was almost ended, certain companies of the Flemings being sent abroad on foraging, brought in a prisoner, who upon his life assured us that there were 15,000 soldiers assembled and encamped very strongly at Puente de Burgos, about five English miles from us, under the conduct and commandment of the Earls of Altomira and Andrada. Whereupon, on Tuesday, the 6th of this present, we marched towards them with 7,000 soldiers, leaving the rest for the guard and siege of the town, and encountering with them, they continued fight the space of three-quarters of an hour ; and then we forced them to retire to the foot of a bridge, whereon not above three could march in rank, and was about ten score in length, from whence (although they were there defended by some fortifications, and had the benefit and succour of certain houses and other places adjoining) they were followed with our shot and pikes, with such courage and fierceness, as, after some few volleys on both sides, they entered the bridge, when in the midst, with the push of the pikes, forced to make retreat into their trenches to the farther foot of the bridge where they encamped, which also (being pursued) they forsook and betook themselves to flight, abandoning their weapons, bag and baggage, and lost about 1,000 in skirmish and pursuit.

"Had we had either horse on hand or some companies of Irish there to have pursued them, there had none of them escaped ; which cannot be but a notable dishonour to the King, and in our opinions no small furtherance to the service intended. We lost not above two common soldiers and one of the corporals of the field. Sir Edward Norris, who led the vanguard, grievously hurt with a blow on the head, and Captain Fulford shot in the arm. Captain George shot in the left eye.

Captain Hind wounded in three places of the head, but no danger of life in any of them.

"Thus it hath pleased God to give her Majesty the victory, which we have great hope to pursue elsewhere with like success, if we may be succoured with such necessaries as are needful; if not, we can but do our endeavours, and leave the rest to the consideration of your lordships, whom we humbly leave to the protection of the Almighty."

On the 10th the fleet sailed along the Portuguese coast, and was joined by the Earl of Essex as a volunteer, bringing with him some war-ships. At Peniche, forty miles from Lisbon, the army was disembarked. Two troops were intrusted to the impetuous Essex, who, leaving one to protect the landing, pushed forward with the other to attack some Spanish companies that had come out of the town. Before the English pikemen these doughty warriors fled at once; the town was entered unopposed, and at the first summons the castle surrendered.

Norris now decided on marching against Lisbon, where, if the weather permitted, Drake promised to join him with the fleet. On the 20th the army arrived before Lisbon, and quickly occupied its suburbs. Here Norris found, to his disappointment, that the people did not welcome the English as deliverers, and fly to arms as Don Antonio had promised, but remained cold and indifferent. He had no sufficient force with which to attack the Spaniards in such a case as this; his supply of ammunition was almost exhausted, and he had not a single piece of artillery for battering purposes. After lingering several days, while his army suffered much from sickness, he resolved on joining Drake at Cascais, of which the great sea-captain had taken possession, as well as of numerous ships laden with stores and munitions for the new armada. Re-embarking, he sailed for Vigo; but the fleet was scattered and crippled in a gale, and it was seventeen days before they reached port, with their crews decimated by sickness and famine. A supply of provisions was indispensable, and the army, reduced to 2,000 effectives, landed to fight for it. The town was taken, and with it a good store of wine. Then the country was ravaged for miles around with fire and sword, and the town having been given to the flames, the army re-embarked. After some further vicissitudes, the expedition returned to Plymouth, having lost one-half of the adventurers, and failed in its chief object; yet not wholly unsuccessful, for it had inflicted a grave amount of injury upon the enemy, and added to the reputation of English seamen for enterprise and prowess. As Camden says, " Most men were of opinion that the English hereby answered all points, both of revenge and honour, having in so short a compass of time taken one town by storm, made a glorious assault upon another, driven before them a very potent army, landed their forces in four several places, marched seven days together in order of battle and with colours flying through the enemy's country, attacked a strong and flourishing city with a small handful of men, and lodged for three nights in the suburbs of it. Besides this, they beat the enemy back to the very gates after they had made a sally, took two castles lying on the sea, and spoiled the enemy of all their stores and ammunition. . . . . And most certain it is that England was so far a gainer by this expedition as from that time to apprehend no incursions from Spain, but rather to grow more warm and animated against that country."

There was, unquestionably, a higher result of such a warfare than the capture of ships or the destruction of towns and villages. The energies called forth in that stirring time, and by so constant a succession of daring adventures, produced "a corresponding elevation of the national character." In one of his earliest comedies, Shakspere, in a scene where a father advises his son " to seek preferment," has briefly pointed out the great principles which at this period fired and sustained the ambition of England's sons :—

> "Some, to the wars, to try their fortune there;
> Some, to discover islands far away." *

It was not until 1596 that Drake went to sea again ; but in the interval he did not allow his active mind to rust inglorious, like a disused weapon, He sat as member for Plymouth in the Parliament of 1592-3, and by no means as a silent member; and steadily urged upon the House the necessity of crippling the power of Spain. He busied himself in enlarging and strengthening the defences of Plymouth ; and, a more permanently useful work, supplied the town with an abundance of fresh water, which he brought by a line of tunnels and aqueducts from the pure fresh springs of Dartmoor. His residence of Buckland Abbey, which he purchased from Sir Richard Trueville in 1587, was situated about two miles from Plymouth, on the wooded banks of the picturesque Tay.

III.

The war with Spain blazed into fresh activity in 1595; and English fleets and armies, both in the Old World and the New, were busily engaged in harassing the enemy. An English armament drove the Spaniards out of Brest; and an expedition under Sir Francis Drake and Sir John Hawkins was dispatched against the Spanish colonies in the West Indies. With the history of this expedition we close the last chapter of our hero's career. It consisted of about twenty private ships, and six of the Queen's ships, viz. the *Defiance*, Admiral Sir Francis Drake ; the *Garland*, Vice-Admiral Sir John Hawkins ; the *Hope*, Captain

---

* *Two Gentlemen of Verona*, act i. scene 3.

Gilbert Stock; the *Bunaventura*, Captain Troughton; the *Foresight*, Captain Winter; and the *Adventure*, Captain Thomas Drake; and it carried a considerable military force under Sir Thomas Baskerville. Its immediate destination was Porto Rico, where, if report might be credited, a great treasure had been accumulated for the King of Spain's use in preparing a third grand armada for the invasion of England.

At the outset Drake designed to land his troops at Nombre de Dios, in the Caribbean Sea, and thence carry them across the isthmus to Panama, in order to pounce upon the ingots of gold and silver annually brought thither from the mines of Peru and Mexico; but, shortly before setting sail, he received letters from the Queen containing information of the arrival in Europe of the West Indian or Plata fleet. It was added, however, that one of the most valuable of the galleons had lost her mast and put into Porto Rico; and the Queen commanded him, therefore, to make Porto Rico his first object of attack. In reply Drake and Hawkins sent the following dispatch, which is worth transcription because it is the last to which these two brave "sea-dogs" put their names:—

"Our duty in most humble manner remembered, it may please your lordship [Lord Burleigh] we have answered her Majesty's letter, we hope to her Highness's contentment, whom we would not wittingly or willingly displease. We humbly thank your lordship for your manifold favours, which we have always found never variable, but with all favour, love, and constancy, for which we can never be sufficiently thankful, but with our prayers to God long to bless your good lordship with honour and health.

"We think it be true that some small men-of-war be taken upon the coast of Spain, but, they are of very small moment. They be for the most part such small caravels as were before this taken from the Spaniards. Some small number of our men are yet in Spain, which is the only loss; but, as we learn, there be not above one hundred left in Spain of them, but many returned already into England.

"And so looking daily for a good wind, we humbly take our leave.   From Plymouth, the 18th of August, 1595.

"Your lordship's ever most bounden,

"FRA. DRAKE.   JOHN HAWKINS."*

Ten days later Drake and Hawkins sailed from Plymouth, and made for the Canaries, where they attempted the reduction of Grand Canary, the largest of the group, but found it impossible to land their troops in the boats on account of the violent surf. On nearing Martinico, Drake, with four or five ships, constituting the van, was separated from the rest of the fleet by a sudden gale; but all reassembled at Guadaloupe. There he took in fresh water, refitted the ships, and lodged his men ashore, that they might recruit their energies. Off the eastern end of Porto Rico gallant old Sir John Hawkins died, prostrated by the unhealthy climate, which carried off numbers of the men. He was succeeded as second in command by Sir Thomas Baskerville; and the fleet in due time dropped anchor about ten miles to the east of San Juan de Porto Rico, exchanging a sharp fire with the Spanish batteries. The English ships received twenty-eight great shot, the last of which struck the Admiral's through the mizen, and the last but one went through her quarter into the chief cabin, the General being there at supper, knocking his stool from under him, but hurt-

---

* From the *Harl. MSS.* (cited by Barrow). In a contemporary hand the following note has been added at the bottom of the letter :—" The Queen sent these two brave sea-captains with a fleet to Porto Rico in America, belonging to the Spaniard, having heard of a great mass of treasure brought thither.   But it proved an unsuccessful attempt, and neither of them returned ever home again, both dying at sea at different places, in this voyage."

ing him not. It wounded, however, seven of his guests, and two of them, Sir Nicholas Clifford and Master (Brute) Browne so seriously that they died of their injuries. Browne was an old comrade and friend of Drake, and as he breathed his last Drake exclaimed, " Ah, dear Brute, I will grieve for thee, but now is no time for me to let down my spirits ! "

On the following morning the fleet took up its position to the westward, and at nightfall twenty-five pinnaces, boats, and shallops, well manned and well equipped, glided into the road-stead. As intelligence of Drake's voyage and destination had reached the island, every precaution had been taken to guard against his attack. The great galleon had been sunk in the mouth of the harbour, and the whole of her treasure removed ashore. A floating boom of masts and spars was laid on each side, near the forts and castles, so as to guard the entrance ; and five ships were moored within the breakwater. As the flotilla advanced it was received with a heavy fire. It pushed forward, however, into the harbour, burnt the five ships, and a large one of 900 tons, and destroyed their cargoes of silk, oil, and wine, before it was driven back by the tremendous cannonade opened upon it from every side.

Steering to the Caribbean shore, Drake took the town of La Hacha, but restored it to its inhabitants on receiving a ransom of 34,000 ducats. The ransom of the town of Rancheria not being forthcoming, it was burned to the ground, and several towns and villages along the coast met with the same fate. At length Drake arrived at Nombre de Dios, which fell into his hands after a short resistance, and was likewise given up to the flames, along with all the vessels, large and small, in the harbour. In these buccaneering achievements much valuable time was lost; and the whole conduct of the expedition shows so many signs of dilatoriness, indecision, and want of

energy, that it is evident that physical weakness, or some unex-
plained cause, had weakened the vigour of the Admiral's cha
racter and broken down his old tenacity of purpose. At
Nombre de Dios the expedition to Panama was organized, and
Sir Thomas Baskerville set out on his march across the isthmus
with 750 soldiers. But the Indians proved hostile, and maintained a harassing fire upon the troops as they threaded the
intricate defiles. Moreover, the Spaniards were fully prepared
for the attempt, and had erected there strong forts to prohibit
an enemy's advance. The task was too big for their leader;
and, famished, footsore, and weary, the adventurers turned
back again, and, with a loss of one hundred men and officers,
withdrew to Nombre de Dios.

This disastrous failure told severely upon Drake in his weakened and dispirited condition, and he fell ill of a sickness which
proved a sickness unto death.

"On the 13th of January, 1596," as Hakluyt tells us, "Sir
Francis Drake began to keep his cabin, and complain of a
scouring or flux. On the 23rd the fleet set sail, and stood up
again for Porto Bello, which is but three leagues to the westward of Nombre de Dios.

"On the 28th, at four of the clock in the morning, our
General, Sir Francis Drake, departed this life, having been extremely sick of a flux, which began the night before to stop on
him. He used some speeches at, or a little before, his death,
rising and apparelling himself, but being brought to bed again
within one hour died.

"They moved on to Porto Bello, and after coming to anchor
in the bay, and the solemn burial of our General in the sea,
Sir Thomas Baskerville being aboard the *Defiance*, where Mr.
Bride made a sermon, having to his audience all the captains in
the fleet."

What more fitting grave could be desired for the great seaman with whom begins the long roll of illustrious English admirals?

" This our captain," to repeat the words of Fuller, " was a religious man towards God and His houses, generally sparing churches where he came ; chaste in his life, just in his dealings, true to his word, merciful to those who were under him, and hating nothing so much as idleness."

ROBERT BLAKE, ADMIRAL AND GENERAL AT SEA.

A.D. 1599—1657.

As in the present volume we are concerned only with the achievements of " Eminent Sailors," we shall pass rapidly over that portion of the caieer of Robert Blake which had no connection with " the service of the sea."

Towards the end of August, 1599, was born at Bridgewater Robert Blake, the eldest son of Humphrey Blake, of Plansfield, and his wife Sara, daughter and coheiress of Humphiey Williams. His early education he obtained at the Bridgewater Grammar School, then considered one of the best in England. At the age of sixteen he was sent to Oxford, where he matriculated as a member of St. Alban's Hall. Little is known of his college life ; but it is recorded of him that he rose early, and was exceedingly diligent at his books, lectures, and devotion ; that he took great delight in field-sports, particularly in fishing and shooting. From St. Alban's Hall he removed to Wadham College, where he applied himself with much assiduity to the acquisition of knowledge. Pecuniary misfortunes had overtaken his father, and young Blake desired to relieve him of the expense of maintaining him at Oxford by securing a fellowship in one of the colleges. In this aim, however, he failed ; and thus England gained, instead of a scholar who would probably have languished in lettered obscurity, a great captain and admiral who led her fleets to victory.

In due time he took the degree of M.A., but was called from the calm and seclusion of a collegiate life by the death of his father in November, 1625. The care of a large family then devolved upon him. He accepted the responsibility with courage, and discharged it with success. Under his loving and firm supervision his seven brothers and two sisters were reared, educated, and placed out in the world in positions of respectability and comfort. Meanwhile he watched with observant eye the progress of public affairs, and gradually developed those political and religious opinions then associated with the names of " Puritan " and " Republican." As the action of Charles I. and his Ministers awakened the just alarm and indignation of all who valued civil and religious liberty, he employed himself with all his force of character and tenacity of intellect to organize in Somersetshire a party of resistance. The extent of his influence is shown by the fact that he was returned to the Long Parliament in 1640 as member for Taunton. But when the appeal to arms was made Blake hastened back from Westminster to Somersetshire, and began to organize an armed resistance. Mr. Dixon tells us that his was one of the first troops in the field, and that both his horse and foot played a conspicuous part in the first action of any importance in the West of England, when Sir John Horner routed the newly raised forces of the Marquis of Hertford at Wells. From that date he was in almost every action of importance in the western counties, fighting his way gradually into military notice. In the sharp encounter at Bodmin he proved his fiery courage ; on the fiercely disputed field of Lansdown his conduct earned the approval of Sir William Waller. His attention, however, was not wholly confined to military affairs. " His knowledge of business, his activity, and his severe integrity pointed him out for other employments, and he was made one of the committee for seizing and sequestrating the estates of delinquents in Somerset—a thankless office, the duties of which he nevertheless discharged for several years without giving rise to a single accusation of partiality, or making for himself one personal enemy. But the camp was his true sphere of action ; his superiority to the men about him lay in the marvellous fertility, energy, and comprehensiveness of his military genius. Before the field of action was as yet occupied by large armies, he scoured the country with his intrepid dragoons, rousing the spirit of his friends, carrying terror to the hearths of his enemies, and levying contributions of money and horses on all towns and hamlets known to be disaffected to the national cause. In the Royalist camp Prince Rupert could alone be compared with him as a partisan soldier ; and that brilliant cavalry officer, fated to be foiled so often on land and sea by Blake, soon made the acquaintance of his redoubtable enemy at the siege of Bristol." *

It was in July, 1643, that he was sent with a reinforcement to the garrison of Bristol, then invested by a Royalist army of 14,000 foot and 6,000 horse under the Princes Rupert and Maurice. In an action with the Royalists outside the walls he was completely successful ; but Nathaniel Fiennes, the governor, lost head and heart, and surrendered to the Royalist chiefs. Blake, who had been promoted to a lieutenant-colonelcy, with a few companies of horse rode away to Bridgewater, and thence to the south coast, where he took part in the defence of Lyme Regis. The little town was besieged by a large force, but with so much skill and courage were the military operations of the Roundheads conducted that the enemy were compelled to retire, with a loss of 2,000 men.

Blake and his veterans, encouraged by this success, marched straight upon Taunton, which was in the hands of a Royalist garrison, and demanded its surrender. Colonel Reeves with a

* HEPWORTH DIXON, *Life of Robert Blake*, p. 38.

good grace yielded, and Blake took possession of the town on the 8th of July, 1644. He immediately proceeded to enlarge and repair its defences, knowing that the Royalists would not fail to make an effort for the recovery of a town of so much importance. His expectation was quickly fulfilled, Sir Richard Grenville undertaking its reduction, and prosecuting its siege with a vast deal of vigour. When he was stricken down by a severe wound, Sir John Berkeley succeeded to the command, and evinced an equal determination. Inch by inch the Royalists pushed their approaches, and even forced their swords and pikes into the outer streets; but the garrison converted every house into a fortress, from the windows of which they delivered an effective fire; and the armed progress of the enemy was not only inconsiderable, but attended with great carnage. More serious far to the besieged was famine; but Blake steadfastly held out until relieved on the 11th of May, 1645, by the arrival of Colonel Walden and four regiments of Fairfax's army.

It was fitting that Blake should be appointed governor of the city he had saved, and he continued to hold the post until the cause of Absolutism perished on the scaffold at Whitehall. From his tranquil Somersetshire home he saw scene after scene in that great tragic drama which terminated in so startling a catastrophe, without himself appearing as an actor on the stage. He disapproved of the execution of Charles I., and would have been content, like many other moderate Republicans, with his deposition and banishment. His calm and serious mind never yielded to fanaticism in religion or in politics; and ambitious only to do as best he could the work that fell to his hands, he cared not for the applause of listening senates or the approval of excited crowds. In the new form of government that was raised on the ruins of the shattered monarchy by the genius of Vane, St. John, and Cromwell, he readily acquiesced.

He sought for no place in it for himself. Foremost he among the patient, silent servants of the State; a tranquil, God-fearing, honourable man; always ready to do his duty, and content with so much public approval as the zealous performance of that duty might secure. His was not the genius that could play the part of a Cromwell. His was not the masterful intellect that could govern and guide a nation. For Robert Blake the imperial purple would have been "a world too wide;" enough for him to carry out those enterprises which the capacity of his rulers designed, and to wield with vigour the sword his country placed in his hand.

One of the earliest objects which commanded the attention of Cromwell and his associates was the establishment of the supremacy of England in the narrow seas, and the defence of her growing commerce against the fleets of Holland or the piratical cruisers of Prince Rupert. They proceeded, therefore, to organize the navy on a large scale. But in the selection of a suitable commander for the navy thus organized they experienced a great difficulty. The Commonwealth had produced many able soldiers, but few successful seamen, the struggle for freedom having been wholly carried on and finally decided by its armies. There were, indeed, some admirable captains of ships—men of whose nautical skill and courage no doubt could be entertained; but the one thing needful—a mastermind, to animate, direct, and govern the whole; to infuse new life into an inert naval administration; to remove the dissatisfaction which rankled in the hearts of the common sailors, and teach them the habit of victory—was the one thing not easily obtainable.

Such a man they found at last in Robert Blake. True, he had had no experience of the sea, knew nothing of ships, was ignorant of naval manœuvres; but he was known to be endowed with resolute purpose, tenacious courage, and a lofty and liberal temper. With him they associated Colonels Deane and Popham. The three commanders were styled "Generals and Admirals at Sea," and invested with ample powers. Moreover, they were instructed to capture all ships-of-war which still carried the royal flag; to drive the corsair princes, Rupert and Maurice, from the high seas; and to co-operate with a suitable land force in that new expedition against rebellious Ireland which was to be led by Cromwell.

Into the great work of reforming the naval service Blake threw himself with immense energy. As soon as it was accomplished, the Commonwealth's naval forces were formed into four great divisions. With one of these Sir George Ascue cruised in the Irish Seas; with a second, Colonel Popham watched Plymouth Sound and the British Channel; Deane, with a third, hovered between Portsmouth and Dover; while Blake himself prepared to follow up and destroy Prince Rupert's piratical squadron.

Blake was fifty years old when, on the 10th of April, 1649, he first hoisted his flag as "General and Admiral at Sea," beginning a new career at an age which, to most men of action, brings an opportunity and a prospect of rest.

He displayed in it even more than his former activity, pursuing Prince Rupert from Kinsale to the Tagus, and blockading him there for a whole winter. Afterwards he hunted him and his cousin Maurice from Majorca to Toulon, and from Toulon to Majorca, entirely breaking up their fleet, and clearing the Channel of their cruisers. For this high service the Council of State appointed him Warden of the Cinque Ports, and Parliament voted him its thanks and a donation of £1,000.

In April, 1651, he reduced the Royalist stronghold of St. Mary's, in the Scilly Isles. The resistance of the Cavaliers was such as might have been expected from English gentlemen, but it availed nothing against Blake's dogged purpose. Moreover, like all great commanders, he possessed the faculty of raising his men—insensibly, as it were, without any direct consciousness on their part—to his own standard of heroism. None could withstand those daring fighting-men of his—the Ironsides of the English navy. He and they, by their united will, got his frigates through the difficult channels which intersect the Scilly Archipelago, and quickly battered down the Royalist defences with their thundering broadsides. For the first time in the history of naval warfare he brought wooden walls against stone walls, and proved their superiority. St. Mary's fell, and the Scilly Islands acknowledged the authority of the Commonwealth.

Passing over his capture of Jersey, which Colonel Carteret held for the King, we come to that portion of his career which has made him famous among English admirals. In 1652 the long smouldering jealousies between England and Holland blazed out into a sudden flame, and the two nations engaged in a deadly and desperate struggle. At bottom it was commercial in character and object—a contention for the carrying trade of Europe ; ostensibly it was caused by the demand of the Commonwealth that any Dutch vessel should do homage to its flag in the narrow seas. Commodore Young, acting on an order of the Council of State, bade the admiral of a Dutch fleet which was returning from Genoa lower his ensign. The latter refused compliance. Young immediately poured in a broadside, and, after a sharp fight, compelled him to strike his flag.

Deeply angered by this open insult, the States-General of Holland ordered their great admiral, Van Tromp, to take command of a fleet of 42 ships, for the purpose of maintaining the dignity of the Dutch flag and protecting the interests of Dutch commerce. And while the Dutch Ambassadors were p ofessedly bent upon amicable negotiations, Van Tromp put to sea, and suddenly appearing in the Downs, seemed to threaten with his frowning cannon the "inviolate shores" of England.

Expecting, and not unprepared or unwilling for war, the Council of State had reappointed Blake to the chief command, and Blake had chosen as his vice and rear admirals two excellent officers, William Penn, the ablest seaman in England, and Major Nehemiah Bourne. The latter was lying in the Downs with eight men-of-war, when Tromp, by stress of weather, was compelled to run into Dover. Tromp immediately sent two frigates to offer an explanation of his conduct, and to promise that he would sail for the North Sea when the hurricane abated. Bourne amicably accepted the explanation, invited the captains of the two frigates to take a glass of wine with him, and at the same time sent a messenger to Blake, who was anchored in Rye Bay. The Admiral came up with all speed, and arrived next day to see Tromp making to the eastward. But suddenly a ship overtook the Dutch fleet; it brought intelligence of the outrage on Dutch honour; and Tromp immediately putting about, ran towards the English, but without lowering his flag.

Wherefore, according to the English account,* Blake fired a signal gun to remind him of his lack of courtesy. A second —a third—to which Tromp replied, as if in scorn, by a single gun, still keeping the Dutch flag flying from his mast-head.

Tromp's fleet numbered 42 ships; Blake had with him only 15, but they were larger, and carried more guns and more men. On the other hand, while a larger proportion of the English crews were new and untried levies, the Dutch were mainly

* The Dutch represent the English as aggressors, and profess that Tromp desired to avoid an engagement.

composed of picked and experienced seamen.   The disparity
of force was great, but it could not influence Blake's determination.   As soon as the two fleets came within musket-range, he
pushed forward in his flag-ship, the *Janus*, to speak with the
Dutch Admiral; but Tromp, it is said, poured in upon him a
destructive broadside, which damaged the poops and shattered
the cabin windows.   Blake and his officers were seated over
their wine in his cabin when the shot rattled about their ears.
" Well," exclaimed Blake, " 'tis not very civil in Mynheer
Tromp to mistake my flag-ship for a brothel and break my
windows."   A second broadside thundered as he spoke.
Then, it is said, the Admiral twisted his black whiskers round
his fingers, as was his wont when he was angry, and bade the
gunners return her enemy's fire.

The battle now became general.   There was no manœuvring,
no combination of dexterous stratagems, no display of intricate tactics.   It was hand-to-hand fighting—each man for
himself, and Providence over all !   The *Janus* was the first
English ship in action ; and out of 250 men lost several
officers and men killed, and about 35 desperately wounded.
By other ships the unequal struggle was stoutly maintained,
until, as the twilight gathered on the water, Bourne and his
squadron, attracted by the echoing cannon, came up under a
cloud of canvas.   His arrival infused a new life into the
English battle, and sorely discouraged the Dutch.   Van
Tromp drew off his fleet and returned to the shores of Holland, having lost a couple of ships, one sunk and one taken,
and 250 prisoners.

In both counties this " untoward event " inflamed the
desire for war, and both set to work with all their energies so
to prepare for battle as to insure victory.   England added 40
new ships to her fleet, raised the wages of her seamen, made a
levy in every port, so that, in one month from the battle in

the Downs, Blake was at the head of a fleet of 105 vessels, carrying 3,961 guns. Nor was Holland less in earnest; she laid down the keels of 60 new men-of-war, and by high rates of pay tempted into her navy the ablest seamen of every nation. Before long a fine armada of 120 ships, well manned and well equipped, was under the command of Marten Harperts Tromp.

The first great operation of the war was directed against the herring fishery in the North Seas, which, at that time almost monopolized by the Dutch fishermen, was a principal source of the wealth of Holland. Ascertaining that the spring flotilla, of more than six hundred "busses," was on its homeward voyage, escorted by twelve men-of-war, Blake left Sir George Ascue in the Channel to observe Tromp's movements, and with sixty ships sailed northwards to intercept it. His van came up with the herring fleet off Black Ness, and after a sharp action sank three and captured nine of the convoy men-of-war. The six hundred busses fell into his hands, but as their destruction would have ruined scores of innocent families, Blake satisfied himself with levying a royalty of every tenth herring, and with delivering a stern warning to the fishermen to refrain from trespassing within British waters.

Tromp, meanwhile, had quitted the Texel with 102 sail and 10 fire-ships, and as before such a force Ascue was compelled to retreat, flying for shelter under the guns of Deal, he rode triumphant in the Downs and threatened the coast of Kent. He was prevented from approaching near enough to do any damage by a strong wind that blew off shore; and, after awhile, returned to port to convoy northward a fleet of Baltic traders, after which he sailed in search of Blake, hoping to crush him with his great preponderance of force.

The two fleets came in sight of each other off the Shetland

Isles early on the 6th of August, and eagerly prepared to
contend for the supremacy of the seas. But a tremendous
storm from the north-west suddenly broke upon them, and the
great ships were scattered right and left, like straws before the
wind. Blake, running at once for the nearest port, escaped
with comparatively little loss ; but the Dutch suffered severely,
and when Tromp reached the mouth of the Texel nearly half
of his fleet was missing, and six of his frigates had fallen into
the hands of the English. Though sorely afflicted by this disaster, the national spirit was not dismayed, and every effort
was made to equip a new fleet. With the characteristic ingratitude of nations, however, the Dutch heaped disgrace and
contumely upon the unfortunate Admiral, and placed in command of their new armament the famous seaman Cornelis De
Witt. Eager to accomplish some great thing which should
prove his superiority to the discredited Tromp, he set sail immediately with 45 men-of-war, and was joined by De Ruyter ;
but the winds and waters were against him, and a heavy gale
beat him back to port, with serious loss and damage. It
seemed as if in the contention between England and Holland
Providence was not disposed to favour the latter.

Having refitted his ships, De Witt put to sea again, with the
view of making for the Downs and attacking the British in
their own waters. But he was anticipated by Blake, who left
his moorings suddenly on the 8th of October, and swooped
down upon the Dutch before they were prepared. The battle
began about three in the afternoon, and was fought with extraordinary determination. The Dutch had more ships than the
English, but those of the latter were on the whole of larger
size, so that the two opponents were tolerably equal. At it
they went—yard-arm to yard-arm—muzzle to muzzle—a sheer
hand-to-hand struggle, in which each individual seemed inspired
with an absolute personal hatred of his adversary ; and it was

only the coming on of night that ended the fierce engagement. Then it was found that three Dutch men-of-war had been sunk, that one had blown up, and that the rear-admiral had been taken. These were small gains ; but the Dutch had sustained a heavy blow in their loss of prestige, as it was evident they had met their match upon the seas.

The true measure of their defeat was shown by their refusal next day to renew the battle. Sullen and discouraged, they retired towards their own shores, closely pursued and severely harassed by the English.

The enthusiasm excited in England by Blake's victory was unbounded ; unfortunately it induced Parliament in its over-confidence to reduce the English fleet by 40 ships. On the other hand, the Dutch Government was conscious of the necessity of a supreme effort to retain its maritime ascendancy ; and having equipped a large fleet with incredible alacrity, recalled the veteran Tromp from his unmerited seclusion, appointing De Witt and De Ruyter to act under him as vice-admirals, and Evertsen and Floritzen as rear-admirals. Jealousy and disappointment, however, had undermined the health of Cornelis De Witt, and at the last moment he was unable to accept the post intrusted to him.

With 80 large ships and 15 smaller vessels, Tromp and De Ruyter appeared in the Dover roads on the 29th of November, 1652.* Blake was lying there with 37 men-of-war, one frigate, and a few fire-ships and boys, the remainder of his fleet being distributed in the ports of the Channel and in Plymouth Sound. His flag was hoisted on board the *Triumph.* It was about noon, and the day was lowering and gusty, when the stately war-ships of Holland hove in sight of the English fleet. To prevent himself from being driven in shore, Blake, despite of his inferiority of force, put out at once into the open sea,

* December 9th, New Style.

resolving to make for Rye, where he would obtain a reinforcement. Tromp, of course, prepared to cut him off, but was prevented from engaging him by a violent gale, which blew all night and the greater part of the following day. At one o'clock on the 10th the van of the Dutch overtook the rearward ships of the English, and a fierce fight began off Dungeness. The two rival admirals first came into collision, and exchanged destructive broadsides. The *Garland* followed Blake into the turmoil, and came into such violent collision with Tromp's flag-ship, the *Brederode*, that she carried away her bowsprit and cat-heads. Assisted by the *Bonadventure,* an armed trader of 30 guns, she plied the Dutch Admiral with such hearty good-will that he was thankful indeed when Evertsen came up to relieve him. Against the two men-of-war the little *Garland*, however, maintained her stand, until, having lost 60 killed and 70 or 80 wounded out of a crew of 200 men, she was forced to strike her colours. The *Triumph*, having lost her fore-topmast, and being herself engaged with an enemy of superior power, could not move to the rescue.

With scarcely any help the stress of the fight had been borne by the *Triumph*, the *Vanguard*, and the *Victory;* and, with gallant tenacity, they had held their defence against a score of adversaries. Thrice did the Dutch obtain a footing on the deck of the *Triumph*, and thrice were they beaten back with great carnage. Her masts tottered, her rigging was cut to pieces, her hull was battered with shot. But the *Vanguard*, of 50 guns, assisted by the *Sapphire*, an armed trader of 30 guns, stuck closely by her Admiral, and saved him from being overwhelmed. Night came on, dark, stormy, and cold ; and without let or hindrance Blake withdrew his shattered ships to the mouth of the Thames, leaving an undoubted victory with the Dutch.

The Council of State was not disheartened by this misfortune,

nor was its confidence in Blake diminished. Vigorous exertions were made to put a fleet to sea capable of coping with
the Dutch. The ships which had been dispersed along the
coast were concentrated in the Downs. The number of seamen
was increased to 30,000. Magazines were replenished, the
dockyards were supplied with fresh stores. Some captains of
whose misconduct Blake complained were cashiered, and
trustier men appointed to their places; while Generals Deane
and Monk were associated with him as his coadjutors.

To and fro in the Channel sailed Marten Harperts Tromp
triumphantly, with a broom at his mast-head to intimate that
he had swept the English off the seas. The States-General
audaciously proclaimed a blockade of the whole coast of
England. The Dutch epigrammatists indulged in jests as flat
as their own Holland, and regarded the islanders from a height
of insolent superiority "They had carried off ' the garland,' "
they said; and there were squibs and jokes about the "bonadventure" having realised the prophecy of its name in falling
into their hands. But the contention between the two
countries was one which ridicule could not decide; and the
Hollanders grew soberer when their resolute enemy reappeared
in the Channel with a formidable fleet of 80 men-of-war, in
which Penn's flag waved as vice-admiral and Lawson's as
rear-admiral.

It was off the glittering cliffs of Portland, on the morning of
February 18th, 1653, that Blake's noble armada came in sight of
their great enemy. Tromp had then under his charge a large
convoy of rich merchantmen bound for the Scheldt, and
having the wind in his favour, might easily have declined the
engagement; but he was too confident in his own strength, and,
as Blake wanted fighting, he told his officers he should have
plenty of it. He rapidly divided his fleet into three squadrons,
under Floritzen, Evertsen, and De Ruyter, and sent his mer-

chantmen, with some ships of war to guard them, into the rear. Then he awaited the shock of battle.

Blake's flag-ship, the *Triumph*, the *Speaker* (Penn), the *Fairfax* (Lawson), and about twenty ships of the advanced division, were several miles ahead and to windward of the main body, but they gallantly pushed forward to begin the action. The *Triumph* was singled out by Tromp in the *Brederode*, and shaken by his heavy artillery from stem to stern. The *Speaker* and her consorts, dashing into the affray, drove off some of the enemy from their Admiral, and the battle became general in spite of the feebleness of the English van. The *Prosperous*, the *Oak*, and the *Assistance* were boarded by the Dutch, but afterwards retaken. The Dutch force, however, was so preponderant that Blake and his followers must have been overborne had not Monk and the main fleet come up.

As the battle grew more equal the Dutch showed a disposition to decline it, hauled to the wind, and endeavoured to draw off; but the English clung closely to their skirts, and would not be denied. Then the action was renewed with increased vehemence. A Dutch man-of-war blew up with a terrible explosion; several were set on fire; others sunk with all on board; and not a vessel in either fleet but bore the marks of battle on its sides or in its rigging. The shores of Kent and Normandy echoed the sounding ordnance. De Ruyter at one time engaged the *Prosperous*, an armed merchantman of 40 guns, but was so steadily withstood that at last he impatiently called for boarders. They sprang upon the Englishman's deck, sword and pistol in hand, as if they were invincible, but were desperately beaten back, and threatened in their turn with a similar compliment. Out spake De Ruyter, "Come, my lads, that was nothing; at them again!" So furious was their second charge that Captain Barton and his men were borne down by it and forced to yield. At this juncture Captain Vesey came up in the *Matin*, and drove the Dutch from their capture, and took refuge with all his men on board it, while his own ship went to the bottom. Thus went the contest until night came on ; when Tromp drew off, spreading his shattered ships in the form of a half-moon round his host of merchantmen, and slowly making for the mouth of the Texel.

So far the battle had gone in favour of the English, who had either captured or destroyed eight Dutch men-of-war. During the night Blake sent ashore his wounded and made good his damages in readiness for a renewal of the struggle. When morning dawned the Hollanders were seen about seven leagues off Weymouth, and Blake made an attempt, first on their left and afterwards on their right, to break through the semi-circular line with which they guarded the traders. Again the fighting lasted until nightfall. The third day decided the issue. The two fleets came into collision off Baveziers (March 2nd), and for two hours the fight equalled in fury any action during the war. Then it languished somewhat, and finally dwindled away, until about four o'clock firing ceased on both sides, from sheer exhaustion and want of ammunition. Blake stood out to sea, leaving fourteen of his frigates to harass the Dutch, who slowly staggered along to the Meuse, having lost 11 men-of-war, taken, burned, or sunk ; 60 merchantmen taken; 2,000 men and officers killed or wounded ; and 700 prisoners.

It was at this time that the Long Parliament, after a glorious career, came to an inglorious end (April 20th and 21st), and Cromwell seized upon the supreme power. Blake had gone northward on a cruise along the Scottish coast, but on his return he gave in his adhesion to the new Government. "It is not for us," he said to his captains, "to mind affairs of State, but to keep foreigners from fooling us." There was enough to be done in the narrow seas, in protecting English commerce and guarding the English shores. Called away to the north, he left Monk in command of a noble fleet of 105 ships, armed with 3,815 guns, and carrying 16,269 men, to watch any renewal of the contention on the part of the Dutch. Early in the summer the latter determined on challenging afresh their English rivals, and Tromp, with De Witt and De Ruyter as his lieutenants, sailed from the Texel. As soon as this intelligence was conveyed to Blake, he crowded on every stitch of canvas his yards would carry in order to meet his old opponent.

Meanwhile, on the morning of the 2nd of June, Tromp engaged Monk near the Galles. In the first hour of the fight fell the gallant Deane, cut in two by a cannon-shot. Monk calmly unfastened his cloak and flung it over the dead body of his brother officer, lest the death of one whom the seamen profoundly loved should act as a discouragement. About three o'clock the Dutch fell into great confusion, and Tromp found himself compelled to make a running fight. At nine in the evening a stout Hollander commanded by Cornelis Van Kelson blew up, and this accident increased their discouragement, in spite of Tromp's vigorous efforts to keep his captains up to their duty.

The next morning was consumed in Tromp's persistent but unsuccessful efforts to obtain the weather-gage. About noon the action recommenced, a fresh impulse being given to it on the English side by the arrival of Blake's squadron. Then indeed the two parties clutched each other, as it were, by the throat, and sought to worry each other into submission. Tromp earned immortal renown by his heroic intrepidity, and his exertions to call forth a spirit of similar resolution in his captains. He laid his ships alongside the *Janus*, which carried Penr's flag, but thirteen English men-of-war came to the

prompt rescue of their Vice-Admiral. Tromp was surrounded—
was almost overwhelmed. The English crews poured in upon
his deck, and, foot by foot, his men were compelled to retire
below. Then arose a great shout among the English—not to be
repeated. For, resolute not to surrender, Tromp, while some of
his men were fighting at the hatchway, dragged two small barrels
of gunpowder to the centre of the middle deck, and set fire to
them. The explosion was terrible. Half the upper deck,
crowded with English sailors, was blown away ; the other half
was wrapped in flames. At this moment De Witt and De
Ruyter, perceiving the strait of their leader, dashed with part
of their squadrons into the thick of the *mêlée*, so that full thirty
ships lay almost board-a-board, and in the dense obscurity of
the smoke that enveloped them friend could scarce be distinguished from foe. So general, however, was the confusion
that a great part of the Dutch fleet hoisted their canvas and
ran for the Texel, compelling Tromp to order a retreat. The
pursuit was hot, and until one o'clock in the morning the
English continued their fire. They abandoned their quarry
only when a further chase would have carried them on the
shoals.

There could be no doubt as to the completeness of the
English victory. Six Dutch ships had been sunk and 2
blown up, 13 had been captured, and 1,350 men been taken
prisoners. The total of the Dutch killed and wounded was
not less than 3,000. On the other hand, the English had lost
only 126 men killed and 236 wounded. No wonder that the
rejoicings were loud in the streets of London, and that the
ballad-singers gained fame and praise as they stood in the
crowded places, and chanted some such rough songs of triumph
as the following :—

> " The moody Dutch are tame and cool,
> They pray and wish for peace ;

Our gallant navy in the Pool
    Has melted all their grease.

" Brave Blake and Ayscue are the men
    Have squeezed their sponge of riches ;
When they have conquered Holland, then
    The Dutch may sell their breeches.

" When they are drunk awhile they fight,
    But after run, swear, mutter ;
Their buns are all too cold and light
    To melt our English butter.

" Turk, Pope, or Devil we defy :
    Courage, brave English, venter !
Since Fate arms you with victory,
    The world lies open—enter."

Blake and Monk now proceeded to blockade the Dutch fleet
in the Texel and to pounce upon the homeward-bound merchantmen of Holland, until the former, by an attack of very
severe illness, was forced to abandon the charge to his colleague
and return to England, where he was received with a noble welcome. It fell to Monk's good fortune to deliver the last blow
of the war, and crush the remnant of Holland's formidable
armada, on the 26th of July, 1653. In this last and most
sanguinary encounter Tromp received a musket-shot in the
heart. Peace was afterwards concluded between the two
belligerents, the States agreeing to the Protector's conditions,
and consenting to do honour to the Red Cross of England.
Cromwell and his Parliament then proceeded to reward the
heroes whose courage and conduct had established our naval
supremacy. Gold chains, each valued at £300, were presented
to Blake and Monk, and chains of £100 value to Penn and
Lawson. A sum of £1,000 was expended in medals for the
officers and men. Bonfires, and illuminated windows, and
public rejoicings in the crowded streets witnessed to the
popular exultation at the victorious termination of England's

first **Punic War**—her first grand struggle with her powerful maritime rival, Holland.

During the closing months of 1653 Blake lay sick at Knoll, his country house near Bridgewater, recovering but slowly, and with a permanently weakened frame, from the malignant fever which had prostrated him. He was able, however, to take his seat, in October, in Cromwell's Parliament, and receive through the Speaker the thanks of the House. In December he was placed at the head of the Admiralty, and he immediately entered with his accustomed energy upon a reform of that important department of the State. The winter of 1653 and part of the spring of 1654 he passed at Bridgewater, but in May was summoned to London, and dined with Cromwell, who was then preparing—with characteristic secrecy of design and tenacity of purpose—a naval expedition of formidable magnitude. All was not ready until the late autumn of 1654, and then the Protector divided his forces into two noble fleets, one of which, under Penn, consisted of 38 sail, carrying 414 guns and 4,410 men, while the other, under Robert Blake, consisted of 25 sail, mounting 874 guns, and manned by 4,100 men. These were the larger ships, and carried the more numerous crews. Penn's armament was dispatched against the Spanish possessions in the West Indies; Blake was reserved for active service nearer home. His was to be the difficult and wearisome task of intercepting the rich merchant fleets which conveyed to Spain the products of her American colonies, and of carefully watching her various ports and harbours. But previous to undertaking this arduous duty, and while as yet the Protector delayed his open declaration of war, he was instructed to demand from certain states in the Mediterranean redress for the injuries they had inflicted upon English subjects and English commerce.

With his flag hoisted on board the *St. George*, of 60 guns,

Blake, early in December, arrived in the roadstead of Cadiz. After a short stay he visited Leghorn, and compelled the Grand Duke of Tuscany to pay a sum of £60,000 as compensation for certain merchant vessels piratically seized by Prince Rupert and sold in Tuscan ports. For a similar peccadillo he extorted 20,000 pistoles from the reluctant fingers of Pope Alexander VII. For some months his further movements were delayed by severe illness and by a succession of violent storms; but in March, 1655, he appeared before Tunis, and demanded that the Bey should surrender his Christian slaves and give satisfaction for his depredations upon English commerce. The Bey refused. To throw him off his guard, Blake sailed away, as if terrified by the formidable character of the defences; but suddenly, on the 3rd of April, he rode straight into the harbour, and opened a furious cannonade on the two castles of Goletta and Porto Ferino that guarded it, and on their lines of communication. The Moors replied with one hundred and twenty pieces of cannon, but were utterly unable to withstand the persistent volleys of the English artillerists; they were beaten from their guns and stricken down by hundreds. To complete their discomfiture, Blake sent the long-boats of his fleet, manned with picked crews, to set on fire the Tunisian pirate vessels.

Having inflicted this heavy chastisement on the Bey of Tunis, Blake next appeared before Tripoli, whose ruler, however, discreetly complied at once with his demands, and made no attempt at resistance. At Algiers the Bey was equally prudent. He sent on board the fleet a welcome gift of live cattle, and released his English captives on payment of a very moderate ransom. Thus the power of England, the glory of Cromwell, and the fame of Blake spread from shore to shore of the Mediterranean—that old historic sea, which has witnessed the downfall of Athens and Rome and Carthage, and the rise and growth of empires greater far than they.

After a visit to England to refit his ships and recruit his crews, Blake, associated with Edward Montague, afterwards Earl of Sandwich, sailed from the Downs in February, 1656, on board the *Naseby*, and cruised in the Channel while his fleet was taking on board fresh stores and supplies. In May he appeared off Lisbon, on receipt of intelligence which seemed to indicate an intention on the part of the King of Portugal to recede from the English alliance. Having compelled him to sign a new treaty and pay a sum of £8,000, he proceeded to station himself off Cadiz, to watch and wait for the treasure-fleet of American galleons. With these a portion of his squadron fell in and made sad havoc, capturing two, and sinking, burning, or driving ashore the remainder. An immense booty fell into the hands of the captors, with which Montague and Stayner were immediately sent home.

Throughout the winter, in spite of storms and heavy seas, Blake blockaded Cadiz, after which he paid a flying visit to Algiers, to insist upon the Dey's rigid fulfilment of his engagements, and · went to Tangier, where the Portuguese were beleaguered by the Moors. He quickly dispersed the enemy, and, returning to Cadiz, prepared to undertake an expedition of the boldest and most hazardous character.

Lord Clarendon, the Royalist historian of the Civil War, or, as he called it, the Great Rebellion, was not too well disposed to do justice to Blake, yet he has drawn his character in very glowing colours. " He was the first man," he says, " that declined the old tracks, and made it manifest that the science (of managing a fleet) might be attained in less time than was imagined ; and despised those rules which had long been in practice to keep his ship and his men out of danger, which had been held in former times a point of great ability and circumspection, as if the principal art requisite in the captain of a ship had been to be sure to come home safe again. He was the first that infused that proportion of courage into the seamen, and making them see by experience what mighty things they could do if they were resolved, and taught them to fight in fire as well as upon water; and though he had been very well imitated and followed, he was the first that drew the copy of naval courage and bold and resolute achievement."

In no exploit of his career was his courage or capacity more conspicuous than in that which proved to be his last. It was in the spring of 1657 that he was apprised of the arrival of the Peru treasure-fleet of Spain, consisting of six " royal galleons " and sixteen other great ships, in one of the Canary Islands. It had resorted thither for safety, its commander being afraid of the " terrible Blake," who at the time was blockading Cadiz. To Blake it at once seemed desirable that so splendid a booty should go to replenish the exhausted funds of the Common-wealth; and accordingly, with twenty-five men-of-war and frigates, he sailed, on the 13th of April, for the Canaries. Every precaution was taken to conceal the destination of this fleet; but Don Diego Diegues, the Spanish governor at Santa Cruz, becoming aware of it, employed the greatest energy and no slight military skill in strengthening the defences of a port which art and nature had already rendered almost impregnable. In shape the harbour resembled a horseshoe. On the west the entrance was defended by a regular castle, armed with heavy ordnance and well garrisoned. The inner side of the bay was lined with seven powerful batteries, connected with the castle and with each other by a series of earthworks, so that the entire circuit bristled with guns and arquebuses. The treasure-fleet was also utilised, its rich cargoes having first been landed, with the exception of such commodities as sugar, spices, hides, and cochineal. On either side of the narrow harbour mouth were anchored the royal galleons, with their broadsides turned towards the sea. The other armed vessels were moored

Inside in a semicircle, but with wide intervals between them to allow of the free play of the land batteries.

On Monday morning, April 20th, a Dutch captain, whose vessel lay in the roadstead of Santa Cruz, discovered the English fleet in the offing, and immediately hurried to the governor to ask his permission to depart. He had had experience of Blake's summary method of chastising an adversary, and felt a hearty disinclination to come again into collision with him. Pointing to his castle, batteries, and galleons, Don Diego haughtily protested that they would effectually prevent an enemy's approach. " Nevertheless," said the Dutchman, " spite of batteries and ships, I am confident that Blake will soon be among you." " Well," replied the Spaniard, " go if thou wilt, and let Blake come if he desire."

For some time Blake had been in feeble health, but the scent of coming battle seemed to inspire him with fresh life. He sprang from his sick bed, and to his captains proposed that they should break into the guarded harbour and destroy the galleons where they lay at anchor if the wind prevented their removal. His own heroism, as in the case of Nelson at a later date, so communicated itself to those under its influence, that his design was promptly accepted. At half-past six prayers were read and breakfast was served on board every vessel in the fleet. A division of the largest ships, under Rear-Admiral Stayner, was then ordered to attack the Spanish galleons, while the remainder of the fleet, under Blake himself, engaged the land defences.

A tremendous fire was opened by the castle and batteries and ships in the harbour, but it could not check the steady advance of Stayner and his comrades, who speedily fell-to with the galleons. Blake meanwhile, in his flag-ship, the *Swiftsure*, with the bulk of his fleet, bombarded the land batteries, and drew off their fire from the Rear-Admiral's flank. For some hours the artillery duel was maintained with desperate vehemence; but eventually the Spanish gunners were quelled by the vigour and obstinacy of the English attack. One by one the batteries ceased firing, until the enemy's fire was so far subdued that Blake was able to proceed to Stayner's support, and pour a hurricane of shot in upon the hapless galleons. Two sank at their moorings; the others were speedily in flames, lighting up the sky and sea for miles around with a lurid glow. Before evening the work was done. Not a sail or mast was left above water. Hither and thither drifted the blackened, mouldering hulks, until they filled, and with a lurch and roll went down like lead. Others were carried ashore. Not a single ship, not a single cargo, escaped destruction.*

It was not less difficult for Blake, after his work was done, to leave the harbour than it had been to enter it. Relays of gunners lined all the fortifications, and, mad with rage and mortification, poured a continuous fire upon their victorious antagonists. They hoped that by destroying the English fleet they might relieve the great defeat they had sustained. Whatever their will or their desire, it was not fulfilled. Their fire was ill directed; and the wind veering to the south-west, Blake carried his fleet out of Spanish waters in comparative safety, having lost, in one of the most daring actions on record, only 50 of his men killed and 150 wounded. All things considered, there seems much justice in Clarendon's stately comment.

"The whole action," he says, "was so miraculous, that all men who knew the place concluded that no sober man, with what courage soever endowed, would ever undertake it; whilst the Spaniards comforted themselves with the belief that they were devils and not men who had destroyed them in such a manner. And it can hardly be imagined how small loss the

* HEPWORTH DIXON, *Life of Blake.*

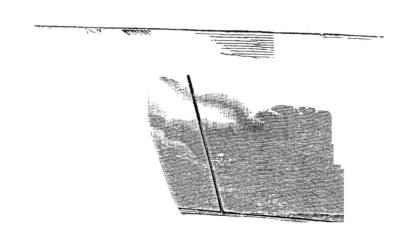

"As his ship came within sight of Plymouth, his attendants lifted his feeble form in their arms."—*Page* 97.

English sustained in this unparalleled action; not one ship being left behind, and the killed and wounded not exceeding two hundred men, when the slaughter on board the Spanish ships and on the shore was incredible." *

Blake's career was now nearly run. His illness daily assumed a more serious form, until it became evident to his sorrowful followers that he had fought his last fight and won his last victory. The devout Puritan confronted death with calm composure, for he was not only a soldier, but a Christian. His sole wish was to see the loved shore of old England once again before he passed away. His wish was gratified. As his ship came within sight of Plymouth his attendants lifted his feeble form in their arms, that he might look out upon the green hills and smiling fields of Devonshire. He gazed eagerly on the well-known landscape, and then lay back to die.

This was on the 7th of August, 1657.

* This splendid achievement is graphically described by Carlyle. "Blake arrives there in time this Monday morning (April 20); finds the fleet fast moored in Santa Cruz Bay: rich silver-ships, strong war-ships, sixteen as we count them; stronger almost than himself, and moored here under defences unassailable apparently by any mortal. Santa Cruz Bay is shaped as a horse-shoe: at the entrance are castles, in the inner circuit are other castles, eight of them in all, bristling with great guns; war-ships moored at the entrance, war-frigates moored all round the beach, and men and gunners at command: one great magazine of sleeping thunder and destruction: to appearance, if you wish for sure suicide to run into, this must be it. Blake, taking measure of the business, runs into it, defying its loud thunder—much out-thunders it—mere whirlwinds of fire and iron hail, the old Peak never heard the like; silences the castles; sinks or burns every sail in the harbour; annihilates the Spanish fleet; and then, the wind veering round in its favour, sails out again, leaving Santa Cruz Bay much astonished at him!"

GEORGE, LORD ANSON.

1697—1763.

AT Shugborough, in Staffordshire, on the 23rd of April, **1697,**
was born George Anson, the son of a country gentleman of
good family. Of his early life no particulars have been
recorded; but it would seem that he entered the navy when
but a boy, for in his nineteenth year he passed the necessary
examination for a lieutenant's commission, and was serving on
board the *Hampshire* frigate in the Baltic fleet, under the command of Admiral Sir John Norris. In **1717** he was appointed
lieutenant of the *Montague,* and underwent his baptism of fire
in Sir George Byng's action with the Spanish fleet off Cape
Parmeo. His thorough seamanship recommended him to
speedy promotion, and as commander of the *Weazel* sloop, in
1722, he displayed much activity in capturing the smugglers
who infested the North Sea. The following year saw him a
captain, and he was dispatched to South Carolina, with instructions to repress the depredations of pirates, to grant convoys
to and from the Bahamas, and to suppress all illegal trading.
He was engaged in this mission until July, **1730,** and that he
executed it with entire satisfaction to the colonists is proved
by the perpetuation of his name in connection with various
towns and districts, such as Anson County, Ansonville. A
Mrs. Hutchinson, of South Carolina, has left on record her
view of his character at this period.

" Mr. Anson," she writes, " is not one of those handsome men whose persons alone may recommend them to the generality of our sex, though they be destitute of sense, good nature, or good manners ; but, nevertheless, his person is what you would call very agreeable. He has good sense, good nature, is polite and well-bred ; free from that loathsome ceremoniousness which often renders many people, who may perhaps rank themselves among the most accomplished, extremely disagreeable. He is generous without profusion, elegant without ostentation, and, above all, of a most tender, humane disposition. His benevolence is extensive, even to his own detriment. At balls, plays, concerts, &c., I have often the pleasure of seeing and sometimes of conversing with Mr. Anson, who, I assure you, is far from being an anchorite, though not what we call a modern pretty fellow, because he is really so old-fashioned as to make some profession of religion ; moreover, he never dances, nor swears, nor talks nonsense. As he greatly admires a fine woman, so he is passionately fond of music ; which is enough, you will say, to recommend him to my esteem ; for you know I never would allow that a character could be complete without a taste for that sweet science.

" Mr. Anson's modesty, inoffensive easy temper, good nature, humanity, and great probity doubtless are the antidotes that preserve him from the poisonous breath of calumny ; for, amidst all the scandalous warfare that is nourished here, he maintains a strict neutrality, and, attacking no party, is himself attacked by none."

This is a character of which almost any man might be proud ; but Mrs. Hutchinson proceeds to note his grave defects, which seem hardly compatible with the " profession of religion " she ascribes to Captain Anson. She speaks of his loving " his bottle and his friend so well," that " he was not soon weary of their company, especially when they happened to be

perfectly to his taste, which is pretty nice as to both ;" and she
adds that, if report might be credited, he was '' very far from
being a woman-hater : "—

> " His heart, his mistress and his friend did share;
>   His time, the Muse, the witty, and the fair."

Probably, however, if we allow for a lady's natural cen-
soriousness on these points, we shall not suspect him of any
actual violation of the laws of religion or morality, or regard him
as addicted to intemperance.

In August, 1734, we find him serving again on the American
coast. In June, 1735, he arrived at Spithead, and for the first
time during the nineteen years since he had received his first
commission was permitted to remain between two and three
years on shore.

In 1739 England declared war against Spain, much to the
regret of Walpole, then the head of the British Cabinet ; but
both countries had been for some time on hostile terms, and in
England the ill-feeling against Spain had spread through all
classes, rousing a national enthusiasm which no Ministry could
hope to repress. When the declaration was issued, a triumphal
procession paraded the streets of London, as if victory had
already been won. From all the metropolitan steeples the
bells sent forth merry peals. " Let them ring," said Walpole
moodily ; " by-and-by there will be wringing of hands." The
spirit of " Jingoism," in truth, was rampant; and England, to
use a well-known phrase, went into war with a light heart, and
in total ignorance of the burden it had undertaken.

I am concerned here, however, with Anson's individual
career, and not with the national history. The Ministry having
determined on an expedition against the Spanish possessions
in the South Sea, Anson was selected to take command of it.
His squadron consisted of the following ships :—

Centurion	. 60 guns	. 400 men	.	George Anson, Commodore.
Gloucester	. 50 ,,	. 300 ,,	.	Richard Norris, afterwards E. Legge.
Severn .	. 50 ,,	. 300 ,,	.	Hon. E. Legge, afterwards Matthew Mitchell.
Pearl . .	. 40 ,,	. 250 ,,	.	Matthew Mitchell, afterwards Danby Kidd.
Wager .	. 28 ,,	. 160 ,,	.	Danby Kidd, afterwards Hon. J. Murray.
Trial sloop	. 8 ,,	. 100 ,,	.	Hon. J. Murray, afterwards Lieut. Cheap.

He was ordered to take on board 500 soldiers, and to proceed to the Pacific, where he was to ravage with fire and sword the western coast of South America, and take or destroy the Spanish settlements. The means provided were totally inadequate to such an end. But not only was his force too small, it was in bad condition. The ships were not well found, and the crews were not up to their present employment; while the 500 soldiers turned out to be 259 out-pensioners of Chelsea College, most of them invalids, all of them old and feeble. For some time the Admiralty had been ill administered and the naval service pitiably neglected, so that Anson's squadron was not the only one dispatched under inauspicious circumstances; probably it was the worst.

Various obstacles, not the least of which was the indecision of the Ministry, prevented the departure of the expedition until the 18th of September, 1740. Adverse winds and the bad quality of the ships lengthened the passage to Madeira to fifty days. While the Commodore recruited his crews at this island sanitarium, Captain Norris resigned the command of the *Gloucester*, which gave a remove to each of the captains, and Lieutenant Cheap was appointed to the *Trial*. On the 3rd of November Anson resumed his voyage; and on May 20th broke out that pestilent sickness, the continuance and fatal effects of which seem to be unparalleled in the annals of navigation. It is stated that " the captains of the squadron represented to the

Commodore that their ships' companies were very sickly, and that it was their own opinion as well as their surgeons' that it would tend to the preservation of the men to let in more air between decks, for their ships were so dry that they could not possibly open their lower ports.   On this representation the Commodore ordered six air-scuttles to be cut in each ship, in such places where they would least weaken it."   Making the island of St. Catherine, on the Brazilian coast, he landed there his invalids, eighty from the *Centurion* alone, and sheltered them in huts ; but in spite of every attention a third of the number died. Meantime, the ships were smoked, cleansed, and washed with vinegar, their sides and decks calked, and new standing rigging set up.   But the disease, which had been probably introduced by the wretched Chelsea pensioners, and aggravated by the bad quality and unsuitable character of the rations then allotted to our seamen, continued to spread.

In January, 1741, Anson again set sail, and keeping down the east coast of South America, entered the Strait of Lemaire on the 7th of March.   After clearing this channel he was met by a terrible storm.   " The wild cloud-drifts," says the historian of the expedition,* came scudding up the horizon ; the winds gathered ; the waters heaved with tumultuous throes ; rain and sleet fell blindingly around them ; the storm-tossed vessels were hurled from side to side with so dread a violence that many men were flung about the decks and killed outright. An affecting incident occurred at this conjuncture.   A sailor belonging to the *Centurion* fell overboard.   He swam well, he swam bravely and strongly, still keeping his face towards the vessel, and straining his aching eyes for the relief his comrades could not afford him.   Such was the fury of the storm, the ship

---

* The well-known "Account of Anson's Voyage " has been generally ascribed to Mr. Walter, Anson's chaplain, but the bulk of it was really written by Mr. Robins, an engineer officer of great talent and ability.

could not be put about, and it sped away with terrible swiftness
from the drowning mariner—

> ' Who still renewed the strife,
> Upheld by buoyant hope and love of life '—

but was at length outworn by the wrestling waters, and compelled to yield the unequal struggle."

Early in April the unfortunate squadron encountered another
and even more terrible hurricane, during the prevalence o.
which the *Wager*, a 28-gun frigate, was driven so far away to
leeward that she was unable to rejoin her consorts.   Her after-
experiences were of a remarkable character, and furnished the
subject of a graphic narrative, written by one of her midshipmen, the Hon. John Byron, to which his grandson, Lord
Byron, was principally indebted for the details of the sea-
scenes in "Don Juan."   The ship was wrecked on the
15th of May off the coast of America, and her crew thrown
upon a lonely desert island, which they expressively named
Mount Misery.   Having sojourned in this ocean-girdled waste
for several months, they embarked in the cutter and long-boat
on the perilous enterprise of returning home through the
Straits of Magelhaens.   The cutter was lost;* but after a singularly painful voyage, extending over a thousand leagues, the
long-boat reached the Portuguese settlements in Brazil; and the
survivors happily returned to England in 1745.

* " 'Twas a rough night, and blew so stiffly yet,
    That the sail was becalm'd between the seas,
  Though on the wave's high top too much to set,
    They dared not take it in for all the breeze:
  Each sea curl'd o'er the stern, and kept them wet,
    And made them bale without a moment's ease,
  So that themselves as well as hopes were damp'd,
  And the poor little cutter quickly swamp'd."
                        BYRON, *Don Juan*, il. 60.

Violent gales continued without intermission for several weeks, in the course of which Anson's ill-fitted ships parted company, the *Severn* and the *Pearl* never to be seen again. Driving blasts of sleet and snow buffeted the unfortunate vessels, whose crews were sore stricken with disease and spent with fatigue. On the 8th of May Anson, in the *Centurion*, had not men able to keep the deck sufficient to take in a topsail, all being violently afflicted with the scurvy, and every day reducing their number by six, and eight, and ten. In this month their sufferings rose to a much higher pitch than they had ever done before, whether the violence of the storms was considered, the shattering of the sails and rigging, or the diminution and weakening of the crew by deaths and sickness. In April no fewer than forty-three persons died of the scurvy on board the *Centurion ;* in the month of May nearly double that number perished ; and as they did not reach land till the middle of June, the mortality went on increasing, and the disease extended itself so prodigiously, that after losing upwards of two hundred men, the crew could not at last muster in a watch more than six foremast men capable of duty.

At daybreak on June 9th the *Centurion* dropped anchor off the island of Juan Fernandez. On that day, says the historian of the expedition, " out of two hundred and odd men who remained alive, we could not, taking all our watches together, muster hands enough to work the ship on an emergency, though we included the officers, their servants, and the boys. In wearing the ship in the middle watch we had a melancholy instance of the almost incredible debility of our people; for the lieutenant could muster no more than two quartermasters and six foremast men capable of working ; so that, without the assistance of the officers, servants, and the boys, it might have proved impossible for us to have reached the island after we had got sight of it—to so wretched a condition was a sixty-gun ship reduced which had passed the Straits of Lemaire but three months before with between four and five hundred men, almost all of them in health and vigour." It was with keen feelings of delight that the weakened survivors beheld the woody hills and the verdant valleys, bright with the glow of streams, of the island which is immortalised in English fiction as the home of " Robinson Crusoe." The sick were speedily removed ashore, and accommodated in huts. Vegetable food, fish, the fresh meat of goats, with the clear pure air of this Eden of the Pacific, soon wrought an improvement in their condition, and they began to recover their health and spirits. The *Trial* arrived a few days after the *Centurion*, and on the 21st of June the *Gloucester* hove in sight, but was again driven off to windward. Anson immediately sent his boat to her assistance, laden with fresh water, fish, and vegetables; a most opportune relief for her distressed crews, who had already thrown overboard two-thirds of their complement, while of the survivors few were capable of doing duty except the officers and their servants. With all the aid Anson could afford her in provisions and water, by boats and men, and all the attempts that were made, she could not be got into the bay for a whole fortnight; and soon after this she disappeared for the space of a week, suggesting the worst apprehensions. However, she again drew in shore, and the long-boat of the *Centurion* was dispatched with a second supply of water and provisions. It was only in time. The ill-fated vessel was converted into a floating hospital; she had lost two-thirds of her crew, and the survivors were gaunt and haggard with famine and disease. The boat returned for additional stores, but meanwhile the ill-starred vessel, for a *third* time, drew out to sea, so that when she rejoined the Commodore on the 23rd of July her condition was indescribably pitiful.

To these wayworn mariners—who, with more truth than

Tennyson's lotos-eaters, and after sadder experiences, might have sung—

" We have had enough of action, and of motion we,
  Roll'd to starboard, roll'd to larboard, when the surge was seething free,
  When the wallowing monster spouted his foam-fountains in the sea "

Juan Fernandez appeared an ocean Paradise. There was a pleasure in the leafy woods and the fragrant shrubs; in the murmur and the sparkle of the brooks; in the profusion of the plants and flowers and fruits; in the pure fresh air and the sunny sky. Their physical weakness disappeared, and their spirits regained their elasticity. The impression produced upon them is visible in the enthusiastic eloquence of the chronicler, who protests that " there can scarce anywhere be found a more happy seat for the Muses, and the flights of fancy, or the pleasures of the imagination." From his description of the island it is evident that Alexander Selkirk, the shipwrecked mariner, whose sojourn here suggested to Defoe his romance of " Robinson Crusoe," must have lived in considerable comfort. Its natural resources were ample: besides fruits and vegetables, seals and sea-lions abounded, the flesh of which was neither unpalatable nor innutritious, and goats also, furnishing a pleasant change in the daily bill of fare. Selkirk has recorded that when he caught more of those animals than he wanted, he slit their ears and let them go; and in Anson's narrative we read that the ears were slit of the first goat killed by Anson's people; whence they concluded that, although thirty-two years had passed over its head, it had once been in Selkirk's hands. It was, indeed, a venerable animal, dignified with a beard of truly majestical aspect.

However delightful might be a life of tranquil ease in this Fortunate Island, there must necessarily come an end to it; and on the 19th of September, with his ships refitted and his crews restored to health, Anson once more put to sea. I have

said that his crews had recovered their health, but their
numerical strength was woefully reduced. The *Centurion*,
having buried 292, had on board only 214. The *Gloucester*,
which had lost the same number as the *Centurion*, mustered
but 82 ; and the *Trial*, having buried 42, counted no more
than 39. It must have been a severe trial, even to the composure and steadfastness of Anson, to reflect that the whole of
the surviving crews, distributed over three ships, amounted to
no more than 335 men and boys ; and that with this small
force he might be called upon to maintain the honour of the
English flag against a powerful Spanish fleet. It was hopeless
to think of attacking any of the Spanish possessions, and even
the Acapulco galleon might prove too powerful for his feeble
little squadron. Allowing no sign of uneasiness to be visible
to his men, he ordered the *Trial* to cruise off Valparaiso, and
the *Gloucester* off the coast of Paita, where in due time the
Centurion and the *Trial* would join her. The sloop fell in with
and captured a Spanish trader, with 25 passengers on board ;
while the *Centurion* on her cruise fell in with another prize
made by the *Trial*, called the *Arranzuga*, of 600 tons
burden. The *Triol* by this time was in so leaky a state that
she was with difficulty kept afloat. Anson, therefore, ordered
her stores, guns, and ammunition to be put into the prize,
which, under the name of the *Trial's* prize, he commissioned
as a frigate in the British navy ; and, the crew being transferred to her, the *Trial* was scuttled and sunk.

Keeping along the American coast, Anson captured a rich
galleon, the *Nuestra Senhora del Carmen*, valued at 400,000
dollars, and from some of her crew obtained information which
led to his planning an expedition against the town of Paita.
With fifty-eight picked men, well armed, Lieutenant Butt was
sent against the fort at midnight on the 11th of November.
It was protected by a strong battery and garrisoned by 300

soldiers. Sweeping into the bay under cover of the darkness, they reached the mouth of the inner harbour before an alarm was given. The crew of a trader anchored in mid-stream raised a shout of " Los Ingleses!" "Los Ingleses!" and springing into their skiff, made for the shore. Our British tars, however, pulled with so much heartiness that they were upon the enemy before they could make any preparations for defence. The inhabitants sprang from their beds and fled in great disorder, most of them without waiting to put on their clothes.

In the morning, as Anson approached the bay, he saw with delight the English flag flying from the fort, and soon afterwards one of his boats came off laden with dollars and church plate. While the treasure and other booty were being embarked, the Spaniards, with some two hundred horsemen, assembled on a hill near the town, with their drums, trumpets, and standards, but never once dared to descend into the plain. Anson sent a message to the Governor offering to ransom the town; but as he sullenly refused to give any answer, Anson ordered it, with the exception of two churches, to be set on fire. The value of the merchandise thus given to the flames was computed at a million and a half of dollars.

The enfeebled condition of his squadron compelled Anson to abandon all hope of a successful attack upon Manilla, which was known to be strongly fortified ; and he resolved on devoting all his efforts to the capture, if possible, of the great galleon, or treasure-ship, which sailed every year with the produce of the Spanish-American mines from Acapulco to Manilla. The pursuit of this rich argosy has in it almost as much romance as Jason's quest of the Golden Fleece. Having obtained information that it was expected to leave Acapulco on the 3rd of March, 1742, Anson immediately sailed in that direction, and on the 1st of the month arrived off the rounded hills known to seamen as the " Paps of Acapulco," disposing his ships, at about fifteen leagues from the shore, in a semi-circle, so as to command a sweep of sea not much less than eighty miles in extent. The Governor of Acapulco, however, had divined Anson's object, and defeated it for the time by detaining the galleon under the guns of Acapulco harbour, until the English were compelled by want of water to abandon their fruitless watch and bear away for China.

During a violent storm on the 26th of July the crazy old *Gloucester* sprang a leak, and was soon reduced to so helpless a condition that Anson removed her crew to the *Centurion.* This was no remarkable addition to his strength, as the crew of the *Gloucester* had been reduced to 77 men and 18 boys, and of these only 16 men and 11 boys were able to keep the deck. Having set the unfortunate ship on fire, Anson continued his voyage, which a return of their old enemy, scurvy, rendered most wearisome and painful. The deaths increased at the rate of eight, or ten, or even twelve a day. "The dirt, nauseous-ness, and stench were almost everywhere intolerable, more people daily disabled by the disease, no sign of land, very little wind, and that not fair, very bad provisions and water, and the ships very leaky."

It must have been an intense relief to Anson when, on the 21st of August, he reached Tinian, one of the Ladrone Islands. Catching sight of a proa, he dispatched his pinnace, with the Spanish colours flying, to overtake her. She proved to be manned by a Spanish sergeant and four Indians, in conversation with whom it was ascertained that the island produced various kinds of fruits and vegetables, sweet and sour oranges, lemons, limes, cocoa-nuts, and the bread-fruit; that it was well watered, and abounded in cattle, hogs, and poultry. Anson hastened to land his wave-worn mariners, and had the satisfaction of per-ceiving a speedy improvement in their condition. "Notwith-standing the great debility and the dying aspects of the greatest part of our sick, it is almost incredible how soon they began to feel the salutary influence of the land ; for, though we buried twenty-one men on this and the preceding day, yet," says the historian of the expedition, "we did not lose above ten men more during our whole two months' stay here ; and in general our diseased received so much benefit from the fruits of the island, particularly the fruits of the acid kind, that in a week's time there were but few who were not so far recovered as to be able to move about without help."

Anson himself was attacked by this fell disease, and to insure his recovery had his hut pitched on the island for a few days. On the 23rd of September, while he was thus recruiting, the *Centurion* was driven out to sea by a furious storm, leaving on the island a company of 113 persons. As Tinian lay out of the track of European vessels, the prospect was sufficiently dispiriting ; but with that coolness of courage and readiness of resource which were Anson's most marked characteristics, he immediately set to work to lengthen a Spanish bark they had captured about twelve feet, so that she might be able to carry them all to China. As the *Centurion* had carried out to sea with her most of the necessary tools and materials, the invention of the carpenters, smiths, sailmakers, and other artisans was severely taxed to supply the deficiencies. One day, while hammers were clinking and saws grinding, a sudden shout arose, " A sail ! a sail !" Eager eyes were turned towards the horizon, and the ship that just hovered on it was pronounced to be the *Centurion ;* another appeared, and then it was known that their first hopeful conjectures must be abandoned. By the help of his glass Anson discovered that the supposed ships were only two sailing-boats : the thought flashed upon him that the *Centurion* must have foundered, and that these were her boats returning with the survivors of her crew—a thought involving so much bitterness that to conceal the overpowering emotion it excited he withdrew to the solitude of his hut. Happily they proved to be a couple of native boats pursuing their way to one of the islands. Once more the hammers clinked and the hum of busy men filled the air ; but when the work was nearly completed, the look-out man from the top of one of the hills sighted the *Centurion* in the offing (October 18th), and raised an enthusiastic cry of " The ship ! the ship !" On hearing this joyful and unexpected news Anson threw down the axe which he was vigorously wielding, and by the fulness of his joy disclosed the real feelings of anxiety and anguish which he had concealed under an equable and composed demeanour. " The others who were with him instantly ran down to the seaside in a kind of frenzy, eager to feast themselves with a sight they had so ardently wished for, and of which they had now for a considerable time despaired."

After thoroughly refitting and provisioning the *Centurion*, Anson set sail on the 21st of October, and on the 12th of November arrived at Macao, on the coast of China. There he remained during the winter season, recruiting his men, and making good all deficiencies of stores and provisions. He also secured a small reinforcement of his crew, entering twenty-three men, a few of them Dutch, and the rest Lascars.

On the 19th of April, 1743, he resumed his voyage. He gave out that he was bound for Batavia, on his way to England ; but with singular and admirable tenacity of purpose he held to his design of intercepting the rich Acapulco ship, which about this time of the year was due at Manilla. Barrow observes * that there never, perhaps, was a stronger instance of firmness of purpose on the part of the commander, coupled with a conviction of the reliance to be placed on the bravery and fidelity of British seamen, than that displayed in the resolution now taken by Anson, who thus gives, in his report to the Admiralty, the

* *Life of Lord Anson*, p. 73.

actual state of his crew :—" The number of men I have now borne is 201, amongst which are included all the officers and boys which I took out of the *Gloucester*, *Tryal* prize, and *Anna* pink, so that I have not before the mast more than 45 able seamen." The complement of one of the Spanish galleons was about 500 or 600 men ; but in Anson's sea-arithmetic 45 English seamen = 500 Spaniards, so that he had no fear of the result. Nor had his men : who, when their commander announced his intention of cruising in search of the treasure-ship, expressed their delight by three hearty cheers. One day, no mutton appearing on his table, Anson inquired the reason, for he was sure that the supply was not exhausted. "True, your honour," replied the cook, "there are still a couple of sheep left in the galley ; but I thought your honour would wish them kept for the dinners of the Spanish captain whom your honour is going to take prisoner !"

On the last day of May the *Centurion* came in sight of the Philippines, and cruised off Cape Espiritu Santo, waiting and watching for her expected prey. The anxiety of his people, who already seemed to hear the chink of Spanish doubloons in their pockets, increased every day until, on the morning of the 20th, the look-out man descried the tall masts of the galleon in the offing.

The reader may imagine with what alacrity all sail was set upon the *Centurion*, which, as if she shared in the excitement of her crew, ploughed the water like " a thing of life "

It is due to the Spaniards to say that they showed no desire to avoid a contest ; when within two miles of the English man-of-war they brought-to to fight her. As they numbered 550 men and carried 44 guns, they might be excused for believing that the result would be in their favour ; and hoisting the standard of Spain at their maintop-gallant mast-head, they confidently defied their adversary. About one o'clock the action began. Anson laid his ship across the galleon's bows, and raked her decks with a terrible fire, which attested the proficiency in gunnery his men had acquired through his foresight in exercising them daily. For two hours the fighting was severe; the masts and rigging of the Spaniard were cut to pieces, and she received one hundred and fifty shots in her hull, many of them between wind and water. Having lost sixty-seven men killed and eighty-five wounded, she hauled down her flag. At the cost of only two men killed and seventeen wounded, Anson had captured one of Spain's golden argosies carrying a cargo valued at £313,000.

The galleon had scarcely surrendered, when one of his lieutenants whispered in Anson's ear that the *Centurion* was on fire, and near the powder-magazine. Without exhibiting the slightest discomposure, he issued orders for not alarming the crew, and for the necessary measures to extinguish the flames. Happily the threatened danger was averted. Several cartridges had blown up and ignited a quantity of oakum, producing a vast quantity of smoke to a small quantity of fire, so that the accident was not as grave in reality as it was in appearance.

Returning with his prize to Mexico, Anson sold her to some merchants for 6,000 dollars, removing her cargo and setting free her crew. Then, on the 15th of December, he sailed for England. After a prosperous voyage, in which Fortune made him amends for her former ill-treatment by carrying him through a powerful French fleet unobserved under cover of a dense fog, he arrived in safety at Spithead on the 15th of January, 1744, after a voyage of three years and nine months, in which he had completed the circuit of the globe. The lesson of his expedition, according to its historian, is, " that, though prudence, intrepidity, and perseverance united are not expected from the blows of adverse fortune, yet in a long series of transactions they usually rise superior to its power, and in the end rarely fail of proving successful."

Though he had brought home a large amount of treasure, he had lost four ships ; and the Government, therefore, was in no haste to confer upon him any reward. He had shown courage and ability, but he had been unfortunate, and Governments do not bestow their favours on the unfortunate. The very fact that his misfortunes were due to the neglect of the Admiralty in sending out ill-found and badly manned ships, did not incline its members to any indulgence towards the leader of an expedition which had so signally demonstrated that neglect. It was not, therefore, until a change of Ministers took place in the early part of 1735 that Anson was promoted to the rank of Rear-Admiral of the White. At the same time he was appointed to a seat on the Board of Admiralty, in which position even the censorious Walpole admits that he discharged his duties efficiently. "Lord Anson," he says, " was reserved and proud, and so ignorant of the world, that Sir Charles Williams said he had been round it, but never in it"—which might perhaps be said with truth of a man who had been almost always engaged in active service, and had spent most of his time afloat. But he adds that " Lord Anson, attentive to and generally expert in maritime details, selected with great care the best officers, and assured the King that, in the approaching war, he should at least hear of no court's-martial."

Early in 1747, however, the French having fitted out an expedition against the British colonies, Lord Anson hoisted his flag as commander-in-chief of a fleet intended to intercept and defeat it, and on the 9th of April sailed from Plymouth with the following ships under his orders :—

Ships.	Guns.	Men.	Commanders.
Prince George .	90	770	Vice-Admiral Geo. Anson ; Capt. Bentley
Devonshire .	66	535	Rear-Admiral P. Warren ; Capt. West.

Ships.	Guns.	Men.	Commanders.
Namur . .	74	650	Hon. Captain Boscawen.
Princess Louisa	60	400	Captain Watson.
Monmouth	64	480	Captain Harrison.
Prince Frederick	64	480	Captain Norris.
Defiance . . .	60	400	Captain Grenville.
Nottingham .	60	400	Captain Saumarez.
Somerset .	64	480	Captain Butt.
Windsor	60	480	Captain Hanway.
Falkland .	50	300	Captain Barradel.
Centurion . .	50	375	Captain Denis.
Bristol . . .	50	300	Hon. W. Montague.
Pembroke	60	400	Captain Fincher.
Ambuscade . .	40	250	Captain J. Montague.

Falcon sloop ; *Vulcan* fire-ship.

On the 3rd of May Anson fell in with the French fleet, under M. de la Jonquière, in the neighbourhood of Cape Finisterre, and attacked and defeated it, under the circumstances described by himself in the following unpretending dispatch :—

" At daybreak," he says, " I made the signal for the fleet to spread in a line abreast, each ship keeping at the distance of a mile from the other, that there might not remain the least probability for the enemy to pass by us undiscovered. At seven o'clock Captain Gwyn of the *Falcon* sloop informed me that he had seen the French fleet the day before, at four o'clock, bearing S.E. by S. four or five leagues from him ; that it consisted of thirty-eight sail, nine of which were large ships, and had the appearance of men-of-war, the rest merchantmen under their convoy, and that they were all steering to the westward

" Upon this intelligence I put abroad the signal for calling in all cruisers, and made sail immediately for the S.W. in order to cut them off. At half an hour after nine the *Namur* made a signal for seeing a fleet in the S.W., which was also seen soon after by the man at the *Prince George's* mast-head, bearing S.W. by S., Cape Finisterre at the same time bearing S. ¾ E., distant twenty-four leagues. I then made the signal to chase with the whole fleet, and by seven plainly discovered the chase to be a French fleet; that nine of the ships had shortened sail, and were drawing into a line of battle ahead, three of which appeared to be smaller than the others; and that the rest of the fleet, whom I judged to be under their convoy, were stretching to the westward with all the sail they could set.

"At one o'clock I made the signal for the line of battle abreast, and in half an hour afterwards for the line ahead. About three I·made the signal for the ship in the van to lead more large, in order to come to a close engagement with the enemy; who, getting their fore-tacks on board, and loosing their top-gallant sails, convinced me that their sole aim was to gain time, and endeavour to make their escape under favour of the night, finding themselves deceived in our strength; upon which I made a signal for the whole fleet to pursue the enemy and attack them, without having any regard to the line of battle.

"The *Centurion* having got up with the sternmost ship of the enemy about four o'clock began to engage her, upon which two of the largest of the enemy's ships bore down to her assistance. The *Namur*, *Defiance*, and *Windsor*, being the headmost ships, soon entered into the action, and after having disabled those ships in such a manner that the ships astern must come up with them, they made sail ahead to prevent the van of the enemy making an escape, as did also several other ships of the fleet.

"The *Yarmouth* and *Devonshire* having got up and engaged the enemy, and the *Prince George* being near the *Invincible*, and going to fire into her, all the ships in the enemy's rear struck their colours between six and seven o'clock; as did all those that were in the line before night. I brought-to at seven, having ordered the *Monmouth*, *Yarmouth*, and *Nottingham* to pursue the convoy, who then bore W. by S. at the distance only of four or five leagues, so that I was in hopes of having a very good account of them.

"The *Falcon* sloop (which I had sent after the convoy during the action, with orders to make signals to the other ships) returned to the fleet the next day with the *Dartmouth* Indiaman. I have taken in all six men-of-war and four Indiamen, of which are the particulars as under :—

Le Sérieux .	66 guns,	M. le Jonquière, chef d'Escadre.	Bound to Quebec.
Le Diamant.	66 „	M. Hoguart	
Le Rulis . .	52 „	M. Oury	
La Gloire .	44 „	M. Salesse	
L'Invincible	74 „	M. St. George	Bound to the East Indies.
Le Jason. .	54 „	M. Berard	
Le Philibert.	30 „	M. Cellié	
L'Apollon .	30 „	M. de Santons	Indiamen.
La Thétis .	20 „	M. Maçon	
Le Dartmouth	18 „	M. Pinoche	

"The *Ruby* had struck several of her guns into the hold, having all the guns and stores on board for a new frigate at Quebec. I have put the prizes into a condition to proceed with me to Spithead, and am in hopes that I shall arrive there in a few days; but it has taken up so much of our time, together with shifting and distributing our prisoners, that I have not hitherto been able to get a perfect account of the killed and wounded on either side. Our loss is not very considerable, except that of Captain Grenville, who was an excellent officer, and is a great loss to the service in general. Captain Boscawen was wounded in the shoulder by a musket-ball, but is almost recovered.

"To do justice to the French officers, they did their duty well, and lost their ships with honour, scarcely any of them striking their colours until their ships were dismasted. M. St. George kept his colours flying some time after the

General had struck. The *Sérieux* and *Diamant* were with great difficulty kept from sinking, which would not have been prevented without throwing great part of their guns overboard, as well as many chests of small arms intended for the expedition. The French general, M. de la Jonquière, is wounded in two places, the captain of the *Gloire* killed, and the second captain of the *Invincible* had his leg shot off."

It was afterwards ascertained that the French loss in killed and wounded amounted to about 700, that of the British to about 520; so that when the great disparity of force is considered, the English fleet being twice the strength of the French, it must be admitted that the French fought gallantly. And, indeed, complete as was the English victory, it was not, for this reason, one to boast of; defeat was impossible; and Anson's real merit lay in the admirable seamanship by which he embraced in his snares the whole of the French squadron. If the English carried off the trophies of victory and its substantial reward, the French must be credited with an elegant compliment which they elicited from it. The *Invincible* struck to the flag-ship, the *Prince George*, and its captain went on board the latter to surrender his sword to the Vice-Admiral. Approaching with an air of dignified courtesy and graceful submission, he said, "Monsieur, vous avez vaincu *l'Invincible*, et la *Gloire* vous suit" (Sir, you have conquered the *Invincible*, and *Glory* follows you).

The treasure captured on board the French squadron and convoy amounted to about £300,000, besides stores of all kinds of immense value. When the victorious fleet reached Portsmouth, the bullion was deposited in twenty waggons, conveyed to London, and with much military pomp paraded through the streets of the City to the Bank, amid the shouts of exultant thousands. The houses were illuminated, and bonfires blazed in every street. To the victorious Admiral the

"Approaching with an air of dignified courtesy and graceful submission, he said,
  Monsieur, vous avez vaincre *l'Invincible*, et *la Gloire* vous suit.'"

Duke of Bedford wrote: "You will easily believe **no one** in this town did with greater joy receive the news of your great success against the French than myself; and universal I may say it is, as I am just come home through illuminated streets and bonfires. The King told me this morning at his levee that I had given him the best breakfast he had had this long time, and I think I never saw him more pleased in my life. He has ordered Captain Davis a reward of £500 for bringing this welcome news."

Twenty waggons of gold are material evidences of success which the mob can thoroughly appreciate. Yet it was not the booty which so strongly excited the national feeling; it was the fact that Anson's was the first victory gained in the war after many reverses, and therefore it revived the hopes of the people, and encouraged their old belief in the prestige of the British flag. They did not stay to reckon odds; the French had been totally defeated, an entire squadron captured, immense treasure seized upon—no more was wanted. The Union Jack was once more in the ascendant, and every Englishman woke next morning a prouder and happier man.

When Anson attended George II.'s levee, the old monarch received him most cordially, and graciously said, " Sir, you have done a great service. I thank you; and desire you to thank, in my name, all the officers and private men for their bravery and conduct, with which I am well pleased." On the 13th o` June Anson was raised to the British peerage by the title of Lord Anson, Baron of Soberton, in the county of Hants.

Anson now resumed his administration of naval affairs, infusing into every department his own patient energy and untiring perseverance, so that squadron after squadron was fitted out promptly and with the most admirable completeness; and the numerous victories which crowned the operations of the British navy were not unjustly referred in part to his credit.

The peace of Aix-la-Chapelle, in 1748, lessened the demands on Anson's energies, and he found time to attend to private affairs. In the month of April he took to wife Lady Elizabeth, daughter of the Earl of Hardwicke, the Lord Chancellor. As he was then fifty-one years of age, we may reasonably conclude that he was no very impassioned lover, though he proved to be an attached and honourable husband.

To Lord Anson's administration of the Admiralty must be credited the Bill for the government of the Navy, in which are found the Articles of War. It was sufficiently stringent, but stringency was required at a time when the laxity of naval discipline had been productive of serious disorders. The most satisfactory proof of the care and ability with which it was drawn is the fact that for nearly a century it underwent no alteration except in two articles, the modification of which was rendered necessary by the hard fate of Admiral Byng *

In June, 1751, Lord Anson, who had for some time been the virtual head of the Admiralty, became First Lord, in name as well as reality, on the resignation of the Earl of Sandwich. His official career presents few incidents of interest or importance until the outbreak of the Seven Years' War, when, to strengthen the fleets of England, he adopted the expedient of establishing a permanent corps of marines to serve on board the royal ships, entirely distinct from the army, and under the command of the Board of Admiralty. The corps consisted at first of 5,000 men, divided into 50 companies, but in less than

---

* " These Articles, the 12th and 13th, which inflict the penalty of death, were then and afterwards considered so severe that, thirty years after the passing of the Act, and twenty-two after Byng's execution, there was added, in the Act of 19 George III. (1779), after the word ' death,' the words, ' or such other punishment as the nature and degree of the offence shall be found to deserve.' "—SIR JOHN BARROW, p. 220.

four years they were augmented to about 18,000. **In 1756,**
while Anson was still at the head of naval affairs, the English
Ministry received information that a formidable expedition was
being organized at Toulon, and that it was probably intended for
the capture of Minorca, an island which for half a century had
been in possession of Great Britain, and the capital of which,
Port Mahon, was considered the best harbour in the Mediterranean. A fleet of ten sail of the line, under Admiral the
Hon. J. Byng, was therefore dispatched for its protection on
the 7th of April. Three days later a French fleet of twelve
ships of the line sailed from Toulon, with transports having
16,000 men on board. On the 18th they arrived off the coast
of Minorca, and began to disembark at the port of Ciudadella.
The sole strength of her defences lay in the castle of St. Philip,
which was garrisoned by about 2,500 men under General
Blakeney, and this was so formidable a post that the French
found themselves compelled to proceed cautiously with its
investment. On the 19th of May Admiral Byng, who had
been reinforced by two more men-of-war, arrived within sight
of St. Philip. Though the French batteries were plying it with
storm of shot and shell, the "banner of England" still blew from
its ramparts. But a man of resolution and daring, a man with
the spirit of a Blake or a Nelson, might easily have effected its
relief. Byng, however, though physically brave, was deficient
in moral courage. A great responsibility was thrust upon him,
and he was unable to cope with it. He had already written
home in a despondent strain; he could not procure, he said,
any necessaries at Gibraltar; the place was so neglected that he
could not clean the foul ships with which he had sailed from
England; had he been sent earlier he might have prevented
the landing of the French, whereas now it was very doubtful
whether an attempt to reinforce the garrison would be successful. There was a note of failure in this feeble threnody.

On the 21st of May, De la Galissionière, the French Admiral, bore down upon the British fleet. Instead of rushing to the attack in the good old English fashion, Byng hesitated; but West, his second in command, with his portion of the fleet, sailed at once into the *mêlée*, broke the French line of battle, and hotly assailed the vessels that came in contact with him. Byng himself was hardly engaged at all except in the early part of the fight, when his ship, being damaged in her rigging, for a time refused to answer her helm. Amazed and confused by the impetuosity of West's attack, De la Galissonière quickly withdrew; and then was seen the strange spectacle of a French fleet retiring leisurely, and in order, unmolested by a British fleet almost its equal in strength! Byng called a council of war, the usual refuge of weak minds, and representing that he was inferior to the enemy in number of men and weight of metal he had, however, more guns, and one more ship—proposed to return to Gibraltar—a proposal accepted by the council, in which a majority of the members were as timid and undecided as himself.

The Admiral then sent home his dispatches; and on the 10th of June Sir Edward Hawke and Admiral Saunders received immediate orders to supersede Byng and his second in command, arrest them, and bring them prisoners to England.

Here it is necessary to furnish a comparative view of the two fleets, that the reader may have some means of forming an accurate judgment of Byng's conduct:—

BYNG'S DIVISION.

	Guns.	Men.			Killed.	Wounded.
Kingston . .	60	400	Capt.	W. Parry	0	0
Deptford . .	50	300	,,	J. Amherst . . .	0	0
Culloden . .	74	600	,,	W. Ward . . .	0	0
Ramillies . .	90	750	{ Hon. J. Byng { Capt. A. Gardiner }	. .	0	0
Trident . .	64	500	,,	P. Darell . . .	0	0

	Guns.	Men.		Killed.	Wounded.
Princess Louisa	60	400	Capt. Hon. J. Noel . .	4	13
Revenge . .	64	500	,, F. Cornwall . . .	0	0

DIVISION :—REAR-ADMIRAL TEMPLE WEST.

	Guns.	Men.		Killed.	Wounded.
Intrepid . .	64	500	Capt. J. Young	9	39
Captain . .	64	500	,, Ch. Catford . . .	6	30
Buckingham .	68	535	{ Rear-Adm. West } { Capt. Everitt } . .	3	7
Lancaster .	66	520	,, Hon. G. Edgecumbe	1	14
Portland . .	50	300	,, P. Baird	6	20
Defiance . .	60	400	,, T. Andrews . . .	14	45
	834	6205		43	168

Frigates :—*Chesterfield*, 40 guns, 250 men ; *Phœnix*, 20 guns, 160 men ; *Fortune*, 14 guns, 100 men ; *Experiment*, 20 guns, 160 men ; *Dolphin*, 20 guns, 160 men.

The list of killed and wounded plainly shows that Byng's division scarcely came into collision with the enemy at all, only one of his ships contributing to the total.

FRENCH FLEET.

	Guns.	Men.		Killed.	Wounded.
Foudroyant .	84	950	{ M. de Galissonière } { Capt. L'Aiguille } . .	2	10
Couronne .	74	800	{ M. de la Clue } { Capt. de Gabanores } . .	0	3
Le Redoubtable	74	800	{ M. de Glendeves } { Capt. de Marconville } .	12	39
Le Guenier .	74	800	,, Villar de la Brosse .	0	43
Le Téméraire	74	800	,, de Beaumont de Matré	0	15
Le Triton . .	64	600	,, de Menier . .	8	14
Le Lion .	64	600	,, de St. Aignan . . .	2	7
Le Content .	64	600	,, de Salien Grammont .	5	19
Le Sage . .	64	600	,, de Revert . . .	0	8
L'Orphée .	64	600	,, de Raimondis . . .	10	9
Le Fier	50	550	,, de Hervillée . . .	0	4
L'Hippopotame	50	550	,, de Rochmère . . .	2	10
	800	8250		41	181

Frigates :—*La Junon*, 46 guns, 300 men ; *La Rose*, 52 guns,

250 men ; *La Gracieuse,* 42 guns, 250 men ; *La Topaze,* 28 guns, 250 men ; *La Nymphe,* 28 guns, 250 men.

From the foregoing tables it will be seen that the French fleet was superior in men, but inferior in guns, though it is understood that their guns were, on the whole, of heavier metal than ours. Certain it is that the disparity between the two armaments was not such as a British admiral of the Rodney or Nelson type would have allowed to discourage him. As it was, the French retired before the impetuous attack of Rear-Admiral West, and there can be no doubt that if it had been adequately supported by Byng the result would have been a signal victory and the relief of Minorca, which, abandoned by the British fleet, was compelled to surrender on the 27th of June.

It is no wonder that a storm of public indignation broke upon Byng's devoted head. The news of his ignominious return to Gibraltar first reached London through the French Admiral's dispatch to his Government. "It is necessary," says Walpole, "to be well acquainted with the disposition of a free, proud, fickle, and violent people, before one can conceive the indignation occasioned by this intelligence." When Byng's own dispatch arrived, in which he wrote with the calm complacency of a man who is satisfied that he has done all that can be expected of him, the popular fury burst all bounds. In every town and city his effigy was publicly burned. The streets rang with ballads in which the keenest contempt and hardest abuse were showered upon his name. Men went about bewailing the degeneracy of the English race, and protesting that they and their brothers were cowards fit only to be enslaved. The walls were covered with furious placards. Caricatures and libels, in which the King and his Ministers were treated with the utmost license, passed from hand to hand. As for example :—" A Rueful Story ; or, Britain in Tears, being the conduct of Admiral **B——g**. London, printed by Boatswain Haul-up, a broken-hearted Sailor ;" and " The Devil's Dance, set to French Music," in which Byng, Fox, and the Duke of Newcastle were represented with cloven hoofs, dancing upon papers inscribed " Justice," " Honesty," " Law," " Magna Charta," " Port Mahon," &c. The only consolation which occurred to the public mind was such as might be derived from the reflection that the French Admiral had exhibited as much reluctance to engage as Byng himself. Hence the epigram—

> " We have lately been told
> Of two admirals bold,
>   Who engaged in a terrible fight;
> They met after noon,
> Which I think was too soon,
>   As they both ran away before night."

A medal was struck, having a figure of the Admiral, with the legend, " Was Minorca sold for French gold ? " In another print he was represented hanging in chains. When he arrived at Portsmouth it was with difficulty that the mob was prevented from tearing him to pieces. Addresses from London and from almost every county and city poured in upon the Throne demanding his condign punishment; and to that from London the King was made to reply, on his royal word, that he would save no delinquent from justice. Walpole relates that when a deputation waited upon the Duke of Newcastle with an accusation against the Admiral, that fatuous minister blurted out, " Oh, he shall be tried immediately—he shall be hanged directly !" But the story is probably an invention.

The Newcastle Ministry, already shaken by internal dissensions, could not withstand this outburst of popular feeling, and a new Cabinet was formed, of which William Pitt, " the great commoner," became the virtual head. Byng was then brought before a court-martial (December the 28th), which held its sittings daily, Sundays excepted, till the 27th of January, 1757, inclusive. After an exhaustive inquiry the court adjudged him to be shot to death, in pursuance of the twelfth article of war, which ran as follows: "Every person in the fleet who through cowardice, negligence, or disaffection shall, in time of action, withdraw or keep back, or not come into the fight or engagement, or shall not do his utmost to take or destroy any ship which it shall be his duty to engage, and to assist and relieve all and every of his Majesty's ships, or those of his allies, which it shall be his duty to assist and relieve, every such person so offending, and being convicted thereof by the sentence of a court-martial, shall suffer death." It is impossible to contend that the court, with these words before it, could have come to any other decision; for nothing is more certain than that Byng did not "do his utmost to take or destroy the French ships." But as the penalty of death seemed severe for an error which might be considered an error of judgment rather than a grave or criminal offence, the court strongly recommended him to the mercy of the Crown.

It then became the business of the Admiralty to convey this recommendation to the King, but they proceeded in a novel and unfortunate manner. They addressed a long letter to the King, enclosing a copy of Byng's instructions, of the resolutions and sentence of the court-martial, and other documents, adding "that doubts having arisen with regard to the legality of the sentence, particularly whether the crime of negligence, which was not expressed in any part of the proceedings, could in this case be supplied by implication, they found themselves obliged most humbly to beseech his Majesty that the opinion of the judges might be taken whether the said sentence was legal." The opinion of the judges was given on the 16th of February. It was of course a unanimous approval of its legality, and a warrant **was** immediately issued for the execution of Admiral Byng on the 28th—a concession to popular clamour, made in the face of the urgent representations of Pitt and Lord Temple. Pitt told George II. that the House of Commons was equally desirous with himself that the royal mercy should be extended to the Admiral. " Sir," said the King sarcastically, " you have taught me to look for the sense of my subjects in another place than the House of Commons."

Eventually, Byng's execution was deferred to the 14th of March. In the last days of his life he behaved with a dignity and an unaffected courage which extorted the admiration even of his enemies. When the fatal morning arrived he welcomed it as the termination of a period of painful delay. He took leave of his friends with easy grace, detained the officers not a moment, repaired directly to the quarter-deck of the ship in which he had been confined, and placed himself in a chair without affectation or levity. Some of the more humane of the officers represented to him that his face being uncovered, as he had desired, his executioners might feel some reluctance, and solicited him to make use of a handkerchief. He replied with indifference, " If it will frighten *them* let it be done, they would not frighten *me*." His eyes were bound—a volley— and he fell at once.*

* **Lord** Holland gives the following account of this painful event from Horace Walpole's MS.: "Admiral Byng's tragedy was completed on Monday —a perfect tragedy ; for there were a variety of incidents—villany, murder, and a hero. His sufferings, persecutions, aspersions, disturbances,—nay, the revolutions of his fate,—had not in the least unhinged his mind ; his whole behaviour was natural and firm. A few days before, one of his friends standing by him said, ' Which of us is tallest ?' He replied, ' Why this ceremony ? I know what it means ; let the man come and measure me for my coffin.' He said, that, being acquitted of cowardice, and being persuaded, on the coolest reflection, that he had acted for the best, and should act so again, he was not unwilling to suffer. He desired to be shot on the quarter-deck, not where common malefactors are ;—came out at twelve—sat down in a chair, for he would not kneel, and refused to

In July, 1757, Pitt prevailed upon Lord Anson to resume his seat as First Lord of the Admirality—a proof that he held his administrative abilities in high esteem. In this capacity it fell to him to prepare the various expeditions which Pitt's activity directed against the French coast and the French possessions in North America. He himself, in May, 1758, hoisted his flag for awhile in command of the general fleet which cruised off Brest, and harassed the shores of France from Brest to Rochefort until the close of the summer. The following year was distinguished by Boscawen's victory over the French fleet under M. de la Clue; Sir Edward Hawke's great defeat of M. Conflans; and the capture of Quebec by General Wolfe and Admiral Saunders—successful operations which glorified the British arms, and shed a reflected lustre on the naval administration under which they had taken place.

In 1760, the naval force of Great Britain consisted of 70,000 men, including 18,355 marines; and it is generally admitted that, owing to Anson's effective and energetic superintendence, the British navy was then in its "most high and palmy state." It well maintained its reputation during this closing stage of the Seven Years' War, contributing largely to the humiliation of France and Spain, capturing their colonies, and destroying their fleets. In February, 1763, peace was concluded at Paris—a glorious peace, which added to the British Empire the whole of the French provinces in North America, the Spanish province of Florida, and the West India islands of Tobago, Dominica, St. Vincent, and Grenada. Lord Anson, however, did not live to see this brilliant termination of a war, the successful conduct of which had been in no small degree owing to his

have his face covered, that his countenance might show whether he feared death; but, being told it might frighten his executioners, he submitted— gave the signal at once—received one shot through the head, another through the heart, and fell."—WALPOLE'S *Memoirs*.

administrative capacity. His health showed signs of giving way in the early part of 1762, and he was advised to try the Bath waters. He appeared to derive considerable benefit from them; but while walking in his garden at Moor Park (his country seat), on the 6th of June, he was seized with violent pains. Returning to the house, he laid himself down on his bed, and almost immediately expired without a struggle.

ADMIRAL LORD RODNEY.

A.D. 1718—1792.

"An officer who fought four general actions as commander-in-chief, and took three admirals of the enemy from the fleets of three of the most powerful nations of his time, one French, one Dutch, and one Spanish; and who, it might be added, took from them in the space of two years twelve sail of the line and destroyed five more, having thus had the singular honour of depriving the common enemy of seventeen out of the twenty-one line-of-battle ships which they lost during the war · "—

Such is the language in which a distinguished writer * refers to Admiral Lord Rodney, and the man of whom such language could justly be employed unquestionably deserves to be ranked among the " Eminent Seamen " of our country.

George Brydges Rodney was born at Walton-upon-Thames on the 19th of February, 1718. His father, through the good offices of his kinsman, the Duke of Chandos, who usually attended George I. on his numerous journeys to and from the continent, obtained the command of the royal yacht; and on one occasion, having been asked what mark of favour he would wish from the King, replied, that his Majesty would stand sponsor to his son. Hence, after his royal and noble godfathers, the King and the Duke, the boy was named George Brydges.

At an early age he was sent to Harrow School, and at an

* *Quarterly Review*, lxxxiii.

early age he left it, for he was only twelve years old when his royal godfather placed him in the naval service. For six years he served on the Newfoundland station under Admiral Medley. In February, 1739, he was in the Mediterranean, and Admiral Haddock appointed him lieutenant in the *Dolphin*. At the age of twenty-four the fortunate young man was promoted by Admiral Mathews to the *Plymouth*, a 64-gun ship, as captain, and intrusted with the charge of a fleet of 300 merchantmen, which a French fleet was cruising in the Channel to intercept. He convoyed it home in safety, and in recognition of this service was confirmed in his rank by the Admiralty, and appointed to the *Sheerness*. Next we find him in command of the *Ludlow Castle*, of 30 guns, in which he fought and captured the great St. Maloes privateer, a vessel of superior strength. Always in active employment, at one time escorting the King from Harwich, at another conveying troops to the siege of Ostend, he had ample opportunities of acquiring experience ; and the rapid promotions which he had owed to his family interest he speedily justified by his skill as a seaman and his energy as an officer. In command of the *Centurion*, he cruised for two years in the North Sea, and was on that station while Prince Charles Edward maintained his mimic state at Edinburgh. His services were rewarded by his removal to the *Eagle*, a line-of-battle ship of 64 guns. On his way to join her, the *Centurion* struck upon a shoal off Orfordness, and lay for nearly five hours six feet deep in the sand, but by good seamanship Rodney contrived to release her with the loss of her rudder and about thirty feet of her false keel, after cutting away part of her masts, and throwing overboard everything but her guns.

In April, 1747, the *Eagle* formed one of a squadron dispatched to intercept the French homeward-bound St. Domingo fleet, which they sighted on the 20th of June off Cape Ortegal. All sail was set, and a spirited chase immediately began. The

French men-of-war contrived to escape during the night, and the British ships then went in pursuit of the traders, of which forty-eight were eventually captured.

On the 14th of October in the same year Rodney took part in the gallant action fought between Rear-Admiral Hawke's squadron off Cape Finisterre, and the French fleet under M. de l'Etendière. It was on this occasion he first earned distinction as a fighting officer. During the heat of the action, Admiral Hawke, observing that Rodney's ship, the *Eagle*, and her consort, the *Edinburgh*, were much crippled, that they had lost their foretop-masts, and were opposed by superior numbers, bore down to their assistance, and after attacking and capturing the *Trident*, of 64 guns, engaged and took the *Terrible*, a 74-gun ship. Rodney, about the same time, compelled his antagonist to haul down her colours, and immediately boarding her, was greeted by her captain, as he gave up his sword, with the graceful remark, that " he would rather have met the *Eagle* in the shape of a dove, carrying the olive-branch of peace." With unusual aptness, Rodney, in reply, quoted his family motto, "Non generant aquilæ columbas" (Eagles do not beget doves).*

Towards the close of the Seven Years' War—a war in which England gained little honour and less profit—the *Eagle* was one of a small squadron which encountered a · Spanish fleet from the West Indies of twelve sail of the line, with a rich convoy, and, though greatly inferior in strength, he and his brother captains made prizes of six of the merchantmen.

* The motto is evidently adapted from the concluding line of a stanza in one of the best-known odes of Horace :—

" Fortes creantur fortibus et bonis,
   Est in juvencis, est in equis patrum
   Virtus, nec imbellem feroces
   Progenerant aquilæ columbas."

On Rodney's return to England the *Eagle* was put out of commission. Shortly afterwards Lord Anson presented Rodney to the King, who pleasantly observed that until then he did not know he had so young a captain in his navy. "Sir," said Lord Anson, " young Rodney has been six years a captain in your Majesty's navy, and without reflection, I wish, most heartily wish, your Majesty had a hundred more such captains, to the terror of your Majesty's enemies." The King answered, " We wish so too, my lord."*

A brief interval of peace followed the Treaty of Aix-la-Chapelle, but an interval employed by both England and France in preparing for a renewal of hostilities, and actually disturbed in the East and West Indies by an incessant struggle, which was only not "a war" because not formally recognised by the two Governments. In May, 1748, Commodore Rodney (for he had again been promoted) was appointed Governor and Commander-in-Chief on the Newfoundland station, and this position he occupied until October, 1752, when he returned home to take his seat in Parliament as member for Saltash. It must be acknowledged that fortune dealt very generously with him, and that in his career he met with none of those bars and impediments, those wearisome lets and hindrances, which so frequently baffle the advance of men of the highest merit.

In February, 1753, Rodney strengthened his social position by his marriage with Lady Jane Compton, sister of the Earl of Northampton. In the following year he was appointed to the *Prince George*, of 90 guns, in which ship he remained until May, 1757, when, on board the *Dublin*, a 74-gun ship, he joined Admiral Hawke's expedition against Rochefort. The expedition did not bombard Rochefort, from a want of harmony between the naval and military commanders, but it

* MAJOR-GENERAL MUNDY, *Life of Lord Rodney*, i. 43, 44.

captured, only to abandon, the small island of Aix, and
then returned home—to be overwhelmed with ridicule by the
wits and pamphleteers and ballad-makers, for seldom had
"mountain" laboured to bring forth a more ridiculous
birth. In 1757 the reins of power were grasped by the great
Pitt, who immediately infused something of his own active and
daring spirit into every department. The country felt that " a
man " was at its head, and responded to his call with joyful
alacrity. A new temper took possession of our soldiers and
seamen, and the era of failures at land and sea was definitely
closed. Rodney seems to have been one of those who felt
the direct influence and inspiration of Pitt's genius. Certain
it is that from this time he displayed a new energy and
resolution; and as his sphere of command enlarged, so
apparently did his capacity for it. Always a good seaman
and capable officer, he now gave proof of those rare and
admirable qualities which have earned him a high and
enduring place among the greatest of our great English
sea-captains.

On the 19th of May, 1759—Rodney was then forty-one years
of age—he was promoted to the rank of Rear-Admiral, and
immediately appointed to the command of a squadron
destined for an attack upon Havre-de-Grâce, where the
French were known to be collecting magazines and stores
preparatory to an expedition against the English coast. He
began the bombardment on the 4th of July, and continued it
for fifty-two hours with such fury as to set fire several times to
the town, destroy all the enemy's stores, and involve their gunboats in a general conflagration. The service with which he
had been charged was thus effectually executed ; and Havre-
de-Grâce, as a naval arsenal, ceased to be of further use to the
French during the continuance of the war. For the remainder of
the year Rodney continued to watch the French coast, harassing

it by frequent attacks, and extending his operations as far as Dieppe.

In 1761 Rodney hoisted his flag on board the *Marlborough*,* having been appointed to the command on the West India station, and the conduct of the naval operations of a great and combined expedition against Martinique, then the most prosperous and wealthy of the French colonies in the Atlantic.

Rodney arrived at Barbadoes on the 22nd of November, collected his fleet without delay, took on board some regiments of troops from North America under Major-General Monckton, and on the 7th day of January, 1762, arrived off Martinique. Next day, having silenced the enemy's batteries, the fleet dropped anchor in St. Pierre's Bay. The coast was carefully reconnoitred, and on the 16th the army was successfully landed without the loss of a single man at a point between Cape Negro and the Cas-de-Pilotte. Fort Royal was carried by assault, and the French authorities then surrendered, though some of the defences were of extraordinary strength, and had been reputed to be impregnable. Rodney and his colleague afterwards proceeded to Grenada, St. Lucia, and St. Vincent, which quickly capitulated, and have since formed part of our vast colonial empire. Jamaica being threatened by a French and Spanish fleet, Rodney hastened to its assistance ; but receiving peremptory orders to co-operate with Admiral Sir George Pocock and the Earl of Albemarle in a formidable expedition against the Havannah, he was obliged to content himself

* "A singular occurrence happened on board the *Marlborough*, at Portsmouth, on the occasion of his Royal Highness the Duke of York's visit to the Admiral. A common sailor got upon the top of the vane of the mainmast and stood upon his head, waving his hat with his feet several times round, to the admiration of his Royal Highness, who made the fellow a handsome present for his extraordinary dexterity."— MUNDY, i. p. 67.

with sending thither a squadron of ten ships under Sir James Douglas. With admirable energy Rodney returned to Martinique, and dispatched reinforcements of troops and ships to Pocock and Albemarle, reserving only 3 ships of the line under his own flag. The expedition, when finally organized, consisted of 19 ships of the line, with numerous smaller vessels; the transports carried 10,000 troops. The defences of the Havannah had been constructed with great skill, and were held with obstinate gallantry. The entrance to the harbour, which contained 12 Spanish men-of-war, was protected by two heavily armed forts, the Pantol and the Moro. From the 12th of June to the 30th of July the siege of the Moro was vigorously pressed, though the soldiers and seamen suffered severely from the pestilential heats of the climate. On the 30th the Moro was captured by assault, after great loss of life; the Havannah was then invested, and it surrendered, with all the vessels in the harbour, on the 12th of August.

On the 10th of February, 1763, peace was concluded; and by the Treaty of Paris Great Britain retained possession of Canada, part of Louisiana, Cape Breton, and other islands in the Gulf of St. Lawrence, as well as of Grenada, Dominique, St. Vincent's, and Tobago, while restoring Guadaloupe, Martinique, and St. Lucia. It is now generally admitted that our Ministers committed a mistake in acceding to terms which were unduly favourable to a beaten and humbled enemy.

On the 21st of January, 1764, Rodney, who in the previous year had been made Vice-Admiral of the Blue, was raised to the dignity of a Baronet of Great Britain. A few months later he was married to Henrietta, only daughter of John Ellis, Esq.; and in November, 1765, he was appointed Governor of Greenwich Hospital, a position in which he added greatly to the comforts of the pensioners. In 1771 a further promotion awaited him : he was made Commander-in-Chief at Jamaica During the three years of his service he exhibited a constant activity in all matters relating to the well-being of the fleet under his command ; and "with unceasing vigilance and firmness of purpose" maintained the honour and dignity of the British flag. He conceived a personal interest in the prosperity of Jamaica, and would fain have had the government of the island conferred upon him ; but in this hope he was disappointed, and, being recalled to England, he struck his flag at Portsmouth on the 10th of September, 1774.

"From this period," says his biographer,[*] "the sunshine which had hitherto cheered his existence became obscured, and for the space of four years the oppressive gloom of want, disappointments, and inaction hung over him like a mist, when again the cheering light of prosperity beamed upon him, and gilded his evening with its brightest rays. It is to be lamented that natures the most generous and ingenuous, from an honest zeal which flows through all their conduct, can bring themselves to bear the dry methodical labour of arithmetical calculation, nor to bestow that attention to their financial concerns which is to a certain degree indispensable in every condition of life. Sir George, it is to be apprehended, was one of this class. Possessing a pleasing and handsome exterior, with the courteous manner and address of the accomplished gentleman (qualities not particularly valued by the navy in those days), he had at all times when on shore been received into the highest circles of fashion, where he took in the draught of pleasure as others did ; and his heart being warm and generous, he not unfrequently found himself involved in pecuniary difficulties." Stripped of its verbiage, this passage simply means that living as a man of fashion, Rodney spent much more than his income, and incurred the humiliation of debt.

* MUNDY, i 162, 163.

A passion for play has been imputed to him, but on no very satisfactory authority; and it seems more just to ascribe the worst of his misfortunes to the expenses he incurred in contesting parliamentary elections. His embarrassments compelled him to withdraw to France, and he took up his abode in seclusion at Paris, where from want of means he was again involved in difficulties, and for some time was virtually a prisoner, until the generous friendship of the Maréchal Biron enabled him to return to his own country.

Writing to Lady Rodney on the 6th of May, 1778, he says, " I have this day accepted of the generous friendship of the Maréchal Biron, who has advanced one thousand louis in order that I may leave Paris without being reproached.

"Nothing but a total inattention to the distressed state I was in could have prevailed upon me to have availed myself of his voluntary proposal; but not having had for more than a month past a letter from any person but Mr. Statham and yourself, and my passport being expired, it was impossible for me to remain in this city at the risk of being sued by my creditors, who grew so clamorous it was impossible to bear it, and had they not been overawed by the lieutenant of the police would have carried their persecutions to the greatest length. Their demands were all satisfied this day; and the few days I remain in this city will be occupied in visiting all those great families from whom I have received so many civilities, and whose attention in paying me daily and constant visits in a great measure kept my creditors from being as troublesome as they otherwise would have been."

The generosity of this chivalrous Frenchman in restoring to England one of her bravest and best sea-captains indirectly prepared for his own country a serious humiliation. When, four years later, intelligence of Rodney's decisive victory over a great French fleet reached Paris, the population were inflamed with rage against the Maréchal, and reproached him with having been, to a certain degree, the author of the calamity. The Maréchal calmly replied that he gloried in the man whose deliverance he had effected, and in the victory which he had so nobly won. It must be confessed that the Maréchal's chivalry seems to have been a stronger impulse with him than his patriotism.

As a contrast to the conduct of the Maréchal, we may cite an instance of lack of delicacy on the part of the Duke of Chartres, afterwards infamous as the Duke of Orleans, and still more infamous as " Citizen Égalité." Shortly before Rodney's departure the Duke called upon him, and informing him that he, the Duke, was to have command of a fleet which would be opposed to the English under Admiral Keppel, with an insulting air asked him what he thought would be the result of their meeting. "That my countryman will carry your Highness home with him to learn English," was the prompt reply.

On his return to England Rodney was enabled at once to repay the loan so generously advanced by the Maréchal, and to effect a satisfactory arrangement with his creditors. He lost no time in applying to the Admiralty for employment, but the principal commands had been filled up, and it was not until the 1st of October, 1779, that his application could be satis-factorily answered. He was then selected for the command of a strong fleet which had been got ready for the purpose of relieving Gibraltar and conveying assistance to our West Indian colonies. Owing to the delays interposed by the dockyard authorities, the fleet was not ready to sail until the very end of December. On the 24th Rodney weighed from Spithead. Next day he put into Plymouth, and collecting the rest of his ships, finally took his departure on the 29th, with his flag flying on board the *Sandwich*. On the 9th of January he fell in with, and captured, a Spanish convoy of twenty-two sail, and a week later fought and defeated the Spanish fleet under Don Juan de Langára. The British on this occasion mustered in the following order :—

Van.	Bedford	. .	74 guns,	600 men,	Captain Affleck
	Cumberland	.	74 ,,	600 ,,	,,	Peyton
	Invincible	. .	74 ,,	600 ,,	,,	Cornish
	Prince George		90 ,,	767 ,,	Rear-Adm. Digby, Capt. Patten
	Terrible	. .	74 ,,	600 ,,	Captain Douglas
	Alcide	. . .	74 ,,	600 ,,	,,	Brisbane
	America	. .	64 ,,	560 ,,	,,	Thomson
Centre.	Resolution	.	74 ,,	600 ,,	,,	Sir Chas. Ogle
	Montagu	. .	74 ,,	600 ,,	,,	Houston
	Dublin	. .	74 ,,	600 ,,	,,	Wallis
	Sandwich	.	90 ,,	732 ,,	Adm. Sir G. Rodney, Capt. Long
	Marlborough		74 ,,	600 ,,	Captain Young
	Ajax	. . .	74 ,,	550 ,,	,,	Purdy
	Shrewsbury	.	74 ,,	600 ,,	,,	Uvedale
Rear.	Defence	. .	74 ,,	600 ,,	,,	Cranstoun
	Culloden	. .	74 ,,	600 ,,	,,	Balfour
	Bienfaisant	.	64 ,,	500 ,,	,,	Macbride
	Monarch	. .	74 ,,	600 ,,	,,	Duncan
	Royal George		100 ,,	867 ,,	Rear-Ad. Sir J. Ross, Capt. Bannister
	Alfred	. .	74 ,,	600 ,,	Captain Bayne
	Hector	. .	74 ,,	600 ,,	,,	Sir J. Hamilton
	Edgar	. .	74 ,,	600 ,,	,,	Elliot

With eight frigates and a cutter. The Spanish force was very inferior, comprising only one 80-gun ship (the Admiral's), ten 70-gun ships, and two frigates. The result of an action between two such opponents could not for one moment be doubtful; the Spaniards were wholly defeated; four of their best ships were taken ; one was blown up ; another, after having surrendered and been taken possession of, went ashore ; and a seventh, drifting among the breakers, perished. The news of this success was very warmly received in the metropolis; it restored the public confidence in the navy, which had been seriously shaken by a succession of untoward events. In the heart of the people Rodney filled the place which was afterwards occupied by Howe and Nelson; and his dash and gallantry were incessantly contrasted with the caution and fear of responsibility exhibited by other English admirals.

His eldest daughter, a girl **of** thirteen, wrote to **him on** the 11th of March as follows :—

"Everybody adores you, and every mouth is full of your praise. . . . The Tower and Park guns were fired last Monday, and that night and the next there were illuminations. On Thursday night there were northern lights seen ; and you will see in the *Morning Post* what fine verses they make upon them to your praise. Indeed, there is nothing but what they find matter to make verses upon about you. There are a great number of songs going about the streets, the choruses always 'Brave Rodney for ever.' I assure you I have had the curiosity to buy them ; such rhymes I never saw ; and if they were not about you I am sure I should not have patience to read them. I congratulate you upon the thanks of both Houses of Parliament. It is nothing new to you, as you had them last war. I have loved Lord North ever since he spoke in the House about you. I hear the King is exceedingly pleased with you. He said at the drawing-room that he knew when Rodney was out everything would go well. Lord Oxford told it to mamma at the Duchess of Chandos's last night. I have had a great many people wish me joy at the dancing academy, and at other places I have been—*very pleasant it is.*"

The City of London resolved on presenting its freedom to Rodney in a box made of gold ; which, as it had bestowed upon Admiral Keppel only a casket of oak, suggested to some wit of he day the following *jeu d'esprit :*—

"Each Admiral's defective part
Satiric lips have told;

That cautious Keppel wanted heart,
  And gallant Rodney gold.

Your wisdom, London's Council, far
  Our highest praise exceeds,
In giving each illustrious tar
  The very thing he needs.

For Rodney brave, but low in cash,
  You golden gifts bespoke ;
To Keppel rich, but not so rash,
  You gave a heart of oak."

Having relieved Minorca and landed the supplies and stores which he had brought out for the garrison of Gibraltar, Rodney sailed for the West Indies to take up his command on that station. Exactly one month after his arrival at Barbadoes he encountered the French fleet of 23 ships of the line, under the Comte de Guichen, his own fleet consisting only of 21. By skilful seamanship he gained the weather-gage, which gave him the advantage of choosing his distance, and by an adroit manoeuvre succeeded in bringing his compact line of battle against about one-half of the enemy, sailing parallel on the same tack ; so that from the close neighbourhood of the two fleets, and the fact that he had the weather-gage, Sir George looked with confidence to an assured and decisive victory. By putting before the wind, he prepared to get alongside one section of the enemy and overpower it before the other could come to its assistance. He accordingly made signal for close battle and for every ship to attack her opposite. Unhappily, owing to the insubordination of some of his captains, and the neglect or grievances of others, neither signal was obeyed. The whole advantage of the day was then lost; the action was fought at long range; and instead of a certain and signal victory, the sole result was a drawn battle.

Never perhaps was a commander—not even Benbow—placed in more embarrassing circumstances. It was not possible to measure the respective delinquency of the great majority of the flag officers and captains so as to bring them to trial; nor had he officers enough whose previous good conduct fitted them to try the others; moreover, to have held a number of courts-martial would have ruined the service. With great judgment he selected the worst offender, arrested him, and sent him for trial by court-martial. He was dismissed the service—a sentence which had a strong effect upon his brother officers. To tighten the bonds of discipline, Rodney put the fleet through a long course of naval evolutions, which taught them obedience and order as well as practical seamanship.

In May, 1780, the French fleet having stolen away to windward of Martinique, in order, it was said, to protect a Spanish convoy, Rodney hastened in pursuit, and beat about for six days and nights in the teeth of a strong east wind. This, says his biographer, afforded an admirable opportunity for maritime practice; for during all the time there was an incessant tacking, sometimes all together, but chiefly in succession—an arduous manœuvre for 20 sail of the line. Of this " admirable opportunity" Rodney availed himself also to infuse into his officers and crews a better *esprit de corps*, and to establish his authority in the fleet, where an impression had prevailed that he was a mere "man of fashion," fresh from the gay circle of the *beau monde*, whose orders might be ignored or neglected with impunity. During the six days we speak of the French so strenuously kept their wind that they could not be brought to close action; and after slight skirmishes on the 15th and 17th, Rodney, perceiving that further pursuit would be useless, returned to Barbadoes.

Rodney's own account of the affair of the 17th is as follows :—

" At daylight on the morning of the 17th we saw the enemy distinctly beginning to form the line ahead. I made signal

for the line ahead at two cables' length distance. At forty-six
minutes after six I gave notice that my intention was to attack
the enemy's rear with my whole force, which signal was
answered by every ship in the fleet. At seven a.m., perceiving
the fleet was too much extended, I made the signal for the line
of battle at one cable's length only. At thirty minutes after
eight a.m. I made a signal for the line of battle abreast, each
bearing from the other N. by W. or S. by E., and bore down
upon the enemy. This signal was penetrated by them, who,
discovering my intentions, wore, and formed a line of battle on
the other tack. I immediately made the signal to haul the
wind, and form the line of battle ahead. At nine a.m. made
the signal for the line of battle ahead, at two cables' length, on
the larboard tack.

"The manœuvres made by his Majesty's fleet will appear to
their Lordships [of the Admiralty] by the minutes of the signals
made before and during the action. At eleven a.m. I made
the signal to prepare for battle, to convince the whole fleet I
was determined to bring the enemy to an engagement. At fifty
minutes after eleven a.m. I made the signal for every ship to
bear down and steer for her opposite in the enemy's line. At
fifty-five minutes after eleven a.m. I made the signal for battle ;
a few minutes after, that it was my intention to engage close,
and, of course, the Admiral's ship to be the example. A few
minutes before one p.m. one of the headmost ships began the
action. At one p.m. the *Sandwich* in the centre, after having
received several fires from the enemy, began to engage. Perceiving several of our ships engaging at a distance, I repeated
the signal for close action. The action in the centre con-
tinned till fifteen minutes after four p.m., when Monsieur de
Guichen, in the *Couronne*, in which they had mounted 90 guns,
the *Triumphant*, and *Fendant*, after engaging the *Sandwich* for
an hour and a half, bore away. The superiority of the fire from

the *Sandwich*, and the gallant behaviour of the officers and men, enabled me to sustain so unequal a combat; though before attacked by them she had beat three ships out of their line of battle, had entirely broken it, and was to leeward of the French admiral.

"At the conclusion of the battle the enemy might be said to be completely beat, but such was the distance of the van and the rear from the centre, and the crippled condition of several ships, particularly the *Sandwich*, which for twenty-four hours was with difficulty kept above water, that it was impossible to pursue them that night without the greatest disadvantage. However, every endeavour was used to put the fleet in order, and I have the pleasure to acquaint their lordships that on the 20th we again got sight of the enemy's fleet, and for three successive days pursued them, but without effect, they using every endeavour possible to avoid a second action, and endeavouring to push for Port Royal, Martinique. We cut them off. To prevent the risk of another action, they took shelter under Guadaloupe. As I found it was in vain to follow them with his Majesty's fleet in the condition the ships were in, and every action of the enemy indicating an intention of getting to Fort Royal Bay, where alone they could repair their shattered fleet, I thought the only chance we had of bringing them again to action was to be off that port before them, where the fleet under my command now is, in daily expectation of their arrival. . . . .

" I cannot conclude without acquainting their lordships that the French admiral, who appeared to me to be a brave and gallant officer, had the honour to be nobly supported during the whole action.

"It is with concern inexpressible, mixed with indignation, that the duty I owe my Sovereign and my country obliges me to acquaint your lordships that during the action with the French fleet, on the 17th, and his Majesty's, the British flag was not properly supported."

·The last paragraph of this dispatch, which really contains its pith and substance, was suppressed by the Admiralty; but we reproduce it here, not only because it explains why the action of the 17th was not, as it might have been, a great victory, but because it helps to dispel a dangerous popular delusion, that all our sea battles have been triumphant, and all our seamen heroes. This assumption is apt to beget a confidence and self-satisfaction on the part of the public which in easily conceivable cases might be attended with almost fatal results. It is a painful fact that our naval history records many unfortunate instances of timorousness, and neglect of duty, and disobedience of orders on the part of British officers. Possibly few instances—with the exception of the battle in which gallant old Benbow was so shamefully betrayed—are more shameful, or throw more discredit on the name and fame of England, than that of the 17th of April, 1780. But all teach the same lesson —the necessity of bringing public opinion to bear directly upon our naval officers, so as to maintain the high standard of discipline and duty with which our ascendancy at sea must always be associated.*

* We are unwilling to overload the text with quotations, and therefore put here in a note some extracts from one of Rodney's private letters (to his wife, dated "Barbadoes, May 27th"), which seem necessary to the full and clear explanation of his difficult position on the 17th of April. There can be no doubt that had his captains done their duty he would have won that day as signal a victory over the Comte de Guichen as two years later he won over the Comte de Grasse. "This is the first opportunity," he writes, "that has offered since I wrote by the *Pegasus*, Captain Bazeley, who has, I hope, by this time been with ѵou, and delivered my letter, and acquainted you with the whole transaction of my battle with the French, and the *gallant behaviour* of my captains, who when victory, the most glorious victory ever obtained by a British fleet over the French, was in their favour, chose to decline accepting it, and to be passive lo kers-on. My public letter will do them ample justice; and I hope the nation will

Having relieved the West Indian Islands from all fear of hostile attack, Rodney in the autumn of 1780 sailed for the coast of Carolina, to co-operate with the British army in its

make them an example to posterity of what those persons deserve who dare to betray their country.

"As you must be anxious to hear of our further operations, and what has happened since my last, when Captain Bazeley left me in pursuit of the enemy's fleet, I have the pleasure to tell you that the French fleet, which had taken a large circuit in the hopes of avoiding us, by the good look-out of my frigates were discovered to windward of Martinique, endeavouring to steal into that island. I immediately put to sea and got sight of them, but no inducement whatever would tempt them to risk another battle; and for fourteen days and nights the fleets were so near each other that neither officers nor men could be said to have had sleep. Nothing but the goodness of the weather and climate could have enabled us to endure so continued a fatigue. Had it been in Europe half the people must have sunk under it. For my part, it did me good; and as I had given public notice to all my captains, &c., that I should hoist my flag on board one of my frigates, and that I expected implicit obedience to every signal made, under the certain penalty of being instantly superseded, it had an admirable effect, as they were all convinced, after their late gross behaviour, that they had nothing to expect at my hands but instant punishment to those who neglected their duty. My eye on them had more dread than the enemy's fire, and they knew it would be fatal. No regard was paid to rank—admirals as well as captains, if out of their station, were instantly reprimanded by signals or messages sent by frigates; and, in spite of themselves, I taught them to be what they had never been before—*officers;* and showed them that an inferior fleet, properly conducted, was more than a match for one far superior; and that France, with all her boasting, must give up the sovereignty of the sea to Great Britain, when, with twenty-three sail of the line opposed only to nineteen, she did not dare either to attack or stand a battle, but basely fled before them, and avoided by all possible means any encounter; but, notwithstanding all their endeavours to the contrary, my van twice had an opportunity of attacking their rear as they passed upon different tacks. The treatment they met with made them so shy, that we never could get near them again; and their ships being all clean, and mine so very foul, it was impossible to follow them with the least probability of overtaking them; and they having sailed out of sight, and three of my ships being sinking, and many incapable of keeping the sea longer, I was under the necessity of sending the sinking ships to St. Lucia, and with the others put into Barbadoes, to send the wounded men on shore, and to refit, as well as I can, my shattered fleet, not ten sail of which are really fit to go to sea."

movements against the forces of the American colonists. After conference with Sir Henry Clinton, the commander-in-chief, he made the necessary naval dispositions, and having stationed a line of frigates along the whole southern coast to check the American privateers, he returned to the West Indian station. During his absence Barbadoes had been visited by a hurricane, which had wrought the most awful devastation. The most substantial public buildings and the whole of the private houses, most of which were of stone, and remarkable for their solidity, had been overthrown ; the forts had crumbled into ruin, and many of the heavy cannons had been carried upwards of a hundred feet from the ramparts. More than 6,000 persons perished, and the condition of the survivors was most pitiable, inasmuch as they had lost everything. The hurricane had proved fatal also to eight men-of-war, and had dismasted the rest of the vessels which Rodney had left there.*

---

* The hurricane began at eight o'clock P.M. on October 10th. It reached its greatest height at midnight, but did not abate considerably till eight o'clock next morning. "During all this time most of the inhabitants had deserted their homes to avoid being buried in the ruins ; and every age, sex, and condition were exposed in the fields to the impetuous wind, incessant torrents of rain, and the terrors of thunder and lightning. Many were overwhelmed in the ruins, either by clinging too long in the ruins for shelter, in attempting to save what was valuable, or by unavoidable accidents from the fall of walls, roofs, and furniture, the materials of which were projected to great distances. Even the bodies of men and cattle were lifted from off the ground and carried several yards. The cries of the helpless wounded and dying could not be heard amidst the crash of ruins and the noise of the elements. . . . . All the fruits of the earth then standing have been destroyed ; most of the trees of the island have been torn up by the roots, and (what will perhaps give as strong an idea of the force of the wind as anything) many of them were stripped of their bark. The sea rose so high as to destroy the fort, carrying the great guns many yards from the platform, and demolishing the houses near the beach. A ship was driven ashore against one of the buildings of the Naval Hospital, which, by this shock and by the impetuosity of the wind and sea, was entirely destroyed and swept away."—*From a Contemporary Narrative.*

The year 1781 was distinguished by **Rodney's** capture of the island of St. Eustatius, which added another valuable possession to the rapidly increasing bounds of the British Empire. The French island of St. Bartholomew was also captured, and the three Dutch colonies of Bahia, Demerara, and Essequibo also surrendered to British arms. Crowned with these successes, Sir George returned to Europe, devolving the temporary command of the West Indian fleet on Sir Samuel Hood. He arrived in Cawsand Bay on the 19th of September, and landing, immediately proceeded to London. A house in Albemarle Street had been taken for his residence, where he arrived amidst the greetings of thousands of his countrymen, the women, as he descended from his carriage, strewing his path with flowers and garlands. After a short residence in London for the benefit of surgical advice, Rodney repaired to Bath to recruit his shattered constitution, and if possible to re-establish his health. But in November he was recalled to his country's service, having received the King's injunctions to return to his station in the West Indies with a powerful reinforcement, the preparations for which he was instructed to hasten with the utmost diligence. The sphere of his command was now extended to the whole West Indies.

With a squadron of 12 ships Rodney sailed in the middle of January, 1782. A powerful French fleet was at that time assembled in Fort Royal Bay, Martinique, consisting of 33 sail of the line and two 50-gun ships; and on board this fleet were embarked 5,400 soldiers, with a heavy siege train, and every other requisite for attempting the reduction of the island of Jamaica. Its admiral's design was to proceed with all possible diligence to Hispaniola, where he would be joined by the forces under the Spanish commander. Combined, they would have presented a superiority which not even a Rodney could have hoped to contest successfully.

The situation of Rodney was one, therefore, of difficulty and danger. The security of Jamaica and of the other West Indian Islands depended upon his exertions. It may even be said that the defeat of the enemy was a matter of imperial interest, as only by some such fortunate and daring exploit would it be possible to revive the national spirit, depressed as it was by the disasters in America, which had followed one another in quick succession. He hastened, therefore, to intercept the Comte de Grasse, before he could unite with the Spaniards, The French fleet sailed from Martinique on the 8th of April, whereupon the British fleet, which Rodney had got into perfect order, weighed anchor, and in less than two hours was standing towards the enemy under a cloud of canvas. De Grasse, whose great object was to effect a junction with the Spanish fleet, en-deavoured to evade his pursuers, and declined the challenge to a general engagement. The British, however, gained so much upon him, that next morning the van and centre of the fleet, including Rodney's flag-ship, had got within cannon-shot of the French rear, and a sharp artillery duel ensued, which, it must be added, was without decisive result, a great part of our fleet lying becalmed under the high hills of Dominique. During the 9th and 10th the Comte de Grasse, by great exertions, suc-ceeded in stretching so far to windward that he would probably have escaped, had he not on the 11th been brought down to save one of his vessels, the *Gelée*, which had fallen to leeward, owing to the damage it had sustained in a nocturnal collision with the French flag-ship, the *Ville de Paris*. Hence, at day-break on the 12th, Rodney discovered that he was in a position to weather a large portion of the hostile armada.

The line of battle was formed with wonderful rapidity—a rapidity which testified to the success of the naval evolutions in which Rodney had practised his captains during the two eventful years of his command.

About half an hour before the action began the Admiral entertained at breakfast on board his ship, the *Formidable*, Sir Charles Douglas, his captain of the fleet; Captain Simmons, commander of the ship ; Lord Cranstoun (a post-captain), his secretary, and Dr. (afterwards Sir Gilbert) Blane, his physician. The conversation naturally turned upon the forthcoming victory, for that such would be the result no Englishman could doubt; and Sir Charles Douglas remarked that if the British fleet maintained its then relative position, steering the same course close-hauled on the opposite tack to the enemy, it would necessarily pass through their line in running along, and closing with it in action. It is said that the Admiral was visibly struck by the idea, and no doubt decided in his own mind at that moment to attempt a manœuvre never before practised in naval tactics. Or it may have been that he had already resolved upon the innovation, and simply caught at a suggestion which showed him that the opportunity for it had arrived.

Here we must put before the reader a list of the ships, English and French, which took part in the great battle of the 12th of April :—

ENGLISH LINE OF BATTLE.

STARBOARD.	Commanders.	Guns.	Men.	Loss in Action. Killed.	Loss in Action. Wounded.
Royal Oak	Capt. Burnet	74	600	8	30
Alfred	,, Bayne	74	600	10	42
Montague	,, Bowen	74	600	12	31
Yarmouth	,, Parry	64	500	14	33
Valiant	,, Goodall	74	650	10	28
Barfleur	{ Admiral Hood. Capt. Knight }	90	765	10	27
Monarch	,, Reynolds	74	600	16	33
Warrior	,, Sir J. Wallace	74	600	5	21
Belligerent	,, Sutherland	64	500	4	10
Centaur	,, Inglefield	74	650		
Magnificent	,, Lingue	74	650	6	11
Prince William	,, Wilkinson	64	500		
Bedford	{ Commodore Affleck Capt. Graves }	74	617	0	17

	Commanders.	Guns.	Men.	Loss in Action. Killed.	Wounded.
Ajax	Capt. Charrington . .	74	550	9	10
Repulse . . .	,, Dumaiez . .	64	500	4	11
Canada . . .	,, Hon. W. Cornwallis	74	600	2	23
St. Alban's . .	,, Inglis	64	500	.	6
Namur . . .	,, Fanshawe . . .	90	750	6	23

LARBOARD.

	Commanders.	Guns.	Men.	Killed.	Wounded.
Formidable .	{ Admiral Sir G. Rodney ,, Sir C. Douglas Capt. Simmons . . . }	90	750	15	39
Duke	,, Gardner	90	750	13	61
Agamemnon .	,, Caldwell . . .	64	500	15	22
Resolution . .	,, Lord R. Manners .	74	600	5	34
Prothée . . .	,, Buchan . . .	64	500	5	25
Hercules . .	,, Savage . . .	74	600	7	19
America . . .	,, J. Thompson .	64	500	1	1
Russell . . .	,, Saumarez . . .	74	600	10	29
Prudent . . .	Not in the action.				
Fame	,, Barber	74	550	3	12
Anson . . .	,, Blair	64	—	3	13
Torbay . . .	,, Gisborn	74	600	10	25
Prince George .	,, Wilhams . .	90	750	9	24
Princessa . .	{ ,, F. Drake . . . ,, Knatchbull . . }	70	600	3	22
Conqueror . .	,, Balfour	74	577	7	23
Nonsuch . .	,, Truscott	64	500	3	3
Celinde . . .	,, C. Thompson . .	74	600	Not stated.	
Arrogant . .	,, Cornish	74	600	0	0
Marlborough .	,, Penny	74	600	3	16

Total: 36 sail of the line (10 frigates not included).

230 killed.
759 wounded.

FRENCH LINE OF BATTLE.

White and Blue Squadron.

1me Division.

Le Souverain, 74; Le Hercule, 74; L'Auguste, 80; Le Northumberland, 74. With four frigates.

2me Division.

Le Zèle, 74; Le Conquérant, 74; Le Duc de Bourgogne, 80; Le Marseillais, 74. With two frigates.

3me Division.

Le Hector, 74; Magnanime, 80; Le César, 74; Le Diadème, 74. With one frigate.

White Squadron.

4me Division.

Le Glorieux, 74; *Le Sceptre,* 74; *L'Eveiler,* 64. With one frigate.

5me Division.

Le Languedoc, 84; *La Ville de Paris,* 106; *La Couronne,* 84. With three frigates.

6me Division.

Le Réfléchir, 74; *Le Scipion,* 64; *Le St. Esprit,* 84; *Le Palmier,* 74. With one frigate.

Blue Squadron.

7me Division.

Le Jason, 64; *Le Citoyen,* 74; *Le Destin,* 74; *Le Dauphin Royal,* 74. With one frigate.

8me Division.

L'Ardent, 64; *Le Neptune,* 84; *Le Triomphant,* 84; *Le Magnifique,* 74. With two frigates.

9me Division.

Le Caton, 64; *La Bourgogne,* 64; *Le Brave,* 74; *Le Pluton,* 74. With one frigate.

In all 34 sail of the line (with 16 frigates).

The action began about seven in the morning, the British fleet advancing in a diagonal line against the enemy, the *Formidable* leading, followed by the *Namur,* the *Duke,* and the *Canada.* Immediately after, breaking through the hostile array, Rodney signalled for the van to tack and gain the wind of the enemy, after which each ship lay-to alongside of its nearest adversary. The *Formidable* in her advance took and returned the fire of one-half of the French force, and "under one general blaze and peal of thunder along both lines," dashed through that of the French, about three ships from the centre, where De Grasse commanded in the *Ville de Paris.* In the act of doing so she swept within pistol-shot of the *Glorieux* (74 guns), and overwhelmed her with such a tornado of shot that all her masts were carried by the board. Dismasted, shattered, and shot-torn, but with the white flag of the Bourbons nailed to a stump, she lay on the placid waters a motionless hulk, presenting a spectacle which, it is said, reminded **Rodney** of a well-known passage in Homer. " Now," he exclaimed, " will take place the contest for the dead body of Patroclus." But the contest was already at an end; for the French fleet, being cut in two sections, fell into confusion, and thought of escape rather than of fighting. During the rest of the day a partial and desultory action was continued, but the French were never able to form, and made no attempt to close with their exultant antagonists.

An eye-witness of the battle writes :—" When the signal for the line was hauled down, every ship annoyed the enemy as their respective commanders thought best, and the French struck their colours in succession to the number of six sail of the line and two frigates. The victory was decided at the moment the *Formidable* broke the French line, but the effect on the spirits of the fleet was not complete until the French flag-ship, the great *Ville de Paris*, surrendered. The thrill of victory that then penetrated every British bosom cannot be described."

The loss of the British was 261 killed and 837 wounded. One of the great advantages of the day was that all the British ships were pretty equally engaged, so that the enemy suffered more or less from each ship. On the other hand, none of the British were wholly disabled, the whole being so disposed that each was ready to support and take off the fire from the other.

The carnage on board the prizes was dreadful ; the *Ville de Paris* alone had nearly 300 killed and wounded. Her sides were riddled with shot, and her rigging was so torn that she had neither a sail left nor mast fit to carry a sail. The *Glorieux* presented a scene of absolute horror; she was a complete floating slaughter-house. So great were the numbers killed, that the survivors, either from want of leisure or through dismay, had not thrown the bodies of the killed overboard ; hence her decks were strewn with the blood and mangled .imbs of the dead, as well as with the wounded and the dying, who lay forlorn and helpless in their great pain.

At the first glance, .this victory would seem to be partly attributable to an inferiority of force on the part of the French, who had 34 ships to our 36; but this numerical superiority was more than counterbalanced by the heavier guns of the French, whose broadside exceeded in weight that of the British fleet by 4,396 lbs. The difference in the number of men was still more considerable ; for not only were the French crews more numerous in proportion to their tonnage, but they had the assistance of a large body of land forces.

It is assumed, therefore, that the only cause for British success in this and many other great sea-fights can be no other than " the closeness of the action—an advantage, how-ever, which, being mutual and equal, can be available only to that party which possesses the moral pre-eminence of un-daunted courage, and the consequent physical superiority of a better sustained fire ; and this was never more fully exemplified and proved "—until Jervis and Nelson introduced a new era—than in the engagement with the French fleet under the Comte de Grasse.

The night after the battle was moonless and cloudy, so that if the pursuit had been continued our ships, in the darkness and confusion, would have been in danger of firing into each other. Owing to this reason, as well as to the necessity of repairing and refitting, to the encumbrance of prizes, and the calm which prevailed for several days, Rodney remained near the scene of action till the 17th, when Sir Samuel Hood was sent ahead with.his division. The fleet afterwards made for Porto Rico, where it was joined by Sir Samuel, with two French 64-gun ships, a frigate, and a sloop-of-war, which he had cap-tured. Then it sailed for Jamaica.

After the surrender of the *Ville de Paris*, the Admiral sent Lord Cranstoun, one of his captains, on board the prize, to beg the Comte de Grasse to remain there at his ease if he chose. Next morning the French Admiral voluntarily went on board the *Formidable*, where he spent a couple of days, "during which time," says Dr. Blane, "I had a great deal of conversation with him and his officers. Sir Charles Douglas did me the honour to introduce me to him, thus : ' C'est le médecin de nos armées navales, qui est presque assez habile pour faire revivre les morts ' [This is the physician of our fleet, who is almost skilful enough to resuscitate the dead] ; to which the Comte, humouring the badinage, replied, ' Et peut-être pour faire mourir les vivants ' [And perhaps to put to death the living]."

The fate of the *César* (74 guns), one of the prizes, was truly pitiable. On the night of the action, soon after dusk, she caught fire, through the carelessness of an English marine who was carrying a candle below in search of liquor. The flames spread with a destructive rapidity which defied every effort to extinguish them. After she had been burning for some time the conflagration spread to the powder magazine, and the ship blew up. Her captain, who had been severely wounded, the English officer who boarded her, and the greater part of the men on board, both British and French, perished. Some few escaped before the explosion ; others who survived it and clung to parts of the wreck were most of them either overwhelmed in the waves or miserably scorched by the flames ; and those who attempted their rescue have left on record that they saw a spectacle beyond all measure horrible—that of the poor wretches who clung despairingly to the wreck being torn off by the voracious sharks which swarm in the West Indian seas, and proved to be not yet glutted with the carnage of the preceding day.*

* We append Rodney's own account of this memorable engagement, in

Among the incidents related of this engagement we may cite the following. When the news of Rodney's victory arrived at Plymouth, some of the French officers detained there as prisoners of war exclaimed, " Impossible ! not the whole British fleet could take the *Ville de Paris !* " The *Ville de Paris,* we may add, as well as the *Glorieux* was lost in a gale off the Newfoundland coast in the following September.

The bold manœuvre of " breaking the line," to which Rodney's decisive success is attributable—a manœuvre after-wards developed by Admiral Duncan at Camperdown, Lord Howe on the 1st of June, and by Nelson at Trafalgar—will always render memorable the action of the 12th of April. Its authorship has been the subject of a prolonged controversy. About the time that Rodney left London to assume the command on the West Indian station was published an " Essay on Naval Tactics," by John Clark, of Eldin, containing a clear and able exposition of the different systems of naval warfare pursued by the French and English ; the one preparing to attack from windward, the other making a leeward position; which difference, according to the author, had produced many of our failures in general actions, neutralising the bravery of our officers

which it is computed that the French lost 10,000 to 12,000 men (one autho-rity says 16,000) :—" The battle began at seven in the morning, and con-tinued till sunset, nearly eleven hours ; and by persons appointed to observe, there never was seven minutes' respite during the engagement, which I believe was the severest that ever was fought at sea, and the most glorious for England. We have taken five, and sunk another. Among the prizes the *Ville de Paris,* and the French Admiral, grace our victory.

" Comte de Grasse, who is at this moment sitting in my stern gallery, tells me that he thought his fleet superior to mine, and does so still, though I had two more in number ; and I am of his opinion, as his was composed all of large ships, and ten of mine only sixty-fours.

" I am of opinion that the French will not face us again this war, for the ships which have escaped are so shattered, and their loss of men so great, that I am sure they will not be able to repair or replace either in the West Indies. Had it not been for this fortunate event Jamaica had been gone."

and seamen. He compared the meeting of the fleets on contrary tacks to an encounter of horsemen, in which the parties pushed their horses at full speed in opposite directions, exchanging only a few pistol-shots as they passed, and thus two great armaments had frequently engaged and separated without any serious damage or loss on either side. He added that if an enemy's line were cut in twain, the portion separated from the rest could more readily be destroyed. In a later edition of his book he declared that before its publication he had made known his views to Mr. Atkinson, a friend of Rodney; and that the Admiral himself, prior to his departure from London, said he would bear them in mind in engaging an enemy. On the other hand, Sir Howard Douglas maintains, by a comparison of dates, that Rodney could not have acquired this information before he left to take his command in the beginning of 1782, and that his father, the captain of the *Formidable,* made the suggestion to the Admiral in the heat of the engagement (see p. 151), when he saw a favourable opportunity of breaking the line.

Rodney himself, in 1789, wrote some marginal notes in a copy of Clark's book, with which he seems then to have first become acquainted, to the effect that it was an admiral's duty "to bring, if possible, the whole fleet under his command to attack half or part of that of his enemy." And he says that, in his action with De Grasse, his own ship began a very close fight within half musket-shot, and continued it close along the enemy's lines under an easy sail, till an opening appeared at the third ship astern of the enemy's admiral, which gave an opportunity of breaking their line, and throwing their rear into the utmost confusion.

On the general subject the remark seems just, that in their rival claims to what is in some degree the character of an invention, most persons will be inclined to consider that the merit really rests with the man who first gives a practical value to a theory, and that this is specially the case with a naval or military commander, who in the fever and tumult of the strife seizes the right moment for carrying a principle into operation. And it may be added that, as a matter of fact, Rodney had already accomplished the manœuvre on a partial scale in his action with the Comte de Guichen on the 17th of April, 1780.*

* The following extract from Richard Cumberland's " Memoirs" may be regarded as conclusive testimony, unless we are to suppose that it is as purely inventive as one of the writer's own dramas—a supposition for which there seems no foundation :—

"It happened to me to be present and sitting next to Admiral Rodney at table, when the thought seemed first to occur to him of breaking the French line by passing through it in the heat of action. It was at Lord George Germaine's house at Stoneleve, after dinner, when, having asked a number of questions about manœuvring of columns and the effect of charging with them in a line of infantry, he proceeded to arrange a parcel of cherry-stones, which he had collected from the table, and forming them as two fleets, drawn up and opposed to each other, he at once arrested our attention, which had not been very generally engaged by his preparatory inquiries, by declaring he was determined so to pierce the enemy's line of battle (arranging his manœuvre at the same time on the table), if ever it was his fortune to bring them into action.

"I dare say this passed with some as mere rhapsody, and all seemed to regard it as a very perilous and doubtful experiment ; but landsmen's doubts and difficulties made no impression on the Admiral, who having seized the idea held it fast, and in his eager, animated way, went on manœuvring his cherry-stones, and throwing the enemy's representatives into such confusion, that, already in possession of that victory in imagination which in reality he lived to gain, he concluded his process by swearing he would lay the French Admiral's flag at his sovereign's feet—a promise which he actually pledged to his Majesty in his closet, and faithfully and gloriously performed.

"That he carried this projected manœuvre into operation, and that the effect of it was successfully decisive, all the world knows. My friend, Sir Charles Douglas, captain of the fleet, confessed to me that he himself had been adverse to the experiment, and, in discussing it with the Admiral, had stated his objections ; to these he got no other answer but that 'his counsel was not called for ; he required obedience only—he did not want advice.' Sir Charles also told me that whilst this project was in operation (the battle then raging), his own attention being occupied by the gallant defence made by the *Glorieux* against the ships that were pouring their

The news of Rodney's victory was received in England with " a tumult of acclaim." All London, we are told, was in an uproar; the whole town was illuminated, bonfires blazed, and when his wife and daughters went to the theatre, pit, gallery, and boxes burst into loud and long-continued huzzas. The Government were not so lavish in their rewards. Sir George received only a barony, with a pension of £2,000 a year to himself and his heirs. Soon afterwards, a change of administration taking place, he was recalled with very little courtesy, and with none of the respect due to his active and valuable services. Sailing from Port Royal Bay on the 22nd of July, he landed at Bristol on the 13th of September, and was welcomed with an enthusiasm which showed that on this point the people were not in accord with their Government.

Thenceforward Lord Rodney lived principally in retirement with his family in the country. He suffered much from attacks

fire into her, upon his crying out, ' Behold, Sir George, the Greeks and Trojans contending for the body of Patroclus! '[1] the Admiral, now pacing the deck in great agitation, pending the experiment of the manoeuvre, which, in the instance of one ship, had unavoidably miscarried, peevishly exclaimed, 'D—n the Greeks, and d—n the Trojans! I have other things to think of.' When, in a few minutes after, the supporting ships having led through the French line in a gallant style, turning with a smile of joy to Sir Charles Douglas, he cried out, 'Now, my dear friend, I am at the service of your Greeks and Trojans, and the whole of Homer's Iliad, or as much of it as you please ; for the enemy is in confusion, and our victory is secure.'

*' This anecdote, exactly as I relate it, I had from the gallant officer, Sir Charles Douglas, untimely lost to his country, whose candour scorned to rob his Admiral of one leaf of his laurels ; and who, disclaiming all share in this manoeuvre, nay, confessing he had objected to it, did, in the most pointed and decided terms, again and again repeat his honourable attestations of the courage and conduct of his commanding officer on that memorable day."

<hr>

[1] According to Sir Gilbert Blane (see p. 154, *ante*), this speech was made by Rodney himself.

of gout, which as he advanced in years increased in frequency and severity. Early in 1792, while on a visit to his son, Colonel Rodney, in London, he was assailed with repeated paroxysms, and on the night of the 23rd of May the disease flew to his stomach with fatal violence. Before morning he expired, without a sigh or a struggle, in the seventy-fourth year of his age, having been in the navy sixty-two years, and upwards of fifty years in commission—a period of service not often equalled, and we should think hardly ever surpassed.

Lord Rodney was of a handsome person, rather tall, with comely and expressive features, and a well-formed figure. In private life he was emphatically the well-bred gentleman, with prepossessing manners, and a polite, dignified, and courteous bearing. His nature was warm, frank, and generous; a kind and affectionate husband, he was also a tender and indulgent parent and a faithful friend. As a commander, he was prompt to reprove, when reproof was called for; but if he held the reins of discipline firmly, he was always considerate and just. His skill as an officer and his bravery as a seaman have been abundantly illustrated in the foregoing pages; and in naval history he will always be remembered as practically the inventor of the celebrated manoeuvre of " breaking the line."

RICHARD, EARL HOWE.

A.D. 1725—1799.

I.

RICHARD HOWE, second son of Viscount Howe of **Langar,** was born in 1725. He appears to have been educated at Eton; but his education must have been of the slightest kind, as he left Eton at the age of fourteen, and was entered as midshipman on board the 50-gun ship *Severn.* This vessel was attached to Commodore Anson's famous South Sea expedition, but in rounding Cape Horn was so disabled in a violent gale as to be compelled to bear up for Rio de Janeiro, whence, after having refitted, she returned to England. The rough experiences which the young midshipman underwent in his first voyage gave him no distaste for the sea. We find him next on board the *Bedford,* which, with a squadron under Sir Charles Knowles, attacked La Guayra, on the Caraccas coast, suffering severely from the heavy fire of its batteries. Thus was he initiated into the dangers of tempest and battle, bearing himself in both so gallantly, that in 1744, at the age of nineteen, he was promoted to the rank of a lieutenant.

In the year of the Rebellion, 1745, Howe, in command of the ship *Baltimore,* served on the Scottish coast; and in a skirmish with a couple of French ships, on the 1st of May, was severely wounded in the head. Soon afterwards he was raised to the rank of captain, a rapid promotion which he probably owed to the influence of his family. We have little to record until the beginning of the Seven Years' War, when, on board the 60-gun ship *Dunkirk*, he joined Admiral Boscawen's fleet ordered to North America for the protection of our settlements against French attack. In a dense fog off the coast of New-foundland, the *Dunkirk* and the *Defiance*, another 60-gun ship, separated from the fleet and fell in with two French men-of-war, the *Alcade* and the *Lys*, the former of 64 guns and 480 men, and the latter, pierced for the same number, but, being armed *en flûte*, mounting only 22; this ship had on board eight companies of soldiers. A smart action followed, in which the *Dunkirk* lost 7 men killed and 25 wounded: both the Frenchmen struck their colours.

In the spring of 1756 we find Captain Howe employed in the Channel service, and displaying an activity and a skill which recommended him to the command of a squadron of ships-of-war, assembled to protect the Channel Islands, and harass and destroy the French coasting trade. Later in the year he was attached to the fleet, under Sir Edward Hawke, destined for an attack upon Rochefort. The characteristics of the naval commanders of this expedition—from which so much was expected, and by which so little was accomplished—have been incisively sketched by Horace Walpole. " Sir Edward Hawke, who commanded the fleet, was a man of steady courage, of fair appearance, and who even did not want a plausible kind of sense ; but he was really weak, and childishly abandoned to the guidance of a Scotch secretary. The next was Knowles, a vain man, of more parade than real bravery. Howe, brother of the lord of that name, was the third on the naval list. He was undaunted as a rock, and as silent. He and Wolfe soon contracted a friendship, like the union of cannon and gunpowder."

After capturing the island of Aix, a service in which Howe greatly distinguished himself, the fleet proceeded to the Channel, and made ready to disembark the troops which it had on board. But the military commanders showed a singular unwillingness to undertake any responsible movement; they held a council of war, which decided, as most councils of war do decide, on doing nothing; and, after a great parade of force, the fleet went " back again "—to the amusement of the enemy, and the angry contempt of all England.

Howe acted as Commodore in the great expedition under Lord Anson which sailed from Spithead on the 1st of June, 1758, to blockade Brest, where the French were understood to have collected a strong fleet. Anson detached Howe, in the *Essex*, with a powerful squadron, to cover the landing in Cancale Bay of an army of 13,000 men under the Duke of Marlborough. The disembarkation was safely effected on the 6th, and next morning the army advanced against St. Maloes, where, however, it accomplished no greater achievement than to burn two or three men-of-war, and some seventy or eighty merchant ships, after which it returned to Cancale Bay, re-embarked, made an equally futile demonstration off Cherbourg, and then sailed for England; having taught the French, as Walpole says, " that they were not to be conquered by every Duke of Marlborough." Comparing the small result of the expedition with its tremendous cost, Henry Fox said that it was " breaking windows with guineas."

Another expedition against the French coast took place in the late summer of the year. This time Howe had the command-in-chief of the naval force; and as Howe, though he spoke little, did much, Cherbourg was captured on the 8th of August, its pier and basins were destroyed, with a hundred and seventy heavy guns. The brass guns were brought to the Tower of London, with their brass mortars, and about one

"Standing upright in the boat, he waved the seamen to follow him."—*Page 165.*

hundred pieces of cannon. An attempt was also made upon St. Maloes, but it was found too strong to be taken by assault, and a large French force appearing in the neighbourhood, the English army re-embarked, though not without a considerable loss (September 5th).

"On this trying occasion," says his biographer, "the conduct of Howe was eminently conspicuous. The grenadiers had nothing left for it but to escape with all speed to the boats, or remain to be killed; they were ordered, therefore, to make to the shore as quickly as possible." A battery thrown up on the hill shattered several of the boats to pieces. As some of these approached the shore, many of the seamen were killed or wounded, which so intimidated the rowers that they hesitated to proceed, and lay upon their oars. Howe, observing this backwardness, and suspecting its cause, sprang into his barge, rowed into the midst of the fire of shot and shells. and, standing upright in the boat, waved the seamen to follow him. His example animated their depressed spirits; no one now thought of shrinking, but all strove eagerly who could pick up the greatest number of poor fellows, some swimming, others wading into the sea. One of the historians of the war, the Reverend John Entick, compares the gallant behaviour of Howe, appropriately enough, to Achilles staying the flying Greeks.

> "So when the Grecians to their navy fled,
> High o'er the brunt Achilles rear'd his head.
> Greece, for one glance of that tremendous eye,
> Straight took new courage, and disdain'd to fly;
> They saw aghast the living lightning's play,
> And turn'd their eyeballs from the flashing ray." *

In the following year (1758) Commodore Howe, who had attained the age of thirty three, was married to Mary Hartop, of

* SIR J. BARROW, *Life of Earl Howe,* p. 52.

Welby, in Leicestershire. Two or three months later, by the death of his elder brother, he succeeded to the title and estate of the family as Viscount Howe of Langar. In June Lord Howe hoisted his flag on board his favourite ship, the *Magnanime*, and joined the fleet under Sir Edward Hawke, then employed off Brest. Thus he came to be engaged in the action of the 20th of November, in which the French, under M. de Conflans, were worsted. His share in the fight was considerable. According to Walpole, "Lord Howe, who attacked the *Formidable*, bore down on her with such violence that her prow forced in his lower tier of guns." He had 13 killed and 66 wounded, out of a total of 39 killed and 202 wounded. His reputation was now firmly established; and the nation had learned to recognise in him an able and energetic officer, who might always be trusted to maintain the honour of the flag; not a man of genius, but a man of character and capacity, of clear judgment and firm resolution. Though a strict disciplinarian, he was a great favourite with the seamen, who knew that he fully sympathized with them, understood their wants and wishes, and at proper times was disposed to concede any reasonable indulgence. After an action he would go below, converse with every wounded man, and sit by the side of their "cradles;" he constantly ordered his live-stock and wines to be applied to their use, at the surgeon's discretion, and always for the sick on board.

The Duke of York, when raised to the rank of Rear-Admiral of the Blue, was appointed to the command of the *Princess Amelia*, an 80-gun ship. He immediately requested that Lord Howe might become his flag-captain, and accordingly Lord Howe removed from the *Magnanime*. While on board the *Princess Amelia*, an incident occurred which brought out strongly his composure in circumstances of danger. He was asleep in his cabin, when the lieutenant of the watch suddenly appeared at his bedside in a state of great agitation, exclaiming—

"My lord, the ship is on fire close to the magazine; but don't be frightened, my lord, it will soon be got under."

"Frightened, sir! what do you mean by that? I never was frightened in my life." And looking his lieutenant full in the face, he said to him coolly—

"Pray, sir, how does a man feel when he is frightened? I need not ask how he looks. I will be with you immediately; but take care that his Royal Highness is not disturbed."*

In 1763 Howe accepted a seat at the Admiralty, and continued to occupy it until 1765, when he was removed to the important and lucrative office of Treasurer of the Navy. In 1770 he was promoted to the rank of Rear-Admiral, and in 1775 to that of Vice-Admiral of the Blue. The following year witnessed his appointment as commander-in-chief on the North American station; and he received a joint commission with his brother, General Sir William Howe, to treat with the American colonists, then engaged in their War of Independence, and to take measures for the restoration of peace. He soon discovered, on arriving at the scene of action, that the Americans were in no mood to listen to pacific overtures, Congress having already issued their famous declaration, "that the United Colonies of America are, and of right ought to be, Free and Independent States, and that they are absolved from all

---

* His biographer records another illustration of his presence of mind. When captain of the *Magnanime*, and serving off the coast of France, a gale of wind on a lee shore induced him to cast anchor. In the course of the night the wind raged violently, but Howe, having made all snug with two anchors ahead, went off deck to his cabin, where he took up a book. Presently, however, the lieutenant of the watch rushed down to him, and with woeful face said, "I am sorry to inform you, my lord, that the anchors are coming home." "They are much in the right," was the curt reply; "I don't know who would stay abroad such a night as this."

allegiance to the British Crown." His first measures, however, were intended to conciliate. Two days after his arrival he dispatched a flag of truce to the American leader, with a letter addressed to " George Washington, Esq." To the officer who bore it one of Washington's colonels replied, that there was no such person in the American army, and that no answer would be vouchsafed until a proper direction was adopted. At the same time Washington wrote to Congress, " I deemed it a duty to my country and my appointment to insist upon that respect which, in any other than a public view, I would willingly have waived." A letter of the 16th from General Howe, with a similar address, was similarly dismissed. The British adjutant-general was sent to offer explanations, but Washington persisted in refusing to receive a letter which ignored his official rank. And thus terminated the unlucky attempt at negotiation.

Throughout the war the part played by the British navy was comparatively unimportant. The Americans had no fleet ; no brilliant engagements, therefore, whetted the public appetite ; and blockading operations possess very little interest. It was not until France espoused the cause of the American revolutionists that the navy was called into active service. In July, 1778, a French fleet, far superior in strength to the force under Lord Howe, appeared off New York harbour, where Lord Howe was lying, charged with the task of forwarding supplies to, and keeping open the communications with, the British army then occupying New York.

D'Estaing, the French Admiral, had under his command twelve sail of the line (including a 90-gun ship, an 80-gun ship, six of 74 guns, and four of 60 guns), with four frigates. Howe had only six 64-gun ships, three of 50, and two of 40 guns, with a few small frigates and sloops ; about 614 guns and 7,000 men against 854 guns and 19,000 men. Nor do these figures represent all the odds; for the French guns were of heavier metal, and the French ships of larger size. The deficiency in point of men was soon made up. A thousand volunteers were found on board the transports, others joined the fleet daily; masters and mates of merchantmen rallied to the old flag. For the security of the fleet and the trading vessels in the harbour, Lord Howe made the most skilful dispositions, in case the enemy should dare to pass the bar ; but, after lingering for eleven days, D'Estaing's heart failed him, and he withdrew to the harbour of Rhode Island. A remforcement of four ships arriving, Howe speedily followed him thither, and spent the 10th and 11th of August in vain attempts to bring him to battle. A violent storm broke out, however, on the 12th, which put an end to all manœuvring, separated the two fleets, and inflicted serious damage on both, though the greater loss fell upon the French.

Shortly afterwards Lord Howe resigned his command. His health had suffered greatly from anxiety and fatigue ; and there seems good reason to believe that the service was distasteful to him—that he would never have entered upon it had he not hoped his part would have been that of a mediator and peace-maker. Moreover, he was not on good terms with the Ministers then in office; and it was not until the Rockingham Administration was formed, in 1784, that he was again employed. In that year he was raised to the rank of a peer of Great Britain, by the title of Viscount Howe of Langar, in the county of Nottingham ; raised to the rank of Admiral of the Blue; and appointed to the command of a fleet then assembling for service in the Channel. On the 20th of April he embarked at Portsmouth for the Texel, to watch the Dutch fleet. Having shut up the Dutch within their ports through the month of May, he was ordered to cruise off Brest, for the purpose of intercepting the combined fleets of France and

Spain, which had sailed from Cadiz on the 4th of June. He was successful in the important object of preventing an attack upon the West Indian convoy; but the hostile armada contrived to avoid a general action, and on the 5th of August Howe returned to Portsmouth.

He was next ordered to proceed to the siege of Gibraltar, which was then beleaguered by the united forces of France and Spain. Its garrison, under General Elliott, maintained a stern and steadfast resistance ; and to the volleys of 170 heavy guns and the menaces of floating batteries of a novel construction, opposed the expedient of red-hot balls. Lord Howe sailed from Spithead on the 11th of September, having under his orders thirty-four sail of the line, six frigates, and three fire-ships, carrying two regiments for the reinforcement of the Gibraltar garrison, and conveying a flotilla of store-ships for their relief. At that time the Bay of Gibraltar was crowded with forty-seven French and Spanish men-of-war, with ten battering-ships, and innumerable small craft, while on shore was stationed an army of 40,000 soldiers, to co-operate in one grand attack on the well-built stronghold. There have been sieges on a larger scale ; but, as Drinkwater says, " such a naval and military spectacle most certainly is not to be equalled in the annals of war."

On the morning of the 13th the ten floating batteries were anchored within about twelve hundred yards of the batteries of " the Rock." The balls were heated in the furnaces of the garrison, and when the first ship dropped her anchors the firing began. Before ten o'clock on that memorable morning four hundred pieces of artillery were joining in the dreadful *mêlée.* The batteries proved not less formidable than the Spanish engineers had expected. The heaviest shells rebounded from their tops ; the thirty-two-pound shot seemed scarcely to dint their massive walls. Sometimes a battering-ship appeared to be on fire, but the flames were quickly extinguished by mechanical contrivances.*

It was about two o'clock when the hopes of the besiegers received their first check. Then the floating battery commanded by the Prince of Nassau (on board of which was also the inventor of the machinery) began to smoke on the side exposed to the garrison, and it was apprehended that she had taken fire. The assailants continued the attack, however, until seven, when their spirits sank to zero. Their floating batteries ceased to fire, and threw up rockets as signals of distress. For by this time the red-hot balls of the garrison—"roasted potatoes," as the English soldiers called them—had taken such good effect, that nothing was thought of but the saving of their crews, and the boats of the combined fleet were immediately sent on that service. A little after midnight the Prince of Nassau's battery ship burst out into flames, whereupon the English gunners redoubled their activity and their fire; the light produced by the conflagration was as vivid as noonday, and greatly exposed the boats engaged in removing the crews. During the night one or other of the batteries was discovered to be on fire; they were so close to the walls that the shot penetrated to a depth of three feet, but their sides were made of green timber, and the holes closed up after the shot, so that for want of air they did not immediately produce an effect. At five in the morning one of them blew up with a tremendous explosion, and soon afterwards the whole, having been abandoned by their crews, were wreathed in flames from stem to stern; and many of their gallant crews were indebted for their lives to the generous exertions of the English.

This glorious repulse of the great combined attack of the two allied powers decided the issue of the siege. Thenceforward the reduction of "the Rock" became simply impracticable.

* DRINKWATER, *Siege of Gibraltar*.

On the 11th of October " Black Dick," as, in allusion to his swarthy complexion, his sailors named him, entered the mouth of the Straits, with his fleet in three divisions; the third and centre squadrons in line of battle ahead; the second squadron in reserve; the *Victory*, Howe's flag-ship, leading ahead of the third division. Under cover of their guns, the transports landed the troops, stores, provisions, and ammunition—an operation not completed until the 17th, but one which was completed without any interruption from the allied fleet. Lord Howe then made ready for his return voyage, having accomplished his object with infinite tact and discretion. A sudden storm drove his fleet into the Mediterranean along with the armada of France and Spain, and he at once drew up in line of battle. An unsuccessful attempt was made to cut off his rear; but his invitations to a general action were all evaded, and after some desultory firing on the part of individual ships, Howe repassed the Straits in safety, and sailed back to England, arriving at St. Helen's, off the Isle of Wight, on the 16th of November.

The masterly manner in which the relief of Gibraltar was effected, in the face of a largely superior force, added greatly to Howe's reputation for skill, courage, and resolution. His appointment, therefore, in January, 1780, as First Lord of the Admiralty was acceptable to the service and popular with the public; and his discharge of the duties of his office was marked by his customary energy and taciturnity. He continued at his post during the early years of William Pitt's administration, and laboured with much vigour to effect a reduction of expenditure without a diminution of efficiency. When he found his efforts counteracted by some of the members of the Government, he at once sent in his resignation. The Crown, however, recognised his services by raising him to an earldom (August, 1788).

After a brief interval of repose and domestic tranquillity, he was invested with the chief command of the Channel fleet, and on the 10th of July, 1793, put to sea from St. Helen's, with 23 sail of the line. Much buffeted about was he for some days by contrary winds, so that it was mid-November before he could get away to the westward; and he failed to come up with the French squadron. His ships having suffered severely in the adverse weather, he returned to port about the 12th of December—a proceeding which involved him in some temporary unpopularity, the public being unable to understand why he had seen a French fleet, and yet not fought and defeated it. This hasty feeling of ingratitude found expression in the following epigram :—

> " Cum Cæsar Romæ Gallos devicerat hostes,
>   Verba tria enarrant fortia facta ducis ;
>   *Howe* sua nunc brevius verbo complectitur **uno,**
>   Et ' vidi ' nobis omnia gesta refert."

Thus Englished :—

> " W en Cæsar had the Roman foe subdued,
>   He told in three short words the deed was done;
>   *Howe,* with more silent modesty endued,
>   Relates concisely what he ' saw ' in one."

II.

Having been repaired and refitted, the ships composing the Channel fleet reassembled at St. Helen's in the middle of April, 1794. On the 2nd of May it put to sea with several outward-bound convoys, which it escorted as far as the Lizard ; and a squadron, under Rear-Admiral Montague, being detached to attend them into the parallel of Cape Finisterre, the remainder of the fleet proceeded for Ushant. It cruised in this vicinity for several days, chiefly in foggy and boisterous weather ; and

on the morning of the 28th was bearing down Channel with a
fresh wind from the south-east, when it came in sight of
the French fleet, under M. Villaret-Joyeuse. Lord Howe immediately signalled to one of his best sailers, the *Bellerophon*, to
stand towards the enemy and reconnoitre; but soon afterwards,
discovering the full force of the French, he issued orders to
his captains to prepare for action.

The ships under Lord Howe's command were as follows :—

Ship	Guns	Men		Captain
Cæsar . . .	80 guns,	730 men,	Captain	Molley
Bellerophon .	74 ,,	617 ,,	,,	Hope ; Rear-Adm. Pasley
Leviathan .	74 ,,	650 ,,	,,	Lord Seymour Conway
Russel . . .	74 ,,	600 ,,	,,	Payne
Marlborough .	74 ,,	600 ,,	,,	Hon. George Berkeley
Royal Sovereign	100 ,,	872 ,,	,,	Nicholas ; Admiral Graves
Defence . . .	74 ,,	600 ,,	,,	Gambier
Impregnable .	90 ,,	767 ,,	,,	Westcot ; Rear-Ad. Caldwell
Tremendous .	74 ,,	600 ,,	,,	Pigot
Invincible	74 ,,	600 ,,	,,	Hon. T. Pakenham
Barfleur	90 ,,	767 ,,	,,	Collingwood ; Rr-Ad. Bowyer
Culloden	74 ,,	600 ,,	,,	Schomberg
Gibraltar	80 ,,	650 ,,	,,	Mackenzie
Queen Charlotte	100 ,,	900 ,,	{ ,,	Sir R. Curtis ; Earl Howe, Commander-in-Chief
			,,	Sir A. Douglas
Brunswick . .	74 ,,	650 ,,	,,	John Hervey
Valiant . . .	74 ,,	650 ,,	,,	Pringle
Orion . . .	74 ,,	650 ,,	,,	Duckworth
Queen . . .	90 ,,	767 ,,	,,	Nott ; Rear-Adm. Gardner
Ramillies .	74 ,,	600 ,,	,,	Henry Hervey
Alfred . . .	74 ,,	600 ,,	,,	Bagely
Montagu . .	74 ,,	600 ,,	,,	Montagu
Royal George .	100 ,	872 ,,	,,	Domett ; Adm. Sir A. Hood
Majestic . .	74 ,,	600 ,,	,,	Cotton
Glory . . .	70 ,,	750 ,,	,,	Elphinstone
Thunderer .	74 ,,	600 ,,	,,	Bertie

The French fleet consisted of the *Trojan, Eole, Amérique,
Téméraire, Terrible, Impétueux, Mucius, Tourville, Gasparin,
Convention, Trente-un Mai, Tyrranicide, Juste, Montagne, Jacobin,*

*Achille, Vengeur, Patriote, Northumberland, Entreprenant,
Jemappes, Neptune, Pelletier, Républicain, Sanspareil,* and
Scipion. These ships, on the whole, were larger than the
English, while they carried more numerous crews, and dis-
charged much heavier broadsides. As thus :—

	British.	French.
Number of guns	2 098	2,158
Weight of metal	21,519 lbs.	25,521 lbs.
Number of men	16,647	19,828
Size in tons	45,338	51,520

"These odds," says Mr. James, our best naval historian,
" are on the side that an Englishman would wish them to be ;
they are just sufficient to shed a lustre upon the victory which
his countrymen gained, and gained too over an enemy who
fought most heroically, and who yielded at last, not to the
superior courage, but to the superior skill and steadiness of
British seamen." We must also remember that Howe's crews
were mostly inexperienced and unaccustomed to act together ;
and that many of his captains were deficient in energy, if not in
courage.

With the *Russel,* the *Marlborough,* and the *Thunderer* moving
ahead to support the *Bellerophon,* Lord Howe formed the
main body of his fleet into two columns, and advanced under
full sail. At ten minutes past eleven he signalled for the crews
to have dinner, knowing that English sailors fight none the
worse for "full stomachs." Meanwhile, the two fleets drew
nearer, and a sharp conflict seemed unavoidable ; when, about
one o'clock, as if to avoid a hostile collision, the French ships
began to tack. Lord Howe ordered a general chase, and his
advanced ships quickly opened a heavy fire on the enemy's rear
division. Scorning to run without an exchange of shots, *La
Révolutionnaire,* a fine French ship of 110 guns, dropped astern
of the nearest two-deckers, and waited for the English to come

up. The *Bellerophon* (of 74 guns) was the first to arrive within
gunshot; and she engaged her formidable adversary for upwards of an hour and a quarter, when the crippled state of her
mainmast compelled her commander to take her out of fire.
The French three-decker had suffered even more heavily from
the well-directed broadsides of the British, and was wearing
round to join her comrades; the *Leviathan* came up and
grappled with her, to be succeeded in turn by the *Audacious*
(74). Then came a sharp exchange of shocks. The contest
was very unequal, but the *Révolutionnaire*, having already under-
gone some severe pounding, was soon seen to be overpowered
by the close and steady cannonade of the British men-of-war.
Having lost 400 killed and wounded, she hauled down her
colours and surrendered; but so much had the victor suffered
in her spars and rigging that she could not take possession,
and next day the French frigate *Audacieux* took her sister-ship
in tow and escaped into Rochefort. By this time it was pitch-
dark night, and a dense rain deepened the gloomy ocean fog.
The *Audacious*, losing sight of Lord Howe's fleet, ran for the
nearest Channel port, and reached Plymouth Sound in safety
on the 3rd of June.

Returning to the events of the 28th, we find that after this
smart brush with the enemy, the *Bellerophon* and her consorts
were recalled to the main body of the fleet, which, with lights
at every mast-head, swept on through the misty darkness of the
night in swift pursuit. At daybreak on the 29th the French
fleet loomed on the horizon about six miles to windward. A
consummate master of naval tactics, Howe manœuvred with so
much skill as to secure that weather-gage which was so essential an advantage in the days before the introduction of steam
as a motive power; and by eight o'clock he got near enough to
open fire. A desultory skirmish ensued, in which the French
continued to avoid coming to close quarters, partly through the

apathy of some of Howe's captains, who do not seem to have understood or relished their commander's determined mode of giving battle.

For the next two days we take Mr. James's record :—

" May 30th and 31st. The weather during these two days was mostly very foggy ; the wind moderate, in the north-west quarter, and the head-sea abated ; the fleet standing always on the lar-board tack, and some parts of the enemy's line seen at times to the north-west. Soon after noon of the 31st, the fog clearing off, the enemy (still consisting of 26 sail of the line, some having separated, and others been added in the intermediate time) were seen to leeward ; but having been dispersed in the fog, were forming again in order of battle, as the fleet advanced to get up abreast of them. But before that could be effected the day was too far advanced for bringing them properly to action. It was therefore judged expedient to keep the wind, with frigates of observation to notify any change in the enemy's motions during the ensuing night. The result of the day's manœuvres was to bring the two fleets considerably nearer to each other."

On the 1st of June, a day long celebrated in naval annals and ballad-lore—

> " Howe made the Frenchmen dance a tune,
> An admiral great and glorious ;
> Witness for that the First of June,
> Lord ! how he was victorious "—

on the 1st of June at daybreak, in lat. 47° 30′ N., and long. 18° 30′ W.—the wind blowing moderately from the south-west, and the sea being " tolerably smooth "—the French were seen about five miles to starboard, steering in line of battle, under heavy canvas. His men suffering from the fatigue of the preceding days, Lord Howe hove-to, and gave them their break-fast, after which, at a quarter-past eight, he set sail and bore down upon the enemy, signalling for each ship to steer for and engage her opponent in the enemy's line The British fleet was drawn up in line abreast  in the following order :—*Cæsar* (van-ship), *Bellerophon, Leviathan, Russel, Royal Sovereign, Marlborough, Defence, Impregnable, Tremendous, Barfleur, Invincible, Culloden, Gibraltar, Queen Charlotte* (Lord Howe's flag-ship), *Brunswick, Valiant, Orion, Terror, Ramillies, Alfred, Montagu, Royal George, Majestic, Glory,* and *Thunderer* (25 in all). The French were formed in close head-and-stern line, W. to E., thus

Trojan, Eole, Amérique, Téméraire, Terrible, Impétueux, Mucius, Tourville, Gasparin, Convention, Trente-un Mai, Tyrannicide, Juste, Montagne, Jacobin, Achille, Vengeur, Patriote, Northumberland, Entreprenant, Jemappes, Neptune, Pelletier, Républicain, Sanspareil, and *Scipion* (26). The frigates attached to both fleets were stationed as usual in the rear.

It was the intention of Lord Howe that each ship should cut the French line *astern* of her opponent, and engage her to leeward; but this intention was partially defeated through the mismanagement of some of his captains. His own ship, the *Queen Charlotte,* was the first to break through the enemy's compact array; and after receiving, and, as she swept by, returning, the broadsides of the *Achille* and the *Vengeur,* she luffed up under the stern of the *Montagne,* into which she poured her fire with terrible effect. Howe, eager to lay his vessel

Course of the *Queen Charlotte.*
1. *Montagne*
2. *Jacobin*
3. *Achille*
4. *Vengeur*

alongside her formidable adversary, ordered Mr. Bowen, the

master—an able, but rough and rugged seaman—to starboard
his helm. "If I do, my lord, we shall run aboard the *Jacobin*,"
which had fallen abreast of the *Montagne* to leeward, and thus
taken up the very position Lord Howe had marked out for himself. "What is that to you?" said "Black Dick" quickly.
"Oh, just as you please," muttered Bowen *sotto voce; "I* don't
care if *you* don't. I'll soon lay you near enough to singe some
of our whiskers." Lord Howe smiled as he overheard the
British seaman's characteristic growl, and turning to his flag-
captain observed, "That's a fine fellow, Curtis."

Driving in between the two Frenchmen, the *Queen Charlotte*
fought them on each broadside with immense vigour. In less
than an hour the *Montagne* (the enemy's flag-ship) had upwards
of one hundred men killed and two hundred wounded; until,
weary of such maltreatment, her Admiral crowded on all sail,
and ranged ahead. Her example was quickly imitated by the
Jacobin. The *Queen Charlotte* then turned upon the *Juste*, and
delivered her fire with such effect that in a few minutes the
Frenchmen's three masts fell. By this time she herself was so
shattered about the spars, and torn in rigging, that she obeyed
her helm with difficulty, and was scarcely in condition to
seek another antagonist; nor was it necessary, for the action,
which had lasted about sixty minutes, was virtually at an
end.

Meanwhile the French Admiral, about three miles to
leeward, had formed with eleven or twelve of his ships not
disabled by the loss of any of their masts. Two of the French
ships, almost totally disabled, were left to windward; but three
of them with their sprit-sails, or sails raised on the stump of
the foremast, joined the French Admiral; the ships of the
British fleet being either so much dispersed, or disabled in their
masts and rigging, as to be in no position to prevent the
escape of the French, or to assemble in force and renew the

engagement.* When these three vessels had joined the others the enemy stood away to the westward, leaving seven of their dismasted ships as trophies to the victors. One, however, the *Vengeur*, sank while the prisoners were being removed, and many of the crew perished with her.

The *Marlborough* and the *Defence* were dismasted on the side of the British; and the *Brunswick*, having lost her mizen and drifted to leeward of the enemy's reassembled ships, bore up, and arrived a few days afterwards at Spithead.

Among Howe's ships the *Marlborough*, the *Defence*, the *Bellerophon*, the *Brunswick*, the *Queen Charlotte*, the *Royal George*, the *Russel*, and the *Ramillies* were splendidly handled; and had the rest of the fleet behaved as well, it is doubtful whether a single Frenchman would have escaped. As it was, the victory was by no means inconsiderable, for Howe had captured six men-of-war and sunk one;† and coming, as it did, at the outbreak of the war, it inspired the whole service with enthusiasm, and the nation with confidence in its navy.

Numerous interesting anecdotes in illustration of the spirit of British seamen have been recorded. A young midshipman on board the *Queen Charlotte* was exposed to so much danger that Lord Howe, out of regard for his tender years, advised

---

* The ships were in a better condition than their captains, who, inexperienced or afraid of responsibility, displayed from first to last a curious apathy and neglect.

† The ships captured were *Le Juste*, 80 guns; *Sanspareil*, 80; *L'Amérique*, 74; *L'Achille*, 74; *Le Northumberland*, 74; and *L'Impétueux*, 74. The *Vengeur*, 74, sank immediately on being taken possession of. The story that she went down with her colours nailed to the masthead, and her crew shouting "Vive la République," has been proved by Carlyle to be an audacious invention. The British loss in the action was 279 killed and 877 wounded, or 1,156 in all; the total French loss is not known, but on board the captured ships the killed were 690, and the wounded 580, besides 320 who perished in the *Vengeur*. There were 5,000 prisoners.

him to go below. The gallant lad, looking up into his face exclaimed, " What would my father say, my lord, were I not on deck during the action ? "

When, on the day after the fight, the full extent of the victory was known, the sailors of the *Queen Charlotte* insisted on being allowed to congratulate their Admiral. He received them on the quarter-deck, and was so overcome by their hearty if rough address that he could not conceal his tears as he replied, " No ! no ! it is *I* who should thank *you*, my brave fellows ; for it was you who won the battle."

Shortly after the return of the flag-ship to Portsmouth, Lord Howe sent for his first lieutenant, Larcom, and said to him, " Mr. Larcom, your conduct in the action has been such that it is necessary you should leave this ship." Larcom, a good officer and brave seaman, felt deeply wounded, and with tears in his eyes cried out, " Good heavens, my lord ! what have I done? why am I to leave the ship ? I have done my duty to the utmost of my power." " Very well, sir," said Lord Howe ; " but leave this ship you must, and I have great pleasure in presenting you with this commission as commander for your conduct on the late occasion."

The *Marlborough* was in the thick of the affray, and suffered heavily. Having been entirely dismasted and torn about the spars and rigging, with her captain and second lieutenant severely wounded, some of the crew, it is said, began to talk of surrender. Lieutenant Monckton overheard them, and burst out indignantly " he would be d——d if she should ever surrender, and he would nail her colours to the stump of the mast." At this announcement a cock, which the wreck had set free from its broken coop, suddenly perched on the stump of the mainmast, clapped his wings, and crowed aloud. In an instant the men broke into three hearty cheers, and no more was heard of the hateful word " surrender."

The figure-head of the *Brunswick* was graced with an effigy of the duke of that ilk, wearing a cocked hat. In the battle the cocked hat was shot away, whereupon the crew sent a deputation to the captain, begging him to give them another "out of respect to the duke." Captain Harvey, much amused, gave them one of his own, which the carpenter immediately nailed to the despoiled figure-head, and there it remained throughout the fray.

In the course of the action, the *Marlborough* dealt severely with her antagonist, the *Impétueux*. One of her seamen grew so excited that he boldly leaped on the French vessel's deck, to "pay the Moosoos a visit;" and when advised to take a cutlass to defend himself, replied, "I'll find one where I am going." And he did, returning in safety with a couple of French swords in his hand.

The *Defence* behaved with great gallantry, and was totally dismasted and rent and torn with shot; she was one of the few ships which broke through the French line, and got into the midst of the enemy's ships. Her commander, Captain James (afterwards Lord) Gambier, was an excellent officer; he was also a sincere Christian. At the close of the fight, Captain Pakenham, a vivacious, good-tempered Irishman, hailed him from the *Invincible:* "Well, Jimmy, I see you are pretty well mauled; but never mind, Jimmy, whom the Lord loveth He chasteneth." The lieutenant of the *Defence*, seeing a large French three-decker, the *Républicain*, suddenly bearing down upon her, struck with a momentary panic, ran up to the quarter-deck, and eagerly addressing the captain, exclaimed, "D—— my eyes, sir, but there is a whole mountain coming upon us; what shall we do?" Captain Gambier, unmoved, and looking gravely at him, replied with much dignity and right feeling, "How dare you, sir, at this awful moment, come to me with an oath on your lips? Go down, sir, and encourage your men to stand **to** their guns like brave British seamen." *

Two days were employed by the victorious fleet in repairing and refitting. On the 10th Howe sailed homeward, and on the 13th arrived at Spithead, where his appearance, with six of the enemy's line-of-battle ships in tow, provoked an outburst of patriotic enthusiasm. Soon afterwards George III. and the royal family paid him the honour of a visit, the incidents and details of which have been very graphically related by Lady Mary Howe, the veteran Admiral's second daughter. The letter is so amusing that we venture to put some considerable extracts from it before the reader :—

"The three younger Princesses and Prince Ernest (Duke of Cumberland)," she says, "arrived on Wednesday. Mamma and I dined and spent the evening with them, and saw them as happy as the general advantage and every consideration of private friendship could make them. I must say the same of the King and Queen and the elder Princesses, who appeared almost to share our feelings. They came to the Commissioner's house, at the Dock, at ten o'clock the next morning. We had been desired to attend and receive them ; and after remaining about half-an-hour in the house they all set out to go on board the *Queen Charlotte*—mamma and I being ordered to go first on board and receive them. On their entering the ship, my father remained on deck, under his own flag. The papers will have described their coming on board in my father's barge, steered by Sir A. Douglas, and attended by the Admiralty in their barge, and all the admirals and all the captains of the fleet in their boats. They were saluted by the *Queen Charlotte* and all the ships of the fleet when the royal standard appeared in sight, and cheered by each ship as they passed. [Sir Roger] Curtis received the King, and led him upon deck. Our

---

* SIR JOHN BARROW, *Life of Earl Howe*, p. 277.

attendance on the Queen and Princesses prevented mamma
and I from seeing the first meeting of the King and my glorious
father, which I am told was the most affecting thing possible.
My father's knees trembled with emotion when he kissed the
King's hand, who presented him with a most magnificent sword
set with diamonds, and afterwards with a gold chain, to which
is to be hung a gold medal struck for the occasion, which is
also given to the other admirals and captains who have contributed to this victory, considered as the greatest ever obtained
on the sea. My father afterwards kissed the Queen's hand ;
and then his flag was lowered and the royal standard raised
to the maintop-mast's head, and saluted by the whole fleet.
The Royal Family then went into the cabin, and appeared
happy and comfortable to the highest degree, giving us a
thousand proofs of the kindest interest. About three o'clock
they went to dinner ; after which the King gave a toast, drank
by all at the table—the Princesses, the Prince, Lady Courtoun,
Lady Caroline Waldegrave, Lady Francis Howard, mamma,
and I, my father waiting on the King and Queen—and this
toast was pronounced in the most solemn manner : ' May her
great Admiral long command the *Queen Charlotte*, and may
she long be an example to future fleets ! ' A short time after
this the whole Royal Family walked through the ship's company, drawn up in line, when my father told the King aloud,
' that their diligence and propriety of conduct in all respects
since the victory. was not less commendable than their resolution and bravery during the action. Nothing during the
day was more pleasing to me than this walk through those
brave fellows, every one of whom I am certain would attend my
father to a cannon's mouth, and all of whom have exposed their
lives for him. We then left the ship with the same ceremonies,
and when we were at some distance, the *Queen Charlotte* began,
and the whole fleet saluted. We attended the Royal Family

to the stairs at the dock, and then returned home perhaps the happiest mortals breathing.

"The attachment of the sailors to my father is, I believe, unexampled. In the fog of the 30th of May, Captain Payne told me he observed a little additional thickness on one side of the *Russel* which he hailed, and it proved to be the *Queen Charlotte.* The ship not having had any communication since the day before, it was asked if all was well, and afterwards how was the Admiral? The moment it was answered Lord Howe was well, all the men of the *Russel* burst into three cheers. I told you before of all his own sailors coming upon deck with the same ceremony to welcome him after the action. Those who were present at the scene tell us nothing was ever equal to it. My father says, ' Poor fellows, I was not prepared for it, and own it almost got the better of me.' What it must have been to those who saw him take off his hat to return the compliment ! My father stood upon the poop the whole time of the action ; and nothing but a shot carrying away his topmast, as he attempted to pursue the *Montagne,* prevented his taking possession of her, after having totally silenced her guns, though so much superior to the *Queen Charlotte* in every respect; she was 800 tons bigger. The 80-gun ships we have taken are ten feet longer than our first-rates, and some inches wider ; and the whole French fleet had 470 guns more than ours, and of much larger calibre. Our superiority, in addition to the skill of our dear commander, lay in the resolution and firmness of the common sailors, of which, amongst many others, one occurred on board the *Marlborough* ; to this ship two of the enemy were so close, that one of the sailors said ' he would visit them on board their own ship.' As he was going to leap over, one of his comrades called after him to take a cutlass with him, which he refused, saying ' he should find one there'; and on being called back, actually returned with two of the enemy's cutlasses in his hands. On board the *Queen* and *Invincible*, the sailors who had their arms taken off in the engagement of the 29th went into the cockpit on the 1st of June to assist the surgeons and encourage the poor men who were to submit to the same operation, by declaring it was much less painful than it appeared to be, and that they felt no pain from the wounds. . . . . .

"It would amuse you to hear the titles which the officers wish my father to have, as they choose him to be a marquis; though some of the sailors when disputing on this point the other day, one of them was heard to say, "A marquis, you blockhead! the King must make him one of the blood royal!' *Entre nous*, if he intends to be anything more, 'Duke de la Montagne' would be a pretty title, if his topmasts had not prevented it. I should prefer that, as it would give me the title of Lady Molly Molehill; but as that title is out of the question, that of 'Duke Sans Pareil' was proposed, there being already a Duke of Northumberland. . . . .

"I think I have now sent you all my stories, except that Tom Pakenham, having fired away in a very wide style on one of the French men-of-war, and observing they did not answer the compliment in the manner he expected, stopped his fire and desired to know if the ship had struck. On being answered they had not, he halloed out in great rage, 'Then d—— ye, why do you not fire?' Remarking that one of the enemy's ships had shot away the topmasts of one commanded by his particular friend, Pakenham declared with an oath, 'I'll pay you for that;' and bearing down on the Frenchman, he gave him a broadside for the affront offered to his friend. After the action of the 29th, he sent word to my father that his men and guns were quite ready for another touch, but they must tow him into the line, for his ship would not stir, and then he would do his duty. . . . .

"I will now only add some of the toasts that have been given, and also used on transparencies:—'May the French ever know Howe to be master of the sea!' 'The two first words of the third Psalm.' The day we sailed in the *Aquilon*, the King gave, 'The Admiral, with the union on the topmast head; he who alone deserves to wear it.' The common acclamation of the mob at Portsmouth was, 'God save the King, and Lord Howe to defend him!'" *

Lord Howe continued to hold his command of the Channel fleet during 1795 and 1796, though increasing infirmities and ill-health compelled him to remain frequently ashore. Towards the end of April, 1797, he insisted on resigning it, as he could no longer discharge his duties actively. His last public service was in the same year, when at the instance of the Government he repaired to Portsmouth, charged with the repression of the mutiny which had broken out in the fleet. No one knew better than himself that it was not without cause, that the grievances of which the seamen complained were real and serious, and that their representations had been neglected by the Government. Their pay was inadequate, their provisions were insufficient and of bad quality, they were tyrannized over by incompetent officers, who resorted to the lash for every petty offence. Alarmed by a demonstration which threatened the peace and security of the country, the Government rapidly passed a Bill through both Houses of Parliament conceding the just and reasonable demands of the seamen; and with this enactment in his hands, and the King's proclamation of pardon to the mutineers on their return to their duty, Howe met the delegates of the fleet at Portsmouth. His personal influence secured their prompt submission; and on his undertaking to remove the officers who had made themselves

* Lady Mary Howe's letter occupies, in Sir John Barrow's *Life of Earl Howe*, nearly eleven pages (pp. 280—290).

ʳpecially obnoxious, order was re-established **in** the fleet (May 13th).

The veteran hero now retired into private life, to spend his few remaining years in the companionship of those who loved him, and by whom he was adored. Severe attacks of gout in quick succession gradually broke down his energy and reduced his strength; but he continued to preserve his eager interest in all matters appertaining to his favourite profession. In the summer of 1799 his disorder rapidly gained upon him, and in the hope of obtaining some relief from its painful attacks he was prevailed upon to try the effect of the then fashionable remedy of electricity. For this purpose he left his seat at Porters, and repaired to Grafton Street, London, where he placed himself under the care of a popular practitioner. After a few trials, however, the gout, it is supposed, was driven to the head, and with such severity that he could no longer bear up against it. Rapidly sinking, he expired on the 5th of August. His remains were removed for interment to the family vault in Nottinghamshire. In pursuance of a resolution of the House of Commons, a public monument from Flaxman's designs was erected to his memory in St. Paul's Cathedral, where to this day the visitor, mindful of the deeds of one of ˋEngland's bravest and most loyal sons, will peruse with sympathetic admiration the following brief inscription —

" Erected at the public expense to the Memory of
ADMIRAL EARL HOWE,
In testimony of the general sense of his great and meritorious services,
In the course of a long and distinguished life, and in particular
For the benefit derived to his country, and the brilliant
Victory which he obtained
Over the French fleet, off Ushant, the 1st of June, 1794.
He was born 19th of March, 1726,* and died 5th of August, 1799,
In his 74th year."

---

* The family records say 1725.

ADMIRAL THE EARL OF ST. VINCENT.

1735—1823.

JOHN JERVIS, second son of Swynfen Jervis, Esq., was born on the 20th of January, 1735, received his early education at the free school of Burton-upon-Trent, and completed his school career " at Swindon's academy at Greenwich." His bias towards a sea life was so strong th. et the close of 1747, he ran away from school with the view of entering the navy. His friends then exerted themselves to obtain him a commission. and he was entered as midshipman on board the *Gloucester*, of 50 guns, which in August, 1748, sailed from Portsmouth for the West Indies. He served on that station until 1754, when, having returned to England and passed his examination for the rank of lieutenant, he was appointed to the *Nottingham*, one of the ships attached to Lord Anson's expedition against Brest. Afterwards he was shifted from vessel to vessel, and saw some service in the Mediterranean, showing himself, it is to be presumed, a good and trustworthy officer, inasmuch as in 1756, when he was only twenty-one years of age, he received the command of the sloop *Experiment*.

When the combined military and naval expedition against the French settlements in Canada, under General Wolfe and Admiral Saunders, was dispatched in February, 1759, Jervis was appointed to the *Porcupine* sloop, and had the honour of piloting the ships and transports that ascended the St. Lawrence as far as Quebec. Wolfe himself embarked on board the sloop. On the night previous to the battle which gave Canada to the British, and closed in glory the young general's brief career, he sent for Jervis; and informing him that he had the strongest presentiment that he should be killed in the morrow's fight, he drew from his breast the miniature of a young lady to whom he was tenderly attached, and placed it in his charge, earnestly soliciting him, if his foreboding were fulfilled, to return it to her on his arrival in England. The trust was faithfully discharged.

After serving in the *Albany* sloop on the American coast, Jervis was promoted to a post-captaincy in October, 1761, and appointed to the *Gosport*, of 60 guns. At the conclusion of the peace of 1763 the *Gosport* was paid off, and Captain Jervis was relegated to an unwelcome inaction until 1769.

He was then commissioned to the *Alarm* frigate, of 32 guns, and sent to the Mediterranean, where he remained until the year 1772. In March, 1770, at the outbreak of the equinoctial gales, the *Alarm* took shelter in the port of Marseilles. But on the 26th the gale was so terrific, and the ship laboured so much, that it was found necessary to throw many of her guns overboard. The next morning the weather moderated, and Jervis prepared to run for Minorca; but in the afternoon, with a sudden change, the wind violently increased, and on the following night it blew a hurricane. The frigate was driven from her anchors, all of them being let go in vain, and she was stranded, a helpless wreck, on a reef of rocks. Assistance was promptly rendered from the shore, and all on board were safely removed ashore. Through great exertions the vessel herself was got into safety, and, being emptied of all her cargo, was " hove down keel out," and completely repaired and refitted. In July, writing to his sister, Captain Jervis said, " The *Alarm* is the completest thing I ever saw on the water, insomuch that

I have almost forgot she was the other day, in the opinion of most beholders, her own officers and men not excepted, a miserable, sunken wreck,—such is the reward of perseverance."

In June, 1772, the *Alarm* was paid off, and Jervis, not expecting any early recall to active service, prepared to devote his leisure to intellectual culture. He was ever of opinion that an officer's zealous application must not abate, but only be directed to fresh though important duty, " when he turns his back upon his ship towards the welcome of his family." To acquire a knowledge of the French language he visited France, and studied so hard as to affect his health. Recovering, he pursued his studies with not less energy, if with more discretion. He visited Paris and all the great manufacturing towns, and examined with acute attention the manners, customs, and characteristics of the people. In the following year he was at St. Petersburg, directing his special inquiries to the condition of the naval resources of Russia. Afterwards he went to Stockholm, to Carlscrona, to the Swedish harbours, to Copenhagen, everywhere, and always diligently observant and intelligently curious.

In 1778 he was appointed to the *Foudroyant*, the finest two-decker in the British navy, and, as her captain, took part in the indecisive action off Ushant between the British fleet, under Admiral Keppel, and the French, under M. d'Orvilliers. The public disappointment at the result led to an angry correspondence between Keppel and Sir Hugh Palliser, his second in command, to whose misconduct it was chiefly attributable. But Palliser was defended by the political party then in power, and so it came to pass that his accusations were taken up and made the ground for demanding a court-martial on Keppel. The reader of history is well aware that the inquiry satisfactorily established the character and vindicated the conduct of Keppel ; he may not know, however, that Jervis was the principal witness in his favour, and that it was he who chiefly prepared his commander's cogent defence. We may add that both Keppel's and Palliser's partisans admitted that the *Foudroyant* had been skilfully handled and gallantly fought.

After serving for two or three years with the Channel fleet, the *Foudroyant* was included in Admiral Barrington's squadron, which came into collision with a French fleet beyond Ushant on the 10th of April, 1782. The signal being made for a general chase, the *Foudroyant*, through her superior sailing and her captain's skilful management, now drew ahead of her consorts, and at midnight overtook a French ship of the line, which proved to be the *Pégase*, of 70 guns. When they were nearly within hail, and before a gun had been fired, the look-out midshipman on the forecastle exclaimed, "She has put her helm up to rake us, sir." Jervis's first impulse was to put the *Foudroyant's* helm a-starboard, and deliver her broadside from her starboard guns; but to young Bowen the thought had already occurred that the opposite manœuvre would enable the *Foudroyant* to give the first fire, and, instead of being raked, to rake her opponent. So forcibly did this strike the lad that he could not help exclaiming, "Then if we put our helm to port we shall rake her." Captain Jervis immediately caught the idea. "You are right, Bowen," he said; and as the Frenchman hauled up, he also clewed up his mainsail, took in his studding-sails, and sweeping under his adversary's stern at a distance of about twenty fathoms, continued his raking fire. The slaughter was so great as to throw the enemy into confusion, and with sails and rigging in the greatest disorder she ran before the wind. Perceiving this, Jervis determined on boarding, and laid the *Foudroyant* on the enemy's larboard side. Headed by young Bowen, the boarders soon obtained possession of the enemy's deck, and with hearty cheers struck her colours, after an engagement of three-quarters of an hour.

The two opponents were fairly matched ; for if the *Foudroyant* had three guns more on her broadside than the *Pégase*, the latter's guns were of heavier calibre, and she carried a much larger crew. Here is Jervis's simple and straightforward account of the affair :—

"At sunset I was near enough to discover that the enemy consisted of three or four ships of war, two of them of the line, and seventeen or eighteen sail of convoy, and that the latter dispersed by signal. At half-past nine I perceived the smallest of the ships of war speak with the headmost, and then bear away; at a quarter-past ten the sternmost line-of-battle ship, perceiving we came up with her very fast, bore away also. I pursued her, and at seventeen minutes past twelve brought her to close action, which continued three-quarters of an hour, when, having laid her on board on the larboard quarter, the French ship of war, *Le Pégase*, of 74 guns and 700 men, commanded by Chevalier de Cillart, surrendered. I am happy to inform you that only two or three of the people, with myself, are slightly wounded ; but I learn from the Chevalier de Cillart that *Le Pégase* suffered very materially in masts and yards, her fore and mizen topmasts having gone away soon after the action."

In September, 1782, the *Foudroyant* was attached to the fleet sent out under Lord Howe to the relief of Gibraltar, and at the end of the year she was paid off, after having been nearly eight years in commission, during which period her crew had been brought by Sir John Jervis—he had been rewarded with the red ribbon of the Bath for his victory over the *Pégase*—to the highest pitch of discipline. Sir John was accustomed to exercise them regularly in gunnery, while he insisted that every manœuvre, however trivial, should be executed with the utmost smartness. He paid great attention to the education and training of his midshipmen ; and in this respect obtained such a reputation that the highest families counted it an honour to have their sons on board the *Foudroyant*.

Soon after the paying-off of the *Foudroyant* Sir John was married to a lady of considerable attractions, Miss Martha Parker, daughter of Sir Thomas Parker, Chief Baron of the Exchequer. A man of active mind, always impatient of an idle life, he embraced with pleasure a Parliamentary career, and sat in the House of Commons as member, first for Launceston, and afterwards for New Yarmouth. He acted with the Whig party, and gave his vote in favour of every measure of a liberal and progressive character. In 1790 he sat for Wycombe; and in all divisions of importance he voted with the Whigs. "He supported Mr. Whitbread's motion against the armament against Russia; he voted with Mr. Grey for reform of Parliament; and he signed the Declaration of the Friends of the People, being one of that small but undaunted band of patriots in the House, who, in those most unfavourable times, gallantly struggled for freedom and for peace. His votes, therefore, were also against England's interference with France in the arrangement of her internal affairs. But when the efforts of his party were ineffectual against Mr. Pitt's influence and Mr. Burke's oratory, when war was decided upon, he, in 1793, quitted Parliament to render more effectual services to his country, and those for which, as from her officer, she had a higher claim "

Towards the close of 1793 the British Government determined on an attack upon the French West Indian Islands, and for this purpose placed Sir John Jervis at the head of a fleet of five sail-of-the-line, four 44's, one 40, and twelve frigates, which embarked 6,000 troops under General Sir Charles Grey, and arrived at Barbadoes in January, 1794. An immediate attack was made upon Martinique, which, after a short resistance, surrendered. St. Lucia was next captured, and the campaign brilliantly concluded with the conquest of Guadaloupe—all these successes having been attained in little more than three months. Sir John remained on the station until November, when an attack of yellow fever compelled him to resign his command and return to England.

Here we may transcribe an anecdote or two in illustration of his characteristics as a commander-in-chief. Setting in his own person the example of great neatness and preciseness of professional attire, he was very particular in insisting upon it in his officers. Commodore (afterwards Sir Charles) Thompson was, however, a great sinner in this respect, and seemed to love to masquerade in a dress scarcely differing from that of a common sailor. One morning, as thus arrayed, he was going in his barge to bathe, when he chanced to pass under the stern of the flag-ship. The Admiral was walking in his stern gallery: in an instant he recognised the untidy Commodore, but pretending ignorance he hailed the boat. "In the barge there! Go and assist in towing in that transport." A troop-ship was shifting her berth at the time. Commodore Thompson at once perceived that he had placed himself in a false position, and received the deserved rebuke with equal tact and good humour. Standing up in his boat, and taking off his hat, he answered with the accustomed "Ay, ay, sir!" and proceeded to execute the order.

Another of his regulations was, that every officer going on duty to the flag-ship should appear with cocked hat and side-arms. Further, that all subordinates, of whatever grade, when addressing, or being addressed by, their superiors in service, should entirely remove the hat from the head, instead of "touching it flippantly"—to use his plain words—to testify respect.

During the whole campaign he slept every night on board his ship, that he might be able to pay constant personal

attention, early and late, to every detail of duty. Though a
strict disciplinarian, he was highly esteemed by his men; while
officers strove energetically to get appointed to his ship, knowing
that they could not fail to gain instruction under his careful
superintendence, and that he was as quick to reward as he was
to detect merit. As we shall see hereafter, he formed quite a
school of captains, all of whom reflected honour upon their
teacher and rose to distinguished positions—such as Halliwell,
Trowbridge, Ball, Berry, Darby, Hood, and Bowen.

The most brilliant portion of Sir John's career was his
command of the Mediterranean fleet; a command which, at
that critical period, when England was putting forth her strength
against the aggressive power of France, directed by the unscru-
pulous genius of Napoleon, called for the exercise of mental
qualities of the highest order. Then and there, under Sir
John's energetic supervision, and attributable to his sagacity
and determination, began the creation of that admirable naval
system to which the efficiency of the British navy was in no
small measure due. The Mediterranean fleet at the time that
Jervis assumed its command was very powerful. It consisted
of two 100 gun ships, five 98's, two 80's, fourteen 74's, two 64's,
and a host of frigates, brigs, cutters, store-ships. Among its
captains were men who afterwards enrolled their names on the
glorious list of England's worthies—Halliwell, Nelson, Trowbridge, Collingwood, Fremantle, Hood, Cockburn, Milen,
Bowen, and many another. Sir John Jervis hoisted his flag in
the *Victory* (100 guns), having under him Vice-Admiral Lonzie,
in the *Princess Royal*, 98; Vice-Admiral the Hon. William
Waldegrave, in the *Barfleur*, 98; Vice-Admiral Sir Hyde
Parker, in the *St. George*, 98; and Rear-Admiral Mann, in the
Windsor Castle, 98.

Sir John arrived off Corsica on the 29th of November, and
immediately set to work.

A blockading squadron was stationed off the port of Toulon; another watched the harbour of Cadiz; a third, under Nelson, operated on the coast of Corsica. Then provision had to be made for the discharge of other duties. The convoys of mer-chant traders all round the Mediterranean and the Adriatic, the protection of British interests in neutral ports, the enforce-ment of the neutrality itself, the inspiring confidence into our allies by the occasional presence of a naval force, the keeping up the communication between those powers, the defence of Corsica, the assistance to Venice and the Adriatic ports, the protection of the British factory at Smyrna, the overawing the Barbary powers, and the watching the French cruisers sent to decoy away the blockading squadron, imposed upon this fleet a variety and severity of service which our sailors alone can estimate ; while to victual and to store so scattered a force, and to provide that everywhere the national interests were constantly supported, was to the Commander-in-Chief one unceasing test of resources, and a task for his vigilant ubiquity.

Such was the work, and there is no doubt the work was well done. Jervis was inferior to Nelson in genius ; he could not win such victories over the enemy as Nelson did ; he could not breathe the same enthusiasm into his followers ; but he was a greater commander-in-chief. Nelson could make his fleet fight, but he could not organize it. His great enterprises were accomplished with officers and crews trained and dis-ciplined by Jervis. Not the slightest detail escaped the attention of this able administrator. The provisions, the health, the comfort, the amusement of the men under his com-mand, were all carefully watched over ; and, in truth, he may claim to have been the first admiral who made the hygiene of his fleet a subject of constant study. Again, disci-pline was developed by him into a perfect system. British

seamen in Jervis's time were drawn from a dwindling mercantile marine and from the dregs of an exhausted population,
and it needed a stern unwavering rule to accustom them to the
restraints of law and order.   He made and fashioned them
into first-rate sailors.   The most mutinous crew, when it came
under his command, soon perceived that it had found its
master, and learned the necessity of prompt submission.

The great naval victory associated with his name was that of
St. Valentine's Day, 1797.   Its completeness was due, perhaps,
to Nelson's bold manœuvre in the latter part of the action.
On the other hand, it was won by crews which Jervis had
disciplined, and captains whom Jervis had trained.   Its details
will be more conveniently given in our life of Nelson than in
the present chapter; and we shall here confine ourselves to
such particulars as attach personally to the Commander-in-
Chief.   The British fleet consisted of fifteen line-of-battle ships
and three frigates ; the Spanish, under Admiral Don Jose
Cordova, of twenty-seven sail of the line, of which thirteen were
three-deckers, and fourteen frigates.   This startling disparity
of force did not affect Jervis's resolution to engage the enemy.
On the morning of the day of battle he was walking the
quarter-deck of his flag-ship, the *Victory*, and, as the Spanish
ships hove in sight, their numbers were duly reported to him
by his captain.

"There are eight sail-of-the-line, Sir John."   "Very well,
sir."

"There are twenty sail-of-the-line, Sir John."   "Very
well, sir."

"There are twenty-five sail-of-the-line, Sir John."   "Very
well, sir."   •

"There are twenty-seven, Sir John!" and this announcement was accompanied by a reference to the great superiority
of the hostile force.

"Enough, sir, no more of that; the die is cast; and if there are fifty sail I will go through them."

An answer which so delighted Captain Halliwell, then walking beside the chief, that in his enthusiasm he forgot the punctilio of etiquette, and patting his Admiral's back, he exclaimed, "That's right, Sir John; that's right; by Heaven, we shall give them a d——d good licking."

While the *Victory* was in the hottest of the fight, the smoke preventing Jervis from seeing the ships as distinctly as he wished, he went to the poop to obtain a clearer view of the progress of the action. While he was coolly making his survey, a marine by his side was struck by a cannon-shot, which smashed his head, and Sir John, from head to knees, was literally covered by the man's brains and blood. Seeing him thus bespattered, and fearing he was wounded, Captain Grey hastened to his assistance. "I am not at all hurt," replied the Admiral calmly, at the same time wiping his mouth, into which a quantity of blood had poured; " but do, George, try if you can get me an orange." A youthful aide-de-camp soon brought one from the cockpit, and Sir John rinsed his mouth with the utmost composure.

In the evening, while discussing the events of the day, Captain Calder hinted that Nelson's spontaneous manœuvre, by which the separated division of the Spanish fleet was prevented from effecting a junction, was an unauthorised departure from the prescribed mode of attack. "It certainly was so," replied Sir John Jervis, "and if ever you commit such a breach of your orders I will forgive you also." Sir John was incapable of jealousy, and took a generous pleasure in bringing forward and presenting those officers who distinguished themselves by their capacity and conduct.

For his share in the victory off Cape St. Vincent he was elevated to an earldom, with the title, chosen by the King himself, of St. Vincent. He still continued in command on the Mediterranean station; and fortunate for the country it was that a man of his firmness and invincible courage held this post when the alarming mutiny broke out in the spring of 1797. With a weaker commander the fleet would have been lost, and the consequences to England must have been disastrous. Having received information of the rebellious outbreaks at the Nore and Spithead, he immediately adopted precautionary measures; among others, appealing to the loyalty and good feeling of the marines, whom he separated from the seamen, and placed in a position of conspicuous importance. And conscious that idleness is the fertile parent of evil, he proceeded to devise the means of keeping his men actively employed, ordering the nightly bombardment of Cadiz, and organizing constant attacks upon the Spanish defences. He dispatched, under Nelson, an expedition against Santa Cruz. The ships were kept in constant movement, and at the same time isolated as much as possible from one another, to prevent any seeds of disaffection being spread from vessel to vessel. The first symptoms of disobedience were sternly and promptly dealt with. Thus, in spite of all his vigilance, an outbreak took place on board the *Marlborough*, which had newly arrived from Spithead, and brought with her the pestilent contagion of mutiny. A court-martial was instantly assembled, and one of the ringleaders tried, found guilty, and sentenced to death. Jervis confirmed the sentence, and directed that it should be executed on the following morning, " and by the crew of the *Marlborough* alone, no part of the boats' crews from the other ships, as had been usual on similar occasions, to assist in the punishment "—Lord St. Vincent's invariable order in the execution of mutineers.

Captain Ellison, of the *Marlborough*, hastened on board the flag-ship to remind St. Vincent " that a determination that their shipmates should not suffer capital punishment had been the very cause of the ship's company's mutiny, and to express his conviction that the *Marlborough's* crew would never permit the man to be hanged on board their ship.

Lord St. Vincent listened attentively until Captain Ellison had ceased to speak. Then, after a pause, he replied gravely—

"What! do you mean to tell me, Captain Ellison, that you cannot *command* his Majesty's ship the *Marlborough?* For if that be the case, sir, I will immediately send on board an officer who can."

The captain requested that, at all events, the boats' crews from the rest of the fleet might, as had always been customary in the service on executions, attend the present to haul the criminal up; for he really did not expect the *Marlborough's* men would do it.

Stern was Lord St. Vincent's answer :—

"Captain Ellison, you are an old officer, sir, have suffered long, suffered severely, in the service, and have lost an arm in action ; and I should be very sorry that any advantage should be now taken of your advanced years. That man *shall be* hanged—at eight o'clock to-morrow morning—*and by his own ship's company*—for not a hand from any other ship in the fleet shall touch the rope. You will now return on board, sir ; and, lest you should not prove able to command your ship, an officer will be at hand to you who can."

Captain Ellison without another word retired, and on reaching his ship received orders to house and secure his guns, and at daybreak to lower the ports. A general order was then issued to the fleet for all launches to rendezvous under the *Prince* at seven o'clock in the morning, armed with carronades and twelve rounds of ammunition for service ; each launch to be commanded by a lieutenant, having an expert and trusty gunner's mate and four quarter-gunners, exclusive of the launch's crew; the whole to be in charge of Captain Campbell, of the *Blenheim*, who was instructed to attend the execution, and if any symptoms of mutiny appeared on board the *Marlborough*, any attempt to open her ports, or any resistance to the hanging of the prisoner, he was to lay his boats alongside, and fire into her until all mutiny and resistance ceased; and even, if it should prove necessary, to sink her in face of the fleet.

These orders were punctually obeyed. At seven the launches appeared, and Captain Campbell, assuming the command, formed them in a line athwart the bows of the *Marlborough*, at rather less than pistol-shot distance off. At half-past seven, all hands throughout the fleet having been " turned up" to witness punishment, every eye was bent on a powerfully armed boat, which, quitting the flag-ship, carried the provost-marshal and his prisoner to the place of execution. The crisis had come, and it remained to be seen whether the *Marlborough's* crew would resist or obey the Admiral's stern injunction.

As the *Marlborough* lay in the centre, between the two lines of the fleet, the boat speedily reached her, and the criminal was placed on the cathead, the rope knotted round his neck. An awful silence ensued, broken at last by the watch-bells of the fleet striking eight o'clock. Instantly the flag-ship's gun fired, and at the sound the criminal was hoisted up; then, visibly to all, he dropped back again ! An intense sensation shot through the fleet, for it seemed as if in this decisive struggle between authority and rebellion the latter was to prevail. By an accident, the men at the yard-rope had unin-tentionally let it slip ; but, recovering themselves, they hauled the mutineer up with a run ; and thus the law was satisfied, authority vindicated, and, in Lord St. Vincent's own words, discipline was preserved.

In all such critical conjunctures, the sharpest and sternest course is ultimately the most merciful. By his promptitude and decision the Admiral soon succeeded in crushing out the embers of disaffection, and the Mediterrenean fleet escaped that pestilence of rebellion and mutiny which had fatally disgraced the fleets at Spithead and the Nore.

His quickness in detecting the right man for the right place, and his generous desire to give full play to the genius of his subordinates, was shown by his appointment of Nelson to the command of the squadron dispatched against the Toulon fleet, though he was the junior of his flag-officers. The appointment so inflamed the anger of Vice-Admiral Sir John Orde that he broke out into violent language, and was summarily deprived of his command and sent back to England— an exercise of authority which elicited the censure of the Admiralty.

His rigorous observance of his duties may be illustrated by an anecdote or two. His intellect was so strong and flexible that it embraced every variety and difficulty of employ; and in spite of failing health and approaching age, his vast powers of application defied the accumulation of arrears. Seldom retiring until two o'clock in the morning, reading and writing his letters and dispatches, his last question to his secretary invariably was, " Now, sir, have I done all my work for the day?" And until he received an affirmative answer he took no rest. Then he would be out and about before daybreak to satisfy himself that watch was properly kept, afloat and ashore; in the dockyard, before the gates were opened to the artificers, to see that all came at the proper time; by daybreak at the Ragged Staff, in Gibraltar, two miles from his house, to learn by inspection what quantity of water for the fleet had been collected in the night; or walking round the jetties to which the ships were lashed, he detected the sluggard from the industrious crew.

That his approach might not be perceived, he requested an
order from the General that sentries should not salute him as
he passed ; and it was on one such very silent ramble, before the
daily din of the dockyard had begun, or even day dawned, that
on reaching the *Majestic*, notwithstanding a light in her cabin
windows, he came to the conclusion that the ship was remarkably still, and hailed her, " *Majestic* ahoy ! *Majestic* ahoy ! "
At last he aroused the sentry, who angrily inquired, " What the
d——l is the matter ? " and was considerably alarmed when he
found that his Admiral stood before him.

Exhausted with toil and heat, every individual on board the
Majestic was sound asleep, the light in the cabin windows
having been placed there to delude the Admiral into a belief
that the officers were up betimes and dressing. The marine
was sent to summon the officer of the watch, who received a
reprimand of the sternest character; and we may be sure that
no more deceptive lights were set up in the cabin windows of
the *Majestic.*

Let us show that the stern commander was capable of the
most generous actions.

One hot and still summer's day he had ordered his crew to
bathe, and for a brief space they enjoyed an aquatic saturnalia
" more easily imagined than described." The word of command recalled them to the restraints of discipline, and then the
Admiral observed a group of blue jackets discussing with
evident animation some subject of apparently engrossing interest.
At once he ordered his secretary to go forward and find out
what was the matter ; for, he added, " there's my delight,
Roger Odell, in tears !" The secretary obeyed, and reported
that Roger, during the sport of bathing, had jumped from the
foreyard with his clothes on ; that of course he had forgotten
that all he possessed in the world was in his trousers pockets
in bank-notes ; that the exertion of swimming had reduced them

to a useless pulp; and that now the man was in despair, for the loss was considerable. Having ascertained the amount, Lord St. Vincent inquired, " What can we do for Roger, Mr. Tucker, for he is a glorious fellow and an invaluable seaman; can we give him a warrant?" Upon reference to the captain it was found that promotion to the rank of a warrant-officer would be injudicious, owing to his yielding too readily to the temptation of liquor. " Well, something or other we must do for him," remarked his lordship, as he withdrew to his cabin.

Returning shortly afterwards to the quarter-deck, he requested the captain to turn the hands up, and, as soon as they were all assembled, desired Odell to stand forward. As soon as the stalwart seaman, hat in hand, had obeyed the order, Lord St. Vincent assumed a stern expression of displeasure, and addressed him in angry tones. " Roger Odell, you are convicted, sir, by your own appearance, of tarnishing the British oak with tears ! Have you aught to say in your defence why you should not receive the punishment you deserve?"

Roger, overwhelmed by the accusation, could urge only " that he had lost all he had in the world; that he knew it was his own fault; but that having been a great many years saving it, he could not help crying a little; but that if his lordship would only forgive him this once, he should never see him cry again," and he appealed to the captain and first lieutenant for a character.

' The loss of money, sir, can never be an excuse to a British seaman for tears. There could be but one—which will never happen to you, Roger Odell—disgrace."

A pause of breathless silence followed; after which, dropping his harshness of tone, St. Vincent proceeded—

" Roger Odell, you are one of the best men in this ship; you are, moreover, a captain of a top; and in my life I never saw a man behave himself better than you in the *Victory* did in the action with the Spanish fleet. To show, therefore, **that** your Commander-in-Chief will never pass over merit, whereso-ever he may find it, there is your money, sir "—giving him £70—"but no more tears, mind, no more tears, sir."

Taking the money in silent astonishment, Odell held it mechanically before him, as if not knowing what to do with it. Now he stared at the Admiral; anon, opening his hand, he looked at the bank-notes; and lastly at the faces of the by-standers, who were all observing him. At length the " Pipe below !" and the rest of the sailors moving to their respective quarters, recalled him to himself; and perceiving that what he held in his hand was really to be his own, he stammered out, " Thank ye, my lord, thank ye," and plunged into the middle of the crowd to hide his emotions.

Yet one more anecdote.

While blockading Cadiz, St. Vincent remarked with warm approval the ability and zeal with which the commander of one of the small brigs maintained his station, during every change of weather, in the most advanced position off the harbour. From unavoidable circumstances the vessel had been kept longer than usual on a service at once anxious and laborious; instead of going into port, she had been supplied with pro-visions and stores from the fleet; but her captain never uttered a complaint nor raised a difficulty. The private merits as well as the public services of this officer had secured the esteem of Lord St. Vincent, who was aware that, with very slender means, and at the cost of much personal privation, he was nobly striving to support in respectability a wife and a numerous young family. At length a relief arrived; and at the same time it was officially reported that, after the usual survey, the brig required very considerable repair. On the day she rejoined the Admiral his lordship had requested his secretary to bring him £100; and when informed that not one-half of that sum was on board, told Mr. Tucker to beg or borrow it by any means. With some difficulty the amount was collected, and the secretary was then desired to make out the necessary orders for the repair of the brig at Gibraltar, and for her proceeding on a cruise, his lordship adding, " If I send him to England now he will be paid off, and he has not wherewithal to buy a gown for his wife and daughters." The commander met with a cordial reception, was invited to that day's dinner, placed by the Admiral at his right hand, and distinguished by marked attention.

After dinner, the Admiral having sent for him to receive his orders, thus addressed him :—

" You have had, sir, a long and severe duty, but I trust it will not prove an unprofitable one in the result, for I have not failed to notice the officer-like, manly way in which you have performed it. I have desired the commander at Gibraltar to give your brig a complete refit; and when she is ready, the orders I shall now give you will carry you to the best position within my command for your chance of picking up some prizes. So be sure you fill your hold at Gibraltar with all the provisions you possibly can stow, for you will be at liberty to cruise as long as you can make them last; and mind, I expect you will stock your own store-rooms, hen-coops, and wine-bin thoroughly."

The commander expressed his warmest gratitude for his lord-ship's kind intentions, but respectfully added that he hoped to be pardoned if he did not avail himself of them, inasmuch as his poverty entirely prevented his laying in the necessary stock, consistently with his duty to his country. And he entreated to be allowed to retire on half-pay, since such was fated to be the end of his career.

" You know," replied the Admiral, " that I always like to be obeyed without a difficulty. Your orders, which are in this

parcel, will, I hope, be found not to prejudice your family
Let me never hear a word in reply, or of any more thanks
about them ; there, go and prosper."

The parcel contained £100.

Failing health, and the mental and physical fatigue induced
by unremitting exertions in a post of high responsibility, compelled Lord St. Vincent to resign his command in August,
1799, and return to England.

For some time after his arrival he was confined by his illness
to the retirement of his seat at Rocketts, in Essex. As soon
as he was known to be recovering, Sir John Orde, who considered himself personally insulted by St. Vincent preferring
Nelson to the command of the expedition against the Toulon
fleet, sent him a challenge. It is needless to say that it was
refused. Not long afterwards, the Admiralty having reason to
apprehend a renewal of mutiny in the Channel fleet, called Lord
St. Vincent from his rural seclusion and placed him in command. With characteristic promptitude St. Vincent repaired
to his new sphere of duty, and hoisted his flag in his old ship,
the *Ville de Paris*. When the news of his appointment had
first reached the fleet, which had been permitted to sink into a
disgraceful laxity of discipline, one of the captains was indis-
creet enough to give as a toast at the table of the Commander-
in-Chief, " May the discipline of the Mediterranean never be
introduced into the Channel fleet !" But he soon discovered
that it *was* to be so introduced. Lord St. Vincent had lost
none of his old energy, and was the last man in the world to
suffer his authority to be set at nought. He issued order after
order designed to put a stop to the excesses that prevailed, to
the insubordination of officers and men, and the general neglect
of duty, and he took care that his orders should be obeyed.
Any violation of them was immediately followed by a sharp
and swift punishment. He then proceeded to station his ships

and frigates so as to insure a close watch and blockade of the French ports, nor did he allow them to quit their stations at the first breath of an adverse wind. At the same time he was sedulously careful of the health of his crews, and it was under his command that lemon-juice was introduced on a large scale as an anti-scorbutic. In his anxiety to secure the proper ventilation and cleanliness of his ships, he anticipated the sanitary reformers of to-day. In a few months, by his decision, his sagacity, and his vigilance, he completely reformed the condition of the Channel fleet, morally and physically, raised the tone of its officers, and infused a new spirit into its seamen. All his admirable administrative and organizing ability was conspicuously displayed in this period of command, which was not the least useful, if not the most brilliant portion of his long and laborious career.

Early in 1801, on the resignation of Mr. Pitt and the accession of Mr. Addington to office, Lord St. Vincent was appointed First Lord of the Admiralty, a post in which his energy and firmness could not but prove beneficial to his country. He was a resolute enemy to negligence and waste. He liked work well done, and insisted that any man who had work to do should do it. A strict economist, he waged active war against jobbery, peculation, extravagance ; while he was too wise and too prudent to sacrifice efficiency. To his administration belongs the credit of dispatching the powerful and well-equipped fleet which, under Hyde Parker and Nelson, bombarded Copenhagen and captured the Danish fleet. To his administration belongs the credit of initiating a reform in the management of the dockyards, and of introducing many improvements into the establishments of the Royal Marines. We have no space, however, to dwell on all the great and useful changes he introduced into every department of the navy. His practical capacity for business, his unwavering resolution, his clear per-

ception, and his resolute integrity were never more conspicuously exhibited.

When the Addington Cabinet resigned, Lord St. Vincent
necessarily vacated office, and joined the Whigs in opposition
to the measures of Pitt. Early in 1806, on the death of Pitt,
the Whigs returned to power, and Lord St. Vincent was
recalled to active service, accepting for the second time the
command of the Channel fleet. An attack upon his official
career in the House of Commons terminated in the unanimous adoption of a motion by Mr. Fox, "That the conduct
of the Earl of St. Vincent in his late naval administration
has added an additional lustre to his exalted character, and
is entitled to the approbation of this House." He was soon
afterwards charged with a special mission to the Court of
Lisbon, the object being, in case Portugal proved indefensible
against the invasion threatened by the French Emperor, to
make the royal family and principal nobility transfer the seat of
government to the Brazils. Says Lord Brougham,* "The
proceedings of this chief, in his twofold capacity of captain
and statesman, were justly remarked for the great talents and
address they exhibited. He began by cutting off all communication between his fleet and the land ; this he effected by
proclaiming an eight-days' quarantine. His colleagues in the
Commission having joined him, he still prevented his officers
and men from landing, but threw open all his ships to the
natives of the place, whose multitudes never ceased pouring
through these gallant vessels, lost in admiration of their beauty,
their resistless force, and the perfect discipline of their crews.
With the Court his intercourse now began ; and the terror of
his name, even without his armament, would there have made
him supreme. The reluctance to remove was, of course,

---

* LORD BROUGHAM, *Historical Sketches,* "Reign of George III.," 2nd
Series.

universal and deep-rooted; nor could any arrangement the expected invader might offer prove less palatable than expatriation and banishment for life across the Atlantic to pampered voluptuaries, the extent of whose excursions had hitherto been the distance between the town and the country palace. But he arranged everything for their voyage, and he was quite ready to compel their embarkation. His plan would have exposed his own person to some danger, but would have required no application of military force if nothing was attempted against the fleet. It seemed to have been borrowed from the celebrated seizure, by Cortez, of the Emperor Montezuma's person in his capital of Mexico, and the very few to whom he communicated it, while struck with the boldness of the design, saw that it was as happy as it was bold, and had no doubt whatever of its perfect success."

The storm, however, did not break over Portugal so soon as was expected; and in October Lord St. Vincent resumed his command before Brest.

Early in 1807 a change of administration took place, and the veteran Admiral immediately resigned his command and struck his flag, never to hoist it again. He was seventy-two years of age, and had spent half a century in the active service of his country, from which he retired, as Sheridan happily said, "with his triple laurel, over the enemy, the mutineer, and the corrupt." His health from this time began to decline rapidly; but it is pleasant to state that to the very last he preserved his strong faculties unimpaired, and never exhibited the sad spectacle of a decaying intellect. He not infrequently took part in the debates of the House of Lords, his speeches being marked by uncompromising liberalism of opinion, and by much force and straightforwardness of expression. In private life he endeared himself to his friends by his ready sympathy, his genial humour, and his unaffected cheerfulness.

While no one could maintain his position with greater dignity, on one could unbend with better grace. His generosity of disposition was constantly being illustrated; the needy and distressed never applied to him in vain;* and to the appeals of indigent members of his own profession his heart and ear were ever open.

"The conduct of Lord St. Vincent," remarks Lord Brougham, "was always high and decorous; and though he had a singular aversion to cant of any kind, nor to any more than to overdone Pharisaical morality, he never lowered in his own person the standard of private any more than of public virtue, wisely holding all conspicuous men as trustees for the character of the people, and, in some sort, representatives of the people's virtues."

A curious testimony to his professional merit was borne by the great Napoleon. One of his pupils, Captain Bowen, was presented to the latter in his exile at St. Helena, and in the course of conversation Napoleon inquired of him—

"With whom have you principally served?"

"I have been chiefly patronised by Lord St. Vincent."

"He is a brave man and a very good sailor; the greatest the English ever had, for he kept his fleet in better order. Did he not command off Cadiz when I went to Egypt, and did he not send Lord Nelson after me?"

"Yes, he did."

"Were you with him in the battle off Cape St. Vincent?"

* "Hearing by chance that Mr. Dibdin, to whose happy and beautiful poetry such excellent nautical songs are due, was in distressed circumstances, Lord St. Vincent immediately sent him £100, and desired an inquiry into the real state of the case to be made: 'For it would be indeed a shame,' he said, 'that the man who has wiled away the midwatch, and softened the hardships of war, should be in want, while a seaman enjoys an abundance.' To the subscription to supply potatoes to the Irish he sent £300, and £500 to the sufferers at Waterloo."— TUCKER, ii. 328.

" No."

" Where does Lord St. Vincent live ? "

" In Essex, about sixteen miles from London."

" When you return, if you go to see Lord St. Vincent, make him my compliments—the compliments of an old soldier to a good old English sailor."

In 1816 Lord St. Vincent lost his wife. He survived her for seven years, and his old age was distinguished by many well-deserved honours. He was made a General of the Marines, a Grand Cross of the Bath, and an Admiral of the Fleet. In 1821 George IV. forwarded to him a naval bâton, corresponding to that of a field-marshal in the army, " as a testimony of his Majesty's personal esteem, and of the high sense his Majesty entertains of the eminent services which his lordship has rendered to his country by his distinguished talents and brilliant achievements."

Lord St. Vincent died on the 13th of March, 1823.

VICE-ADMIRAL LORD NELSON.

A.D. 1758—1805.

I.

HORATIO NELSON, fifth son of the Rev. Edmund Nelson, rector of Burnham Thorpe, by his wife Catherine, daughter of the Rev. Dr. Suckling, was born at the parsonage of Burnham Thorpe on Midsummer's Day, 1758.

The anecdotes preserved of his early years are few in number; but, such as they are, they testify to his constitutional courage and daring temper. At the age of five or six, when on a visit to his grandmother, he went in search of birds' nests, lost his way, and did not return as was expected. Messengers were dispatched in quest of him, to find him sitting alone by the side of a stream which he had been unable to cross. His grandmother, reproaching him for rambling so far and so long, concluded by saying, "I wonder that fear did not drive you home." "Fear, grandmamma!" replied the boy indifferently. "I never saw *fear;* what is it?"

In 1767 he lost his mother, and it seems to have been at this time that he was removed from Norwich High School, his earliest place of education, to the grammar-school at North Walsham, which, under the care of a Rev. Mr. Jones, had obtained some degree of celebrity. His progress here is described as satisfactory; but when only twelve years old he was entered as a midshipman on board his maternal uncle's ship, the *Raisonnable*, of 64 guns, then fitting out for an expedition to the Falkland Islands. The expedition never sailed ; the *Raisonnable* was laid up, and the young Horatio, in order to gain some knowledge of his intended profession, was placed on board a merchantman bound for the West Indies. With a considerable store of practical information, he returned to England about the middle of 1772. What was to prove so brilliant a naval career then began, the boy of fourteen being appointed to his uncle's ship the *Triumph*, whence, in the following year, he volunteered to serve as coxswain to Captain Lutwidge, who, with Captain Phipps, had been chosen by the Admiralty to conduct an expedition of discovery towards the North Pole. The two ships chosen for this purpose, the *Racehorse* and the *Carcass*, each with a complement of 80 or 90 picked men, sailed from the Nore on the 4th of June. On the 30th of July the explorers found themselves among the Arctic ice. They proceeded to work their way through the floes with considerable labour, and on the 11th of August reached Amsterdam Island, formerly a place of resort for the Dutch whalers. The state of the ice beyond, a vast and impassable barrier, extending for upwards of ten degrees between the latitudes of 80° and 81°, convinced the two captains that a north-east passage into the Pacific Ocean was at the time impossible, and they determined on returning to England. The homeward voyage presented no incidents of importance, and the two ships reached England on the 24th of September.

This expedition failed to enlarge the bounds of geographical discovery, and is principally remembered in connection with an anecdote of Nelson's intrepidity. On one of the clear Arctic nights common in those high latitudes Nelson was missing from his ship, and a careful search having been made after him in vain, he was given up as lost. At sunrise, how-

ever, to the general astonishment, he was seen afar off on the
ice, hotly pursuing a large polar bear.   He carried a musket in
his hand, but the lock being injured he could not fire it; and
he was endeavouring, therefore, to weary the animal that he
might be able to kill it with the butt-end.   Captain Lutwidge,
on his return, censured him for quitting the ship without leave,
and asked what could be his motive for committing so rash an
action.   " I wished, sir," he replied, " to get the skin for my
father."

In the *Sea-horse*, a 20-gun frigate, commanded by the gallant
Captain Farmer, Nelson sailed to the East Indies, where he
availed himself of every opportunity of improving in seamanship, and commended himself to his superiors by his active
discharge of his duties.   But the climate broke down his
health, and he was compelled to return to England.   In September, 1776, through the influence of his uncle, who had
become Comptroller of the Navy, he was appointed acting-
lieutenant in the *Worcester*, of 64 guns, and in this ship he
remained at sea, with various convoys, till the spring of 1777.
Passing his professional examination for a lieutenancy, he
received his commission as second lieutenant of the *Lowestoffe*,
32 guns, under Captain Locker, and sailed for Jamaica.   In a
strong gale of wind and a heavy sea the *Lowestoffe* fell in with
an American privateer, and compelled it to strike its colours.
Captain Locker ordered his first lieutenant to board her and
take possession ; but, owing to the tremendous sea, the officer,
though a gallant man, could not approach sufficiently near,
and pulled back to the *Lowestoffe*, discomfited.   Captain Locker,
much disappointed, exclaimed, " Have I, then, no officer who
can board the prize ? "   The master immediately ran to the
gangway that he might jump into the boat, but young Nelson
suddenly stopped him : " It is my turn now," he cried ; "if I
come back too, it will be yours."   Leaping into the boat, he

managed it with the skill acquired by long experience, laid it alongside of the prize, and took possession

Nelson's reputation for energy and seamanship attracted the attention of the Commander-in-Chief, Sir Peter Parker, who appointed him third lieutenant on board his own flag-ship, and recognising his superior abilities, as well as his professional ardour, rapidly promoted him to the rank of first lieutenant, and before the conclusion of the year gave him the command of the *Badger* brig. In this he did good service in the Bay of Honduras and on the Mosquito coast, protecting English commerce from the depredations of the American privateers. On the 11th of June, 1779, while yet in his twenty-first year, he obtained his post-captaincy, and in the following year commanded the *Hinchinbroke*, which was selected to convoy a military expedition against the Spanish settlement of San Juan. On the 10th of April the troops arrived before the castle, which is situated on the river San Juan, about thirty-two miles from the Lake of Nicaragua. Nelson advised an immediate assault ; but Colonel Polson proceeded in accordance with the old traditional military routine, and the consequent delay proved fatal to the success of the expedition. The castle was taken ; but the malarious climate told fatally on the health of the troops and seamen, who died by scores; the survivors were feeble and sickly ; Nelson himself was stricken with disease, and it was only his opportune promotion to the *Janus* (of 44 guns) which saved his life by recalling him to a healthier station. The air of Jamaica, however, is never very favourable to European constitutions, and assuredly not adapted to invigorate the feeble. It was soon apparent that Nelson made no sensible progress, and his friends and physicians at length compelled him, though sorely against his will, to return home.

On his arrival in England, his professional zeal induced him, though he had almost lost the use of his limbs, and existed rather than lived, to apply to the Board of Admiralty for a ship. " This they readily promised me," he afterwards observed with sly humour, " thinking it not possible for me to live."

After spending three months at Bath he found his health considerably improved, and was able to visit his aged father at Burnham Thorpe, and other relatives and friends in the county of Norfolk. In August, 1781, he was appointed to the *Albemarle,* and throughout the winter was actively employed in cruising and convoying in the North Seas. In the following year he was sent to Quebec, and afterwards arrived off Boston harbour, destroying several American vessels, and having his first " brush " with a Frenchman. " On the 14th of August," he says, " we fell in with, in Boston Bay, four sail of the line and the *Iris* frigate, part of Monsieur Vaudreuil's squadron, who gave us a pretty dance for nine or ten hours. But we beat all except the frigate ; and though we brought-to for her, after we were out of sight of the line-of-battle ships, she tacked and stood from us. Our escape I think wonderful. They were, on the clearing up of a fog, within shot of us, and chased us the whole time about one point from the wind." It was due to Nelson's admirable seamanship that his ship escaped the French fleet. He stood right in among the shoals of St. George's Bank, where they were unable or afraid to follow him.

Soon afterwards Nelson joined Lord Hood's fleet in the West Indies, and continued actively employed with it until the conclusion of peace in 1783. After his return to England he went to reside for a short time in France, for the purpose of acquiring a knowledge of the language. In his linguistic studies, however, he ma le but small progress ; and he probably rejoiced when, in the spring of 1784, he was recalled to his professional duties and commissioned to the *Boreas* frigate, of 28 guns.

On the same day, the 20th of March, he was attacked by ague and fever, which lasted for a fortnight. On his recovery he sailed at daylight, just after high water; but the pilot ran the ship aground, and it lay there with so little water that the people could walk round her till the tide again rose. That night and part of the following day the frigate lay behind the Nore, buffeted by a severe gale of wind and snow.

Writing to a friend from Portsmouth on the 21st of April, he says, " I got into the Downs. Wednesday I got into a quarrel with a Dutch Indiaman who had Englishmen on board, which we settled, though with some difficulty. The Dutchman made a complaint against me; but the Admiralty, fortunately, have approved my conduct in the business, a thing they are not very guilty of when there is a likelihood of a scrape. And yesterday, to complete me, I was riding a blackguard horse that ran away with me at Common, carried me round all the works into Portsmouth by the London gates, through the town, out at the gate that leads to Common, where there was a waggon in the road, which is so very narrow that a horse could barely pass. To save my legs, and perhaps my life, I was obliged to throw myself from the horse, which I did with great agility, but, unluckily, upon hard stones, which has hurt my back and my legs, but done no other mischief. It was a thousand to one that I had not been killed. To crown all, a young girl was with me; her horse ran away as well as mine, but, most fortunately, a gallant young man seized the horse's bridle a moment before I dismounted, and saved her from the destruction she could not have avoided."

In the middle of May Nelson sailed from Spithead for the Leeward Islands, where he remained for several months, but the record of his services presents nothing to call for special notice. In March, 1787, he was married to Mrs. Nisbet, the widow of a physician, the Duke of Clarence (afterwards William IV.), with whom Nelson had had much friendly intercourse, officiating as the bride's father. As is only too well known, the marriage did not prove a happy one. In November of the same year his ship was paid off at Sheerness, and he was free to retire to the parsonage at Burnham Thorpe, where he cultivated a few acres of land, and enjoyed an occasional shot at a hare, a woodcock, or a partridge.

One of the most amusing of his biographers describes his rural retirement in highly coloured language :—*

" In cultivating the friendship of respectable neighbours, who laudably courted his society ; in rendering kind offices to the humbler inhabitants of his vicinity, by whom he was universally beloved; in enriching his mind by reading and reflection, and improving his land by cultivation—this great man employed most part of the leisure which peace afforded him. Sometimes, indeed, he went to Bath, or other fashionable resort, during the season, where he might meet with his old friends ; and sometimes sought them in the metropolis, when he occasionally paid his respects at the Admiralty. His heroic mind, no doubt, amidst the calm of peace, prepared for the storm of war ; and, though he disdained not the culture of the ploughshare, he looked forward to the day when it would become necessary to exchange it for the sword. He was particularly fond of geographical studies ; few men were so well acquainted with maps and charts ; and his accurate eye frequently traced with eagerness the various parts of the globe which he had passed with difficulty or delight, and the spots at which he had successfully or unpleasantly paused."

On the 30th of January, 1793, Nelson was appointed to the *Agamemnon*, of 64 guns, which was then under orders of equipment for the Mediterranean. He raised his crew chiefly from his own neighbourhood, and from the counties of Norfolk and Suffolk ; and drew together a sturdy band of gallant fellows, united by their strong confidence in their leader, and

* HARRISON, *Life of Lord Nelson*, i. 97.

prepared **to** attempt any enterprise to which he might call them. For some months he cruised about the Mediterranean, under Lord Hood's orders, accustoming his men to a steady discipline, and practising them in gunnery and seamanship. In September he was dispatched on a confidential mission to the Court of Naples. It was on this occasion that he made the acquaintance of Lady Hamilton—an acquaintance destined to exercise so great an influence on his future life. He appears at once to have been profoundly impressed by her remarkable personal charms and her considerable talents, though he can hardly have been ignorant of the irregularities of her career prior to her marriage to the English ambassador at Naples, Sir William Hamilton. She on her part, with a woman's fine perception, detected the boldness and originality of his genius, sympathized with his ambitious hopes, and responded to the fervour of his friendship.

Intrusted by Lord Hood with the command of a squadron of frigates, to be employed in cruising operations on the coast of Corsica and the adjoining shore of Italy, he began a series of active, successful, and brilliant operations against the enemy. He exerted himself on land with scarcely less energy than at sea : getting out guns, erecting batteries, reducing fortresses, infusing into all with whom he came in contact something of his own ardour and irrepressible activity, and succeeding in everything he undertook by virtue of a patience that never failed and a courage that never despaired. His exertions at the siege of Bastia commanded the admiration of the army as well as of the navy ; and when troops were to be landed or disembarked, his measures were always found adapted to every emergency.

Not less conspicuous was the part he played in the siege of Calvi. He not only took charge of the disembarkation of the troops, but landed a body of seamen, who under his direction

constructed and worked one of the attacking batteries. Cool
and composed under fire, his example had always and everywhere an inspiriting effect, and his voice acted upon his men
like the sound of a trumpet. In this siege he lost the sight of
his right eye. A shot from one of the enemy's guns struck the
ground near the battery which he commanded, and dashed
some minute particles of sand or gravel into it. But he subdued all signs of pain, refused to leave his post, and with
a ribbon bound over the wounded eye continued to direct the
fire of his men until the enemy surrendered.

Scant acknowledgment of his pre-eminent services was made
either by the naval or military commander-in-chief. "They
have not done me justice," said Nelson, writing to his eldest
sister, "in the affair of Calvi; but never mind," he added,
with a proud confidence of genius, "I'll have a Gazette of my
own."

We have not the space for a detailed account of the operations of the British fleet in the Mediterranean at this period of
the war. In all the most important Nelson was foremost, and
his "Agamemnons" secured a wide renown for intrepidity and
daring under his leadership. It may be asserted, without fear
of denial, that no other officer inflicted on the enemy so vast
an amount of injury. His reputation rose rapidly, and the
country began to turn its eyes upon this dashing and able
captain, whose energy was so irrepressible, whose vigour
seemed never to know diminution.

In November, 1795, Sir John Jervis assumed the command-
in-chief of the Mediterranean fleet. A first-rate seaman, he was
fully capable of appreciating the worth of an officer like
Nelson; and one of his earliest acts was to promote him
temporarily to the rank of Commodore, with permission to hoist
a distinguishing pennant on board the old *Agamemnon*. But
this ship being in need of repair, Nelson shifted his flag in May,

1796, to the *Captain*, of 74 guns, and sent back the weather-beaten, wave-battered, and shot-torn *Agamemnon* to England. In August his appointment as Commodore was confirmed and made permanent. It was on board the *Captain* that he contributed so largely to the glorious victory of St. Valentine's Day, February 14th, 1797, over the united French and Spanish fleets.

On this memorable occasion the British fleet consisted of the following ships :—

Victory	. . 100 guns	{	Admiral Sir John Jervis ; Captains Calder and George Grey.
Britannia.	. 100 „		Vice-Admiral Thompson ; Captain Foley.
Barfleur	. . 98 „		Vice-Adm. Waldegrave ; Captain Dacres.
Prince George	98 „		Rear-Admiral Parker ; Captain Irwin.
Blenheim .	98 „		Captain Frederick.
Namur	. . 90 „		„ Whitshed.
Captain	. . 74 „		Commodore Nelson ; Captain Miller.
Goliath	. . 74 „		Captain Sir Charles Knowles.
Excellent.	. 74 „		„ Collingwood.
Orion .	. . 74 „		„ Sir James Saumarez.
Colossus	. . 74 „		„ Murray.
Egmont	. . 74 „		„ Sutton.
Culloden .	. 74 „		„ Thomas Trowbridge.
Irresistible	. 74 „		„ Martin.
Diadem	. . 64 „		„ Torvey.
Minerva .	. 38 „		„ Cockburn.
Lively .	. . 32 „		„ Lord Garlies.
Niger .	. . 32 „		, Foote.
Southampton	32 „		„ Macnamara.

Frigates. { *Minerva*, *Lively*, *Niger*, *Southampton*

With this armament it was Sir John Jervis's object to prevent the fleets of France, Spain, and Holland from effecting a junction; and hearing that a Spanish fleet of twenty-six ships of the line and two frigates were steering for the Mediterranean, he immediately sailed to intercept it. On the evening of the 13th of February his advanced ships came in sight of the enemy within about eight leagues of the bold bluff of Cape St. Vincent. Immediately he hoisted the signal, ever welcome to English sailors, to prepare for battle, and to keep close order during the night. Meantime the Spaniards staggered along under press of sail, hoping **to** steal into the harbour of Cadiz.

The morning of the 14th was dim and hazy, but as the sun rose the mist cleared off, and revealed the Spanish fleet on the starboard tack. Owing to various changes, the enemy mustered twelve 34-gun frigates, besides twenty-five men-of-war (one of 136 guns, six of 112, two of 80, and sixteen of 74). The Admiral's flag was hoisted in the *Santissima Trinidada*, a huge four-decker, reported to be the largest war-ship afloat.

About 9.30 the *Culloden*, *Blenheim*, and *Prince George* were ordered to chase in the south-west, but on the *Bonne Citoyenne* signalling that she saw eight sail in that quarter, the advance was strengthened by the *Irresistible*, *Colossus*, and *Orion*.

Soon after ten the *Minerva* made the signal for twenty sail in the south-west, and a few minutes after for eight sail in the south-by-west. Half an hour later the *Bonne Citoyenne* signalled that she could distinguish first sixteen and afterwards twenty-five of the strange ships to be of the line. But by this time the whole of the Spanish armament was visible to Sir John Jervis's squadron.

The Admiral now ordered his ships to form in line of battle ahead and astern of the flag-ship, as might be most convenient, a course which kept the enemy's lee division, consisting of one three-decker (carrying a vice-admiral's flag), five two-deckers, and a few frigates, upon the lee or larboard bow.

The British fleet then stood close-hauled on the starboard tack in this order : *Culloden*, *Blenheim*, *Prince George*, *Orion*, *Colossus*, *Irresistible*, *Victory*, *Egmont*, *Goliath*, *Barfleur*, *Britannia*, *Namur*, *Captain*, *Diadem*, and *Excellent*. To the Spanish Admiral it seemed certain that the British intended to attack his separated ships ; but such was not Sir John Jervis's design. At a few minutes past noon, having passed the sternmost ships of the Spanish weather division, the *Culloden*, in obedience to signal, tacked to the larboard, a manœuvre so skilfully and rapidly accomplished that Jervis involuntarily exclaimed, " Look, look at Trowbridge ! Does he not manœuvre as if all England were looking at him ? Would to Heaven all England *were* present to appreciate, as I do, the gallant captain of the *Culloden*."

The firing began about half-past eleven, when the *Culloden* exchanged shots with the enemy's headmost ship to windward. As the British fleet advanced it became more general, and soon the fact was evident that the Admiral had succeeded in his intention of passing through the enemy's line.

" The animated and regular fire of the British squadron," says Drinkwater, " was but feebly returned by the enemy's ships to windward, which, being frustrated in their attempts to join the separated ships, had been obliged to haul their wind on the larboard tack. Those to leeward, which were most effectually cut off from their main body, attempted also to form on their larboard tack, apparently with a determination of either passing through or to leeward of our line and joining their friends ; but the warm reception they met with from the centre ships of our squadron soon obliged them to put about, and, excepting one, the whole sought safety in flight, and did not again appear in the action till the close of the day. This single ship, which persevered in passing to leeward of the British line, was so covered with smoke that her intention was not discovered till she had reached the rear, when she was not permitted to pass without notice, but received the fire of the sternmost ships ; and, as she luffed round the rear, the *Lively* and other frigates had also the honour of exchanging with this two-decker several broadsides."

The British Admiral, having succeeded in his first design, now directed his whole attention to the enemy's main body to windward, consisting at this juncture of eighteen sail of the line ; and accordingly, at eight minutes past twelve, signal was made for the British fleet to tack in succession, and shortly afterwards to again pass the enemy's line.

On the other hand, the Spanish Admiral aimed at effecting a junction with his leeward division by wearing round the rear of the British line, and those of his vessels which had passed and exchanged fire with our squadron had actually borne up for this purpose.

But the keen eye of Nelson detected, and his readiness of resource frustrated, this manœuvre. He had no sooner passed the rear of the enemy's windward division than he ordered his ships to wear, and stood towards the enemy on the other tack, a manœuvre as bold as it was decisive.

If it had failed, the consequences to himself of such a disobedience of orders must have been serious ; but Nelson was not the man to be deterred by any consideration of personal risk. "They can but hang me, after all," he exclaimed; and his ship gliding between the *Excellent* and the *Diadem*, he coolly placed her across the bows of the huge Spanish flag-ship, the *Santissima Trinidada*, a four-decker of 136 guns, said to be the largest ship in the world. He thus stopped the way against her, forcing her to haul to the wind, and driving her back upon the English advanced ships. A portion of the latter then swept to leeward of the enemy's line, to prevent a repetition of the attempt which Nelson had so splendidly baffled ; while the others, led by the *Victory*, careened along the Spanish array to windward, and placed Cordova's van-ships between the twofold fire. Thus the tactic of Nelson, with its brilliant audacity, had proved a complete success; but he himself, separated from his consorts, was for some time exposed to the volleys of the *Santissima Trinidada*, 136 guns; the *San Josef*, 112 guns ; the *Salvador del Mundo*, 112 guns ; the *San*

Nicolas, 80 guns ; and the *San Isidro*, 74 guns. That **he** survived their concentrated fire is a proof that it must have been ill-directed. After awhile the *Culloden* came to his assistance, but she soon passed on, leaving him hand-to-hand with his numerous antagonists. Having exhausted his supplies of shot by the rapidity of his fire, he was compelled to get fresh supplies out of the hold, so that he was doubtlessly glad when the *Blenheim* ranged up and diverted the attention of his enemies.

The latter at once challenged the Spanish Admiral, and as she suffered much in sails and rigging her captain resolved to close. Backing his maintop-sail, he cried, " Fire away, my brave fellows, and let us take the Spanish Admiral !" His men heartily responded to his words, and for their utmost ardour the need was urgent, inasmuch as the *Blenheim*, like the *Captain*, lay in the centre of a terrible circle of fire. The English tenacity, or " pluck," carried her safely through the trial. About three, some of her consorts came up to her help, and shortly afterwards the tall masts of the *Santissima Trinidada* went by the board. She hauled down her colours sullenly, and a rolling, blackened, shot-torn hulk was towed out of the fight.

The *Victory*, when she tacked to the larboard, made to windward of the Spanish fleet, followed by the *Barfleur, Namur, Egmont,* and *Goliath*, but the latter two vessels were so crippled in their top-gear that they gradually fell astern. Shortly after one o'clock Sir John Jervis signalled to the *Excellent* to break through the enemy's line, and one hour later Collingwood placed his ship abreast of the three-decker, *Salvador del Mundo*, with which the *Captain* and the *Excellent* had been engaged. He poured into her several staggering broadsides, and passed on to the *San Isidro*, which had already received a terrible mauling, and speedily struck her colours to this new opponent.

Then, taking note of Nelson's critical position, he steered up on the starboard side of the *San Nicolas*, drawing off her fire from the *Captain*, a welcome service which Nelson afterwards acknowledged *more suo*. "Dear Collingwood," he wrote, "'A friend in need is a friend indeed.'—HORATIO NELSON."

Having lost her foretop-mast, and most of her rigging having been cut away, the *Captain* was scarcely manageable; and as it was clear that she must soon drop astern of the Spanish fleet, Nelson resolved on delivering a final blow. The *San Nicolas*, with which he had been engaged, had fallen aboard the *San Josef*, so that the latter became the Commodore's antagonist. Upon her, therefore, he directed a crushing fire; nor was it feebly returned, as the loss on board the *Captain* showed, nearly twenty men being killed and wounded in a few minutes. "It was now," says Drinkwater, "that the various damages already sustained by that ship through the long and arduous conflict which she had maintained, appearing to render a continuance of the contest in the usual way precarious, or perhaps impossible, that Commodore Nelson, unable to bear the idea of parting with an enemy of whom he had so thoroughly assured himself, instantly resolved on a bold and decisive measure, and determined, whatever might be the worst, to attempt his opponent sword in hand. The boarders were accordingly summoned, and orders given to lay his ship, the *Captain*, on board the enemy." Her course was so skilfully directed that she was laid aboard the starboard quarter of the Spanish eighty-four, with her spritsail-yard hooked in the enemy's mizen-shrouds. What followed is best described in Nelson's own words.

"Calling for the boarders, I ordered them to board. The soldiers of the 69th, with an alacrity which will ever do them credit, and Lieutenant Pearson of the same regiment, were almost the foremost on this service. The first man who

jumped into the enemy's mizen-chains was Captain Berry, late
my first lieutenant. Captain Miller was in the act of going
also, but I directed him to remain. He was supported by our
spritsail-yard, which hooked in the mizen-rigging. A soldier of
the 69th having broken the upper quarter-gallery window, I
jumped in myself, and was followed by others as fast as possible. I found the cabin doors fastened, and some Spanish
officers fired their pistols, but, having broken open the doors,
the soldiers fired, and the Spanish brigadier—commodore, with
a distinguishing pendant—instantly fell, as retreating to the
quarter-deck. I pushed immediately onwards for the quarter-
·deck, where I found Captain Berry in possession of the poop
and the Spanish ensign hauling down. I passed with my
people and Lieutenant Pearson on the larboard gangway to
the forecastle, where I met two or three Spanish officers,
prisoners to my seamen. They delivered me their swords.
A fire of pistols or musketry opening from the Admiral's stern-
gallery of the *San Josef*, I directed the soldiers to fire into her
stern, and, calling to Captain Miller, ordered him to send more
men into the *San Nicolas*, and directed my people to board the
first-rate, which was done in an instant, Captain Berry assisting
me into the main-chains. At this moment a Spanish officer
looked over the quarter-deck rail and said they surrendered.
From this most welcome intelligence it was not long before I
was on the quarter-deck, where the Spanish captain, with a
bow, presented me his sword, and said the Admiral was dying
of his wounds. I asked him, on honour, if the ship surrendered. He declared she was. On which I gave him my
hand, and desired him to call in his officers and ship's company, and tell them of it; and, on the quarter-deck of a
Spanish first-rate, extravagant as the story may seem, did I
receive the swords of vanquished Spaniards, which as I
received I gave to William Fearney, one of my bargemen, who

put them with the greatest *sang-froid* under his arm. I was surrounded by Captain Berry, Lieutenant Pearson of the 69th, John Sykes, John Thompson, Francis Croke, all old Agamemnons, and several other brave men, seamen and soldiers. Thus fell these ships.

"N.B.—In boarding the *San Nicolas*, I believe, we had about seven killed and ten wounded; and about twenty Spaniards lost their lives by a foolish resistance. None were lost, I believe, in boarding the *San Josef.*" *

---

* Some additional particulars of this striking episode are recorded by Colonel Drinkwater:—" In a short time, the *San Nicolas* was in the possession of her intrepid assailants. The Commodore's impatience would not permit him to remain an inactive spectator of this event. He knew that the attempt was hazardous, and his presence, he thought, might contribute to its success. He therefore accompanied the party in this attack; passing from the fore-chains of his own ship into the enemy's quarter-gallery; and thence, through the cabin, to the quarter-deck, where he arrived in time to receive the sword of the dying commander, who was mortally wounded by the boarders. For a few minutes after the officers had submitted, the crew below were firing their lower deck guns; this irregularity, however, was soon corrected, and measures taken for the security of the conquest.

"But this labour was no sooner achieved than he found himself engaged in another, still more arduous. The stern of the three-decker, his former opponent, was directly amidships on the weather-beam of the *San Nicolas;* and from her poop and galleries the enemy sorely annoyed with musketry the British who had boarded the *San Nicolas*. The Commodore was not long in resolving on the conduct to be adopted on this momentous occasion. The two alternatives that presented themselves to his unshaken mind were to quit the prize or instantly board the three-decker. Confident in the bravery of his seamen, he determined on the latter. Directing, therefore, an additional number of men to be sent from the *Captain* on board the *San Nicolas*, the undaunted Commodore headed himself the assailants in this new attack, vehemently exclaiming, ' Westminster Abbey or glorious victory!'

" Success, in a few minutes, and with little loss, crowned the enterprise. Such, indeed, was the panic occasioned by his preceding conduct, that the British no sooner appeared on the quarter-deck of their new opponent, than the commandant advanced, and, asking for the British commanding officer, dropped on one knee and presented to him his sword, mentioning at the same time, as an excuse for the Spanish admiral not appearing, that

The loss of the Spaniards in this sharply fought action must have been very considerable. As on board the four prizes it amounted to 261 killed and 342 wounded, we may estimate it for the whole fleet at 450 killed and 600 wounded. The

he was dangerously wounded. For a moment Commodore Nelson could scarcely persuade himself of this second instance of good fortune ; he therefore ordered the Spanish commandant, who had the rank of a brigadier, to assemble the officers on the quarter-deck, and direct steps to be instantly taken for communicating to the crew the surrender of the ship. All the officers immediately appeared, and the Commodore had the surrender of the *San Josef* duly confirmed by each of them delivering to him his sword.

"William Fearney, one of the Commodore's bargemen, had attended close by his side throughout this perilous adventure. To him the Commodore gave in charge the swords of the Spanish officers as he received them ; and the jolly tar, as they were delivered to him, tucked these honourable trophies under his arm with all the *sang-froid* imaginable. It was at this moment also that a British sailor, who had long fought under the Commodore, came up, in the fulness of his heart, and, excusing the liberty he was taking, asked to shake him by the hand, to congratulate him on seeing him safe on the quarter-deck of a Spanish three-decker.

"This new conquest had scarcely submitted, and the Commodore returned on board the *San Nicolas*, when the latter ship was discovered to be on fire in two places. At the first moment appearances were alarming ; but presence of mind and resources were not wanting to the British officers in this emergency. The firemen were immediately ordered from the *Captain*, and, proper means being taken, the fires were soon got under.

"A signal was now made by the *Captain* for boats to assist in separating her from her two prizes ; and as the *Captain* was incapable of further service till refitted, Commodore Nelson hoisted his broad pendant for the moment on board *La Minerve* frigate, and in the evening shifted it to the *Irresistible*, of 74 guns, Captain Martin.

"Four of the enemy's ships were now in the possession of the British squadron—two of three decks, the *Salvador del Mundo* and the *San Josef*, of 112 guns each ; one of 84, the *San Nicolas ;* and the *San Isidro*, of 74 guns—and the van of the British line still continued to press hard the *Santissima Trinadada* and others, in the rear of the enemy's flying fleet.

"The close of the day, before the four prizes were secured, undoubtedly saved the Spanish Admiral's flag from falling into the hands of the victors. The *Santissima Trinadada*, in which he carried it, had been so much the object of attention, that the ship was a perfect wreck when the action ceased. May, indeed, aver that she actually struck both her flag and ensign, hoisting a white flag as a signal of submission ; but as she con-

British killed numbered 73, and the wounded 227, of whom the greater proportion fell to the *Captain*, the *Excellent*, and the *Culloden*. The four prizes were the *Salvador del Mundo*, 112 guns; the *San Josef*, 112 guns; the *San Nicolas*, 80 guns; and the *San Isidro*, 74 guns.

That an English fleet of only fifteen sail of the line should attack and defeat a Spanish fleet of twenty-seven was in itself a moral victory of the highest importance, far superior to the material victory represented by the few captured vessels, and it necessarily produced a very deep impression on the mind of Europe. It strengthened our seamen in their confidence, their habit of victory, while it taught foreign navies more and more keenly to dread the English at sea—to expect as the certain result of encountering our fleets a signal discomfiture. It was right, therefore, that Sir John Jervis, with whom lay the merit of the bold resolution to engage so superior a force, should be rewarded with an earldom; while Nelson, who had so largely contributed to the victory, received the Red Ribbon of the Bath.

The Spaniards having collected a large number of gunboats and launches to harass the blockading ships which Sir John Jervis had stationed off Cadiz, Nelson received orders to bombard the city. At the same time (July 3rd) he directed a vigorous attack on the enemy's flotilla, pressing it with such determination that it was driven and pursued close to Cadiz. Sir Horatio fought hand-to-hand with the Spanish commandant; and though the crew of his barge consisted only of himself, Captain Fremantle, the coxswain, and two bargemen, they killed or wounded the whole of the twenty-six men who, with

tinued her course, and afterwards hoisted a Spanish jack, others doubt this circumstance. It is, however, an indisputable truth that her fire had been silent for some time before this event is reported to have occurred. It was a defensive combat entirely, on their parts, after Commodore Nelson obliged them to haul their wind on the larboard tack."

the commandant, were in the Spanish launch. In this affray Nelson exposed himself to great personal danger, and would probably have lost his life had not his coxswain, John Sykes, interposed his head and received from the uplifted Spanish sabre the blow intended for his leader. Said Lord St. Vincent, " The Rear-Admiral, who is always present in the most arduous enterprises, with the assistance of some other barges, boarded and carried two of the enemy's gunboats and a barge-launch belonging to some of their ships-of-war, with the commandant of the flotilla. Rear-Admiral Nelson's actions speak for themselves ; any praise of mine would fall very short of his merit."

The Admiral receiving intelligence of the arrival of a precious argosy, *El Principe d'Asturias,* in the harbour of Santa Cruz, the capital of the island of Teneriffe, dispatched thither a squadron, under Sir Horatio Nelson, consisting of three ships of the line, the *Theseus, Culloden,* and *Jealous,* and three frigates, the *Terpsichore, Emerald,* and *Seahorse,* with the *Fox* cutter. These were afterwards joined by the *Leander,* of 50 guns. Arriving off Santa Cruz on the 20th of July, Nelson sent a summons to the Governor of Santa Cruz, demanding " the immediate surrender of the ship *El Principe d'Asturias,* from Manilla, bound to Cadiz, belonging to the Philippine Company, together with her whole and entire cargo ; and also all such other cargoes and property as may have been landed in the island of Teneriffe, and not intended for the consumption of its inhabitants." This summons was conveyed by Captain Troubridge at the head of a force of 900 seamen and marines, who were to disembark in the north-east part of the Bay of Santa Cruz. But the enemy were in such numbers and so well prepared that the attempt failed. On the 24th Nelson anchored his ships about two miles to the northward of the town, and made every show as if he intended to attack the heights. At eleven o'clock at night the boats of the squadron, containing between 600 and 700 men, with 180 men on board the *Fox* cutter, and about 70 or 80 in a boat that had been captured the day before, and led by Nelson himself, proceeded towards the mole, where they were to land, and thence pass forward into the great square of the city. The boats were not discovered until within half gun-shot of the landing-place. Nelson then directed them to cast off from each other, give a hearty hurrah, and make for the shore.

But the enemy were in greater force than was supposed. A tremendous fire from thirty or forty pieces of cannon, with musketry, from one end of the town to the other, opened on the British, but failed to daunt their ardent resolution. Unhappily, in the dense darkness, most of the boats failed to see the mole, and, caught in a boiling surf, were thrown ashore and dashed to pieces.

Nelson, supported by Captains Fremantle and Bowen, with four or five boats, stormed the mole, and carried it, though opposed by four or five hundred men. They spiked all the guns; but such a storm of musketry and grape-shot was hurled from the citadel and the houses at the head of the arch, that they could not advance, and, after suffering severely, they re-embarked and rowed back to the ships.

The *Fox* cutter, in pulling towards the town, received a shot under water from one of the enemy's distant batteries, and sank immediately; her commander with 17 men perished.

The boats of the *Theseus* lost 12 killed, 25 wounded, and 34 drowned.

The boats of the *Culloden*, 3 killed, 18 wounded, and 36 drowned.

The boats of the *Jealous*, 5 killed, and 21 wounded.

The boats of the *Leander*, 6 killed, 5 wounded, and 1 missing.

The boats of the *Seahorse,* 2 killed, and 14 wounded.

The boats of the *Terpsichore,* 8 killed, 11 wounded, and 4 missing.

The boats of the *Emerald,* 8 killed, 11 wounded, and 10 drowned.

And the *Fox* cutter, 17 drowned.

Thus this fatal attempt, the disastrous issue of which seems to have been due to the circumstance that the boats did not hit the mole,* entailed a loss of 251 killed, wounded, and missing, besides officers—a dark night's work. Nelson in the affray lost his right arm. He had only one foot out of his boat, and was in the act of landing on the mole, when the fatal shot struck him, and he fell back. His sword dropped as he fell, but with singular coolness he groped for it at the bottom of the boat, speedily recovered it, and clutched it in his remaining hand. He called to his brave fighting-men, who had already landed, and directed them to force the gate of the citadel. His son-in-law, Lieutenant Nisbet, then took his handkerchief and bound it round the shattered arm a little above where it had been shot. Meanwhile, under a terrific cannonade from the batteries, the boat hastened to return on board the *Theseus.* It soon drew near the spot where the *Fox* cutter had foundered, and its unhappy crew were still struggling in the waters. This was a scene of distress too dreadful for Nelson to pass with indifference, and as many as the boat would hold were immediately taken into it, Nelson with his remaining arm lending eager assistance, despite the anguish of his wound, which, indeed, he barely felt in his agony at being compelled to leave so many goodly fellows to perish. Every possible effort was made to gain the *Theseus,* so that the boat might be in time to rescue a

---

* At the same time it must be owned that there seems to have been a serious want of accurate information as to the strength of the enemy; the enterprise was too much of " a leap in the dark."

few more of the victims; and, a chair being called for to assist the wounded hero in getting on board, his impatience was such that he refused to wait for it, twisted a rope round his left arm, and was thus hauled up into the ship. Amputation immediately took place, but owing to some mistake in taking up a nerve with one of the arteries Nelson for a long time experienced the severest torture.

The nature of the wound necessitated his immediate return to England, and he arrived in London about the middle of September. It is needless to say that the nation rose like one man to bid him welcome, and every class, from the highest to the lowest, did homage to his conduct and character, the brilliancy of his services, and the heroic temper of his courage. The City of London presented him with its freedom in a gold box, and the Crown granted him a pension of £1,000 per annum. By November he had perfectly recovered from his wound, and on the 19th of December he hoisted his flag on board the *Vanguard*. His Christmas he spent with his aged father, his spring at Bath, and then, his ships being completely equipped, he sailed from St. Helen's on the 9th of April, and on the 29th joined the Mediterranean fleet, under the Earl of St. Vincent, off Cadiz.

The "situation," as men say, was critical. A large French fleet, under Admiral Brueys, had escorted Napoleon's expedition to Egypt, having escaped the notice of the cruising ships which blockaded Toulon. Lord St. Vincent immediately dispatched Nelson in pursuit with fourteen line-of-battle ships; and after rapidly scouring the Mediterranean and once putting into Alexandria, our hero discovered that the whole fleet was anchored in the Bay of Aboukir (August 1st). This indentation begins at a point about twenty miles to the north-east of Alexandria, and sweeps in a bold semicircle from the castle of Aboukir to the Rosetta mouth of the Nile. Though the circuit is so considerable, the two horns of the crescent are not more than ten miles apart. Line-of-battle ships cannot anchor within a league of the shore, owing to the presence of a great shoal or sandbank, on which there are not more than twenty-four feet of water. On the north-west side lies a small island, about two miles from the castle point, and connected with it by a chain of rocks and sandbanks; it is almost the sole shelter the bay enjoys.

The French fleet was in line of battle within this deep bay, but outside the shoal already spoken of. Its seaward flank, so to speak, was covered by the island, on which had been planted a battery of four twelve-pounders, some light guns, and a couple of mortars. The ships were moored in the following order :—

Guerrier, 74 guns; *Conquérant*, 74; *Spartiate*, 74; *Aquilon*, 74; *Peuple Souverain*, 74; *Franklin*, 80; *L'Orient*, 120; *Tonnant*, 80; *Heureux*, 74; *Mercure*, 74; *Guillaume Tell*, 80; *Généreux*, 74; *Timoléon*, 74.

Between this noble array and the sandbank were stationed the frigates *Sérieuse*, 36; *Artémise*, 36; and *Diane*, 40. A couple of gun-brigs, seven gun-boats, and three fire-ships completed the French armament. The Vice-Admiral Brueys flew his flag in the *Orient;* the *Franklin* carried that of Rear-Admiral Blanquet ; and the *Guillaume Tell* that of Rear-Admiral Villeneuve. In all the fleet was armed with 1,196 guns, and carried 11,820 men. Brueys regarded his position as impregnable, and he had good reason for so thinking. But Nelson no sooner surveyed it than he determined to attack "Before this time to-morrow," he exclaimed, "I shall have gained a peerage or Westminster Abbey." The enthusiasm of the commander communicated itself to his men. Every heart was afire with the hope of victory. Hatred of the French was then a part of the national religion, and there were few who did not look forward to the coming battle with an emotion of ardent patriotism.

The aspect of the French fleet as it lay in the calm shelter of Aboukir's crescent shore has been graphically described by Blackmore, who, in his "Maid of Sker," makes one of his characters, an old seaman, say—

"I shall never forget how beautiful those ships looked, and how peaceful. A French ship always sits on the water with an elegant quickness, like a French woman at the looking-glass. And though we brought the waving breeze in with us very briskly, there was hardly swell enough in the bay to make them play their hawsers. Many fine things have I seen, but it was worth any man's while to live to the age of three score years and eight, with a sound mind in a sound body, and eyes then almost as good as ever, if there were nothing for him more to see than what I saw at this moment. Six-and-twenty ships of the line, thirteen bearing the tricolour, and . . . . cleared for action. The other thirteen, with the Red Cross flying, the Cross of St. George on the gunnel of white, and tossing the blue water from their stems under pressure of canvas. Onward rushed our British ships as if every one of them were alive and driven out of all patience by the wicked escapes of the enemy. And now, at last, we had got them tight, and mean we did to keep them."

The wind at this time was north-north-west, and blew what seamen call a top-gallant breeze. It was necessary to take in the royals, to haul up on a wind. The Admiral made the signal to prepare for battle, and that it was his intention to attack the enemy's van and centre as they lay at anchor, according to a plan previously developed, the nature of which will presently be apparent. In disposing his force his idea was, first, to secure the victory, and next to make it complete. A bower-cable of each ship was immediately got out abaft and bent forward. They continued carrying sail, and stood in for the enemy's fleet in close line of battle. As all the officers of the squadron were totally unacquainted with Aboukir Bay, each ship kept sounding as she stood in.

At this moment the French ships were lying **at** single anchor, without springs on their cables, and each had a watering party on shore. Brueys recalled these detachments by signal, and further strengthened his fighting force by drawing some men from his frigates. He then signalled to prepare for action, but observing that the British fleet hove-to, he concluded that Nelson would not attack until the following morning, and signalled to remain at anchor, in the hope that, under cover of the night, he might be able to obey Napoleon's instructions and steal out to sea.

The enemy's position, as we have said, presented the most formidable obstacles, but Nelson was resolute to attack it. Where there was room for an enemy's ship to swing, he said, there was room for one of ours to anchor; and he formed the determination of passing between the shoal and the French fleet, and attacking the latter on its unprepared side. Having signalled his ships to form in line of battle ahead and astern of the flag-ship, he hailed the *Zealous* to know if there were sufficient depth of water. "I don't know, sir," answered Hood, "but, with your permission, I will stand in and try."

Here let us pause to enumerate the vessels which composed the British squadron.

Vanguard	74 guns	{ Rear-Admiral Sir Horatio Nelson,	}	595 **men.**
		{ Captain Berry		
Minotaur .	74 ,,	,,	Louis	640 ,,
Audacious .	74 ,,	,,	Gould	59c ,,
Defence . .	74 ,,	,,	Peyton	590 ,,
Zealous . .	74 ,,	,,	Hood	590 ,,
Orion . . .	74 ,,	,,	Sir James Saumarez . .	590 ,,
Goliath . .	74 ,,	,,	Foley	590 ,,

Majestic			74 guns	Captain	Westcott								590 men.
Bellerophon		.	74 ,,	,,	Darby	.	.	.		.	.	.	590 ,,
Culloden		.	74 ,,	,,	Trowbridge	.	.	.			.		590 ,,
Theseus		.	74 ,,	,,	Miller	.	.	.	.	.	.	.	590 ,,
Alexander		.	74 ,,	,,	Ball	.	.	.	.	.		.	590 ,,
Swiftsure		.	74 ,,	,,	Halliwell	.	.	.	.	.	.		590 ,,
Leander		.	50 ,,	,,	Thompson				.	.	.	.	343 ,,

Total: 1,012 guns and 8,068 men.

Taking repeated soundings, the *Zealous* carefully cleared the shoal, with the *Goliath* slightly ahead on her larboard bow. The remainder of the fleet followed in order—*Orion, Audacious, Theseus, Vanguard, Minotaur, Defence, Bellerophon, Majestic,* and *Leander.* The *Culloden* was under press of sail to the northward, while to the west, making equal efforts to join the fleet, were the *Alexander* and *Swiftsure,* with colours hoisted and the union-jack waving from their rigging.

At about half-past six the action began, the *Conquérant* and the *Guerrier* opening a distance cannonade on the slowly advancing *Goliath* and *Zealous.* Two minutes more and the *Goliath,* ranging ahead of the *Guerrier,* which in passing she hailed with a tremendous broadside, bore up for that vessel's mainbow; but her anchor not dropping soon enough, she drove on until abreast of the larboard quarter of the second of the French line, the *Conquérant.* The *Zealous* then glided into the station on the larboard or mainbow of the *Guerrier,* which Foley had intended to take. These four ships were speedily at work, while the island battery contributed to the terrible din. The broadside of the *Zealous* brought down the *Guerrier's* foremast, an omen of good fortune which was hailed by three enthusiastic cheers from the whole British line.

Next came up the *Orion,* which, running past the *Zealous* and the *Goliath,* made for the bow of the *Aquilon,* but as she bore down the *Sérieuse* frigate ventured to open fire upon her. The audacious challenge met with an immediate response, the

Orion pouring in her starboard guns, dismasting the venture-some frigate, and shattering her hull so terribly that, drifting back upon the shoal, she filled and partially went down. Eventually the man-of-war brought up her head to wind, and assailed on the one side the *Peuple Souverain*, and on the other the *Franklin*.

In standing in, the leading ships were unavoidably obliged to receive into their bows the whole fire of the broadsides of the French line till they could take their respective stations ; and it is but justice to observe that the enemy encountered their opponents with great firmness and deliberation, no colours being hoisted on either side, nor a gun fired till our van ships were within half gun-shot. At this time the necessary number of our men were engaged aloft in furling sails, and on deck in hauling the braces and other requisite employments, preparatory to casting anchor. As soon as this took place a most animated fire opened from the *Vanguard*, which continued to cover the approach of those in the rear, as they followed in close line. The *Minotaur*, *Defence*, *Bellerophon*, *Majestic*, *Swiftsure*, and *Alexander* came up in succession, and, passing within hail of the *Vanguard*, took their respective stations opposed to the enemy's array. All our ships anchored by the stern, by which means the British line became inverted from van to rear. Captain Thompson, of the *Leander*, of 50 guns, with a degree of judgment highly honourable to his professional character, advanced towards the enemy's line on the outside, and most judiciously dropped his anchor athwart hawse of *Le Franklin*, raking her with great success ; the shot from the *Leander's* broadside, which passed that ship, all striking the flag-ship *L'Orient*, of the French commander-in-chief.*

It was then about seven o'clock, and the glories of the sunset were fading slowly on the purple rim of the distant desert.

* From Sir Edward Berry's narrative in the *Naval Chronicle*.

A part of each fleet was fiercely engaged; the thunder of their guns rolled with heavy reverberations through the echoing streets of Alexandria; while the heights around the bay were crowded with excited spectators of the naval battle. The ardour with which it was fought seems almost inconceivable. In a few minutes every man stationed at the first six guns in the fore part of the *Vanguard's* deck was down, killed or wounded, and one gun in particular was repeatedly swept clear; a midshipman was just exulting over his remarkable escapes when a shot came and struck him in two. Nowhere did the fray rage more fiercely than round Nelson's flag-ship, which was made conspicuous by the six ensigns, red, white, and blue, fluttering from various parts of its rigging. Assailed both by the *Spartiate* and the *Aquilon*, even Nelson must have felt relieved when the *Minotaur* came up and took off the fire of the latter.

With lofty courage Captain Darby laid his ship, the *Bellerophon*, alongside the great French three-decker, the *Orient*, while the *Majestic* challenged the *Tonnant*, an 80-gun ship.

In his eagerness to take part in the glorious conflict, Captain Trowbridge ran the *Culloden* upon the Aboukir shoal. Neither the exertions of her men and commander nor the ready help of the *Leander* could get her off. She acted as a beacon, however, to save the *Swiftsure* and the *Alexander* from a similar misadventure. The former came into action at about half-past eight, and Captain Halliwell aimed her shot, within a range of 200 yards, at the French flag-ship. On the larboard side of the latter the ordnance of the *Alexander* did considerable execution.

As the darkness of the night spread over the scene of carnage, our British ships, in obedience to their Admiral's signal, hoisted their distinguishing lights. Victory was with them from the beginning; three French vessels, the *Guerrier*,

Conquérant, and *Spartiate*, being dismasted in the first thirty minutes. The *Aquilon* and the *Peuple Souverain*, the fourth and fifth ships of the enemy's line, were taken possession of at half-past eight. Captain Berry, at that hour, sent Lieutenant Galway, of the *Vanguard*, with a party of marines, to take possession of the *Spartiate;* and that officer returned by the boat the French captain's sword for immediate presentation to Nelson, who was then below suffering from a severe wound in the head received during the heat of the attacks.

While he was standing on the quarter-deck of the *Vanguard*, a langridge-shot, or small iron bar, struck him in the forehead, and he would have fallen but for the prompt action of Captain Berry, who caught him in his arms. So great was the effusion of blood that those around feared the wound must be mortal, and such was the hero's own impression. A large flap of the skin of the forehead, cut from the bone, had fallen over one eye, so that he was completely blinded. On being carried down into the cockpit, where the wounded were lying in their agony, the surgeon hastened to attend upon him. " No, no," he replied with the utmost composure, " I will take my turn with my brave fellows."

As the agony of his wound increased, he yielded to an old presentiment that he should die in battle, and began to prepare for death. He desired his chaplain to bear his best remembrance to Lady Nelson ; and signed a commission appointing his friend, the gallant Hardy, to the rank of post-captain in the *Vanguard*. Soon afterwards, at his express desire, Captain Louis, of the *Minotaur*, came on board, Nelson desiring to thank him personally for the assistance which he had rendered to the *Vanguard*. " My dear Louis," said the Admiral, "farewell! I shall never, should I survive, forget the obligation I am under to you. Whatever may become of me, my mind is at peace." By this time the surgeon was at liberty to

attend to him.   While he examined the wound a deep silence
prevailed ; but no sooner did he pronounce it to have been
merely superficial, and not dangerous in character, than a loud
murmur of delight arose, which gave Nelson infinitely more
pleasure than the assurance that his life was safe.

As the *Swiftsure* sailed statelily into the press of the battle,
her path luridly lighted up by the flashes of the guns, she fell in
with a dismasted ship, which was slowly dragging its shot-torn
hull out of fire.   She was about to cannonade her, when
Captain Halliwell bethought himself of hailing to ask what
vessel she was.   " *Bellerophon*, going out of action disabled,"
was the reply.   The *Swiftsure* immediately let go her anchor,
and dropping into the place just quitted by the *Bellerophon*,
crashed her broadside into an enemy's ship, which afterwards
proved to be the *Tonnant*.   The *Bellerophon* had stoutly held
her own against the great French flag-ship, the *Orient*, for three-
quarters of an hour ; but having lost her mainmast and mizen-
mast, with 29 men killed and 148 wounded, had been compelled at last to withdraw from the unequal combat.   As she
ranged ahead her foremast went by the board, and it was in
this condition that the *Swiftsure* found her.

The *Orient*, however, was not fated to escape.   The *Leander*
harassed her with occasional shot, and about half-past eight
the *Swiftsure* opened upon her with her larboard guns.   The
Alexander, on coming into the *mêlée*, took up a position to rake
her with her starboard broadside.   A few minutes after nine
the crew of the *Swiftsure* detected signs of fire in the mizen-
chains of the great flag-ship, and pointed their guns towards the
spot with tremendous effect.   The flames crept swiftly along
the deck, ran up the masts, and wreathed the yards and
rigging, reflecting a dreadful lurid glow on the dense clouds of
battle, and bringing into startling relief, as in the pageant of
a festal illumination, the spars and shrouds of the contending

vessels. At about ten o'clock the fire reached the magazines, and then the huge three-decker blew up with a tremendous crash, which shook the neighbouring men-of-war from stem to stern, and filled the air with burning beams and pieces of blazing timber. "The whole sky," it is said, "was blotched with the corpses of men, like the stones of a crater cast upward; and the sheet of fire behind them showed their arms, their bellies, and streaming hair. Then with a hiss, like electric hail from a mile's height, all came down again, corpses first, and timber next, and then the great spars that had streaked the sky like rockets."

This awful catastrophe was followed by a sudden silence, and the boldest held their breath for a time. It was fully ten minutes before a gun was fired on either side. Meanwhile a boat, the only one that could swim, was dispatched from the *Vanguard* to rescue the survivors of the explosion; other ships, when able, followed the example, and altogether about seventy Frenchmen were saved.

The firing was resumed about half-past ten. The *Defence* and the *Swiftsure* soon silenced the guns of the *Franklin,* bringing down her masts and compelling her to surrender. It was early morning when the French frigate, *Artémise,* hauled down her colours; her captain, after having thus surrendered, set fire to his ship, and, with part of his crew, made his escape ashore. Another of the French frigates, *La Sérieuse,* had been sunk by the fire from some of our men-of-war; but, as her poop remained above water, her men were saved on it, and taken off by our boats in the morning. At eleven o'clock the *Généreux* and *Guillaume Tell,* with two frigates, *La Justine* and *La Diana,* cut their cables and stood out to sea, pursued by the *Zealous,* which endeavoured to prevent their escape. But, as there was no ship in a condition to support her, she was recalled.

The whole of the 2nd of August was employed in securing the prizes, which were all in possession of the British, except the *Tonnant* and *Timoléon*. As they were both dismasted and could not escape, they could safely be left until the following morning. The *Timoléon*, however, was set on fire by her own crew; the *Tonnant* was seized on the 3rd. Thus, of all the splendid fleet which had accompanied Napoleon from France, and was designed to maintain his communications with the mother-country, only two line-of-battle ships and two frigates escaped. This momentous victory, however, had more than annihilated a fleet; it had checkmated the ambitious design of the French general, and effectually baffled his scheme of Oriental supremacy.

The loss of the British in the battle of the Nile amounted to 218 killed and 678 wounded. That of the French must have exceeded 3,000. Amongst the killed was the French commander-in-chief, Vice-Admiral Brueys, who about two o'clock received a shot that almost cut him in two. He refused to be taken below, exclaiming, " Un amiral français doit mourir sur son banc de quart," and survived his wound only some fifteen minutes. In the explosion of the *Orient* perished Commodore Casa-Bianca and his son, a lad of only ten years of age. According to a story popularised by Mrs. Hemans, he refused to quit his post, even when the flames of the burning ship rolled around him, because he had not received his father's permission :—

> " The boy stood on the burning deck,
> Whence all but he had fled;
> The flame that lit the battle's wreck
> Shone round him o'er the dead.
>
> The flames rolled on—he would not go
> Without his father's word;
> That father, faint in death below,
> His voice no longer heard.

There came a burst of thunder-sound,
　　The boy—ah! where was he?
Ask of the winds that far around
　　With fragments strewed the sea—

With mast and helm, and pennon fair,
　　That well had borne their part;
But the noblest thing that perished there
　　Was the young and faithful heart."

The rough grasp of matter of fact has torn away the veil of romance with which poetry had draped this incident, and it is now known that, at the time of the explosion,* the elder Casa-Bianca was below, having his wound dressed, with his son in attendance upon him.†

* A French authority gives a different version:—" Commodore Casa-Bianca and his son, who was only ten years old, and who gave, during the ac·ion, proofs of bravery and intelligence far above his age, were not so fortunate. They were in the water, on the wreck of *L'Orient's* masts, not being able to swim, seeking each other, till three-quarters past ten, when the ship blew up, and put an end to their hopes and fears."

† To this account of the battle of the Nile it will be convenient to add Coleridge's description of the action between Captain Ball's ship, the *Alexander*, and the *Orient*, as derived from Captain Ball himself:—

" It was already dalk when Captain Ball brought his ship into action, and laid her alongside the *Orient*.

" He had previously made a combustible preparation, which, from the nature of the engagement to be expected, he had proposed to reserve for the last emergency; but just at the time when, from several symptoms, he had every reason to believe the enemy would soon strike to him, one of the lieutenants, without his knowledge, threw in the combustible matter; and this it was that occasioned the tremendous explosion of that vessel, which, with the deep silence and interruption of the engagement that succeeded to it, has been fitly deemed the sublimest war incident recorded in history.

" At the renewal of the battle, Captain Ball, though his ship was then on fire in three different places, laid her alongside a French eighty-four, and a second long obstinate contest began. The firing on the part of the French ship having at length, and for some time, slackened, and then alto-gether ceased, and yet no sign being given of surrender, the senior lieutenant of the *Alexander* came to Captain Ball and informed him that the hearts of his men were as good as ever, but that they were so com-

II.

Leaving a squadron to cruise off Alexandria, Nelson sailed on the 18th of August for Naples, where, it is needless to say, he was received with befitting splendour by the King and Queen, and with true southern enthusiasm by the population. There, too, he resumed that acquaintanceship with Lady Hamilton which has left so unfortunate a shadow on his career. It cannot be doubted that the admiration which was at this time lavished upon him had a deteriorating effect on his moral character, and developed in him an arrogance and an egotism which provoked the regret of judicious friends. The honours and rewards with which he was freely loaded helped to swell this intemperance of pride. He was created a peer of Great Britain, by the title of Baron Nelson of the Nile, and of Burnham Thorpe, in the county of Norfolk; and a pension of £2,000 per annum was granted to him and his two next successors in the title. A gold medal was struck in honour of his victory. The Irish Government bestowed upon him an annuity of £1,000. The East India Company voted him a gift of £10,000; while so many towns and cities voted him

pletely exhausted that they were scarcely capable of lifting an arm. He asked, therefore, that as the enemy had ceased firing, the men might be permitted to lie down by their guns for a short time. After some reflec- tion, Captain Ball acceded to the proposal, taking, of course, the proper precaution to rouse them again at the moment he thought requisite.

"Accordingly, with the exception of himself, his officers, and the appointed watch, the ship's crew lay down, each in the place at which he was stationed, and slept there twenty minutes.

"They were then roused, and started up, more like men out of an am- bush than from sleep, so co-instantaneously did they all obey the summons. They recommenced their fire, and in a few minutes the enemy surrendered ; it was soon after discovered that during the interval, and almost imme- diately after the French ship had first ceased firing, her crew had sunk down by their guns, and there slept, almost by the side, as it were, of their sleeping enemies."

their freedom that he was overwhelmed by the shower of gold boxes. Moreover, the Crown granted him a most honourable augmentation of his armorial bearings, including the well-known motto, "Palmam qui meruit ferat."

The successes of the French armies in Southern Italy rendering necessary the departure of the King and Queen from Naples, Nelson, on the 22nd of December, embarked them and their suite on board the *Vanguard*, and conveyed them to Palermo. He himself remained at Palermo, directing British naval operations in the eastern Mediterranean, for seven months. Meanwhile the French evacuated Naples, which was occupied by Cardinal Ruffo, with an army of 20,000 Calabrese and other royalists, and by the summer of 1799 a prospect was opened up of the return of their Sicilian Majesties to their capital. Nelson, accompanied by Sir William and Lady Hamilton, accordingly proceeded in the *Foudroyant*, on board of which he had hoisted his flag, to Naples, charged with full power by the King, and set to work to restore order. This unfortunate mission, one which no English admiral ought to have undertaken, involved him in painful complicity with what cannot be otherwise regarded than as a judicial murder—the execution of Prince Caraccioli, on a pretended charge of high treason. Even Southey speaks of this as "a deplorable transaction, a stain upon the memory of Nelson and the honour of England." Nelson was too honest and too just not to see the gross defects of the Neapolitan Government; but his hatred of the French was as absorbing a passion as Hannibal's hatred of the Romans; and to deliver Naples from their influence, though he threw it back into the cruel arms of the Bourbons, seemed to him an absolute duty. He was rewarded for his exertions with the dukedom and estate of Bronte, worth about £3,000 a year, and the Circean smiles of Lady Hamilton.

Returning to England towards the close of 1800, he met with

a reception worthy of the English people and of himself—
worthy of the greatest maritime nation of the world, and of
"the greatest sailor since the world began." The influence of
Lady Hamilton was at this time daily increasing, and its extent
was marked by his separation from his wife, under circumstances which Nelson's biographer cannot attempt to excuse or
defend. On the 1st of January, 1801, he became a Vice-
Admiral of the Blue, and on the 12th of March sailed as
second in command to Sir Hyde Parker, who had been placed
at the head of a great naval expedition destined to act against
Denmark. Briefly it may be stated that Napoleon had induced the northern powers, Russia, Denmark, and Sweden, to
join with him in an effort to extort from England a surrender
of her traditional naval rights. To break up this confederacy
was the object of the expedition, of which, if Parker were the
head, Nelson was the heart and soul. The British fleet passed
the Sound in safety, and on the morning of the 2nd of April
began the attack upon Copenhagen. The Danish force consisted of six sail of the line, 11 floating batteries, numbering
from 26 24-pounders to 18 18-pounders, one bomb-ship, and
several schooner gun-vessels. These were supported by the
batteries on the Crown islands, amounting to 88 cannon, and
four sail of the line moored in the harbour's mouth, and some
batteries in the island of Amak. Nelson's force consisted of 12
sail of the line, four frigates, four sloops, two fire-ships, and seven
bombs ; three of the men-of-war, however, ran ashore. A terrible
contest ensued, the Danes fighting with great gallantry and
determination ; and so uncertain seemed the result, that Sir
Hyde Parker about one o'clock made signals for the action to
cease. "Leave off action?" said Nelson, when informed of the
signal ; "now d—— me if I do ! " "Shall I repeat it ? " said
the signal lieutenant. "No, acknowledge it ; " and turning to
his captain, he said, " You know, Foley, I have only one eye ;

I can't see it;" and he put his glass to his blind eye. "Nail my signal," he added, "for close action to the mast." About two the gunnery of the British prevailed, and the Danes ceased firing along nearly the whole line. Captain Fremantle says, "When the ships abreast of the *Elephant* and *Ganges* were completely silenced, Lord Nelson desired me to go to him. He was in his cabin, talking to some Danish officers out of one of the ships captured, saying how anxious he was to meet the Russians, and wished it had been them instead of Danes we had engaged. At this time he put into my hand a letter, which he meant immediately to send to the Crown Prince of Denmark in a flag of truce." This letter he refused to seal with a wafer, and called for wax and a candle· "It was no time," he said, "to appear hurried and informal." It ran as follows :—

"Vice-Admiral Lord Nelson has been commanded to spare Denmark when she no longer resists. The line of defence which covers her shores has struck to the British flag ; but if the firing is continued on the part of Denmark, he must set on fire all the prizes he has taken, without having the power of saving the brave men who have so nobly defended them."

At this time the British ships were all cut to pieces, and Nelson knew that it would be a difficult task to get them out of the shoals. But in about half an hour a Danish superior officer brought a reply from the Crown Prince, desiring to know Nelson's particular object in sending a flag of truce. The British Admiral answered that his object was humanity ; that he was willing hostilities should cease ; that he would remove his prisoners out of the captured vessels, which he would burn or carry off, as he thought fit; adding that he should consider it the greatest victory he had ever gained if it should effect a reconciliation between his own sovereign and the King of Denmark. The firing having entirely ceased, Nelson lost not a moment in extricating his squadron from its dangerous position among the shoals. The ships cut their cables and ran out, but were so crippled as to be unmanageable. Four were ashore, and had to be got off during the night by the boats of Sir Hyde Parker's division. A suspension of hostilities was, however, agreed to, and this was followed by an armistice for fourteen weeks, the precursor of a treaty of peace which detached Denmark from the French alliance.

For his victory at Copenhagen Nelson received the thanks of both Houses of Parliament, and was raised to a viscountcy. On his return to England he was appointed to a command extending from Orfordness to Beechy Head, that he might watch and defeat Napoleon's extensive preparations for the invasion of England. After the peace of Amiens he lived for some time in seclusion at Merton Abbey, in Surrey, where he had purchased a small estate. Sir William and Lady Hamilton were his constant guests, until the death of the former on the 6th of April, 1803.

On the renewal of the war with France, Nelson was appointed, in May, 1803, Commander-in-Chief of the Mediterranean station, and hoisted his flag in the *Victory*, of 110 guns, which for some months continued to watch the French fleet in Toulon. Nelson repudiated the notion that he " blockaded " Toulon. In his own words, writing in August, 1804, "Every opportunity has been offered the enemy to put to sea, for it is there that we hope to realise the hopes and expectations of our country." In the January of 1805 war broke out between England and Spain, and in the same month Villeneuve and the Toulon fleet put to sea in order to effect a junction with the Spanish fleet. Stress of weather forced them back to port, but on the last day of March they slipped out again, and were joined by the Spanish contingent, with 4,500 men on board. The combined fleet numbered 20 sail of the line and

10 frigates; Nelson had only 10 sail of the line and three frigates. His quick sagacity conjectured Villeneuve's destination, and he wrote accordingly to the Admiralty, that "he was sailing after the combined fleet to the West Indies, and if he did not find them there he would follow them to the Antipodes." The enemy, however, had the start of him by more than a month. Nelson reached Barbadoes on the 4th of June; but inaccurate information misled him. Villeneuve had appeared before several West Indian islands, Grenada, Antigua, and Martinico, and then at the news of Nelson's approach hastened back to Europe. Nelson pursued them, as the hound pursues the hare, having saved the West Indies literally by the prestige of his name.

Worn out with anxiety and fatigue, Nelson returned to England, and withdrew to his country seat to recruit his shattered health. Then, in early September, the news reached him that the French and Spanish fleets, after an indecisive action with Sir Robert Calder, had entered Cadiz in safety. The war-horse scented the battle afar off, and could rest no longer. He repaired to the Admiralty and offered his services, which were accepted with alacrity. He would fight the twofold armada, and "depend upon it," he said, "I shall yet give De Villeneuve a sound drubbing." During the few weeks allowed for preparation he formed his plans of attack; and Lord Sidmouth has left it on record that, in the course of a visit he received from Nelson, three weeks before the battle of Trafalgar, the great Admiral described his scheme with bits of paper on a table as it was afterwards fought. But if confident of victory, he was not without a presentiment of his own fate. After the battle of the Nile, Sir Benjamin Halliwell had caused a coffin to be wrought out of the mainmast of the *Orient*, and presented it to him. He now desired its history to be engraved on its lid, saying that he should probably want it on his

return.   Arriving at Portsmouth on the 14th of September,
he was made the object of an almost unparalleled demonstration of popular enthusiasm.   The immense crowds that
lined the streets wept and knelt as he passed along, and
overwhelmed him with blessings.   They bade him God
speed with a cheer which had in it all the might and majesty
of a nation's love and gratitude.   As his barge pushed off
to the flag-ship he waved his hat: it was his last farewell to
England.

On the 29th of September, his birthday, Nelson arrived off
Cadiz, where Collingwood was closely watching the combined
fleet.   He had sent forward the *Euryalus* frigate to inform
Collingwood of his advance, and to direct that no salute should
be fired to reveal to the enemy that the British fleet had been
reinforced.   On assuming the command he had 27 sail of the
line, with which he retired to a station upwards of sixteen
leagues from Cadiz, leaving two frigates to watch the harbour,
and stationing a line of three men-of-war to maintain the communication between them and the main fleet.   On the day
that Nelson joined the fleet Napoleon dispatched positive injunctions to Villeneuve to carry his squadron into the Mediterranean, and, clearing it of British cruisers and merchant vessels,
to proceed to Toulon.   Villeneuve prepared to obey orders,
but did not venture to put to sea without his Spanish auxili-
aries.   He moored his fleet at the mouth of the harbour, and
waited there for a fair wind.   Eight days elapsed before he got
what he wanted, but on the 19th and 20th of October he
weighed anchor and set sail, having with him 33 sail of the
line, five frigates, and ten brigs.

Nelson's force consisted of 27 sail of the line and four
frigates, drawn up in two lines or columns, as hereinunder set
forth :—*

* JAMES, *Naval History of Great Britain.*

BRITISH VAN, OR WEATHER COLUMN.

Victory . . .	110 guns	Admiral Lord Nelson and Captain Hardy.	
Téméraire . . .	98 „	Captain Harvey.	
Neptune . . .	98 „	„	Fremantle.
Conqueror . .	74 „	„	Pollen.
Leviathan . .	74 „	„	Bayntorn.
Ajax	74 „	Lieutenant Pilfold.	
Orion	74 „	Captain Codrington.	
Agamemnon	64 „	„	Sir Edward Berry.
Minotaur .	74 „	„	Mansfield.
Spartiate . . .	74 „	„	Sir Francis Laforey.
Britannia . . .	100 „	Rear-Ad. Lord Northcote and Capt. Bullen.	
Africa	64 „	Captain Digby.	

REAR, OR LEE COLUMN.

Royal Sovereign.	100 guns	Adm. Collingwood and Capt. Rotherham.	
Mars	74 „	Captain Duff.	
Bellisle . . .	74 „	„	Hargood.
Tonnant . .	80 „	„	Tyler.
Bellerophon . .	74 „	„	Cooke.
Colossus . .	74 „	„	Morris.
Achille . .	74 „	„	King.
Polyphemus	64 „	„	Redmill.
Revenge . . .	74 „	„	Moorsom.
Swiftsure . . .	74 „	„	Rutherford
Defence . . .	74 „	„	Hope.
Thunderer . .	74 „	Lieutenant Stockham.	
Defiance . . .	74 „	Captain Durham.	
Prince	74 „	„	Grindall.
Dreadnought .	98 „	„	Conn.

FRIGATES.

Euryalus . . .	36 „	The Honourable Captain Blackwood.	
Sirius	36 „	Captain Prowse.	
Phœbe	36 „	„	Capel.
Naiad	36 „	„	Parker.
Pickle (schooner)	10 „	Lieutenant Laponitiere.	
Entreprenante (cutter) }	10 „	„	Payer.

The British fleet was, therefore, numerically inferior to the allies; but it was still more signally inferior in number and calibre of guns, as well as in men. On board the allied fleet were distributed 10,000 veterans to insure success in boarding, and the ships were furnished with fire-balls and combustible materials of every description. The French commander-in-chief was Admiral Villeneuve, with Rear-Admirals Dumanoir and Magnon as seconds. The Spaniards were commanded by Admiral Gravina, with Admirals Don Ignaiez Morea D'Alva, Don Domingo Guadalharas, and Commodore Don Baltazere, under him.

On the 9th of October Nelson sent his plan of attack to Collingwood. It was a development and a scientific application of Rodney's principle of breaking the line. His fleet was to move towards the enemy in two divisions, with an advanced squadron of eight of the fastest two-deckers. Collingwood, at the head of one division, was to break through the enemy about the twelfth ship from their rear, Nelson would strike at the centre, and the advanced squadron was to cut off three or four ships ahead of the centre. The plan would necessarily vary according to the strength of the enemy, but its governing principle was that the British should always be one-fourth superior to the ships they cut off. "Something," he added in explaining this plan, "must be left to chance. Nothing is sure in a sea-fight, beyond all others ; shots will carry away masts and yards of friends as well as foes. But I look with confidence to a victory before the van of the enemy could succour the rear, and then that the British fleet would be ready to receive the twenty sail of the line, or to pursue them should they endeavour to make off. If the van of the enemy tacks, the captured ships must run to leeward of the British fleet. If the enemy wears, the British fleet must place themselves between the enemy and the captured and the disabled British ships ; and should the enemy close, I have no fear as to the result. The second in command will in all possible things direct the movements of his line by keeping them as

compact as the nature of the circumstances will admit. Cap·
tains are to look to their particular line as their rallying-point,
but in case signals cannot be seen or clearly understood, no
captain can do wrong if he places his ship alongside that of an
enemy."

"When," says Nelson, "I came to explain to the commanders of the fleet the *Nelson touch*, it was like an electric
shock. Some shed tears; all approved. It was new, it was
singular, it was simple; and from admirals downwards it was
repeated, 'It must succeed if ever they will allow us to get
at them! You are, my lord, surrounded by friends whom you
inspire with confidence.'"

On the 19th Nelson learned that his hope had been fulfilled, and that the combined fleet had put to sea. He concluded at once that their destination was the Mediterranean
and made all sail for the entrance of the Straits of Gibraltar.
At daylight on Monday, the 21st, they were discovered when
some leagues from Cape Trafalgar, six or seven miles to the
eastward. Nelson was then upon deck, and regarded the
enemy with the victor's prophetic eye. Signal was made to
bear down in two lines according to arrangement, and prepare
for battle, after which he descended to his cabin, and at seven
o'clock wrote down the following prayer :—

"May the great God whom I worship grant to my country,
and for the benefit of Europe in general, a great and glorious
victory! and may no misconduct in any one tarnish it! and
may humanity, after victory, be the predominant feature in the
British fleet! For myself, individually, I commend my life to
Him who made me, and may His blessing light upon my endeavours for serving my country faithfully! To Him I resign
myself and the just cause which is entrusted to me to defend.
Amen! Amen! Amen!"

He wrote also a memorandum recapitulating the public services of Lady Hamilton, and bequeathing her as well as his adopted daughter to the generosity of his country.

It was noticed that on this occasion he showed none of that joyousness of spirit peculiar to him on the eve of a great enter-prise. He was serenely calm ; but evidently a presentiment of coming death guided all his thoughts. Of Captain Blackwood he asked what he should cónsider as a victory. There was no sign of hesitancy or weakness on the part of the enemy, and Blackwood answered, therefore, that the capture of fourteen sail of the line would be a grand result. " I shall not be satisfied with less than twenty," replied Nelson. Soon afterwards, Blackwood, in taking leave of his Admiral to return on board his own frigate, observed that he hoped they should in a few hours meet again. Nelson answered calmly, " My dear Black-wood, I shall never again speak to you." Probably he spoke in this way because he had estimated the inequality of the con-test, and felt that the inequality could be met only by a daring and an intrepidity inspired to an extraordinary degree of fer-vour by his personal example. Hence he determined on an exposure of his life which amounted to chivalrous recklessness. He wore his admiral's uniform, with four stars embroidered on its left side, the emblems of the orders to which he had been admitted. His officers solicited him to put on a plainer dress, as it was known that there were many riflemen amongst the 4,000 troops on board the French ships. But no, what he had won he would not lay aside, and there he stood on the quarter-deck of his stately flag-ship, a mark for the enemy —one whose life was worth a legion of common lives.

In advancing, Lord Nelson, as commander-in-chief, led the weather column in the *Victory*, and Collingwood, as second in command, the lee column in the *Royal Sovereign*. Nelson's last signal was the immortal one, " England expects every man to do his duty "—a signal which, when made known, was hailed by every man with a hearty cheer.*

This signal flew from the mast-head of the *Victory* exactly at twelve o'clock, and the action instantly began by the leading ships of the British columns attempting to break the enemy's compact array, the *Victory* about the tenth ship from the van, the *Royal Sovereign* about the twelfth from the rear. When Collingwood began the attack and forced his passage, Nelson turned round to his officers and exclaimed, "Look at that noble fellow! Observe the style in which he carries his ship into action!"

At four minutes past twelve the *Victory* opened its fire on the enemy's van while ranging along their line, and in almost a quarter of an hour afterwards, finding a gap through which she could pass, she fell on board the eleventh and twelfth ships. She was followed by the *Téméraire*, which also fell on board one of them. Thus these four ships were for a considerable time huddled up into a knotted group, so that the flash of almost every gun fired from the *Victory* set fire to the *Redoubtable*, her more immediate adversary. In this juncture a curious spectacle might be seen; that of numerous British seamen, in the midst of a tremendous fire, coolly pouring buckets of water to extinguish the flames on board their enemy's ship, that both might not be involved in one common destruction.

Nelson would fain have opened the contest by ranging ahead of Admiral Villeneuve's flag-ship, the *Bucentaure*, in order to have placed the *Victory* ahead of her, and astern of his old opponent, the huge *Santissima Trinidada*. The *Bucentaure*, however, shot ahead, and compelled the *Victory* to pass

* It is thus expressed in numbers :—

England expects that every man will do his d—u—t—y.
253   269   533 261 471 250 200 570 4 21 19 24

under her stern, raking it heavily, and to luff-up on the starboard side.   The *Bucentaure* poured four broadsides into the
British flag-ship before Nelson ordered his ports to be opened.
Then, indeed, all his guns, double-shotted, crushed in such a
storm of deadly missiles that the French vessel literally heeled
with the concussion.   But he sought even higher game ; he had
selected for his target the *Trinidada*, and laying the *Victory*
alongside of her, he ordered the ships to be lashed together.
The *mêlée* now grew fast and furious ; the dense clouds of battle
were lighted up incessantly by the flashes of cannon and
musketry, and with the crash of falling masts and yards
mingled the cheers of the British seamen at every fresh
indication of coming victory.   As was his wont when the
conflict deepened, Nelson was light of heart and gay of spirit.
His fin, as he pleasantly termed the stump of his right arm,
moved the shoulder of his sleeve up and down with the utmost
rapidity, a sign that he was greatly pleased.   Captain Hardy,
fearful that Nelson's star-embroidered uniform would point him
out as a special object to the French marksmen, again entreated
him to change his dress or assume a great-coat ; but he simply
observed that he had not yet time to do so.   In the meantime
the enemy's fire continued very heavy and well directed.   Of
110 marines stationed on the poop and quarter-deck, upwaids
of 80 were either killed or wounded.   Mr. Pascoe, the first
lieutenant, was severely wounded while conversing with the
Admiral, and John Scott, his secretary, was shot through the
head while standing by his side.   Captain Adair, of the
marines, almost at the same moment, experienced a similar
fate.   This was about a quarter-past one ; a few minutes later
Captain Hardy observed a marksman on the rigging-top of the
Bucentaure, which there lay on the *Victory's* quarter, taking
deliberate aim at Nelson, and had scarcely time to exclaim,
"Change your position, my lord !   I see a rascal taking aim at

you!" when the fatal bullet struck the hero. Entering over the top of his left shoulder, it penetrated through his lungs, carrying with it a portion of the epaulette, and lodging in the spinal marrow of the back. It is said that the French immediately raised an exultant shout. What is certain is that the marksman was instantly brought down by a well-directed shot from Mr. Pollard, a young midshipman of the *Victory*, who thus became his Admiral's avenger. Nelson was prevented from falling by Captain Hardy, who caught him in his arms, and to whom he said with a smile, "They have done for me at last."

As he was being removed below he covered his face and his stars with a handkerchief that his crew might not recognise him, and observing that the tiller-rope was too slack, requested that Captain Hardy should be told to get it tightened. All the surgeons being busily engaged with the wounded, he insisted, with his usual generosity, on waiting until his turn. A brief examination revealed the fatal character of his wound, and Nelson, remarking the change in the surgeon's countenance, calmly said, "It is, I perceive, mortal!"

The Rev. Dr. Scott, the chaplain, now came to attend him. Nelson, who was racked with physical anguish, gradually lost his collectedness, and uttered incoherent sentences in reference to Lady Hamilton and his adopted daughter. At times he expressed an eager desire for drink, and continually partook of lemonade. Towards the close his mind recovered its serenity, and he sent for Captain Hardy, inquiring how many of the enemy's ships had been captured. On being told that twelve had certainly struck, he exclaimed, "What, only twelve! there should have been at least fifteen or sixteen by my calculation. However," he added after a short pause, "twelve are pretty well." He desired Captain Hardy to bear his affectionate remembrance to Lady Hamilton and his adopted daughter, Horatia; and to inform them that he had left them as a legacy to his King and country, in whose service he willingly yielded up his life. "Will you, my dear Hardy?" he anxiously inquired, and, on receiving an immediate promise, he said, "Kiss me, then." Kneeling, Captain Hardy respectfully pressed his lips to the wan cheek of the dying hero. Nelson then requested that his affectionate regards might be presented to his brave officers and men, and said that he could have wished once more to have beheld his beloved relatives and friends, or even to have remained till he had seen the fleet in safety; but, as neither was possible, he felt resigned, and thanked God for having enabled him to do his duty to his King and country. He had lingered for nearly three hours, when the approach of death became rapid and decided. "Doctor," he said to his chaplain, "I have not been a great sinner, and, thank God, I have done my duty!" Then, as if asking a question and seeking consolation, he repeated with sorrowful pathos, "Doctor, I have not been a great sinner?" And when the Doctor was too deeply affected to reply immediately, "Have I?" he eagerly interrogated. In a final access of pain he cried aloud and impressively, "Thank God, I have done my duty! Thank God, I have done my duty!" These were his last words. Consciousness seemed afterwards to leave him, and he gradually passed away like one who falls slowly into a profound sleep.

Nelson was dead.

In a few words we may indicate the completeness of the victory which was thus solemnly consecrated by the great seaman's blood. Twenty of the French and Spanish men-of-war surrendered; and of those that escaped the destruction of Trafalgar, four were captured on the 6th of November by Sir Richard Strachan. The navies of France and Spain never recovered during the war from this heavy blow, which cast adrift all Napoleon's schemes of an invasion of England, and assured to the British an undisputed maritime as-ccndancy.

"We have lost more than we have gained!" said George III., when the twofold intelligence reached him of the victory of Trafalgar and the death of Nelson. And this was the feeling of the British people, with whom the " hero of the Nile" had always been an idol. They forgot his minor defects of charac-ter, and remembered only that he was a great seaman, the greatest, perhaps, the world had ever produced, the one man who brought to bear upon war at sea a genius as brilliant as that which Marlborough and Wellington displayed in military operations. Lord Malmesbury writes,* " I never saw so little public joy. The illuminations seemed dim, and, as it were, half-clouded by the desire of expressing the mixture of con-tending feelings, every common person in the streets speaking first of their sorrow for him, and then of the victory." The day of the hero's funeral—January 9th, when through streets crowded with saddened and weeping spectators the procession passed on to St. Paul's—was a day of such general and profound grief as England has seldom known. To this feeling one of our minor singers has given expression in verse which emotion raises above his ordinary level :—†

> " To thy country thou cam'st back,
> Thou conqueror, to triumphal Albion cams't
> A corse. I saw before thy hearse pass on
> The comrades of thy perils and renown.
> The frequent tear upon their dauntless breasts
> Fell. I beheld the pomp thick gather'd round
> The trophied car that bore thy grac'd remains
> Through arm'd ranks, and a nation gazing on.
> Bright glow'd the sun, and not a cloud distain'd

---

* *Correspondence of Earl of Malmesbury,* **iv. 319.**
† SOTHEBY, *Saul: an Epic Poem,*

Heaven's arch of gold, but all was gloom beneath.
A holy and unutterable pang
Thrill'd on the soul. Awe and mute anguish fell
On all. Yet high the public bosom throbb'd
With triumph."

It has been well said of Nelson that, in deed as in speech, he was intuitive and impetuous. His genius had a strong strain of originality; it rebelled against tradition and conventionalities; it spurned professional restraints as hotly as it levelled its attacks against the foe. It was a bold, daring, independent genius, which no danger could daunt and no responsibility intimidate. At the fight off Cape St. Vincent, without waiting for orders, Nelson seized the moment of victory, darted out of the line, and swooped down on the enemy like an eagle. At Copenhagen he absolutely ignored Sir Hyde Parker's signal of recall. And he was justified in doing this by his confidence in his power to do great things. All his sayings were in keeping with his fiery, romantic, invincible spirit—the spirit of one of Plutarch's heroes, or rather, perhaps, of one of the Paladins of chivalrous legend. "When in doubt, fight!" he said to young Lord Cochrane, afterwards a naval commander of no ordinary distinction. "Victory or Westminster Abbey!" "Laurel or cypress!" "England expects every man to do his duty!" His hatred of the French was like that of the Crusader of old against the Mahommedan; it was almost a religion. It lent a fierce defiant glow to his patriotism, and responded to the sympathies of a people then engaged in a war for very existence with an aggressive, tyrannical, and Napoleonic France. He had a wonderful power of inspiring affection and confidence; there was not an English sailor who would not have followed blithely wherever Nelson led. His capacity for command was unbounded; his seamanship was great; his tactical skill unequalled. The completeness of his victories ıs the most striking thing about them ; he did something more than *defeat* the enemy's fleet, he *destroyed* it. And because of all he did and all he was, he remains to this day the one naval commander whose name and fame are enshrined in the national heart.

> "Thine island loves thee well, thou famous man,
> The greatest sailor since our world began."*

* TENNYSON. *Ode on the Death of the Duke of Wellington.*

ADMIRAL SIR W. SIDNEY SMITH, G.C.B.

A.D. 1764—1840.

WILLIAM SIDNEY SMITH, born 1764, was the son of Captain
John Smith, at one time gentleman-usher to Queen Charlotte,
and of his wife Mary, the daughter of Mr. Pinkney Wilkinson,
rich London merchant.   At an early age he was sent to Tun-
bridge Grammar School, then under the direction of Dr.
Vicesimus Knox, the essayist, and afterwards to a boarding
school at Bath ; but his regular education must have been of
the scantiest, as he was not twelve years of age when he was
placed in the navy.   His first service was on the American
coast, under Lord Howe.   In November, 1779, he joined the
Sandwich, and, under Rodney's victorious flag, took part in the
victorious action with the Spanish fleet under Don Juan de
Langara. The gallantry he displayed on this occasion obtained
him, at Rodney's hands, his promotion as lieutenant of the
Alcide, though he was then (September, 1780) nearly three years
under the regulation age.   He was in the battle which Rear-
Admiral Graves fought with the French fleet off the mouth of
the Chesapeake ; and he also served in Rodney's crowning
engagement with the French fleet under the Comte de Grasse on
the 12th of April, 1782.   A few days afterwards Lord Rodney
made him commander of the *Fairy* sloop ; and in May, 1783,

he was commissioned as captain to the *Alcmene*, when only nineteen years of age.

While on board the *Alcide* he wrote to his father the following letter, which is animated by the lively spirit and joyous indifference to danger characteristic of his whole career. We give it in a condensed form :—

"DEAR FATHER,

"After having the lower deck ports barred-in these four days on account of bad weather, the water is smooth enough to-day to get the aftermost port (where my cabin is) hauled up. I have hung up all my wet things to-day around one, and am sit down to lay the keel of a letter to you. On the night of the 16th, about two o'clock, a terrible gale of wind came on faster than we could get our sails furled; it carried away our fore and maintop-masts, part of the foretop and foreyard, killed two men, and wounded several others. The next morning we could see nothing of the fleet, the wreck beating alongside; the ship (from her ports and upper decks) making as much water as we can clear her of with four chain-pumps, the wind (as it luckily was) driving us *along* shore; if it had come more to the S.E. we must all have gone *on* shore, and of course inevitably perished. But it is all over now. . . . I have now brought you up to the present hour, and am not sorry that I have done, for she rolls so, that my ink is spilled and my wrist aches.

"Thursday 7th, off Lucia.—Well, after the 20th, as above, nothing remarkable, but one continued *roll* even in the trades. On the 1st of December (now look at your red pocket-book), in company with the *Resolution* and *Triton*, we crossed the Tropic of Cancer, which makes the third time this year—a curious way of travelling. On the 4th we met the *Triton* in chase of a brig, which she took (*we* share), loaded with fish and timber, valuable here. About ten in the forenoon we anchored at Barbadoes, when, lo and behold! we found that in our absence this *fine-weather* country, as I have called it, has been turned topsy-turvey by a hurricane and earthquake, worse than all our American gales put together. Bridgetown is in ruins, and if we inquire for anybody we know they are either buried in the ruins or drowned. What is very remarkable, the *Greyhound*, who sailed with the packet from New York to see her clear of the coast, escaped the American gale, and did not arrive in the West Indies till after the hurricane, so that she had a more pleasant voyage. If she had been here she would probably have shared the fate of the rest of our poor frigates and the *Egmont*. The *Andromeda*, 28 guns, and 200 men, foundered; *Laurel*, 28 guns, and 200 men, foundered; *Beaver's Prize*, 20 guns, and 160 men, foundered; *La Blanche*, 220 men, and 32 guns, foundered; *Cameleon*, 16 guns, and 125 men, foundered; *Endymion*, 60 guns, and 350 men, foundered; *Deal Castle*, Captain Hawkins, 20 guns, and 160 men, foundered; *Egmont*, 74 guns, and 600 men, gone to the bottom. I feel worse now than when I saw the *St. Domingo* blow up. We weighed from Barbadoes to-day, and are running in with St. Lucia, where I suppose *we* shall stay, whatever the fleet may do. . . . .

" Now for your letters. I wish everybody that calls Sir George Rodney's temper and judgment in question had been in the fleet those thirteen days, to windward of Martinique, in chase of the enemy's superior fleet. They often bore down, and would have engaged if they could have taken advantage of a wrong manœuvre. . . . .

" My answer to what you tell me about losing her time with a 60-gun ship is this. The Admiral meant to attack the enemy's centre; their line was superior to ours; when the lines were in this direction——

French.

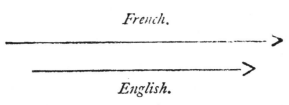

English.

—**he** made the signal for each to bear down to engage his opponent, and as an example bore down to his opposite 60-gun ship, and banged her and another out of the line. Instead of our headmost ship bearing down to his *opposite*, he made sail for the headmost ship in the enemy's line, contrary to the Admiral's signal, intention, and example. All hands bring ship to an anchor. Adieu.

"Sunday, 10th of December, 1780.—We are now all in Grosilet Bay, and, as I have just heard a packet is going to England, I sit down to put a period. In the first place the French are in Port Royal Bay, and if, when we were running down here, we had stood a little further to the northward, we should have seen a French convoy, all of which are now anchored safe in Port Royal. We are refitting here. . . . . This island is strangely altered. Coming in here, we struck upon a bank that never was here before; we were fast about ten minutes. Love to the people."

Sidney Smith remained in the West Indies until the 21st of January, 1784, when he sailed from Barbadoes homeward bound. He arrived at Spithead on the 25th of February.

Taking advantage of the "piping times of peace," he set out on a continental tour, for the purpose, to use his own words, "of further qualifying himself for his country's service." At Caen, in Normandy, he remained about two years, gaining a thorough command of the French language and an intimate acquaintance with French manners. Afterwards he visited Cherbourg, and thence proceeded to Gibraltar and Galicia. His experiences he described in a very graphic and amusing style in letters to various members of his family. Making his way to Stockholm, he conceived a desire to enter the Swedish service, in consequence of a complimentary letter he received from the King of Sweden; but the Admiralty refused him permission. Sidney Smith, however, remained at the Swedish Court, and accompanied the King on his expedition against the Russian Cronstadt fleet in the capacity of a friend and adviser. He seems to have been highly valued in this capacity, and by the force of his character to have made a deep impression on all with whom he came in contact. In June, 1790, he appears, from the " order" issued by the King, to have actually held command in the Swedish service. The King says that he has instructed Colonel Sidney Smith, by word of mouth, concerning the operations undertaken against the Russian coasting fleet in Wiborg harbour; and that his commanders and chiefs of division are therefore commanded to follow all such orders as the said Colonel Sidney Smith issued in his name. These operations were of a dashing kind. With a flotilla of galleys, tourommes (light frigates), and large gunboats, Sidney Smith entered the harbour, and at one o'clock in the morning arrived before a point called Actislapet, where the Russians were erecting a battery.

All was still; the Swedes advanced; suddenly the Russians unmasked their guns and opened fire. They singled out Sidney Smith's yacht as the vessel which evidently carried the commander, and saluted it with a storm of shot. The Swedish gunboats responded to the challenge briskly, and a sudden explosion taking place in the battery, the assailants leaped into the water and dashed in upon the Russians. There was some sharp fighting, and then the battery was won.

In the month of August an armistice was agreed to between the belligerents, which resulted in the conclusion of a treaty of peace; and Sidney Smith's occupation being gone, he returned to England. He was rewarded for his services in the Swedish war with the Royal Swedish Order of the Sword.

His bold and energetic character indicated him as a man for immediate employment, and he was dispatched on a secret mission to Constantinople, with instructions to inquire into the nature of the French intrigues at the Turkish coast, and to examine into the defensive capabilities of the Turkish seas and islands. In December, 1793, he appeared at Toulon, which was then held by an English garrison and fleet against the forces of the French Republic. Its evacuation having been determined upon, Lord Hood, the commander of the English fleet, resolved in the first place to destroy the French ships, powder-ships, arsenal, and storehouses, and for this work Sidney Smith was selected. The suggestion is said to have come from Sidney Smith. On seeing everybody busily engaged in saving himself and his property, he inquired, " What do you mean to do with all those fine ships of the enemy ? Do you mean to leave them behind ? " Some one responded, " What would you propose to do with them ? " The reply came short and sharp, " Burn them to be sure." When this was reported to Lord Hood, he immediately sent for Sir Sidney, and intrusted him with the execution of his design.

Losing not a moment, Sir Sidney proceeded with the *Swallow* tender, three English and three Spanish gunboats, to the arsenal, and made the necessary preparations for his work of destruction. The galley-slaves, to the number of 600, looked on with jealous eyes ; but Sir Sidney's resolute bearing daunted them from actual interference. The Republican troops maintained a cross fire of shot and shell on the spot from Malborquet and the neighbouring hills, which helped to quiet the galley-slaves, and operated in every way favourably for the destroying party, by keeping the Republican portion of the population within their houses. So complete was the steadiness of the small body of seamen under Sir Sidney's command, that their work occasioned little interruption to the labour of preparing and placing combustible matter in the different storehouses and on board the ships. A great multitude of the enemy continued to move down the hill towards the dockyard wall, and as the night closed in they drew near enough to pour in a quick but irregular fire. Sir Sidney kept them at bay by volleys of grape-shot from time to time, and prevented them from advancing to a point whence they might discover the smallness of his force and its inability to repel a close attack.

About eight o'clock the *Vulcan* fire-ship arrived, and was moored across the line of men-of-war. This addition to his strength diminished Sir Sidney's apprehensions of a rising of the galley-slaves, whose cries and tumult ceased as soon as she made her appearance. The only noise he heard among them after-wards was the clash of the hammer knocking off their fetters, and this Sir Sidney was too humane to oppose. It was well they should be able to save themselves from the conflagration that was about to shoot up around them. At a given signal the flames shot up in every quarter. Lieutenant Tapper fired the general magazine, the pitch, tar, tallow, and oil houses, and the lamp magazine. The mast-house was not less merci-lessly given to the flames by Lieutenant Middleton.

The guns of the fire-ship as they heated went off on both sides, baffling the enemy in their intention to advance nearer; their shouts and Republican songs could be distinctly heard, until they, as well as the English, were hushed to silence by the explo-sion of some thousand barrels of powder on board a frigate in the river road, which had been set on fire, instead of being sunk as ordered. The concussion of air, and the showers of burning barrels and spars, threatened the ruin of the whole of Sidney Smith's party. Lieutenant Patey, of the *Terrible*, with his boat's crew, nearly perished ; the boat was blown to pieces, but the men were picked up alive.   Another gunboat, which lay nearer to the frigate, suffered considerably, her officers with three men being killed, and the vessel shaken to pieces.

An attempt was made to reach the ships in the basin before the town, but Sir Sidney was defeated in his efforts to cut the boom by repeated volleys of musketry from the flag-ship and the *Batterie Royale.*

" The rear of our column," says Sir Sidney, " being by this time out of the eastern gate, the horrid cries of the poor in-habitants announced that the villainous part of the community had got the upper hand; boats, full of men, women, and chil-dren, pushed from the shore, even without oars, claiming our protection from the knife of the assassin by the most sacred of all ties, professed friendship. We accordingly kept our station for the purpose of affording them an asylum.   Many straggling Neapolitan soldiers, whose undisciplined conduct had separated them from the main body, were among the number thus driven into the water.   We received them as more particularly belonging to us, repulsing their pursuers by our fire; nor did we quit the shore till we had received all who were there to claim our assistance."

They next proceeded to burn the *Hero* and *Themistocles,* two 74-gun ships, lying in the Inner Road.   Near approach to them had hitherto been impracticable in boats, as the French prisoners left on board the latter still held possession of her, and had shown a determination to resist the English if they attempted to board.   But the flames had spread all around them like an outburst of hell, and the shock of the late tremendous explosion had awakened their fears for their lives; and when Sidney Smith offered, if they submitted, to carry them to a place of safety, they tendered their abso-lute capitulation and gratefully acknowledged his humanity.

T

The unexpected explosion of a second powder-vessel, with a shock even greater than that of the first, placed them again in urgent peril; and when it is considered that they were within the range of the falling timber, we must pronounce it wonderful that no one of the many brands which fell hissing and spluttering in the water around them happened to touch either the boats or their crews.

Having set fire to everything within his reach, exhausted all his combustible preparation, and spent the strength of his men to such a degree that they absolutely dropped on their oars, Sir Sidney directed his course towards the fleet, which he reached without the loss of a single life. Seldom has gallant exploit been more successfully performed.

In the following summer Sir Sidney, whose energy and originality were by this time fully recognised, received his commission as captain of the *Diamond* frigate, in which he was actively employed in sweeping the Channel clear of French privateers and cruisers, and, with a flotilla of frigates, sloops, batteries, fire-vessels, gun-boats, and other small craft, in harassing the French coast with fire and sword. On one occasion Commodore Sir John Warren ordered him to reconnoitre Brest, to ascertain if the French fleet had sailed. This service he performed with his usual dash, daring, and skill. By a succession of ingenious manœuvres he stole past a great line-of-battle ship, and by dawn on the 1st of January gained a position whence he could survey the anchorage of Brest, and assure himself that no men-of-war were lying there. Having acquired this information, he proceeded to make his way out of the entrance channel, taking a direction to repass the line-of-battle ship. A corvette, which was steering out in a parallel course, took alarm at his change of movement, brought-to, made signals energetically, and communicating her alarm to two other ships, both hoisted their topsail-yards immediately and began to get under sail. His situation was now extremely critical. He saw, by the course the line-of-battle ship had adopted, that she intended to cut him off in his passage between her and the rocks, and there seemed no alternative but, by an affectation of innocent unconcern, to dispel their suspicions. He accordingly steered down directly within hail. By this time he could see that she was a disabled vessel, pumping from leaks, with jury topmasts, and that some of her upper-deck ports were without guns. To avoid being questioned in any way that might cause embarrassment, Sir Sidney began to converse in French with the captain, who stood in the stern-gallery. He accounted for his change of course by professing that he had observed his disabled condition, and had come down to see if he could render any assistance. The French-man thanked him, but said he had men enough, which, indeed, Sir Sidney could plainly perceive, as they crowded the gunwale and quarter, looking at the English ship.

From the disabled state of the vessel, Sir Sidney hoped he might retain his position under her stern, so as to rake her repeatedly, and thus begin an action with an advantage which would compensate for his inferiority of strength. His guns were ready pointed, but, with a touch of chivalrous generosity, he reflected that such an action would be useless, as he could not hope to secure the ship and carry her off in the face of the two others, while to fight the three would have been an heroically absurd measure, to which no successful issue could be expected. The utmost he could do would be to pour in a destructive raking fire and sail away. For this his men were ready, you may be sure, and eager as well as ready, but Sir Sidney overruled the proposal. He knew that the carnage would be awful, and it seemed to him that to cause such havoc while speaking in friendly terms and professing assistance would be treacherous and unmanly. His country might have

indirectly derived some trivial benefit from the act, but **it**
would have been obtained at the expense of the national
character.   After a long conversation the two captains parted
with mutual compliments ; and the other ships, observing that
the stranger had been spoken with by the . *Caton*, discon-
tinued the pursuit.

To dwell upon Sir Sidney's various exploits in the kind of
guerrilla warfare he maintained along the French coast would
occupy too much of our space.   They amply illustrated his
extraordinary daring, activity, and wealth of resource.   We
pass on to the event which interrupted his brilliant career for a
couple of years.   A certain French piratical lugger had so
repeatedly evaded the pursuit of the fastest English frigates by
her fine sailing qualities, and had done so much mischief among
our trading ships in the Channel, that Sir Sidney determined to
capture her in the first port in which he could find her.   After
a long search, she was found at anchor under a ten-gun battery.
He accordingly ordered the *Diamond's* boats to be manned and
armed, and, his lieutenant being unable from various causes to
take the command, determined to lead them in person.   He
therefore went on board his Thames wherry, and with his four
boats in two lines, and the wherry in the centre, started at
about two in the morning.   A couple of the boats were ordered
to board the lugger on each side, while the wherry assailed
her by the stern.   The crews were all upon deck at the same
moment, and gained immediate possession of the lugger,
driving the prisoners down the main hatchway, and securing
the hatchways by loading them with guns.   Attended by
an old and true servant, John Phillips, Sir Sidney went
down into the cabin, where he found the four officers of
the lugger just roused from their sleep by the clang and
clamour upon deck.   They were sitting up in their beds, each
loading his pistol.   Sir Sidney at once addressed them, ad-

rising them to surrender, as he was supported by a force sufficient to compel them. Discretion is the better part of valour, and they agreed.

But meanwhile, the cable having been cut, the lugger with a strong flood-tide had been carried up the Seine considerably above Havre ; and when Sir Sidney, having overpowered the crew, began to make preparations for carrying off his prize, he found himself in a critical position. His frigate lay at the mouth of the harbour, becalmed, and could not come to his assistance ; and now, by the increasing light of day, the enemy discovered him from the shore, and immediately sent out four gun-boats, a large lugger, and a number of small craft, all armed, to attack him. The unequal contest was prolonged for two hours ; he was then obliged to yield, much to his digust at so sudden and unexpected a revolution of Fortune's fickle wheel.

The circumstances under which he was made prisoner are thus described in his letter to his father :—

"You, who know me, will not wonder when I tell you that I am in better health than usual from having nothing to fatigue me, and in excellent spirits, finding amusement in the novelty of my situation ; the whole is so like a very interesting play, 'the characters, dresses, and scenery entirely new;' but whether tragedy or comedy, I cannot yet pronounce, as we are only at the third act. The first and second, although 'not without the clash of arms and din of war,' could not be called tragic, while there were so many tragic faces on the stage ; no lives were lost on either side, which is always a good thing in the round reckoning of humanity. I wish I could say there was no bloodshed, but the grape-shot flew too thick for that to be possible. Those you knew most of are not among the wounded

"The end of the second act, when my brave fellows collected

round me on the enemy's closing on us, swearing **to die**
fighting by me, was the most affecting and interesting scene I
ever saw of the many which have passed under my eye; the
servants behaved admirably, and the boys acted like men. In
this disposition were we when the enemy, far superior in
number, prepared to board us, sword in hand, refusing us
quarter with insults and imprecations. Our firm posture
checked them, and my harangue to their chief relented their
fury and turned their resentment into admiration. It was
acknowledged that we could not get away, and that further
resistance would not avail; but we were determined to die
with our arms in our hands if they would not give us quarter;
and this determination saved us. The menacing attitude of our
enemy was instantly changed into that of cordial salutation;
we met shaking hands, and I have since had every reason to
thank the military part of those into whose power we are
fallen for very generous treatment. Separation and confinement is all we have to complain of, but the fortune of
war is imperious, and I learn patience every day by the
practice."

The British Government, on hearing of his capture, immediately proposed to exchange him for a French officer of equal
rank; but the Directory, remembering the destruction he had
wrought at Toulon, and irritated by his recent exploits, refused
to release him. He was therefore removed to Paris, and
imprisoned in the Abbaye, along with his clerk and a Royalist
émigré who had been on board the *Diamond*. For obvious
reasons this gentleman was represented to be Sir Sidney's servant. From the Abbaye the three prisoners were removed to
the Temple, where Sir Sidney gained the good-will and confidence of the governor, and received at his hands very kindly
treatment. When it became evident that the French authorities
were indisposed to liberate him, Sir Sidney, and some Royalist

friends whose acquaintance he had formed, began to concert measures for effecting his escape through the instrumentality of the pretended servant, who was allowed considerable liberty. But for some time no definite plan could be decided upon, and after a year's imprisonment the servant was released, and allowed to return to England.

Sir Sidney remained in confinement—a confinement not undisturbed by alarms and apprehensions. On one occasion he heard his gaoler shouting to him to come down-stairs: " On vous demande en bas." Upon reaching the bottom of the staircase he found him standing with a pistol in each hand. " Monsieur," he cried, " voilà tout ce que je puis vous faire ; c'est pour vous défendre la vie." (This is all I can do for you, sir; it is for you to defend your life.) Sir Sidney asked him what he meant. " Voilà la garde en insurrection," he replied ; and he went on to explain that the prime object of the insurgents would be to release the criminals, and then he, as a state prisoner, would be the first to fall a victim. Said Sir Sidney, " Well, then, I must defend your life as well as mine." And, looking around, he said, " This is an ancient fortress of the Templars. There must be a well within the walls, as also without them ; and we have some bread. Take care not to open the gate, and we can defend ourselves against all attack but that of artillery, and that can come only from a constituted authority, to which we shall be bound to yield."

Advancing to the gate, the insurgents shouted to the gaoler, " Ouvrez la porte."

The gaoler answered gruffly, " Forcez-vous le dehors, je répondrai pour l'intérieur." (Attend you to the outside, and I will answer for the interior.)

A voice was heard to say, " Ah, s'il ouvre je répondrai bien pour lui."

A vigilant watch was maintained until the tumult subsided and order was restored. Sir Sidney's conduct was reported next day by the gaoler to the Directory, and called forth loud expressions of approval.

The man employed to carry fuel and water to the different apartments of the prison would stop to chat about current events and the frequent changes of Government to Sir Sidney. He was wont to say philosophically, "Tenez! ah! ils passeront tous; il n'y a que vous et moi qui restons." (Well, they all pass away; only you and I remain.)

In the spring of 1791 a new proposal was made to Sir Sidney for his escape, which he adopted as "his last resource." It was simply to obtain a forged order for his removal to another prison, and then to arrange for his being privately carried off. The order was accurately imitated, and by means of a bribe the actual stamp of the Minister's signature procured; so that nothing remained but to find men bold enough to put the scheme into execution. These were quickly found in two gentlemen of Royalist proclivities, noted for their high courage. Dressed, the one as an adjutant, and the other as a military officer, they presented themselves at the gate of the prison. The keeper, having perused the order and tested the signature, sent for Sir Sidney, who, when informed of the order of the Directory, professed to be very much concerned. The pretended adjutant, however, gravely informed him that the Government were far from intending to aggravate his misfortune, and that he would not fail to be comfortable at the place whither he was instructed to convey him.

The greffier, who was present, observed that at least six men from the guard must accompany the prisoner. The adjutant, preserving his impassiveness, acquiesced in the justice of the remark, and gave orders that they should be called out. But, in a moment, as if he had been reflecting, he addressed Sir

Sidney, saying, "Commodore, you are an officer; I am an officer also; your parole will be enough. Give me that, and there will be no necessity for an escort." "Sir," replied Sir Sidney, "if that be sufficient, I swear on the faith of an officer to accompany you wherever you choose to conduct me."

The keeper then asked for a discharge. The registrar gave the book, and Mons. B—— boldly signed it with a flourish—*L'Oger, Adjudant-Général.* Meanwhile Sir Sidney kept the turnkeys employed, and loaded them with favours, to prevent them from having time to consider. The registrar, or greffier, and the keeper accompanied them to the second court, and at length the last gate was opened, and the parties separated with a profuse exhibition of ceremony and politeness.*

In a fiacre, driven by one of Sir Sidney's friends, he started from the Temple. At a very short distance the coach ran up against a passer-by, and much confusion ensued, in the midst of which Sir Sidney and his companion, M. Phelypeaux, got out, mingled with the crowd, and afterwards made their way on foot to the house of a member of the Clermont-Tonnerre family, where he spent the night. Early next morning they

---

* "When the day of Sidney's escape was fixed, at eight in the morning the turnkey entered with his hat on, which he had never been in the habit of keeping on his head. He appeared much embarrassed and affected, and said, 'Monsieur, en vous demande en bas.' Sir Sidney Smith was reading his Spanish edition of *Gil Blas*, and, looking up, he said, 'Mais qu'est que c'est donc?' The turnkey said, 'On vous dira cela en bas.' The poor man had a fearful misgiving about the fate of his prisoner, as few of those ordered to be transferred had again been heard of. He asked him where he was to be transferred. The turnkey replied, 'To Fontainebleau;' and then Sir Sidney Smith said, 'Oh, that is not far! You will come and see me there, won't you? and my things, books, &c., you can send after me; there is no occasion to take them with me to-night.' The turnkey promised to go and see him, and to have his things safely conveyed to his new prison." The story of Sir Sidney's imprisonment in the Temple, and of his escape, is given in the *Naval Chronicle.* It was also published separately in pamphlet form.

took their departure. It was arranged that two travellers should arrive at the house from Nanterre, and that the return horses should take Sir Sidney and Phelypeaux the first stage. On turning out of the courtyard the pole of the carriage was broken, and a delay took place by which the two friends profited to get out and go on foot outside the barrier. When the carriage arrived at the barrier it was stopped and examined by the police, who, finding it empty and driven by Nanterre postboys, believed it to be a return carriage, and allowed it to pass on.

Having parted from their two native and disguised friends, Sir Sidney and De Phelypeaux, with Sir Sidney's secretary, proceeded to Rouen. There they were obliged to stay several days for their passports. In company with his friend Captain Wright, Sir Sidney one day had occasion to pass the barrier, where some sentinels were stationed; and the expedient he adopted, if it did not savour of discretion, bore witness to his extraordinary coolness and presence of mind. Neither he nor his friend had a passport, and the difficulty was to pass the sentinels without being examined or questioned. Sir Sidney, who was well accustomed to the usages at the barrier, arranged that Wright should go first, and that if he were stopped by the guard, Sidney should advance and endeavour to impose upon him by a bold assumption of authority. Wright did as he was instructed, and when he was asked for his passport, Sir Sidney advanced, and with an air of dignity, said, "Je réponds pour le citoyen, je le connais." Fully satisfied, the sentinel answered, "C'est bien, citoyen," and the two went their way.

At length all arrangements were completed for crossing the Channel. They quitted Rouen, and in due time drew towards Honfleur. As they obtained a view of Havre and of the mouth of the Seine, the postillion turned round and remarked to

Phelypeaux, " Ah, voilà, citoyen, où nous avons pris l'Amiral Smith," and then, with a significant smile, said, " Mais nous le tenons à présent."

At Honfleur, while, concealed in a fisherman's hut, he waited for the .tide, Sir Sidney heard one of the men exclaim, " Je connais celui-là, c'est l'Amiral Schmit." Sir Sidney was naturally alarmed, and beginning to think he had been betrayed, he kept a rigorous watch on his way to the boat lest he should be seized from behind. He embarked in the fishing craft which had been prepared for him ; still breathless with anxiety, he passed a line of gun-boats at anchor, not knowing but that at any moment he might be forced on board one of them. They hailed, but being answered " *Pêcheur, No. —,*" allowed them to proceed. One of the crew, as they stood out to sea, recognised Sir Sidney, having often been on board the *Diamond*, and liberally entertained with rum and biscuit. " Monsieur l'Amiral," said the honest mariner, " c'est inutile de vous cacher de nous ; nous vous connaissons bien ; nous avons été souvent abord votre frégate le *Diamant*, et vous nous avez toujours bien traité ; vous n'avez souvent donné un verre d'eau de vie et encore des biscuits, et nous avons toujours tenus compte de ces bons offices." (Monsieur Admiral, it is useless to hide yourself from us, we know you well ; we have often been on board your frigate, the *Diamond*, and have always been well treated. You have often given us a glass of brandy and some biscuits, and we have never forgotten those good offices." In a few minutes they came in sight of the *Argo*, and signalling her as best they could, she bore down upon them, took Sir Sidney and his friends on board, and crowded on all sail for Portsmouth.

Sir Sidney was made prisoner on the 18th of April, 1796, and arrived in London on the 8th of May, 1798. Needless to say that he at once became a social " lion," and was caressed

and flattered in every drawing-room.   The romance of his ad‑
venture is much diminished, however, if we accept his biographer's suggestion that the French Governm ent connived at
his escape ; and on any other supposition it seems difficult to
account for their extraordinary apathy.   There was certainly
time to have stopped him before he reached Honfleur ; but they
set no one on his track, issued no offers of reward for his capture, and, indeed, took none of those steps which are usually
taken on the occasion of the flight of an important prisoner.

II.

The British Government lost no time in employing an officer
of such fertility of resource, brilliant courage, and determined
resolution.   Appointed to the command of the 8o-gun ship
Tigre, he was ordered to repair to the Mediterranean and place
himself under the orders of the Earl of St. Vincent.   At the
same time, through some inexplicable blunder, he was named
joint minister plenipotentiary with his brother, Mr. Spencer
Smith.   This latter dignity clashed with his rank and duty as
an officer of the navy, and led to a very angry feeling towards
him on the part of Lord St. Vincent and Lord Nelson, who
resented the exceptional confidence thus placed in a junior
officer, and were not disposed to allow him an independent command.   Lord Spencer, First Lord of the Admiralty, eventually
explained matters in a way satisfactory to the two admirals, and
Nelson thereafter exhibited towards Sir Sidney the utmost good
feeling and good-will.   To Constantinople Sir Sidney proceeded
with all due celerity, and learning there the condition of affairs
in Palestine and Syria, and the ravages committed by Napoleon's
army, he set out with his small squadron for St. Jean d'Acre, to

assist in its defence. The advanced guard of the French arrived
at the port of Mount Carmel in the night of the 17th.   Unaware
of the presence of British ships upon the coast, the troops took
up their ground close to the water's side, and were immediately
mowed down by a fire from the boats of the Admiral's flag-ship,
which put them to the rout and drove them headlong up the
green acclivities of the sacred mountain. The main body, to
avoid attack from the sea, took the Nazareth road, and invested
the town on the east.   The next day Sir Sidney intercepted a
flotilla bound for Joppa with a heavy siege-train on board.
Then, with characteristic activity, he proceeded to stimulate
the Djezzar Pasha, the governor of the town, to carry out the
necessary arrangements for strengthening the fortifications,
landed the cannon which he had captured, and gave the Pasha
as military adviser Colonel Phelypeaux, the companion of his
imprisonment and the faithful assistant of his escape. The
defence was as spirited as the attack, and Sidney Smith was
the life and soul of it. A successful sortie was made on the
7th of April, and four attempts to escalade the walls were suc-
cessively repulsed, the enemy suffering heavily from the flanking fire of Sidney Smith's two men-of-war.   On the 7th a fleet
of corvettes and transports with reinforcements on board for
the hard-pressed garrison led Napoleon to hazard another
attack in the hope of securing the town before they could
disembark.

The French artillery increased the violence of their fire
tenfold, and under cover of it advanced the attacking column.
The shells from the *Tigre* tore great gaps in its solid ranks, but
the Frenchmen went sullenly forward, drove back the garrison
foot by foot, and made good their lodgment in the north-east
tower.

The fire of the besieged now slackened notably in comparison with that of the besiegers, and the flanking fire from

the ships lost much of its effect, the enemy having covered themselves in this lodgment and in its approaches by two traverses across the ditch, which they had built up of sandbags and the bodies of the dead.

The troops brought by the flotilla were in the boats, and about half-way to the shore. This was the most critical point of the contest, and a bold effort was necessary to hold the place until they could arrive. Sir Sidney accordingly directed his boats to disembark at the mole, and then led his men armed with pikes up to the breach. The enthusiasm of the Turks at the sight of this naval and unexpected reinforcement was boundless; many fugitives turned back with them to the breach, which a few brave Turks were lustily defending with no better weapons than heavy stones. Djezzar Pasha, hearing of the bold action of the English tars, quitted his station where, according to ancient Turkish custom, he sat to reward every soldier who brought to him the head of an enemy, hastened to the spot, and, coming behind them, pulled them down with violence, declaring that if any harm befell his English friends all was lost.

This friendly contention who should defend the breach occasioned a rush of Turks to the stirring scene, and thus time was gained for the arrival of the first detachment of Hassan Bey's troops.

Sir Sidney had now to conquer the Pasha's repugnance to the admission of any troops except his own Albanians into the garden of his seraglio, which, as it occupied the *terre-plein* of the rampart, was necessarily an important point of the defence. Sir Sidney promptly overruled his objections, and threw into it a Turkish regiment of a thousand men armed with bayonets and disciplined on the English system. Soon afterwards the gates were thrown open and a sally ventured; but they could not cope at close quarters with

Napoleon's veterans, and were driven back into the town with loss.

A group of generals and aides-de-camp had by this time assembled on the eminence known as Richard Cœur de Lion's Mount. In their centre stood Napoleon vehemently gesticulating. The defenders conjectured that he intended to renew the attack, and his dispatch of an aide-de-camp to the French camp showed that he tarried only for a reinforcement. Sir Sidney immediately directed Hassan Bey's ships to take their station in the shoal water to the southward, and made the *Tigre's* signal to weigh and join the *Theseus* to be northward.

" A little before sunset," we quote Sir Sidney's own narrative, " a massive column appeared advancing to the breach with solemn steps. The Pasha's idea was not to defend the breach this time, but rather to let a certain number of the enemy in, and then close with them, according to the Turkish mode of war. The column thus mounted the breach unmolested, and descended from the rampart into the Pasha's garden, where, in a very few minutes, the bravest and most advanced amongst them lay headless corpses, the sabre, with the addition of a dagger in the other hand, proving more than a match for the bayonet ; the rest retreated precipitately, and the commanding officer, who was seen manfully encouraging his men to mount the breach, was carried off, wounded by a musket-shot. General Raubaad was killed. Much confusion arose in the town from the actual entry of the army, it having been impossible, nay impolitic, to give previous information to anybody of the mode of defence adopted, lest the enemy should come to a knowledge of it by means of their numerous emissaries. •

" The English uniform, which had hitherto served as a rallying point for the old garrison wherever it appeared, was now in the dusk mistaken for French, the newly arrived Turks not distinguishing between one hat and another in the crowd. Thus many a severe blow of a sabre was parried by our officers. Calm was restored by the Pasha's exertions ; and thus the contest of twenty-five hours ended, both parties being so fatigued as to be unable to move.

"Bonaparte will no doubt renew the attack, the breach being perfectly practicable for fifty men abreast ; indeed, the town is not, nor ever has been, defensible according to the rules of art, but according to every other rule it must and shall be defended ; not that it is in itself worth defending, but we feel that it is by this breach Bonaparte means to march to further conquest. 'Tis on the issue of this conflict that depends the opinion of the multitude of spectators on the surrounding hills, who wait only to see how it ends to join the victor ; and with such a reinforcement for the execution of his known projects, Constantinople and even Vienna must feel the shock."

In addition to his extraordinary activity in the direction of the defence, Sir Sidney Smith's energy was equal to the circulation of proclamations among the French troops in order to shake their confidence in their leader. Napoleon replied with "an order of the day" which insinuated that, owing to the heat of the climate and the excitement of war, the British Commodore had become insane, and all communication with him, therefore, was prohibited. It was at one time believed that Sir Sidney sent to Napoleon a challenge to fight a duel. And according to O'Meara, Napoleon, referring to the incident, said, "I laughed at this, and sent him back an intimation that when he brought Marlborough to fight me I would meet him. Notwithstanding, I like the character of the man." Sir Sidney, however, declared that there was not a word of truth in the statement, and that he knew his duty better than to have committed himself and the army he commanded by any such petulant vapouring.

Writing to his brother on the 14th of May, Sir Sidney records that the enemy had been repulsed in eleven different attempts to assault the place. " But they are not," he adds, "in possession of Acre, although they have a lodgment in the north-east angle of the north-east tower, one half of which is theirs, and the other half ours ; while we keep possession of the two new English ravelins which flank the approach to this lodgment, and have raised batteries within the breach, which is wide enough for fifty men abreast, the fire from which completely cleared it the last assault, and increased the number of dead, bodies in the ditch.   Our labour is *excessive*, many of us among whom our anxious, zealous friend, Phelypeaux, have died of fatigue.   I am but half dead, but Bonaparte brings fresh troops to the assault two and three times in the night, while we are obliged to be always under arms.   He has, lost the flower of his army in those desperate attempts to storm."

Critical, indeed, was Napoleon's situation.   He had lost upwards of 4,000 men ; the plague raged in his hospitals ; provisions began to fail.   The courage and resources of a British officer, at the head of a handful of seamen, had baffled the conqueror of Italy, and though he knew all that he was relinquishing he was compelled, on the 20th of May, to own himself beaten and to raise the siege.   " The fate of the East,' he said at St. Helena, " lay in that small town.   Had St. Jean d'Acre fallen I should have changed the face of the world." Having previously removed his sick and wounded, he began his retreat upon Jaffa, and thence rapidly withdrew into Egypt, marking his track by a ghostly line of the dead and dying, and by the smoke of burning towns and villages.

Such is the story of the defence of St. Jean d'Acre, as sus-

tained for sixty days by a young naval officer of no higher
rank than captain, at the head of the seamen and marines of
three British ships-of-war, and a body of Ottomans, brave, but
undisciplined and newly levied. Our naval history scarcely
preserves the record of a more brilliant achievement, or of one in
which many of the highest qualities of a military commander
were more vividly displayed. Courage is not everything ; in
warfare conduct is not less necessary nor less admirable ; and
mere courage could not have saved St. Jean d'Acre. The
work to be done was eminently anxious and difficult, and
could be successfully wrought only with the aid of immense
fertility of resource, unvarying firmness of resolution, great
tenacity of purpose, wonderful power of endurance, unfailing
patience and promptitude, and the faculty of inspiring, encouraging, and commanding men.

His services received the unusual reward of the thanks of
both Houses of Parliament, and were acknowledged in the
Speech from the Throne. Earl Spencer, in moving the thanks
of the Lords, very neatly and forcibly said, " The merit of
all actions depended on the means for effecting them. In no
case were they ever so disproportionate ; the means of Sir Sidney
Smith were very small, while the service performed was of the
greatest magnitude. St. Jean d'Acre, the theatre of this
brilliant scene, was not a regular fortress. The garrison was
dispirited by the renown of the enemy, and unacquainted
with the mode of defence ; and yet, notwithstanding all these
disadvantages, by the energy and intrepidity of that gallant
officer, the French army, which had conquered a great part of
Europe, overrun the east of Africa, and made a considerable
impression on Asia, was arrested in its progress for two
months, and afterwards forced to retreat in a disgraceful
manner."

The Corporation of London and other public bodies seized

the earliest opportunity of formally proclaiming their sense of Sir Sidney's merits.   The Sultan sent him a rich pelisse and an aigrette, together with the diamond chalingk, or plume of triumph ; and, finally, the House of Commons, in response to a message from the Crown, granted him a pension of £1,000 per annum.

Contemporary poetry did not forget to pay the tribute of eulogistic verse to the hero of Acre.   The following is a passage from Heber's prize poem of " Palestine : "—

> " When he from towery Malta's yielding isle,
> And the green waters of reluctant Nile—
> Th' apostate chief—from Misraim's ancient shore
> To Acre's walls his trophial banners bore ;
> When the pale desert mark'd his proud array,
> And desolation hoped an ampler sway ;
> What hero then triumphant Gaul dismayed ?
> What arm repelled the victor renegade ?
> Britannia's champion !—Bathed in hostile blood,
> High on the beach the dauntless seaman stood ·
> Admiring Asia saw the unequal fight,—
> E'en the pale Crescent bless'd the Christian's might.
> Oh, day of death !   Oh, thirst beyond control
> Of crimson conquest in the invader's soul !
> The slain, yet warm, by social footsteps trod,
> O'er the red moat supplied a panting road ;
> O'er the red moat our conquering thunders flew,
> And loftier still the grisly vampire grew ;
> While proudly glow'd above the rescued tower
> The wavy cross that mark'd Britannia's power."

There is a good deal of patriotic enthusiasm in these lines, but very little power of poetic expression, and we apologize to the reader for digging them out of the oblivion into which they long ago fell.

The next duty of Sir Sidney was to make preparations for the disembarkation at or near Alexandria of the army under Sir Ralph Abercrombie, which, in the spring of 1801, the British Government dispatched for the expulsion of the French from Egypt.   The work was accomplished with characteristic energy.

On the 2nd of March the British fleet anchored in the Bay of Aboukir, and on the morning of the 8th the troops landed after a sharp struggle with the French, under Sir Sidney's im- mediate direction. Covered by the fire of a flotilla of gun-boats and small armed vessels, the army advanced towards Alexan- dria. Early on the morning of the 21st they were attacked by the French under General Menou, and a desperate contest ensued, resulting in the complete success of the British. Un- fortunately, Sir Ralph Abercrombie received a wound of which he died on the 20th. Sir Sidney, who had been foremost in the affray, was slightly hurt in the right shoulder by a musket- ball. The battle of Alexandria effectually dispelled the belief that the French soldiers were "invincibles," with whom our British troops could not cope in the open field ; and the army moved forward with alacrity to invest Cairo. The French com- mander finally abandoned the struggle, and signed a capitula- tion by which he agreed to evacuate Egypt. Throughout this successful campaign the energy of Sir Sidney was unconquer- able, but he embroiled himself in a dispute with General Hutchinson, who, on the death of Abercrombie, had succeeded to the command-in-chief, and in September he returned to England. There he met with a reception which amply com- pensated for any mortification he had experienced in his com- munications with superior authorities. From all quarters addresses and congratulations were lavished upon him, and even *his* indomitable spirit could hardly bear up against the pressure of public and private banquets and entertainments. Rochester sent him to Parliament as its member, and the Cor- poration of London bestowed upon him the freedom of the City and a valuable sword. The East India Company gave him its thanks and a gratuity of £3,000 ; the Levant Company its thanks and a gratuity of £1,500 , and the Corporation of Plymouth honoured him in the usual civic fashion.

Early in 1803 he was again summoned into active service. and placed in command of a squadron intended to watch the operations of the enemy along the Dutch and Flemish coasts, where they were believed to be making extensive preparations for the invasion of Great Britain. Hoisting his broad pennant in the *Antelope*, of 50 guns, he took up his station off Flushing, and maintained a close and vigilant watch, though the work was uncongenial to his active and restless disposition, and was but occasionally relieved by dashing attacks upon the enemy's flotilla. His inventive mind found employment in the construction of a vessel or raft for the conveyance of large bodies of troops over shallow parts of the sea, to attack forts, or land them on shores inaccessible to large vessels. He constructed also a couple of gun-boats on a novel pattern, intended for the navigation of shallow waters.

In May, 1804, he went ashore, and on striking his broad pennant was promoted to a colonelcy of the Royal Marines. In November, 1805, he was made a Rear-Admiral of the Blue, and in January, 1806, hoisted his flag on board the *Pompée*, of 84 guns, to join the Mediterranean fleet under Lord Collingwood. Thence he was detached on a special service for which he had been recommended by Lord Nelson: "that a British naval force should be appropriated and employed to act offensively on the coasts of Italy, in such manner as to operate as a powerful diversion in that quarter, and so as to prevent the occurrence of similar events to those which had driven the King of the Two Sicilies from Naples in the former war, or at any rate to secure the island of Sicily to that sovereign."

Arriving at Palermo on the 21st of April, 1806, he found himself in command of a squadron of five men-of-war, the *Pompée*, the *Excellent*, the *Athénienne*, the *Intrepid*, and the *Eagle*. His first operation was the expulsion of the French from the island of Capri. Afterwards he proceeded to

Gaeta to co-operate in its defence against the French, and next
we find him present at the battle of Maida (July 4th), where
General Stewart defeated the French under Regnier. From
point to point he continued to move, always energetic in
devising and carrying out measures for the harassment of the
enemy, until in January, 1807, he was ordered to place himself
under the command of Sir John Duckworth, and his scene of
action was changed from the Straits of Messina to those of the
Dardanelles.

With seven sail of the line and some smaller vessels, Duckworth forced the passage of the Dardanelles in the teeth of
the Turkish batteries. The Turkish fortifications along the
Dardanelles were grievously dilapidated, and when the British
fleet appeared before Constantinople, the Sultan in his intense
alarm was prepared to concede anything demanded of him.
But Sebastiani, the French ambassador, encouraged him to
gain time in the well-known Turkish fashion, by pretended
negotiations, and Duckworth, a man wanting in decision,
resorted first to menace and next to persuasion, but did nothing.
Meanwhile, under the direction of General Sebastiani, the
Turks repaired and strengthened the defences of their shores,
lining them with powerful batteries, which the population
zealously laboured at day and night, and concentrating troops
at every vantage point. Thus the passage of the Dardanelles
came to assume a very different aspect from that which it had
presented when the British entered it; but it was evident that
the longer the fleet stayed before Constantinople the greater
would be the danger of its being shut up within a *cul-de-sac*,
and on the 1st of March it ran the whole course of thirty miles
in the teeth of an incessant and a heavy fire. From the twin
strongholds of Sestos and Abydos, which guard the mouth of
Helle's "stormy water," enormous granite shots, missiles which
no British mariner had ever before seen, were hurled at the

retreating ships, crashing in their decks, snapping their masts, and producing an unusual sense of alarm among their crews.

The only officer who won distinction in this untoward affair was Sidney Smith, who with his division had attacked and overwhelmed and burned a Turkish squadron lying off Point Perquies, consisting of a 64-gun ship, four frigates, three corvettes, one brig, and two gun-boats, and had also carried off a gun-boat and a corvette. Had he been in command of the fleet we may feel assured that the expedition would not have terminated in so inglorious a fiasco. It has justly been said that his name alone would have operated as a charm with the Turks, by whom he was respected and beloved. The moral influence which he possessed over them to an extraordinary degree was here thrown away by the then councils of England, and the greatest fault of all was that of placing the naval power under the direction, as it were, of the diplomatic agent. The fleet ought not to have passed the Dardanelles until diplomatic measures had been brought to an end, and the object should then have been Constantinople, and the action against it that of direct hostility. Things, however, were ordered otherwise, as they too often are in our military and naval expeditions.

In November, 1807, Sir Sidney was appointed to the command of a squadron destined to blockade the mouth of the Tagus. Portugal had been invaded and overrun by the armies of Napoleon; and its ruler, the Prince Regent, resolved to retire from a kingdom which he could no longer retain except as a vassal of France. After some negotiation through Lord Strangford, the British Ambassador, Sir Sidney agreed to escort him to Rio de Janeiro, the capital of the Brazils, which he had chosen as his place of refuge, until the imperial tyranny should be overpast. Accordingly the British fleet sailed from the river Tagus on the 29th of November, having in charge the Portuguese squadron, with the Prince Regent, the whole of the royal family of Braganza, and many of their principal adherents and councillors on board.

" This fleet of eight sail of the line," says Sir Sidney, " four frigates, three brigs, and one schooner, with a crowd of large armed merchant ships, arranged itself under the protection of that of his Majesty's . . . . the scene impressing every be-holder, except the French army on the hills, with the most lively emotions of gratitude to Providence that there yet existed a power in the world able as well as willing to protect the oppressed, inclined to pardon the misguided, and capable by its fostering care to found new empires and alliances from the wreck of the old ones, destroyed by the ephemeral power of the day, on the lasting basis of mutual interests."

Sir Sidney saw the royal squadron safely into the Atlantic, and then detached four of his men-of-war to attend it to Rio de Janeiro, while with the rest of his fleet he returned to his position off the Tagus. There he remained until the beginning of 1808, when he was succeeded by Sir Charles Cotton, and ordered to repair without delay to take the command of the whole naval force on the Brazil coast. He held this appointment until the spring of 1809, but it was not distinguished by any incident worthy of record, further than a disagreeable difference of opinion between himself and the British Ambassador, Lord Strangford, due, we fear, to Sir Sidney's besetting weakness, an ungovernable temper. He was not a man who acted well with colleagues of his own standing ; and while rigorously insisting upon implicit deference and obedience from his inferiors, towards his own superiors he by no means exhibited those admirable qualities. We have often been struck by the points of comparison between Sir Charles Napier and Sir Sidney Smith. Both were men of original mind and great force of character, abundant in resource, tenacious of purpose, with high capacities for command, perfectly fearless, honourable, just, and generous; but both were men who impaired these splendid gifts by a painful infirmity of temper and impatience of control. We have not thought it necessary here to dwell upon the various contentions m which Sir Sidney involved himself. It is very possible that in all he was not in the wrong; it is certain that in some he was not in the right.

Sir Sidney Smith's professional career was terminated on the 1st of July, 1814, when he struck his flag in the *Hibernia*, after having served for a couple of years as second in command of the Mediterranean fleet under Sir Edward Pellew (afterwards Lord Exmouth). His active mind, however, could not be at rest, and he applied himself with great energy to the formation of the " Knights Liberators and Anti-Piratical Society," which was composed of knights of the various European orders and of other dignified personages, and had for its object the abolition of Christian or white slavery in the Barbary States.

When, in 1815, on Napoleon's return from Elba, the Hundred Days' War broke out, Sir Sidney hastened to the scene of action, was present as a non-combatant at the battle of Waterloo, and afterwards laboured with rare zeal and disinterestedness to relieve the wounded, assisting in their removal to Brussels. Here is a characteristic anecdote told in his own characteristic style :—

" Meeting Sir George Berkeley returning from the field, wounded, and thinking his sword a better one to meet my old antagonist *on horseback*, I borrowed it. Things went ill and looked worse at that time in the afternoon of the 18th of June, 1815. I stemmed the torrent of the disabled and *givers-in* the best way I could, was now and then jammed among broken waggons by a *drove* of disarmed Napoleonist janissaries, and finally reached the Duke of Wellington's person, and rode in with him from St. Jean to Waterloo; thus, though I was not allowed to have any of the fun, not to be one too many

(*vulgo*, a fifth wheel in a coach), I had the heartfelt gratification of being the first Englishman, that was not in the battle,
who shook hands with him before he got off his horse, and of
drinking his health at his table—a supper I shall no more
forget than I can the dinner at Neuilly, when Fouché came out
to arrange the quiet entry into Paris *without more bloodshed;*
or the banquet the Duke considerately and kindly gave to the
Knights of the Bath when I received at his hands the second
rank of the order of the Bath." *   This banquet took place on
the 29th of December, 1815, in celebration of the investi-
ture of Sir Sidney as Knight Commander of the Bath.

Our story is nearly told.   It would scarcely interest the
reader if we dwelt on the latter events of Sir Sidney's career,
which, towards its close, was not without a vein of absurd
Quixotism.   Owing to his carelessness in money matters, an
unthrift which took no account of the actual limit of his income,
he was compelled to escape the pressure of his creditors by a
prolonged residence in Paris.   There he become a member of
the " Order of the Temple," of which he was made Regent in
1838, when he was seventy-four years old.   Of the exact
privileges and powers which appertain to that distinguished rank
we confess ourselves ignorant, but it seems to have gratified the
romantic element of Sir Sidney's character.   In the same year
that he obtained this shadowy distinction he received the
better-understood and more real honour of the Grand Cross of
the Bath.   In the early part of 1840 his faculties, both mental
and physical, began perceptibly to decline, and on the 9th of
May he received a stroke of apoplexy, which was followed by
paralysis.   With this fatal cloud overhanging him he lingered
until the 21st, when he passed away peacefully, in the seventy-
sixth year of his age.

* J. BARROW, *Life and Correspondence of Sir Sidney Smith*, ii. 394,
395.

Bishop Luscombe, in preaching his funeral sermon, alluded to the hero's career and character in terms not less accurate than graceful. He spoke of his "long life of glorious and hardy enterprise," through every scene of which he was distinguished not more by deeds of heroism than by mercy and forbearance to the vanquished—generous in victory and intrepid until he obtained it. He referred to the numerous and amiable qualities which in private life had endeared him to all, to the warmth and sincerity of his friendship, his entire freedom from cold and selfish feelings, his even lavish bounty to all who solicited and whom he believed to deserve support and assistance, his ardent zeal in promoting every humane and charitable institution, his honest enthusiasm in any generous undertaking, his singleness of heart, his genius, and his activity. *De mortuis nil nisi bonum ;* and forgetting the defects of his disposition and temperament, we may well accept the eulogism embodied in these words. Sir Sidney Smith was not a great man, but he was a brave and good man ; he cannot be placed in the front rank of naval commanders, but he was a skilful seaman and capable officer ; and England has just cause to be proud of the romantic enterprise **and chi**valrous daring of "**the hero of Acre.**"

VICE-ADMIRAL LORD COLLINGWOOD.

1750—1810.

CUTHBERT COLLINGWOOD came of an ancient and reputable family in Northumberland. He was born on the 26th of September, 1750, and at an early age was sent to a school at Newcastle, where among his comrades were the two Scotts, afterwards so distinguished in the legal profession as Lord Stowell and the Earl of Eldon. He was sent to sea when only eleven years old, under the care of his cousin, Captain, afterwards Admiral, Brathwaite; and in later life used to relate how, when weeping bitterly at his separation from home, the first lieutenant observed and cheered him with kindly words, and how, in the gratitude of his heart, he seized the sympathetic officer's hand, took him to his box, and pressed upon him a large piece of plum-cake, which was one of his chief treasures (A.D. 1761).

Under the tuition of his kinsman he made excellent progress in a knowledge of his profession. He served with him for many years, and afterwards with Admiral Roddam. In 1774 he went to North America with Admiral Graves, who, in the following year, promoted him to a lieutenancy in acknowledgment of his services with a party of seamen at the battle of Bunker's Hill. In 1776 he went to Jamaica in the *Hornet* sloop; and it was there that a previous acquaintance with Nelson, then lieutenant of the *Lowestoffe*, ripened into a firm and lasting friendship. Both the friends were known to the Admiral, Sir Peter Parker, and hence, whenever Nelson got a step in rank, Collingwood succeeded him, first in the *Lowestoffe*, then in the *Badger*, of which ship Collingwood was made commander in 1779, and afterwards in the *Hinchinbroke* frigate, in which both Nelson and Collingwood were made post-captains.

"The *Hinchinbroke*," writes Collingwood, "was, in the spring of 1780, employed on an expedition to the Spanish main, where it was proposed to pass into the South Sea by a navigation of boats along the river San Juan and the lakes Nicaragua and Leon. The plan was formed without a sufficient knowledge of the country, which presented difficulties not to be surmounted by human skill or perseverance. It was dangerous to proceed on the river, from the rapidity of the current and the numerous falls over rocks which interrupted the navigation ; the climate, too, was deadly, and no constitution could resist its effects. At San Juan I joined the *Hinchinbroke*, and succeeded Lord Nelson, who was promoted to a larger ship ; but he had received the infection of the climate before he went from the port, and had a fever, from which he could not recover until he quitted his ship and went to England. My constitution resisted many attacks, and I survived most of my ship's company, having buried in four months 180 of the 200 who composed it."

Collingwood was removed from this painful scene in August, 1780, and in the following December was appointed to the command of the 24-gun frigate *Pelican*.

In August, 1781, the *Pelican* was wrecked in a severe storm on the rocks of the Morant Keys. The next day her crew contrived to reach the shore on rafts made of the small and broken yards ; and on these sandy islets they remained for ten days, with but little food, until a boat could be sent to Jamaica,

and the *Diamond* frigate came to their rescue and carried them
to Kingston.

The *Samson*, a 64-gun ship, was Collingwood's next com·
mand.   At the peace of 1783 she was paid off, and he was
appointed to the *Mediator*, in which he served for nearly three
years on the West Indian station.   Nelson was on the same
station in the *Boreas ;* and the two friends enjoyed abundantly
their opportunities of intercourse.   Collingwood admired
Nelson's genius, fervour, electrical energy ; Nelson appreciated
Collingwood's firmness of purpose and integrity of motive.
Both, moreover, were thorough patriots and skilful seamen.
The two friends were alike, yet with many points of·difference ;
so that there was no imitation of the one by the other, but the
two, taken together, represented or made up a perfect whole
toti teretes que in se ipsis.

Returning to England in 1786, Collingwood enjoyed a
lengthened residence at home, of which he had seen and
known but little since his boyhood.   In 1790 he married
Miss Sarah Blackett, of Newcastle, a lady worthy of all the
affection he bestowed upon her.   She bore to him two
daughters—Sarah in May, 1792, and Mary Patience in 1793.

Of most of our naval heroes we have to gather their views
and judgments of life and men from the anecdotes preserved by their biographers, or the estimates formed by their
friends.   But in Collingwood's case we have the advantage
of his admirable letters, in which the purity and loftiness of
his mind and his high sense of duty are strikingly illustrated.
Here is one which he wrote to a young officer in 1787 :—

" It gives me great pleasure to find by your letter that your
situation is agreeable to you, and I hope it will always be so.
You may depend on it that it is more in your own power than
in any one else's to promote both your comfort and advance·

ment. A strict and unwearied attention to your duty, and a complaisant and respectful behaviour, not only to your superiors, but to everybody, will ensure you their regard; and the reward will surely come, and I hope soon, in the shape of preferment; but if it should not I am sure you have too much good sense to let disappointment sour you. Guard carefully against letting discontent appear in you; it is sorrow to your friends and a triumph to your competitors, and cannot be productive of any good. Conduct yourself so as to deserve the best that can come to you, and the consciousness of your own proper behaviour will keep you in spirits if it should not come. Let it be your ambition to be foremost on all duty. Do not be a nice observer of turns, but for ever present yourself ready for everything, and if your officers are not very inattentive men they will not allow the others to impose more duty on you than they should; but I never knew one who was exact to do no more than his share of duty, who would not neglect that when he could do so without fear of punishment.

" I need not say more to you on the subject of sobriety than to recommend to you the continuance of it as exactly as when you were with me. Every day affords you instances of the evils arising from drunkenness. Were a man as wise as Solomon and as brave as Achilles, he would still be unworthy of trust if he addicted himself to grog. He may make a drudge, but a respectable officer he can never be, for the doubt must always remain that the capacity which God has given him will be abused by intemperance. Young men are generally introduced to this vice by the company they keep; but do you carefully guard against ever submitting yourself to be the companion of low, vulgar, and dissipated men; and hold it as a maxim that you had better be alone than in mean company. Let your companions be such as yourself, or superior, for the worth of a man will always be ruled by that of his company.

You do not find pigeons associate with hawks, or lambs with bears; and it is as unnatural for a good man to be the companion of blackguards.

"Read—let me charge you to read. Study books that treat of your profession and of history. Study Faulkner's Dictionary, and borrow, if you can, books which describe the West Indies, and compare what you find there with your own observations. Thus employed you will always be in good company. Nature has sown in man the seeds of knowledge, but they must be cultivated to produce fruit. Wisdom does not come as instinct, but will be found when diligently sought for; seek her, she will be a friend that will never fail you. . . . . Remember, Lane, before you are five-and-twenty you must establish a character that will serve you all your life."

It will be seen that Collingwood was a master of the graces of literary composition; that he not only thought justly, but could express his thoughts in clear and elegant language. While the military profession has produced a host of writers whose books, apart from their professional value, claim attention on the score of literary merit, the navy has given birth to but few, and among these few Collingwood may deservedly claim a high place. Evidences of culture and intellectual refinement abound in his private correspondence, nor are they wanting, indeed, in his public dispatches.

The outbreak of the great Revolutionary War recalled Collingwood to active service, and in 1793 he was appointed captain of the *Prince*, Rear-Admiral Bowyer's flag-ship. He afterwards followed that gallant commander into the *Barfleur*, and thus came to take part in the action of the 1st of June, distinguishing himself by his cool courage and unflinching resolution. We have already described this famous sea-fight at length in a memoir of Lord Howe; and we shall therefore content ourselves here with transferring Collingwood's personal narrative to our pages.*

After seeing the convoys, he says, down the Channel as far as the Lizard, and detaching Rear-Admiral Montague with six sail of the line for their further protection, they stretched across the Channel to Brest, and sent in two frigates covered by two ships of the line to see what force was there, when they found the French fleet at anchor, and counted twenty-four sail of large ships. Unsettled weather, and the wind hanging to the north-eastward, set them to the southward, so that it was four-teen days before they got off Brest again, and then found that the enemy's fleet was gone. How the Admiral got his intel-ligence Collingwood says he does not know, but he did get a very exact account of their course. The British fleet imme-diately crowded on all sail for 150 leagues to the westward, recovering about fifteen English merchant vessels and some Dutch, and capturing a few French cruisers on the way, all of which were at once burnt, as, in the circumstances, Howe could not spare a man nor embarrass himself with prizes. "In that situation," says Collingwood, " we cruised for a few days, like disappointed people looking for what they could not find, *until the morning of little Sarah's birthday* (the seaman's duties could not stifle the father's feelings!), between eight and nine o'clock, when the French fleet of twenty-five sail of the line was discovered to windward." It was then within about five miles of the main body of the English, but much nearer to Admiral Pasley's advanced squadron — *Bellerophon, Russel, Marlborough, Thunderer* — which about three P.M. exchanged fire with the enemy's rear. The contest increased in severity as they drew nearer, and waxed very hot until nine at night, when the detached ships rejoined the fleet.

* NEWNHAM COLLINGWOOD, *Life of Lord Collingwood,* pp. 19—23.

On the 29th the French were about three miles to windward, but as they showed no disposition to offer battle, Howe
tacked about six in the morning, with the hope that his van
would force their rear into close action; but they could get only
within a long shot. About eight they wore, and forming in a
line parallel to the English, their van kept up a sharp cannonade
for upwards of two hours; when Howe, plainly perceiving that
they could not be brought to close quarters except by a dash,
signalled for the van to tack, and the rest in succession to
follow, whereupon our ships plunged in amongst them "in a
very fine style." Admiral Gardner, who led, suffered a good
deal, but the French rear was cut off effectually.

On the 30th they were seen far to leeward, but the weather
became bad and foggy, so that it was scarcely possible to see a
ship's length; nor did it clear until the afternoon of the 31st,
when they could be observed in the act of forming their line.
Howe bore down towards them, and was engaged in forming
the English line all the evening.

"The night," says Collingwood, "was spent in watching and
preparation for the succeeding day, and many a blessing did I
send forth to my Sarah, lest I should never bless her again.
At dawn we made an approach on the enemy, then drew up,
dressed our ranks, and it was about eight when the Admiral
made the signal for each ship to engage her opponent and
bring her to close action; and then down we went under a
crowd of sail, and in a manner that would have animated the
coldest heart and struck terror into the most intrepid enemy.
The ship we were to engage was two ahead of the French
Admiral, so that we had to go through his fire and that of two
ships next him, and received all their broadsides two or three
times before we fired a gun. It was then near ten o'clock.
I observed to the Admiral that about that time our wives
were going to church, but that I thought the peal we should

ring about the Frenchmen's ears would outdo their parish bells."

Lord Howe began his fire some time before Collingwood's ship did ; but it soon got up to its adversary, and then its men plied their guns with a will. During the whole action they preserved the most complete order, obeying every command with punctuality, coolness, and precision. In ten minutes Admiral Bowyer was wounded, but Collingwood caught him in his arms before he fell ; the first lieutenant was hurt by the same shot, and it looked as if Collingwood were in a fair way of being left on deck alone ; but the lieutenant, after having had his head dressed, refused to stay below. Soon afterwards a cry arose on the forecastle that the Frenchman was sinking, whereupon the men started up, and broke into three hearty cheers.

At about twenty minutes past twelve the fire slackened, and the French fled, leaving seven fine men-of-war in the hands of the victorious English. One of these, however, as already stated, sank before night.

"We left off," writes Collingwood, "in admirable good plight, having sustained less loss than could be expected, considering the fire we had so long on us. We had nine men killed and twenty-two with severe wounds, a few others slightly hurt ; our masts, &c., all in their places, though much wounded. We have not obtained this victory without losses that must long be lamented. Admiral Bowyer and Admiral Pasley have each lost a leg ; Admiral Graves is severely wounded in the arm, and as he is seventy years of age, or nearly, it is hard to say what will be the consequence. Captain Montague was killed, and Captain Strutt, of the *Queen*, lost his leg. Several lieutenants are killed and wounded ; and this altogether has been the severest action that has been fought in our time, or perhaps ever. It did not last very severely much more than two hours, when ten of the enemy's ships were dismasted, and two of ours. They were superior to us in ships, men, and guns, sent out for the express purpose of destroying us. Four of their ships were provided with furnaces for red-hot shot, one of which stuck in the *Royal Sovereign*, but I have not heard that they did any mischief in any part of the fleet by them. We understand their orders were to give us no quarter; and, indeed, they fought as if they expected none."

It was the subject of considerable surprise, and to Collingwood the cause of considerable mortification, that Lord Howe in his dispatch made no mention of his services; nor did he receive until 1797 one of the medals struck in commemoration of the victory. This act of injustice we may suppose to have been undesigned; but to Captain Pakenham, of the *Invincible*, it seemed so grievous that he was wont to say, " If Collingwood has not deserved a medal, neither have I, for we were together the whole day."

From the *Barfleur* Collingwood was removed to the *Excellent*, a ship with which his name will always be associated. It became famous for the admirable discipline of its crew, so that Lord St. Vincent, then commander-in-chief on the Mediterranean station, was accustomed to send on board the most refractory spirits in the fleet, saying, " Send them to Collingwood, and he will bring them to order." It was not, however, by a frequent use of the cat-o'-nine-tails that he maintained his authority; nor did he have recourse to capital punishment except for the gravest crimes; nor was he continually harassing his men by minute interference. It was his firmness, his justice, his humanity, his personal influence, that worked so wonderful an effect. On one occasion a seaman was sent to him from the *Romulus;* he had pointed one of the forecastle guns, shotted to the muzzle, at the quarter-deck, and,

standing by it with lighted match, had declared that he would
fire at the officers unless they promised not to inflict any punishment upon him. On his arrival on board the *Excellent*,
Captain Collingwood took occasion to address him with a
serious brow : " I know your character well, but beware how you
attempt to excite insubordination in this ship, for I have such
confidence in my men, that I am certain I shall hear in an hour
of everything you are doing. If you behave well in future I
will treat you like the rest, nor notice here what happened in
another ship ; but if you endeavour to excite mutiny, mark me
well, I will instantly bend you up in a cask and throw you into
the sea." It should be added that this man became an excellent
sailor, favourably known for his obedience and good conduct.

As Collingwood learned more fully the responsibilities of
command, and obtained a deeper insight into the characters of
men, his abhorrence of the brutalising practice of corporal
punishment grew stronger, so that at last he ceased to have
recourse to it, a fact which may be commended to the consideration of contemporary advocates of flogging. Said Lieutenant Clavell one day to some of the crew who were not
working as he wished, " Would I were the captain for your
sakes !" A person touched him on the shoulders, and, looking
round, he saw it was Collingwood, who had overheard him.
" And if you had been captain, Clavell, what would you
have done ?" " I would have flogged them well, sir." " No
you would not, Clavell ; no, you would not ; I know you
better."

He used to inform the ship's company that he would have
the youngest midshipman obeyed as promptly as himself ; but
he was careful to discourage the midshipmen from constant
"meddling and muddling." When a midshipman made a
complaint he would order the offender for punishment next

day, and in the interval, calling the boy down to him, would say, "In all probability the fault was yours; but whether it was or not I am sure you would be grieved to see a man old enough to be your father disgraced and punished on your account. It will give me a good opinion of your disposition, therefore, if when he is brought out you ask for his pardon." As this recommendation had the force of an order, it was necessarily complied with, and the lad duly interceded for the prisoner. The captain would appear to yield with much difficulty, but at length would remark, "This young gentleman has pleaded so humanely for you, that in the hope you will feel a due gratitude to him for his benevolence I will for this one occasion overlook your offence."

There was much good sense as well as ingenuity shown in the punishments which he substituted for the lash. One of these was watering the grog; another, even more effectual, was the exclusion of an offender from his mess, and his employment in every kind of extra duty, so that at any moment he was liable to be called upon deck for the meanest service, amid the inextinguishable laughter of men and boys. The men were often heard to say that they would prefer three dozen lashes to this punishment. But he knew that prevention was more effectual than punishment, and adopted every possible expedient to occupy and amuse the attention of his men. Moreover, when any of them were sick he visited them daily, and supplied them from his own table; and as soon as they became convalescent the lieutenant of the morning watch took them under his charge, and daily brought them before the Admiral to be examined by him. This thoughtful sympathy secured the affection of the sailors, who considered him and called him their "father;" so that when he changed his ship many of those he left behind him were seen with tears rolling down their rugged, weather-beaten countenances.

Yet Collingwood was not the man to court popularity. He remembered that familiarity breeds contempt, and always maintained that dignity which is consistent with self-respect commands the respect of others. At the same time he never addressed his men in coarse and unbecoming language. "If you do not know a man's name," he would say to his officers, "Call him 'Sailor,' and not 'You sir,' and such other appellations; they are offensive and improper."

Towards his officers his conduct was marked by similar characteristics. He was so thorough a seaman, and his eye was so quick and exact, that in a moment he discovered the existence of any disorder or irregularity in his ship; whereupon he would administer a reproof to the officer in fault couched in perfectly courteous language, but so grave and serious as always to produce a deep impression. He was never tolerant to any breach of discipline. "I have given you, sir, a commission," said Lord St. Vincent to Lieutenant Clavell, "into the *Excellent*, but remember that you are going to a man who will take it away from you to-morrow if you behave ill." His biographer records that he treated his midshipmen with parental care, examining them over a week, and declaring that nothing would give him greater pain than that any young man in his ship should be unable to pass. When they were off duty he did all he could to place his officers at their ease and to promote their welfare.

While yielding to his superiors the deference to which their position entitled them, he insisted that they, in their turn, should treat him with proper respect. On one occasion the *Excellent*, when off Cadiz, was directed to weigh and close with the Admiral's ship: as she was running down the signal was made five or six times for altering the course, first on one side and then on the other, and finally for a lieutenant. Collingwood, who had been observing this in silence, ordered his

boat to be manned, as he would go too. On arriving on
board the flag-ship he desired the lieutenant, when the order
was copied, to bring it to him, and he read it while he was
pacing the quarter-deck with Lord St. Vincent and Sir
Robert Calder. It was neither more nor less than an order for
the *Excellent* to receive on board two bags of onions for the
use of the sick, and on seeing it he exclaimed, "Bless me!
is this the service, my lord?—is this the service, Sir Robert?
Has the *Excellent's* signal been made five or six times for two
bags of onions? Man my boat, sir, and let us go on board
again." And though Lord St. Vincent earnestly pressed him
to stay to dinner, he refused and retired.

We may now venture upon some extracts from his correspondence while the *Excellent* was attached to the Mediterranean fleet, both because they are illustrative of character,
and because they refer very frequently to events of historical
interest and importance.

Writing in January, 1798, he says—

"My wits are ever at work to keep my people employed,
both for health's sake and to keep them from mischief. We
have lately been making musical instruments, and have now a
very good band. Every moonlight night the sailors dance;
and there seems as much mirth and festivity as if we were in
Wapping itself. One night the rats destroyed the bagpipes
we had made by eating up the bellows; but they suffer from
it, for in revenge we have made traps of all constructions, and
declared a war of extermination against them."

In June, 1798:—

"We have not heard from Admiral Nelson since he left us,
but he is in a field for the exercise of his great talents, and I
hope his good fortune will not forsake him on this occasion.
The Admiral has received advice that the armament which
the French have been so long preparing at Toulon and

Marseilles has sailed on an expedition, which is confidently asserted to be to Egypt. It consists of several sail of the line—how many is not known—and a great number of transports, containing many thousand troops, besides entire families, men, women, and children, in short a complete colony, to take possession and people a country at a stroke. It is, I believe, the execution of a plan, which has been long in contemplation in France, for the opening of a trade from India by the Red Sea, and supplying Europe with the produce of the East without that long circuitous voyage round the Cape of Good Hope. Whatever it is, I hope Sir Horatio Nelson will dispose of their army and fleet in a way to be no longer troublesome to Europe."

He writes to Captain Ball, in October, 1798, after Nelson's great victory of the Nile :—

"I cannot express to you how great my joy was when the news arrived of the complete and unparalleled victory which you obtained over the French, or what were my emotions of thankfulness that the life of my worthy and much-respected friend was preserved through such a day of danger to his family and his country. I congratulate you, my dear friend, on your success. Oh, my dear Ball, how I have lamented that I was not one of you ! Clearly a victory has been won, and many are yet to come, but there never has been, nor will perhaps again, one in which the fruits have been so completely gathered, the blow so nobly followed up, and the consequences so fairly brought to account.

"I have been almost broken-hearted all the summer. My ship was in as perfect order for any service as those which were sent ; in zeal I will yield to none ; and my friendship, my love for your admirable Admiral gave me a particular interest in serving with him. I saw them preparing to leave us, and to leave me, with pain ; but our good chief found employment for

me, and to occupy my mind sent me to cruise off St. Luccars
(San Lucar), to intercept—the market boats, the poor cabbage-
carriers. Oh, humiliation ! But for the consciousness that
I did not deserve degradation from any hand, and that my
good estimation would not be depreciated in the minds of
honourable men by the caprice of power, I should have died
with indignation. . . .

" I have heard with great pleasure that your squadron has
presented Sir Horatio Nelson with a swoid; it is the honours
to which he led you reflected back upon himself—the finest
testimony of his merits for having led you to a field in which
you all so nobly displayed your own. The expectation of the
people of England was raised to the highest pitch; the event
has exceeded all expectation." *

In the spring of 1799 Collingwood enjoyed for a few weeks
those sweet domesticities and simple home joys for which he
had so hearty a relish ; but he was soon recalled to active
service. The times were not such that men of his mark could
be suffered to rust in inglorious ease, nor was his the spirit
that could stand aloof when his country needed the brains and
hearts and arms of all her sons. Promoted to the rank of
Rear-Admiral, he hoisted his flag in the *Triumph*, and joined
the Channel fleet. Thence he was dispatched, under Sir
Charles Cotton, to reinforce Admiral Lord Keith, who, in the
Mediterranean, was guarding the shoies of Italy and Sicily,
and watching the armadas which France and Spain had
assembled at Brest. Collingwood was stationed off the harbour
to prevent their escape—a duty which, performed in all
weathers, day after day, week after week, month after month,
oppressed him with its monotony, and by all our seamen
was felt as a heavy burden, though one that for the safety of
their country must needs be borne. "We are wandering

* *Correspondence and Memoir of Lord Collingwood*, pp. 64—74.

before this port," he writes on the 15th of August, 1800, "with no prospect of change for the better. Nothing good can happen to us short of peace. Every officer and man in the fleet is impatient for release from a situation which daily becomes more irksome to all." And again on October 4th:— "This unremitting hard service is a great sacrifice, giving up all that is pleasurable to the soul or soothing to the mind, and engaging in a constant contest with the elements, or with tempers and dispositions as boisterous and untractable."

After a short visit to Plymouth, we find him again engaged in the weary work of blockading in 1801, until released from it by the conclusion of peace between England and France at Amiens. In February, 1802, he returned to England, and immediately repaired to join his family at Morpeth. Here, during the brief interval of repose permitted by Napoleon's ambition, he was occupied in directing the education of his daughters, and in renewing those literary pursuits which he had always found congenial. His reading was extensive, particularly in history ; and he was accustomed to exercise himself in composition by writing abstracts from or abridgments of the books he read, distinguished by their force and conciseness. "I know not," said a distinguished English diplomatist, "where Lord Collingwood got his style, but he writes better than any of us." His severer studies were diversified by the practice of drawing and conversation with his family, and much spare time was given to the cultivation of his garden, which lay on the banks of the beautiful Wansbeck.

In the spring of 1803, when the brief peace or armed truce which had followed the treaty of Amiens was broken up, Collingwood was once more summoned from his home, to which he was never to return. It gives us a vivid idea of the stress and storm to which England was exposed in the latter years of the eighteenth and the earlier years of the nineteenth century, when

we reflect that out of fifty years spent by Collingwood in the
naval profession, about forty-four were spent in active employment! In those critical times, from 1793 to 1810, he was
mainly engaged in tedious and arduous blockades, seldom
visiting a port; and on one occasion he actually kept the sea
for the almost incredible space of twenty-two months without
once dropping anchor. "Since 1798," he writes, "I have
been only one year at home. To my own children I am
scarcely known; but while I have health and strength to serve
my country, I consider that health and strength to be its due;
and if I serve it successfully, as I have ever done faithfully, my
children will not want for friends."

In the early part of May, with his flag flying in the *Venerable*,
Collingwood joined Admiral Cornwallis's squadron off Brest, to
watch the motions of the French fleet, and prevent it, if possible,
from putting to sea. During this anxious time, when Napoleon
was understood to be meditating the invasion of England if he
could get command of the Channel, Collingwood frequently
passed the whole of the night on the quarter-deck. On some
of these occasions, observing the fatigue of his chief officer,
Lieutenant Clavell, he would say, "You have need of rest, so go
to bed, Clavell, and I will watch by myself." Very frequently
they slept together on a gun, from which Collingwood would
frequently rise to sweep the horizon with his night glass, lest
the enemy should steal out in the dark.

Early in 1805 a French fleet sailed from Toulon in the hope
of effecting a junction with the Brest squadron, and Collingwood received immediate orders to sail in pursuit of it.
Arriving off Cape Finisterre on the 27th of May, he took up a
station off Cadiz to prevent the escape of the Spaniards. In
September he was joined by Lord Nelson with the fleet which
had been in search of Villeneuve, and, by that great admiral
being appointed second in command, shifted his flag to the

Royal Sovereign. The battle of Trafalgar followed, under the circumstances already related in our memoir of Lord Nelson, so that here we have to deal only with Collingwood's share in it. On the morning of the day of battle, his valet says that he entered the Admiral's cabin about daylight, and found him already up and dressing. "He asked if I had seen the French fleet, and on my replying that I had not, he told me to look out at them, adding that in a very short time we should see a great deal more of them. I then observed a crowd of ships to leeward, but I could not help looking with still greater interest at the Admiral, who during all this time was shaving himself with a composure that quite astonished me." The Admiral dressed himself with great care, and soon afterwards meeting Lieutenant Clavell, he advised him to pull off his boots. "You had better," he said, "put on silk stockings as I have done, for if one should get a shot in the leg they would be so much more manageable for the surgeon." Then he visited the decks, encouraged the men in doing their duty, and addressing his officers said to them, "Now, gentlemen, let us do something to-day which the world may talk of hereafter."

Lord Nelson signalled for the *Royal Sovereign* to pass through the enemy's line at the twelfth ship from the rear; but Collingwood perceiving that she was only a two-decker, while the tenth was a first-rate carrying the Spanish Admiral Alava's flag, so far deviated from the Commander-in-Chief's order as to select the latter for his antagonist. While they were running down to engage the enemy the well-known signal was hoisted on Nelson's ship, "England expects every man to do his duty." On Collingwood's first observing it he expressed a wish that Nelson would make no more signals, for they all understood what they were to do; but when its purport was made known to him he was surprised and delighted, and immediately repeated it to his officers and crew.

Soon afterwards it was seen that all sail was being crowded on the *Victory* to give her the lead; whereupon Lieutenant Clavell, in a spirit of noble emulation, begged permission to set the *Royal Sovereign's* studding-sails. "The ships of our line," replied the Admiral, "are not yet sufficiently up for us to do so now, but you may be getting ready." Accordingly the studding-sails and royal halliards were manned, and in about ten minutes the Admiral, catching Lieutenant Clavell's expectant look, bent his head, and almost immediately a mass of canvas hung from every yard and spar of the *Royal Sovereign*, which forged ahead with rapidity, while the men lay down on the decks, and in silence waited for the beginning of the struggle. At this time the *Fougueux*, the ship astern of the *Santa Anna*, had closed up in order to obstruct the passage of the English flag-ship, but Collingwood immediately ordered his captain to steer for the Frenchman and carry away his bowsprit. To avoid this manœuvre the *Fougueux* backed her maintopsail and suffered the *Royal Sovereign* to pass, at the same time opening fire. The Admiral then caused a gun to be fired at her occasionally so as to cover his ship with smoke, and baffle her aim.

The *Royal Sovereign* was now about a mile ahead of the nearest English ship, and as she stood out conspicuous on the sunlit surface of the waters, Nelson, watching her from the *Victory's* quarter-deck, remarked to his captain, "See how that noble fellow, Collingwood, takes his ship into action. How I envy him!" As if possessed by a simultaneous feeling of sympathy, Collingwood himself at this moment exclaimed, "What would Nelson give to be here!" Such is the intimate fellowship that exists between two spirits of equal bravery and loftiness! On the other hand, Villeneuve, the commander-in-chief of the allied French and Spanish fleets, observing with what fervour and daring the leading ships of the English squadrons advanced to battle, felt that they would snatch the victory from him. As she swept past the *Santa Anna*, Collingwood's ship delivered a crashing broadside and a half right into her stern, tearing it down as if it had been made of paper, and killing and wounding 400 of her men ; then with helm hard-a-starboard she ranged up alongside so closely that the lower yards of the two vessels were locked together. The Spanish Admiral, divining Collingwood's intention of engaging to leeward, had collected all his strength on the starboard, and such was the weight of the *Santa Anna's* metal, that her first broadside made the *Royal Sovereign* heel two streaks out of water. Her studding-sails and halliards were torn to rags, and as a top-gallant studding-sail hung over the gangway ham cks, the Admiral called to Lieutenant Clavell to help him take it in, observing with characteristic economy that they should want it again some other day. And so they rolled it up carefully, and stowed it away in a boat.*

Fifty minutes had passed, and no other English ship had as yet taken part in the action, when Collingwood's captain came up to him, and, grasping his hand, exclaimed, " I congratulate you, sir ; she is slackening her fire and must soon strike." It was, in truth, the hope and belief of the *Royal Sovereign's* heroic crew that theirs would be the honour of capturing the Spanish Admiral, in the midst of a fleet of thirty-three men-of-war, before another English ship came up; but though suffering grievously from the *Royal Sovereign's* continuous fire, and not able to do more than return a gun at intervals, the *Santa Anna* maintained the desperate conflict, relying doubt-lessly on the assistance of her numerous consorts, which crowded round the English flag-ship like hounds around an ensnared lion. The *Fougueux* took up a position on her lee-quarter ; another French two-decker lay across her bow, as

* *Correspondence and Memoir of Lord Collingwood*, pp. 126, 127.

well as two Spanish ships; in this, however, there was a decided advantage, for they could not fire without injuring each other.

Descending from the poop to the quarter deck, Collingwood visited his men, urging them not to waste a single shot, watching to see that the guns were properly pointed, encouraging and commending the sailors, particularly a black man, who was afterwards killed, but who, while his Admiral stood beside him, fired ten times directly into the *Santa Anna's* porthole. The *Fougueux* at one time lay so close upon the quarter of the *Royal Sovereign* that she almost touched, but the English quarter-deck carronades were brought to bear on her forecastle with such effect that she gladly dropped a little astern, maintaining from that position a raking and destructive fire until the *Tonnant* came up and drove her away.

At half-past two o'clock, about the time when Collingwood received information of Nelson's mortal wound, the *Santa Anna* struck, but the *Royal Sovereign* had been so crippled in her masts and spars by the enemy's ships that had crowded round her as to be unable to alter her position. Collingwood therefore summoned the *Euryalus* frigate to take her in tow and make his signals. He sent Captain Blackwood to remove the Spanish Admiral on board the *Euryalus*, but as Alava was supposed to be dying from his wounds he returned with the Spanish captain. That officer had already visited the *Royal Sovereign* to surrender his sword, and on reaching her deck had asked one of the English sailors the name of the ship. When told it was the *Royal Sovereign* he replied in broken English, patting one of the guns with his hand, " I think she should be called the ' Royal Devil.' "

On the death of Nelson Lord Collingwood assumed the command, and proceeded to gather up the fruits of victory. Twenty French and Spanish ships had struck, and as of those that escaped four were afterwards captured by Sir Richard Strachan, it may be said that the allied fleet was almost destroyed. Certain it is that no more complete victory was ever won at sea, and that from a blow so crushing the French and Spanish navies never recovered during the war. Even to this day its moral effect is still felt, and no one can doubt that the prestige which surrounds the British navy dates from Trafalgar.

The morning after the victory a strong southerly wind arose, and Collingwood employed the officers and men of such ships as were manageable in getting hold of thirteen or fourteen of the prizes, and towing them to the westward. On the 23rd the fury of the gale increased, and the sea ran so high that many of them broke the tow-rope and drifted far to leeward before they could be recovered, and some of them, in the dark and boisterous night, drove ashore and were sunk. The general result is thus stated by Collingwood himself :—

"Twenty sail of the line surrendered to us, out of which three, in the furious gale we had afterwards, being driven to the entrance of the harbour of Cadiz, received assistance and got in. These were the *Santa Anna*, the *Algesiras*, and *Neptune* (the last since sunk and lost); the *Santa Anna's* side was battered in. The three we have sent to Gibraltar are the *San Ildejonso, San Juan Nepomuceno,* and *Swiftsure;* fourteen others we have burnt, sunk, and run on shore, but the *Balavea* I have yet hope of saving; she is gone to Gibraltar. Those ships which effected their escape into Cadiz are quite wrecks; some have lost their masts since they got in, and have not a spar or a store to refit them. We took four admirals—Villeneuve, the commander-in-chief; Vice-Admiral D'Alava; Rear-Admiral Cisneros, Spanish; and the French Admiral Magon, who was killed—besides a great number of brigadiers (commanders). D'Alava [dangerously], wounded, was driven into Cadiz in the *Santa Anna;* Gruvoria, who was not taken, has lost his arm. Of men, their loss is many thousands, for I reckon in the captured ships we took 20,000 prisoners, including the troops. This," adds Collingwood, in language which all England has adopted, " this was a victory to be proud of !"

For his share in it Collingwood was deservedly raised to the peerage by the title of Baron Collingwood of Caldburne and Hethpoole, in the county of Northumberland. He received the thanks of both Houses of Parliament, and the thanks and freedom of the principal cities and towns of Great Britain. A pension was granted by Parliament of £2,000 per annum for his own life, and in the event of his death of £1,000 per annum to Lady Collingwood, and of £500 per annum to each of his two daughters.

Here it may be noted that Collingwood was never a popular hero in the same manner as Nelson or St. Vincent, Rodney, Duncan, or Howe. His name was not familiar to the lips of the public of his own day; and to the present generation—we speak of course of the masses—if it be known at all, it is not as one of the finest seamen and most capable officers of his age, but as Nelson's second at Trafalgar. Fortune was not kind to him. He never commanded a fleet in battle, he never captured an enemy's ship in single combat, he led no dashing boat attack, made no interesting or important capture ; and it is of such conspicuous services as these that the multitude take account. His able career as captain, commodore, and second in command, his merits as an enlightened disciplinarian and practical seaman, his vigilant discharge of the laborious duty which devolves on the chief of a blockading squadron, would necessarily pass unnoticed by the crowd, whose attention is caught only by work of a more exciting and romantic character. Fortune, we repeat, was not kind to

Collingwood. He never had independent command of a fleet until after the victory of Trafalgar, which swept the enemy's navies from the sea, and left him no chance of winning the glory that is always to be acquired by successful battle.

The admirable qualities of Collingwood's character come out very forcibly in the following letter, which he addressed to his wife a few weeks after the great victory, while he was enjoying the fulness of triumph, and receiving from all quarters a tribute of applause and congratulation ; while, too, he was in anxious discharge of the multifarious duties of the admiral of a large fleet in time of war :—*

" All this," he writes, " is very pleasing; but alas ! my love, until we have peace I shall never be happy ; and yet how we are to make it out in peace I know not, with high rank and no fortune. At all events, we can do as we did before. It is true I have the chief command, but there are neither French nor Spaniards on the sea, and our cruisers find nothing but neutrals, who carry on all the trade of the enemy. Our prizes, you see, are lost ; but was there ever so complete a break-up of an enemy's fleet ? If we have not saved them to ourselves, we have at least put them out of the power of doing further mischief. Villeneuve's ship had a great deal of money in her, but it all went to the bottom. I am afraid the fees for this patent [of his peerage] will be large, and pinch me ; but never mind ; let others solicit pensions, I am an Englishman, and will never ask for money as a favour. How do my darlings go on ? I wish you would make them write to me by turns, and give me the whole history of their proceedings. Oh ! how I shall rejoice, when I come home, to find them as much improved in knowledge as I have advanced them in station in the world ; but take care they do not give themselves foolish airs. Their excellence should be in knowledge, in virtue, and

* *Correspondence and Memoir of Lord Collingwood*, pp. 160—168.

benevolence to all; but most **to** those who **are** humble and require their aid. This is true nobility, and is now become an incumbent duty on them.

" I am out of all patience with Bounce. The consequential airs he gives himself since he became a right honourable dog are insufferable. He thinks it beneath his dignity to play with commoner dogs, and truly thinks that he does them grace when he condescends to lift up his leg against them. This, I think, is carrying the insolence of rank to the extreme; but he is a dog that does it.

"**25**th December.—This **is** Christmas day; **a** merry and cheerful one, I hope, to all my darlings. May God bless us, and grant that we may pass the next together. Everybody is very good to me; but his Majesty's letters are my pride; it is there I feel the object of my life attained."

Lord Collingwood now entered upon a new sphere of activity, the maintenance of the political relations between England and the powers whose territories border on the Mediterranean. From the rest of Europe England was at this time virtually excluded by the Napoleonic system, which had bound together in temporary alliance France, Prussia, Austria, Russia, and Sweden. It was all the more needful, therefore, that she should keep up a friendly intercourse with Naples and Sicily, and prevent their absorption in the French Empire. Collingwood's duties were necessarily of a very delicate character, but he discharged them with great tact and judgment, and his dispatches to the Queen of Naples, the Emperor of Morocco, the Bey of Tunis, and other princes and authorities, are marked by political sagacity as well as elegance of diction. It is interesting to observe that in the midst of these anxious employments his heart was constantly travelling homewards, and his mind busying itself with the education of his daughters or the improvement of his little estate. We see how conscientious he

was, how serious and sensible, how thorough an Englishman of
the best type ; but we see also why he never became a popular
hero—from the lack of a dramatic element in his character, of the
dash and fervour which always arrest and command the popular
imagination. To continue our extracts from his letters will, we
think, be more interesting to the reader than a detailed account
of negotiations and political transactions which are of little importance except in their connection with the history of the
time.

In June, 1806, he writes—

" How do the dear girls go on ? I would have them taught
geometry, which is of all sciences in the world the most entertaining ; it expands the world more to the knowledge of all
things in nature, and better teaches to distinguish between
truths and such things as have the appearance of being truths,
yet are not, than any other. Their education and the proper
cultivation of the sense which God has given them are the
objects in which my happiness most depends. To inspire them
with a love of everything that is honourable and virtuous,
though in rags, and with contempt for vanity in embroidery, is
the way to make them the darlings of my heart. They should
not only read, but it requires a careful selection of books, nor
should they ever have access to two at the same time ; but
when a subject is begun it should be finished before anything
else is undertaken. How would it enlarge their minds if they
would acquire a sufficient knowledge of mathematics and as-
tronomy to give them an idea of the beauty and wonders of the
creation ! I am persuaded that the generality of people, and
particularly fine ladies, only adore God because they are told
it is proper and the fashion to go to church ; but I would have
my girls gain real knowledge of the works of the creation, that
they may have a fixed idea of the nature of that Being who
could be the author of such a world. Whenever they have that

nothing on this side the moon will give them much uneasiness of mind. I do not want that they should be Stoics, or want the common feelings for the sufferings that flesh is heir to, but they would then have a source of consolation for the worst that could happen.

"Tell me how do the trees which I planted thrive? Is there shade under the three oaks for a comfortable summer seat? Do the poplars grow at the walk, and does the wall of the terrace stand firm?"

To Mr. Blackett, his brother-in-law, he writes on New Year's Day, 1807 :—

"I cannot begin this new year so much to my satisfaction as by offering my congratulations to you on your birthday, and my best wishes that you may enjoy health to see many happy returns of it. I hope you are with my beloved family enjoying yourselves in great comfort, and long may you live uninvaded by the sounds of war. What a blessed day it will be to me when we shall all meet together to celebrate the new year, to talk of the privations we have suffered in times past, and have only to look forward to blessings for the future. I have lived now so long in a ship, always engaged in serious employments, that I shall be unfit for anything but the quiet society of my family; it is to them that I look for happiness if ever I am relieved from this anxious and boisterous life, and in them I hope for everything. Tell the children that Bounce is very well and very fat, and yet he seems not to be content, and sighs so piteously these long evenings that I am obliged to sing him to sleep, and have sent them the song :—

> " Sigh no more, Bouncey, sigh no more,
>   Dogs were deceivers never ;
> Though ne'er you put one foot on shore,
>   True to your master ever.
> Then sigh not so, but let us go,
>   Where dinner's daily ready,

> Converting all the sounds of woe
> To heigh phiddy diddy."

On the 26th of December, in the same year, he addressed a letter to his " dearest children : "—

" A few days ago I received your joint letter, and it gave me much pleasure to hear that you were well, and I hope improving in your education.   It is exactly at your age that much pains should be taken, for whatever knowledge you acquire now will last you all your lives.   The impression which is made on young minds is so strong that it never wears out ; whereas, everybody knows how difficult it is to make an old snuff-taking lady comprehend anything beyond Pam or Spadilee.   Such persons hang very heavy on society; but you, my darlings, I hope, will qualify yourselves to adorn it, to be respected for your good sense, and admired for your gentle manners. Remember that gentle manners are the first grace which a lady can possess.   Whether she differs in her opinions from others, or be of the same sentiment, her expressions should be equally mild.   A positive contradiction is vulgar and ill-bred; but I shall never suspect you of being uncivil to any person. . . . .

" Your application must be to useful knowledge.   Sarah, I hope, applies to geometry, and Mary makes good progress in arithmetic.   Independently of their use in every situation in life, they are sciences so curious in their nature, and so many things that cannot be comprehended without them are made easy, that if it were only to gratify a curiosity which all women have, and to be let into secrets that cannot be learned without that knowledge, it would be a sufficient inducement to acquire them.   Then do, my sweet girls, study to be wise."

He writes to them again in July, 1808 :—

" It is at this period of your lives that you must lay the foundation of all knowledge, and of those manners and modes of

thinking that distinguish gentlewomen from the Miss Nothings.
A good woman has great and important duties to do in the
world, and will always be in danger of doing them ill and without
credit to herself unless she have acquired knowledge. I have
only to recommend to you not to pass too much of your time
in trifling pursuits, or in reading books merely of amusement,
which afford you no information nor anything that you can
reflect upon afterwards, and feel that you have acquired what
you did not know before.

" Never do anything that can denote an angry mind ; for
although everybody is born with a certain degree of passion,
and from untoward circumstances will sometimes feel its
operation, and be what they call ' out of humour,' yet a
sensible man or woman will not allow it to be discovered.
Check and restrain it ; never make any determination until you
find it has entirely subsided ; and always avoid saying anything
that you may afterwards wish unsaid. . . . .

" Do you study geometry? which I beg you will consider as
quite a necessary branch of knowledge. It contains much
that is useful and a great deal that is entertaining, which you
will daily discover as you grow older. Whenever I come home
we will never part again while we live."

One more extract, and we have done. It is from a letter
written on board his flag-ship, the *Ville de Paris*, when off
Minorca, on the 17th of April, 1809.

" The education of a lady, and indeed of a gentleman too,
may be divided into three parts, all of great importance to
their happiness, but in different degrees. The first part is the
cultivation of the mind, that they may have a knowledge of
right and wrong, and acquire a habit of doing acts of virtue and
honour. By reading history you will perceive the high estimation in which the memories of good and virtuous people are
held ; the contempt and disgust which are affixed to the base,

whatever may have been their rank in life. The second part of education is to acquire a competent knowledge how to manage your affairs, whatever they may happen to be ; to know how to direct the economy of your home, and to keep correct accounts of everything which concerns you. Whoever cannot do this must be dependent on somebody else, and those who are dependent on another cannot be perfectly at their ease. I hope you are both very skilful in arithmetic, which, independently of its great use to everybody in every condition of life, is one of the most curious and entertaining sciences that can be conceived. The characters which are used, the 1, 2, 3, are of Arabic origin; and that by the help of them, by adding them, by subtracting or dividing them, we should come at last to results so far beyond the comprehension of the humar mind without them is so wonderful, that I am persuaded that if they were of no real use they would be exercised for mere entertainment; and it would be a fashion for accomplished people, instead of cakes and cards at their routs, to take coffee and a difficult question in the rule of three or extracting the square root. The third part is, perhaps, not less in value than the others. It is how to practise those manners and that address which will recommend you to the respect of strangers. Boldness and forwardness are exceedingly disgusting, and such people are generally more disliked the more they are known ; but, at the same time, shyness and bashfulness, and the shrinking from conversation with those with whom you ought to associate, are repulsive and unbecoming.

"There are many hours in every person's life which are not spent in anything important, but it is necessary they should not be passed idly. Those little accomplishments, as music and dancing, are intended to fill up the hours of leisure, which would otherwise be heavy on you. Nothing wearies me more than to see a young lady at home sitting with her arms across or twirling her thumbs for want of something to do. Poor thing! I always pity her, for I am sure her head is empty, and that she has not the sense even to devise the means of pleasing herself."

'Tis a strange picture this; the commander-in-chief of a great fleet, watching the movements of a powerful enemy, calmly sitting down in the cabin of his flag-ship to embody in clear and ordinary language the most sensible reflections on the education and home duties of his daughters, and supply them with sound, practical advice on their daily conduct in life. The homeliness of tone in these letters impresses me greatly. And I cannot but think that the writer did not fall into his right career; that, brave man as he was, and able seaman, and good officer, Fortune had never intended him for the part which circumstances forced him to play. However this may be, the literary merit of his correspondence is indisputable, and the light it throws on a strong, true, manly character endows it with a peculiar interest.

We have already dwelt upon the contrast between Collingwood, with his calm, equable temperament and sober intellect, and Nelson, with his impulsive nature and quick, audacious genius. Mr. Myers has recently found in Wordsworth's "Happy Warrior" the portrait of Nelson; but surely all the lineaments do not fit that hero. Some of them seem rather to convey the likeness of Collingwood, with his well-balanced nature; and the whole has about it an aspect of tranquillity and seemliness which we cannot understand as belonging to the ardent and forceful hero of the Nile and Trafalgar. The following lines, for example, find many an illustration in Collingwood's letters :—

> " He who, though thus endued as with a sense
> And faculty for storm and turbulence,
> Is yet a soul whose master-bias leans
> To home-felt pleasures and to gentle scenes;

> Sweet images ! which, wheresoe'er he be,
> Are at his heart, and such fidelity
> It is his darling passion to approve ;
> More brave for this, that he hath much to love."

And the brief sketch we have given of Collingwood's career prepares the reader, we think, to acknowledge in the subjoined passage a just and appropriate panegyric which we may without violence apply to him :—

> " Who, if he rise to station of command,
> Rises by open means, and there will stand
> On honourable terms, or else retire,
> And in himself possess his own desire ;
> Who comprehends his trust, and to the same
> Keeps faithful with a singleness of aim ;
> And therefore does not stop, nor lie in wait
> For wealth, or honours, or for worldly state ; . . . .
> Whose powers shed round him in the common strife,
> Or mild concerns of ordinary life,
> A constant influence, a peculiar grace . . . .
> Who, whether praise of him must walk the earth
> For ever, and to noble deeds give birth,
> Or he must fall, to sleep without his fame,
> And leave a dead unprofitable name—
> Finds comfort in himself and in his cause :
> And, while the mortal mist is gathering, draws
> His breath in confidence of Heaven's applause :
> This is the Happy Warrior ; this is He
> That every Man in arms should wish to be."

Towards the end of 1808 we meet with frequent allusions in his letters to his serious bodily infirmities. As he became conscious of enfeebled health and failing energy, he solicited the Admiralty to accept the resignation of his laborious post, but was constantly urged to retain it on the ground that no competent successor was available. He might well wish for repose. For nearly five years he had been constantly at sea, succouring and supporting feeble allies, watching the movements or counteracting the projects of formidable enemies, and keeping his fleet in a condition of most absolute readiness. To this prolonged labour was due the disease from which he suffered—an aggravated form of dyspepsia, which gradually induced emaciation and feebleness. But his mental energy did not give way; and in the summer of 1809, the fleet, under his direction, carried on a series of brilliant operations in the Adriatic and on the coast of Italy. "All our frigate captains are great generals," he writes, "and some in the brigs are good briga-diers. They have taken seven forts, garrisons, or castles within the two last months; and scaling towers at midnight and storming redoubts at mid-day are become familiar occur-rences. The enemy cannot stand a galling fire from the launch's carronade, or a sharp fire of grape and musketry from the jolly-boat."

When at Port Mahon, on the 25th of February, 1810, he suffered greatly, and his medical advisers urging him to try gentle exercise on horseback, he went on shore for that pur-pose. But it was too late; he could no longer bear the slightest fatigue. Apprised that his return to England was his only chance for life, he surrendered his command on the 3rd of March to Rear-Admiral Martin. On the 6th he sailed for England; but so rapid at last was the progress of his malady that at six o'clock on the following evening he passed away without a struggle.

"Those who were about his lordship's person," says the surgeon who attended him,* "and witnessed the composure and resignation with which he met his fate, will long remember the scene with wonder and admiration. In no part of his lord-ship's brilliant life did his character appear with greater lustre than when he was approaching his end. It was dignified in the extreme. If it be on the bed of sickness and at the approach of death—when ambition, the love of glory, and the

* *Correspondence and Memoir of Lord Collingwood*, pp. 563, 564.

interests of the world are over—that the true character is to be discovered, surely never did any man's appear to greater advantage than did that of my Lord Collingwood. For my own part I did not believe it possible that any one on such an occasion could have behaved so nobly. Cruelly harassed by a most afflicting disease, obtaining no relief from the means employed, and perceiving his death to be inevitable, he suffered no sigh of regret to escape, no murmuring at his past life, no apprehension of the future. He met death as became him, with a composure and fortitude which have seldom been equalled, and never surpassed."

· Lord Collingwood, at the time of his death, had attained the age of fifty-nine years and six months. His body was conveyed to England, and interred in St. Paul's Cathedral by the side of his friend and chief, Lord Nelson. A cenotaph was raised to his memory in his native town of Newcastle, which rightly speaks of him as "a pious, just, and exemplary man."

OLIVER HAZARD PERRY.

A.D. 1786—1820.

THE temples reared to their deities by the pious inhabitants of Greece and Rome, and even *the* temple erected and devoted to Jehovah by Solomon, have been razed to their foundations ; but the memories of their patriotic warriors still live in the minds, not only of their countrymen, but of all civilized men. The martial deeds of Leonidas and Alexander, of Cincinnatus and Scipio, of the Maccabees and their like, have outlasted the granite and the marble, the silver and the bronze. The United States, brief as has been her existence as a nation, has not lacked martial spirits to carry her beautiful banner into the fiercest frays, and in no battles have finer traits of valour been displayed than in her naval wars.

Among her foremost naval heroes may well be rated Oliver Hazard Perry.

The beautiful county of Devon, in England, gave birth to Edmund Perry, the ancestor of this officer in the fifth generation, about 1630. Like many others of his God-fearing persuasion, nicknamed Quakers, Edmund Perry arrived in Plymouth, Massachusetts, some quarter of a century after the founding of that settlement.

He soon removed to Kingston, on Narragansett Bay. Here, both the red and the white men were more truly Christian in their actions than others who made greater profession of their saint-like dispositions.

In February, 1732, Freeman Perry, great-grandson of the Edmund Perry alluded to, and grandfather of the naval hero, was born. When twenty-four years of age he wedded the daughter of Oliver Hazard, likewise a Narragansett Quaker.

This Perry's third son, named Christopher Raymond, father of Oliver Hazard Perry, was born in December, 1761. Notwithstanding his pure Quaker lineage, he fought the battles of his native land throughout a pretty long life. This gentleman was one of the few survivors left to recount the sad stories of the cruel captivity on board the prison-ship *Jersey*. During one of his many sea-voyages Raymond Perry became acquainted with a Miss Sarah Alexander ; and three years after, when he assumed command of a merchant vessel, he married her, in Philadelphia. For many years the happy couple took up their abode with the captain's father, who lived on a fine farm that was originally cultivated by their ancestors.

All acquainted with the family unite in speaking in the highest terms, not only of the personal attractions, but also of the admirable mental qualities of Mrs. Perry — another instance showing how much the maternal character has to do in moulding the disposition and talents of a child.

To their first-born son was given the name borne by both his great-grandfather and his uncle, Oliver Hazard.

Young Oliver was sent to a good private school kept by an old Scotchman named Kelly, at Tower Hill, about four miles from the Perry homestead.

A fair fortune for those frugal days repaid Oliver's father for his numerous trips backwards and forwards to different countries, and he moved to Newport, then an important commercial town.

His principal object was to take advantage of the excellent schooling there to be obtained. Here, as at the old home, Oliver won admiration by his handsome looks, and respect by his good sense and gentlemanly behaviour. About this time Bishop Seabury, visiting Newport, was so much taken by the youth's good manners and great intelligence that, notwithstanding his extreme youth, he requested that Oliver should be confirmed.

At thirteen, when his father retired to Westerly, a small village, Oliver could boast of being exceedingly well educated for one of his few years. He was an inveterate reader—fortunately of the best class of books, by which his mind was expanded, while his morals were improved.

We have now reached within three years of the termination of a most eventful century—the year 1797. Our relations with France were becoming very much strained, and battle-clouds seemed to be gathering on the horizon. Citizen Genet, the French minister to our government, was carrying things with a high hand. Presuming upon the undemonstrative character of President Washington, he issued letters of marque to armed vessels to cruise against English shipping, and contrived to get some of these vessels away in spite of the vigilance of the government. But, not satisfied with preying upon British commerce, the French privateers even took some American ships when they came athwart their course.

The President called the attention of Congress to this state of things, and was empowered to increase our little navy, which consisted of but three frigates actually afloat.

But the first step was to build vessels, and Captain Perry, filled with the same ardent courage that actuated him during the Revolutionary struggle, and having made a study of the building and equipping of ships as well as the navigating of them, offered his services in any capacity to the government. His application for employment was strongly indorsed by first-class citizens of Rhode Island.

On the 7th of June, 1798, he received his commission as post-captain in the navy. No fit vessel could be found, and he was directed to begin building one at once. The keel was soon laid in Warren, R. I. In this neighbourhood good ship-timber was plenty. Captain Perry and his wife took up their abode near the yard, so that a constant supervision could be had of every timber fitted.

Meanwhile young Oliver, though scarce thirteen years of age, stopped at the family homestead, taking care of everything, buy-ing all things needed, seeing that the other children attended to their schooling, and writing at stated times to his parents, giving detailed accounts of his juvenile stewardship.

He, however, did not settle down into a demure kill-joy ; he was as fond of innocent sport as any of his companions, and freely participated in all that was going on among his boyish associates, particularly in rowing and sailing. But this love of sport did not make Oliver indifferent to the future. On the contrary, the future hero was deeply thinking about his future profession. His mother's ancestors had many of them been engaged in warlike deeds, and her animated recitals of the bat-tles in which they had figured had filled the lad's soul with longings to participate in similar adventures.

As he was scarcely ever out of sight of the sea in daylight, a person of his active habits and fearless disposition naturally de sired to be a sailor, while his father's eminence as a nautical man put it in his way to enter the navy.

As soon as his father received his commission, Oliver sent a letter to his father desiring to be allowed to enter the navy. So sensibly did he write, and so cogent were the reasons he gave for his choice of the marine profession, that all who were lucky enough to see the letter united in praising the good sense displayed by the youthful aspirant for a sea life.

It took all of one year for Captain Perry to construct the little frigate *General Greene*. She carried about thirty-six guns.

As Oliver's mother fully approved of her son's wish to become a sailor, it soon followed that he received his warrant and in April, 1799, he joined his ship, and soon afterwards sailed with his father towards the island of Cuba.

It was on the 9th of February, 1800, that the young midship-man was first under fire, during an action off Cape Tiburon, St. Domingo. Captain Perry, in the *General Greene*, silenced some forts in a few minutes, sustaining only a trifling damage, but killing quite a number of the enemy.

On returning from his cruise, the *General Greene* was put out of commission, as the times looked peaceful. Most of the offi-cers were retired. But among the midshipmen retained, fortu-nately for himself and his country, was the youthful Oliver Perry.

After remaining for some twelve months unattached to any ship, Oliver was taken on board the *Adams*, Captain Hugh G. Campbell, as a midshipman. In this ship a long cruise was made in the Mediterranean ; but nothing occurred of particular moment to Oliver Perry, except that he received his commission as lieutenant at the age of seventeen.

The young lieutenant visited his family at Newport, after being away about a year and a half. He thoroughly studied astron-omy and other high branches at this time, and was known as an accomplished and agreeable gentleman, with a taste for music, and as being quite a fine performer on the flute.

Commodore Preble had gained distinction by his skill and dauntless bravery on the Moorish coast, and when the *Constella-tion* was ordered to sail for that station she was commanded by

Captain H. G. Campbell, who succeeded in having his young friend Oliver attached to his ship as a lieutenant.

The *President* and the *Constellation* arrived off Tripoli together, the former bearing the flag of Commodore S. Barron.

Soon after young Perry was appointed to the schooner *Nautilus* as first lieutenant. Nothing particular came of this appointment but that young Perry had an opportunity of becoming an adept in handling small vessels.

In 1806 the lieutenant was again at Newport, and again he devoted much time to study.

A year later, at a social entertainment, Oliver first became acquainted with the young lady whom he afterwards married. Miss Elizabeth Champlin Mason was only sixteen, but already she displayed much of the beauty, talent, and many other admirable qualities which afterwards characterized her through life.

About this time Perry was associated with his friend Lieutenant Samuel G. Blodgett, to attend to the building of seventeen gunboats at Newport. This marks the high opinion already entertained in Washington of his abilities and reliableness. In June of 1807 Perry proceeded to New York with his fleet of gunboats, but not before he had been accepted by Miss Mason as her lover.

It was while Perry was in New York that the affair of the *Leopard's* attack upon the *Chesapeake* took place. Like all patriotic men, the young lieutenant felt keenly the outrage and the insult. Here is what he wrote on the subject to his father, who was absent :

"You must, ere this, have heard of the outrage committed by the British on our national honour, and feel with us all the indignation that so barbarous and cowardly an act must naturally inspire. Thank God, all parties are now united in the determination to resent so flagrant an insult ! There is but one sentiment pervad'ng the bosom of every American, from North to

South.   The British may laugh, but let them beware ! for never has the public indignation been so completely aroused since the glorious Revolution that made us a nation of freemen.   The utmost spirit prevails throughout the United States in preparing for an event which is thought inevitable, and our officers wait with impatience for the signal to be given to wipe away the stain which the misconduct of one has cast on our flag.''

The elder Perry fully sympathized with his son in his strongly expressed sentiments.

So well satisfied was the government with Lieutenant Perry's management of the gunboat building at Newport, that they forthwith ordered him to begin the construction of a flotilla of similar vessels at Westerly.

This employment lasted until April, 1809, when the construction was finished.

It was at this time resolved to do away with the gunboat service, and bring together the best officers and men in comparatively large vessels.   Most of these ships were put under command of Commodore Rodgers, an admirable officer for that purpose.

While Perry was proceeding in the *Revenge* to Washington, it is put down in the log that in passing up the Potomac his schooner was the first vessel to fire a salute in passing the tomb of Washington.

While his schooner, the *Revenge*, of fourteen guns, was cruising off the coast of Georgia, a United States marshal boarded her, to give the information that a ship miscalled the *Diana* was lying in Spanish waters, off Amelia Island.   She carried British colors, but was really an American vessel, her captain, an Englishman, having run away with her.   The Spanish governor gave permission to the Americans to seize her, as he believed her to honestly belong to that nationality.   Although the *Diana* lay under the guns of two British war-ships and displayed the English flag, Perry took possession of her, and carried her off to Cumberland Island. The *Diana* sailed for Europe, under command of the sailing-master of the *Revenge*.

Before the *Revenge*, which was convoying the *Diana*, had lost sight of land, a large British sloop-of-war, the *Goree*, hove in sight, and Captain Perry at once cleared for action. The British captain rounded to his ship and sent a boat, with an officer, stating that his ship was the *Goree*, and requested that the captain of the *Revenge* would come on board and satisfy him of her character. Perry refused to go on board, and while his answer was being returned to Captain Byng, got his crew ready to rush on board the *Goree*, as he intended to lay the *Revenge* alongside of that vessel if her captain resorted to violence.

Happily, Captain Byng merely desired that an officer would come on board his ship. This was acceded to, and all passed off peacefully. But those on board the *Revenge* were satisfied that Perry would have carried out his design of boarding his formidable antagonist, as her superior weight of metal would have given him no other possible chance.

Lieutenant Perry's conduct in this affair greatly enhanced his reputation both as an officer and a man. The subject became generally well known in consequence of the Secretary of the Navy having made public the annexed letter, sent to Lieutenant Perry by the underwriters of the vessel :

" The *Diana* having arrived at Savannah in safety and sailed again upon her destined voyage, we avail ourselves of the opportunity to inform you thereof, and to tender to yourself and to the gentlemen of the squadron in the river St. Mary's, under your command while there, in behalf of ourselves and the owners of the ship, our warmest thanks for the zeal and anxiety manifested by you for the honour and prosperity of the American flag. We cannot close this letter of thanks without expressing our admiration of the firmness and decision, properly tempered with moderation, evinced by you, when it seemed probable, from the reports in circulation, that a hostile course might have been adopted against the *Diana*, and of the complete state of preparation in which you constantly held yourself to repel any attack upon the sovereignty of the United States."

Upon Perry's return to New London he was selected to make a chart of New London, Newport, and the adjacent coasts. His selection for such an important duty was a high compliment ; but the season (December) was very unpropitious for such an enterprise.

On the 8th of January, 1811, he weighed anchor, in the *Revenge*, with a first-class pilot, as sailing-master. During a heavy fog the vessel was run upon a reef near Point Judith. In spite of the most able seamanship, the schooner was lost. The customary investigation followed, and the court found that the loss of the vessel rested on the pilot, and that Lieutenant Perry had done all that could have been done under the unfortunate circumstances to save the crew and preserve all that could be saved. Incidentally it was brought out that he was the last to leave the vessel.

During a visit to Washington, Perry obtained a year's leave of absence, and availed himself of that honourable leisure to make Miss Mason his wife.

While the brave officer and his young wife were enjoying themselves on their wedding tour, the probabilities of trouble with England daily increased. The British cruisers continued to overhaul and search American vessels, even in our own waters, and seizing seamen under various pretexts, frequently alleging that they were English deserters. Not only were the outrages most illegal, but they were generally accompanied with aggravating insolence or downright brutality.

Toward the close of the year Perry endeavored again to get into active service, not only engaging the offices of influential friends, but addressing the. Secretary of the Navy personally, thus :

" I have instructed my friend, Mr. W. S. Rodgers, to wait on you with a tender of my services for the Lakes.   There are fifty or sixty men under my command that are remarkably active and strong, capable of performing any service.   In the hope that I should have the honour of commanding them whenever they should meet the enemy, I have taken unwearied pains in preparing them for such an event.   I beg, therefore, sir, that we may be employed in some way in which we can be serviceable to our country."

On February 1st, 1813, Perry received a communication that greatly cheered him.   Commodore Chauncey, in reply to a letter of his, said that he had urged the Secretary to order him to the Lakes.   This letter conveyed a high compliment from the Commodore.   " You are the very person that I want for a particular service, in which you may gain reputation for yourself and honour for your country."

He was to be given command of the fleet which it was determined to organize on the waters of Lake Erie.   Accordingly, Perry was directed to proceed with all due haste to the lake, taking with him a detachment of his best sailors from Newport. Two powerful brigs were to be built, and launched on the lake. " You will, doubtless, command in chief.   This is the situation Mr. Hamilton mentioned to me two months past, and which, I think, will suit you exactly ; you may expect some warm fighting, and, of course, a portion of honour."   So wrote his friend Rodgers.

On the auspicious 22d of February Captain Perry started for Sackett's Harbor.   It was a difficult, disagreeable, and even hazardous journey.   At the very outset a violent tempest met him in crossing to Narragansett.   But difficulties inspired instead of daunting him.   He spent but a few hours taking leave of his family—as it seemed, possibly forever.   He had for companion his brother Alexander, a boy of twelve ; they travelled in an open sleigh great part of the route.

The interval between Perry's arrival at Sackett's Harbor and the 4th of February was spent by the vigilant and painstaking officer in a series of operations as important, if not as brilliant to read of, as winning battles.   He had to be continually urging lagging officials to forward supplies and men.   More particularly was he deficient in medical men, and officers, both commissioned and warrant.   It must be remembered that he had to meet a squadron of the British navy, and that that power had just come out of a series of naval wars in which their officers had had a practical education in maritime fighting, in which the greatest navies of the old world had been completely annihilated.   The English sailors were mostly veterans, trained to the use of large and small guns ; while the marines proper have always been deservedly classed as the flower of their country's infantry.   With us, on the contrary, the few officers that survived from our small wars on the Mediterranean pirates had been honourably dismissed from the navy, had obtained situations in mercantile service, and were scattered in sailing vessels over distant seas.   Our marine corps scarcely amounted to a corporal's guard to every vessel. As we had no navy-yards like England's, France's, or even Sweden's—in which millions upon millions of dollars' worth of timber, canvas, cordage, chains, anchors, guns, and such necessary munitions had been accumulating for decades of years, it fell to Perry's lot to be builder, provider, purveyor, and even paymaster for the whole expedition.

Meanwhile General Harrison, commanding the Western levies, was impatiently urging the young naval officer to break the British power on the Lakes, and thus afford his army an opportunity to commence active operations against the common enemy.

It was about this time that Perry obtained reliable news as to the strength of the British squadron under Captain Robert H. Barclay :

" The *Detroit*, of five hundred tons and nineteen guns, all long except two twenty-four pound carronades ; the ship *Queen Charlotte*, of four hundred tons and seventeen guns, three of them being long guns, the *Detroit* and *Queen Charlotte* having each one of the long guns on a pivot ; the schooner *Lady Prevost*, of two hundred and thirty tons and thirteen guns, three being long guns ; the brig *Hunter*, of one hundred and eighty tons and ten guns ; the sloop *Little Belt*, of one hundred tons and three guns, two long twelves and one long eighteen ; and the schooner *Chippeway*, of one hundred tons, mounting one long eighteen ; making in all sixty-three guns, thirty-five of which were long."

Captain Barclay was one of Nelson's officers at Trafalgar, and was badly wounded in that battle ; he was known to be skilful, courageous, and ambitious of honourable renown. The officers under him were of approved capacity and courage. By official report his crews consisted of four hundred and seventy sailors and marines. Add the officers, and the count stood at full five hundred men.

The fleet under Oliver Hazard Perry consisted mainly of vessels of less than five hundred tons ; the *Lawrence* and *Niagara* were the only ships that exceeded that tonnage, and consequently could not be rated as men-of-war. The bulk of the American squadron were weakly built, and had not even bulwarks of any strength. Their principal armament was long guns. The brigs mounted each twenty guns, two long twelves and eighteen thirty-two-pound carronades. It was only by forcing the fighting and coming quickly to close quarters that these could be made to tell. Captain J. D. Elliott commanded the *Niagara*. The other officers were excellent seamen and of unquestioned courage, but they were mere tyros as naval officers. "The whole force, in officers and men, of our squadron amounted to four hundred and ninety; of these, one hundred and sixteen were on the sick-lists of the different vessels on the morning of the action, seventy-eight cases being of bilious fever." In tonnage, guns, and men, the British force outnumbered ours.

Just previous to the 10th of September, Perry became satisfied that Barclay intended to give battle. Accordingly he summoned his officers to meet him on the quarter-deck of his ship the *Lawrence*, and furnished them each with their corrected instructions—we quote from Mackenzie's spirited recital—and he further explained to them verbally his views with regard to whatever contingency might occur. He now produced a battle-flag, which he had caused to be privately prepared by Mr. Hambleton before leaving Erie, and the hoisting of which to the main royal mast of the *Lawrence* was to be his signal for action : a blue flag, bearing in large white letters, "Don't give up the ship !" the dying words of the hero whose name she bore. When about to withdraw, he stated to them his intention to bring the enemy from the first to close quarters, in order not to lose by the short range of his carronades, and the last emphatic injunction with which he dismissed them was that he could not, in case of difficulty, advise them better than in the words of Lord Nelson, "If you lay your enemy close alongside, you cannot be out of your place !"

On the 10th of September Barclay's fleet was observed coming toward ours. After some very delicate evolutions, Perry told his sailing-master to lead in a certain direction. The officer showed that such a plan had its disadvantages. "I care not," said Perry, "let to leeward or to windward ! they shall fight to-day."

The *Lawrence* was ready for action by ten o'clock, when the enemy hove to in line of battle on the larboard tack, advancing at about three knots an hour. The weather was glorious, and the British vessels, with their royal ensigns and newly painted hulls glistening in the bright sunshine, formed a magnificent spectacle. Never had two braver fleets contended for the mastery.

Controversialists have sought to diminish the skill and bravery of either of the officers and men ; but the gallant heroes who had done all the fighting did but little of the writing.

The English commander had arranged his fleet with the *Chippeway*, of one long eighteen pivot, leading ; the *Detroit*, of nineteen guns, next ; the *Hunter*, of nineteen guns, third ; the *Queen Charlotte*, seventeen guns, fourth ; the *Lady Prevost*, of thirteen guns, fifth ; and the *Little Belt*, of three guns, last. Captain Perry, passing ahead of the *Niagara*, got into position to match the *Detroit*, placing the *Scorpion*, of two long guns, ahead, and the *Ariel*, of four short twelves, on his weather bow, where, with her light battery, she might be partially under cover. The *Caledonia*, of three long twenty-fours, came next, to encounter the *Hunter;* the *Niagara* next, so as to be opposite her designated antagonist, the *Queen Charlotte ;* and the *Somers*, of two long thirty-twos, the *Porcupine*, of one long thirty-two, *Tigress*, of one long twenty-four, and *Trippe*, of one long thirty-two, in succession towards the rear, to encounter the *Lady Prevost* and *Little Belt*. The line being formed, Perry now bore up for the enemy, distant at ten o'clock about six miles. He now produced the lettered burgee which he had exhibited as the concerted signal for battle. Having unfurled it, he mounted on a gun-slide, and, calling his crew about him, thus briefly addressed them : " My brave lads ! this flag contains the last words of Captain Lawrence ! Shall I hoist it ?" " Ay, ay, sir !" resounded from every voice in the ship, and the flag was briskly swayed to the main-royal masthead of the *Lawrence*. The answer was given by three such rousing cheers as few but American sailors know how to give.

Slowly but steadily our fleet went on in the direction of the leading line of the foe, the leading vessels under reefed sails, but the remainder having every yard of canvas set that could possibly draw. No preparations remained to make at this hour.

Captain Perry, now having made all right in reference to his public duties, seized a few moments to attend to his private matters, giving instructions what was to be done provided he fell in the approaching action. All official papers were prepared with sinkers, to be thrown overboard, while he destroyed all his private documents. "It appeared," says Mr. Hambleton, "to go hard with him to part with his wife's letters. After giving them a hasty reading he tore them to ribbons, observing that, let what would happen, the enemy should not read them, and closed by remarking, ' This is the most important day of my life.' "

A thrilling bugle blast from the *Detroit* rang over the waters, and was followed by vehement cheering from the British sailors.

It was now within a few minutes of noon, the *Detroit* having reached within between one and two miles of our leading vessel. The *Detroit* began the fight by sending a round shot at the *Lawrence*. It, however, fell short of its mark. The proper signals were now flown for every ship to engage her designated antagonist. The *Ariel, Scorpion, Lawrence*, and *Caledonia* were in their proper stations, in the rotation given, distant from each other less than a cable's length. Some distance astern, the other vessels were drawing into action.

In a few moments the *Detroit's* second shot came hurtling over the waves, striking the *Lawrence* and tearing through the bulwarks. Instantly the long guns of the British squadron sent their shot in the direction of the American ships, some of them missing, but some carrying death in their train.

Just at noon the *Lawrence* was suffering from the severe fire of the British, which she returned from her twelve-pounder

Perry now, by speaking-trumpet, ordered the *Caledonia* and the *Niagara* to discharge their long guns. The vessels still further astern also commenced cannonading, but they were too far off to do any material injury.

The *Lawrence* was at a great disadvantage in fighting the *Detroit*, as this latter vessel was armed almost entirely with long guns, while Perry had to depend almost entirely on the carronades. For this reason Perry was impatient for his own ship and his consorts to close with all possible haste. Elliott, of the *Niagara*, received and transmitted the order to the line, but for some inexplicable reason he did not apply the order to his own conduct, but held off, occasionally discharging shots from her twelve-pounder.

The *Lawrence* kept firing on toward the British line, every moment receiving shot in her hull and spars. Trying the experiment, he found that his shot fell short ; so he ceased firing until quarter past noon ; then he let fly his entire starboard broadside when he was less than four hundred yards away. Then, as he neared the *Detroit*, he discharged a quick and murderous fire into her. The *Lawrence*, however, had meanwhile been terribly riddled by the *Detroit* and her sister craft. But now the action was continued by her with augmented fury ; and, notwithstanding the overpowering odds with which she was assailed, the whole battery of the enemy, amounting, in all, to thirty-four guns, being almost entirely directly against her, she continued to assail the enemy with steady and unwavering effort. In this unequal contest she was sustained by the *Scorpion* and *Ariel* on her weather bow, which were enabled to direct their fire upon him with sure aim. The commander of the *Caledonia*, animated by the same gallant spirit and sense of duty, followed the *Lawrence* into close action, and closed with her antagonist, the *Hunter ;* but the *Niagara* had not made sail when the *Lawrence* did, but got embarrassed with the *Cale-*

donia. One of the British vessels, in the smoke, had closed up behind the *Detroit*, and opened her fire at closer quarters upon the *Lawrence*. In this unequal contest the *Lawrence* continued to struggle desperately against such overpowering numbers. The first division of the starboard guns was directed against the *Detroit*, and the second against the *Queen Charlotte*, with an occasional shot from her after-gun at the *Hunter*, which lay on her quarter, and with which the *Caledonia* continued to sustain a hot though unequal engagement. The *Scorpion* and *Ariel*, from their stations on the weather bow of the *Lawrence*, made every effort that their inconsiderable force allowed. The smaller vessels away in the stern of Perry's line were far too distant to be of any service. The will was not wanting, but the ability was not there. Terrific as were the odds against the *Lawrence*, being in the ratio of thirty-four guns to her ten in battery, she continued, with the aid of the *Scorpion*, *Ariel*, and *Caledonia*, to sustain the contest for more than two hours. At this time, however, her rigging had been much shot away, and was hanging down or towing overboard; sails torn to pieces, spars splintered and falling upon deck, braces and bowlines cut, so as to render it impossible to trim the yards or keep the vessel under control. Such was the condition of the vessel aloft ; on deck the destruction was even more terrible. One by one the guns were dismounted until only one remained that could be fired ; the bulwarks were riddled bv round shot passing completely through. The slaughter was dreadful.

All this while Perry continued to keep up a fire from his single remaining carronade, though to man it he was obliged to send repeated requests to the surgeon to spare him another hand from those engaged in removing the wounded, until the last had been taken. It is recorded by the surgeon that when these messages arrived, several of the wounded crawled upon deck to lend a feeble aid at the guns.

The conduct of Perry throughout this trying scene was well calculated to inspire the most unbounded confidence in his followers, and to sustain throughout their courage and enthusiasm. When a gap would occasionally be made among a gun's crew by a single round shot or a stand of grape or canister, the survivors would for a moment turn to Perry, exchange a glance with him, and step to fill the place of their comrades.

In the hottest of the fight, Yarnall, the first lieutenant, came to Perry and told him that the officers in the first division under his command were all killed or disabled. Perry sent him the required aid ; but soon after he returned with the same complaint of a destruction of his officers, to which he replied, "You must endeavor to make out by yourself ; I have no more to furnish you." We may give another incident to show the carnage which occurred on the deck of the *Lawrence*, and the destruction by which her commander was so closely surrounded. The command of the marines of the *Lawrence* was intrusted to Lieutenant John Brooks, a gay, amiable, and intelligent young officer, whose numerous good qualities were enhanced in their effects by the rarest personal beauty. He was addressing Perry with a smile and in an animated tone, with regard to some urgent point of duty, when he was struck down by a shot. The terrible hurt made him utter an agonized cry, and he besought Perry to shoot him dead. He was tenderly taken below deck. Little Midshipman Perry, then but twelve years old, had his clothes rent, and received more than one ball through his hat, when a part of a hammock was torn from its netting and dashed against the lad's side. As it luckily happened he was merely stunned, and the captain saw him again on duty in a few minutes.

The critical moment had now arrived which was to call out all the best qualities of a great commander. Nothing like it had ever occurred before in a the strange mutations of a naval action. When the last cannon of the *Lawrence* had been rendered unserviceable ; when but twenty persons, including his little brother and himself, were able even to make a show of being able-bodied, it became evident that some new measure must be resorted to. Heretofore, in such a case, there had been but one way : to strike the flag. And such a course could have been honourably taken. But Perry was " made of sterner stuff," and his whole soul seemed imbued with Lawrence's noble motto, " Don't give up the ship." He had striven with might and main to get his vessels built and launched ; he had hurried his superiors into furnishing him with supplies and men ; he had given General Harrison to hope that his squadron would strike a blow that would cut the Gordian knot by which the eager armies of the West were bound, as Samson by the green withes ; he had evidently made up his mind that he would never be *taken* out of his ship unless he was sewed up in a hammock.

Moments now were priceless, and Perry rapidly made up his mind what to do.

The *Lawrence* was helplessly drifting, sailless and rudderless, when, as for a moment the smoke was blown away, he was able to take the bearings of his surroundings. Lieutenant Forrest called his attention to the queer way in which the *Niagara* was handled. She was well on the larboard beam of the *Lawrence ;* the *Caledonia*, at the same time, was passing on the starboard beam, between the enemy and Perry's stricken ship. Forrest said plainly that the *Niagara* was evidently determined not to help them ; as she seemed to carefully avoid coming into close action. " Then I must fetch her up," was Perry's sententious remark. And he quickly called his boat. He was convinced that the *Niagara* was scarcely injured at all ; and he vowed that the flag of his country should not be pulled down on any vessel that he was on board of. His reliable second was at once placed in command of what was now little more than a floating hulk. The boat was at the larboard gangway, the word was given, the oars took water, but ere they shoved off, Perry exclaimed, "If a victory is to be had, I'll have it!"

When Perry shoved off in the boat that bore "Cæsar and his fortunes," it was just half past two. The *Niagara* was at that moment passing her larboard beam, some half mile away. The wind had increased, and she was quickly going away from the British fleet. Perry stood at his full height, his breast charged with the grandeur of his design : to take a fresh vessel, and dash back in the midst of the enemy, who had already deemed him whipped, and once again try conclusions with his stubborn adversary. Had not Perry been something more than merely a brave officer, the idea would never have occurred to him. But, as we have seen, almost from his infancy he had been on the water. He had played on the rolling logs in the harbor before he ever had any experience in managing a skiff, and he had rowed and sailed in every sort of craft that could be kept afloat on the stormy, tide-vexed shores of Narragansett. So that it was second nature for him, for the nonce, to leap into a boat, and stand proudly erect in her. Nelson, it is said, used to get sea-sick in a gun-brig, so he certainly would never have thought of an admiral taking to a barge in the height of a furious battle.

So it will be seen that it was almost providential that Perry possessed the qualifications that he owned.

Quick as had been the captain's resolve and its execution, the enemy almost as quickly saw his design.

Great guns and musketry were rapidly sending their missiles, in the hope of sending the little boat to destruction. In vain Perry's crew begged of him to be seated, and it was only when they declared that they would not pull another stroke while he remained standing that he finally yielded. It hardly needs telling that the brave fellows, some wounded and dying, followed every movement of Perry and his brave crew as they made the desperate passage from ship to ship ; and as they saw him step on the deck of the *Niagara* they saluted him with soul-fraught cheers.

As there was nothing to be gained by keeping the *Lawrence* a mere floating target for British guns, her few remaining officers held a brief consultation and resolved to surrender. As the colors fluttered down, their descent was saluted with cheers by the foe, who knew too well the stuff of which her gallant defenders were made. About this time young Brooks died, and Mr. Hambleton, the purser, volunteering to a post of danger, had his shoulder fearfully torn. He was working at the last gun that fired a shot.

The British had their hands too full in working out their own safety to give any further heed to the condition of the *Lawrence*. When Perry reached the deck of the *Niagara*, he was met at the gangway by Captain Elliott, who " inquired how the day was going. Captain Perry replied, Badly ; that he had lost almost all of his men, and that his ship was a wreck ; and asked what the gunboats were doing so far astern. Captain Elliott offered to go and bring them up ; and, Captain Perry consenting, he sprang into the boat and went off on that duty.''

Perry at once ordered that the *Niagara* should be prevented from escaping out of action. The top-gallant sails were set, and the signal for '' close action'' was given. As the pennants were seen, loud cheers resounded down the line.

By great efforts Lieutenant Holdup Stevens, who had been astern of the line in the *Trippe*, soon closed up to the assistance of the *Caledonia*, and the remaining vessels approached rapidly, to take a more active part in the battle, under the influence of the increasing breeze.

The helm had been put up on board the *Niagara*, sail made, and the signal for close action hove out at forty-five minutes after two, the instant after Perry had boarded her. With the increased breeze, seven or eight minutes sufficed to traverse the distance of more than half a mile which still separated the *Niagara* from the enemy.

The *Detroit* made an effort to wear, in order to present her starboard broadside to the *Niagara*, several of the larboard guns being disabled. As this evolution commenced on board the *Detroit*, the *Queen Charlotte* was running up under her lee. The evolution of wearing, which was not quickly enough done on board the *Queen*, resulted in the latter running her bowsprit and head-booms foul of the mizzen rigging of the *Detroit*. The two British ships were thus foul of each other, and they so remained, when the *Niagara*, shortening sail, went slowly under the bows of the *Detroit*, within short pistol-shot, and sent a broadside into each vessel ; so that, entangled as they were, they received fearful showers of grape and canister. The sterns of the *Little Belt* and the *Lady Prevost* were treated to the same awful fire, while the marines, by their skilfully aimed shots, swept their decks. At this juncture the small vessels also came into close action to windward, and poured in a destructive fire of grape and canister ; their shot and that of the *Niagara*, whenever it missed its mark, passing the enemy and taking effect reciprocally on our own vessels.

All resistance now ceased ; an officer appeared on the taffrail of the *Queen* to signify that she had struck, and her example was immediately followed by the *Detroit*. Both vessels struck in about seven minutes after the *Niagara* opened this most destructive fire, and about fifteen minutes after Perry took command of her. The *Hunter* struck at the same time, as did the *Lady Prevost*, which lay to leeward under the guns of the *Niagara*. The battle had begun on the part of the enemy at a quarter before meridian ; at three the *Queen Charlotte* and *Detroit* surrendered, and all resistance was at an end. As the cannonade ceased and the smoke blew over, the two squadrons, now owning one master, were found completely mingled. Now a glorious yet sad time had come. The form of taking possession of the British captured ships was to be gone through with. When our boarding officer reached the *Detroit* she was in a fearful state. Her bulwarks were in slivers, strong oak as they were ; the *Lawrence's* carronade shots were sticking in her sides. The deck looked like a veritable slaughter-house.

A grapeshot had lodged in Captain Barclay's thigh, making a fearful wound.

The brave man had been taken below when senseless but on recovering consciousness he was carried on deck to see with his own eyes if resistance was hopeless. Then the *Niagara* threw in her fire, and a second grapeshot, passing through the right shoulder, fractured the blade to atoms.

The rest of the enemy's vessels were found to be also much cut to pieces, especially the *Queen Charlotte*, which had lost her brave commander, Captain Finnis, very early in the action ; her first lieutenant had been soon after mortally wounded, and the loss of life on board of her was very severe ; she was also much cut to pieces both in hull and spars. The other vessels suffered in like proportion. The *Lady Prevost* had both her commander and first lieutenant wounded, and, besides other extensive injury, was become unmanageable from the loss of her rudder. Lieutenants Bignal, commanding the *Hunter*, and Campbell, the *Chippeway*, were also wounded, thus leaving only the commander of the *Little Belt* fit for duty at the close of the action. Indeed, in the official account of Commodore Barclay, it is stated that every commander and every officer second in command was disabled. The total of killed and wounded rendered by Commodore Barclay in his official report was forty-one killed, including three officers, and ninety-four wounded, nine of whom were officers. The returns, on account of the condition of the commanders and their seconds in command, could not have been very complete, and the numbers of killed and wounded are believed to have been greater. The killed of the British squadron were thrown overboard as they fell, with the exception of the officers.

On every side were to be seen objects calculated to harrow the most obdurate heart. And our own vessels were full of scenes that made the boldest shudder. Our whole fleet had lost twenty-seven brave men killed outright, while ninety-six had been wounded.

But the lamentation over the heroic victors and their worthy antagonists could not lessen the brilliancy of this splendid victory. The British were superior in almost every way : their vessels were larger, their guns heavier, their sailors better trained, and their marines were veterans ; while the commander and many of his subaltern officers had been in many battles under the glance of " Britannia's god of war," as Byron styled Horatio Nelson. To the nautical skill, ready invention, and indomitable prowess of one man the victory was in great part due, and that man had but just attained his twenty-seventh year ; and, strangest fact of all, he had never seen a naval battle ! He had dashed boldly into action with the *Lawrence*, counting upon the support of those immediately around him, and trusting that the rear of his line would soon be able to close up to his support.

Passing from the *Lawrence* under the enemy's fire, saved from death, as if miraculously, by the protecting genius of his country, he reached the *Niagara*, and by an evolution unsurpassed for genius and hardihood, bore down upon the enemy, and dashed with his fresh and uninjured vessel through the enemy's line. It was thus that the battle of Lake Erie was won, not merely by the genius and inspiration, but eminently by the exertions of one man.

As soon as Perry had taken all precautions for securing his numerous prisoners and seeing to the comfort of the wounded, he lost no time in communicating the result of the battle to the expectant General Harrison. For this victory was of paramount importance to the furtherance of his plans. The great victory was announced in this brief way :

" DEAR GENERAL : We have met the enemy, and they are ours. Two ships, two brigs, one schooner, and one sloop. Yours, with very great respect and esteem,

" O. H. PERRY."

To the Secretary of the Navy he also wrote at once. His despatch read thus :

" U. S. Brig Niagara, off the westernmost Sister, head of Lake Erie, Sept. 10, 1813, 4 P.M.

" SIR : It has pleased the Almighty to give to the arms of the United States a signal victory over their enemies on this lake. The British squadron, consisting of two ships, two brigs, one schooner, and one sloop, have this moment surrendered to the force under my command, after a sharp conflict.

" I have the honor to be, sir, very respectfully, your obedient servant,

" O. H. PERRY."

Not a solitary syllable of self-glorification. He tamely terms that a " sharp conflict" which bears comparison with any naval conflict ever fought.

The ships were as speedily as possible brought to anchor. So few were his guards that he had to take extra precautions to prevent a possibility of the prisoners rising during the night,

It was on the quarter-deck of his own *Lawrence* that Perry received the formal surrender of the prizes. It was but fair that the heroes who aided so much to gain the victory should witness the harvesting of its fruits. Dr. Parsons communicated to Lieutenant Mackenzie the annexed description : " It was a time of conflicting emotions when the commodore returned to the ship. The battle was won ; he was safe. But the deck was slippery with blood and brains, and strewed with the bodies of twenty officers and men, some of whom had sat at table with us at our last meal, and the ship resounded everywhere with the groans of the wounded. Those of us who were spared and able to walk approached him as he came over the ship's side, but the salutation was a silent one on both sides : not a word could find utterance.''

Perry, at the request of his officers, had hitherto worn a uniform round jacket ; he now resumed his undress uniform, and, standing on the after part of the deck, received the officers of the different captured vessels as they came to tender the surrender of their vessels and their own submission as prisoners. At the head of them was an officer of the Forty-first Regiment, who acted as marine officer on board the *Detroit*, and was charged by Commodore Barclay with the delivery of his sword ; he was in full dress. When they had approached, picking their way among the wreck and carnage of the deck, they held their swords with the hilts towards Perry, and tendered them to his acceptance. With a dignified and solemn air, the most remote possible from any betrayal of exultation, and in a low tone of voice, he requested them to retain their side-arms ; inquired with deep concern for Commodore Barclay and the wounded officers, tendering to them every comfort his ship afforded, and expressing his regret that he had not a spare medical officer to send to them.

As it was impossible to reserve all the killed of the *Lawrence* for burial on shore, the seamen were buried at nightfall alongside, the able-bodied of the crew, so much less numerous than the killed, being assembled around to perform the last sad offices. His little brother, though he had received several musket-balls through his dress, had met with no injury, and was now dozing in his hammock. An allusion to these facts awakened the same sense of a controlling Providence which, in beginning his report, had led him to ascribe the victory to the pleasure of the Almighty. " I believe," he said, " that my wife's prayers have saved me."

On the next morning the commodore removed to the *Ariel*, having determined, as the *Lawrence* was completely disabled for all further service, to make her a hospital ship, and despatch her with our wounded to Erie.

The wounded were fortunate in the surgeon, Dr. Parsons of the *Lawrence*, who was as skilful as he was devoted. No man on board deserved better of his country on that eventful day.

At ten o'clock in the evening a few of the more slightly wounded still remained unattended to, when the surgeon was obliged to desist, from inability longer to sustain himself in a stooping position, and from mere physical exhaustion. The remaining wounded of the *Lawrence*, with the wounded of the rest of the squadron, were only seen on the following day. It is conclusive as to the rare skill of Dr. Parsons and his humane attentions to the wounded, that out of the whole ninety-six, only three died ; one of these was Midshipman Thomas Claxton, a young officer of merit and great promise.

In the course of this day Perry visited Commodore Barclay on board of the *Detroit*, and from that visit, so tragically ushered in, began a warm and enduring friendship. Every comfort that Perry could procure for his wounded prisoner was freely placed at his disposal. He became responsible for a considerable sum of money required by Barclay for his own use and that of his officers. Strange! years afterward Perry's generosity and humanity were in a slight degree repaid, on as sad an occasion, by the countrymen of Barclay. But this is anticipatory.

After a sail of two hours the victor and the vanquished fleets arrived at Put-in Bay. The interment of the officers who had fallen in battle took place on the morning of the 12th.

The day was serene, and the lake unruffled by a breeze. The boats, with their crews neatly dressed and their colours half-masted, conveyed the bodies to the shore, keeping time, with a measured stroke, to the mournful death-dirge. The procession formed, as it reached the shore, according to rank, in reversed order. The youngest of the killed was borne first, then the lowest in rank of the other squadron, and so on alternately, an American and a British corpse, the body of Captain Finnis coming last. As the corpses moved on, the officers fell into procession, two Americans and two English, according to rank reversed, Perry himself closing the procession. As the mournful pageant advanced, keeping time to the measured cadence of a dead march from the drums and fifes of both squadrons, minute guns, fired alternately from each, offered the appropriate tribute of respect to the remains of the departed.

At length the procession reached the spot, near the margin of the lake, where the graves had been prepared for the reception of the dead. The funeral service was read over them, and they were lowered into the earth in the order in which they had been borne. Volleys of musketry over the graves closed the mournful ceremony.

Captain Perry did not lose a moment in preparing to give all the aid in his power to the army of General Harrison. It was the intention to move the army to Malden and there attack the British army, as it was necessary to capture that place before proceeding to Detroit. The *Niagara* and the light vessels of the fleet were at once got ready for service. All our wounded were placed on the *Lawrence,* while the British were taken care of on the *Detroit.* Care was taken to properly moor the two vessels.

A terrific gale came on from the south-west on the 13th of September, and tossed up a fearful sea in the bay. The tottering masts of the *Detroit* went by the board, although great pains had been taken to brace them in every way. As they crashed down on the deck they put the finishing touch to the appalling picture of ruin and desolation. The prize crew very providentially had got out of harm's way. A similar mishap befell the masts of the *Queen Charlotte.*

Perry found time in the midst of all this confusion to write and forward his official account of the battle, with as perfect lists as could be obtained of the forces engaged in either squadron. He kept his own doings as much in the background as he could with propriety, while he gave every one else his due meed of praise.

Considerable feeling and a great deal of correspondence arose from Captain Jesse D. Elliott having taken offence at what he deemed Perry's unfair treatment of his services in the battle of Lake Erie. But as far as all the accounts of the battle give the circumstances, they are fairly narrated in the account which we have given.

A pleasing incident may be here related, among the weightier matters we have been recording, as exhibiting Captain Perry's goodness of heart and thoughtfulness for others. A couple of dozen soldiers, composing the remnant of a gallant company of young Virginians who had joined the army the year before under the name of the Petersburg Volunteers, and who had been reduced by battle and disease to their present number, had accompanied General Harrison on board the *Ariel.*

On the passage to Put-in Bay, supper was served in the cabin, and after the commodore and his numerous guests had partaken of it, they resumed their seats on deck to enjoy the evening air. Major Chambers was conversing with Lieutenant Packett, who commanded the *Ariel*, when one of the young Virginians, whom a spirit of adventure had led to abandon a life of ease for the hardships of the camp, and who was just recovering from severe illness, approached Major Chambers, whom he knew, and asked, in an undertone, if it would be possible for him to obtain a cup of coffee from the cabin, saying that his stomach rejected the cold and coarse food to which the army had necessarily been confined. Being a stranger to Perry, Major Chambers felt reluctant to trouble him with such a request, and therefore explained it to Mr. Packett. He hesitated to say anything, and the subject was dropped. But Perry, who was sitting near, had overheard the remark, and quietly given directions to his steward. In half an hour Major Chambers had the gratification of seeing the whole of the young Virginians seated round an excellent supper in the cabin, and the warm-hearted host attending to them in person. Perry had heard the character and gallantry of the little band assigned as the reason for taking them on board the *Ariel*, that they might be under the eye of the general, and kindly rebuked Major Chambers for having hesitated to explain what accident alone had revealed to him—the longing of these poor fellows for a cup of hot coffee.

On the 23d day of the month, after General Harrison and Captain Perry had reconnoitred the harbor of Malden (by the British called Amherstburg), it was determined to attack the place. Accordingly, on the morning of the 27th the vessels were ranged in order of battle, something better than a mile to the eastward of Bar Point, and within quarter of a mile of the shore. Everything had worked well, but when the boats landed they found no garrison. The place was evacuated. No clearly satisfactory reason was ever given for the British General Proctor's abandoning his chosen position without a battle.

Tecumseh, his famous Indian ally, strongly combated the idea of retreating, and delivered the following speech—more remarkable for its strength than its polish : " Listen, Father !" said he ; " our fleet has gone out. We know they have fought ; we have heard the great guns, but know nothing of what has happened to our Father with one arm. Our fleet has gone one way, and we are very much astonished to see our Father tying up everything, and preparing to run away the other, without letting his red children know what his intentions are. You always told us that you would never draw your foot off British ground ; but now, Father, we see that you are drawing back, and we are sorry to see our Father doing so without seeing the enemy. We must compare our Father's conduct to a fat animal that carries its tail upon its back, but, when affrighted, it drops it between its legs and runs off. We wish to remain here and fight the enemy, should he appear. If he conquers us, we will then retreat with our Father."

But General Proctor retreated from position to position without striking a blow. The various Indian tribes who had been in amity with the British fell off from their allegiance and offered their services to the Americans, so that a proclamation was shortly published re-establishing the civil authorities in Michigan, as the enemy had been repulsed.

As there was nothing more to call for Perry's action in naval affairs, he volunteered as an aide-de-camp to General Harrison. It is needless to say that the hero of Lake Erie was received with vehement rapture by the bold frontiersmen, and our small but far from insignificant nucleus of a regular army, which formed part of Harrison's command, and which rendered such effective service under their gallant leader, Colonel Snelling. The army was soon in motion, and in spite of many difficulties a fierce battle ensued on the banks of the Thames. It was in this action, when victory hesitated on which side to declare, that Colonel Johnson made such a brilliant charge at the head of his mounted Kentuckians, and, if popular legends are to be relied on, the great Tecumseh—lawgiver, orator, and general of the bravest of the Indians—fell by the unerring bullet of the Kentucky colonel. The ultimate result was that the British grounded their arms, and the great North-West, now the habitat of millions of prosperous freemen, was untrodden by any foeman of the Thames.

During the battle Perry as much astonished the Kentuckians by his horsemanship as he had astonished his country's enemies by his seamanship a few short weeks before.

Nor were there wanting opportunities for Perry to display those benevolent qualities which are often found the adjunct of the fiercest bravery. In one case, the circumstances of which only became known by the testimony of an eye-witness, he gave time and money in alleviating the hardships entailed upon innocent women and children by the inevitable results of the most necessary and glorious wars.

During our possession of the Moravian town of Christianized Indians on the banks of the Thames, Perry interested himself so deeply and so effectually to help the worthy Moravians and their poor disciples to such an extent as to call forth the following letter. It is signed John G. Cunow, and dated Bethlehem :

"HONOURED AND DEAR SIR : The directors of the Society of the United Brethren, commonly called Moravians, residing at this place, have been informed by the Reverend Mr. Schnall, late one of our missionaries in Upper Canada, of the friendly offices and generous protection which you have had the goodness to afford to our missionaries when the settlement of our Christian Indians on Thames River was taken possession of by the army of the United States under General Harrison,

"Impressed with the most lively sense of gratitude for the numerous proofs of your benevolent disposition towards our missionaries when in distress and danger, the directors beg leave to present to you their sincerest and most cordial acknowledgments. · May the Lord, whose servants you have taken pleasure to protect, be your shield and your exceeding great reward, have you in his holy keeping, and bless you in life, in death, and throughout eternity."

Soon after the victory of the Thames, Captain Perry returned to Detroit, and the two brave officers issued a proclamation to the people of Upper Canada, in which the safety of life and property was guaranteed to all living quietly, and leaving them to their own local authorities in all the ordinary affairs of life.

Hardly ever has any nation received its greatest hero with more heartfelt enthusiasm than greeted the hero of Lake Erie when he made a trip to Washington at the call of the authorities. In every city, town, and village he was almost deafened with the salute of cannon and loud huzzas, and ladies showered the choicest flowers upon him. Nor were more substantial marks of approbation bestowed with a niggard spirit. Rich plate and other valuable offerings were liberally bestowed upon the still youthful commander.

Captain Elliot was by no means pleased at the way that Perry ignored his complaints about what he termed the unfair way in which he had been treated, and his friends and himself continued to write disparaging letters regarding Perry.

Barclay, however, who was so gallantly vanquished by Perry, and not only lost his five ships and scores of brave officers and valiant seamen, entertained the very highest regard for his chivalric conqueror. In a letter written by Captain Barclay to his brother in England, and which fell into the hands of a United States marshal on its transmission, occurs this passage :

"The treatment I have received from Captain Perry has been noble indeed. It can be equalled only by his bravery and intrepidity in action. Since the battle he has been like a brother to me. He has obtained for me an unconditional parole. I mean to make use of it to get to England so soon as my wound will permit." At a public dinner, followed by a ball, given in honour of this gallant officer at Terrebonne, in Canada, he took occasion, in reply to a complimentary speech, to notice the unusual kindness which he had received from Captain Perry. He said that his humanity to his prisoners would alone have immortalized him, and he gave as a toast, in conclusion, "Commodore Perry, the gallant and generous enemy."

On taking leave of Perry, Barclay had presented him with his sextant as a memento of his regard ; and some months after Perry forwarded to Barclay a highly-finished American rifle, made with the greatest possible care by a celebrated gunsmith of Albany, expressly for him.

Although, as has been said, honours were literally showered upon him, dinners, balls, and receptions awaited him in every place and on every hand. None were too rich or too poor not to feel it an honour to get a word or a smile from the man who had in a moment, in the hour of his country's greatest need, stemmed the torrent of defeat and brought victory once more to the standard that had been partially dishonoured by the incapacity if not the cowardice of some commanders.

But one thing was wanting to complete his happiness, and that was to meet his admirable and dearly-loved wife and his equally loved children. He found that "one lamb had been taken from the fold during his absence"— an infant had died while he was at Lake Erie.

Even while he was resting in the midst of his family, tributes of admiration and respect poured in upon him. He still made his home at Newport.

He was soon called to Washington and appointed to the command of the frigate *Java*. There was every likelihood of his once more seeing very active service.

The British, although they had played a losing game in Canada, were by no means inclined to admit that all was lost. They did all in their power to spread alarm upon the Atlantic seacoast, measurably confining their attacks upon places in the vicinage of the national capital. A force was landed from the British fleet, which attacked and burned Washington. Perry, with such slight force as could be hastily gathered, aided in seriously injuring the hostile fleet as it went down the Potomac from its hostile mission. The attack made on Baltimore was bravely repulsed, and among other of its effects was the production of our immortal national hymn, " The Star-Spangled Banner." To Key, " England, with all her faults," would have given burial in Westminster Abbey ; where is our national minstrel laid ?

The too successful attempt on Baltimore showed the necessity of our being prepared to give the enemy a different reception, should he feel inclined to make us another predatory visit, and accordingly a number of small vessels were got ready to meet any such attack. Perry received the temporary command of one of them.

The Treaty of Ghent put an end to hostilities between the United States and Great Britain. It was signed on the 24th of December, 1814, and was soon after officially ratified.

The formal wording of the treaty did not imply that we had gained much by the war, but those who look closely at after events will perceive that there were some strong intimations between the lines. From the moment that that treaty received its signatures it will be noticed by the student of history that the most powerful nation upon earth and sea spoke to and of us as an admitted equal. There was no more firing of cannon for our cruisers to come to and send an officer on board. The right of search had disappeared from the ocean and the lakes with the smoke of the cannon fired by Oliver Hazard Perry and his valiant fellow-sailors.

There were not many days of peace in the midst of his family for Perry. It is the penalty of greatness that it must put its talents to the service of the country. Perry was once more in demand. A voyage of discovery was projected, but Perry did not relish going in a secondary position, so declined to go.

It was then determined to send the *Java* to the Mediterranean, with Perry in command. The passage was a very stormy one, and in its course the captain displayed his usual capacity and coolness in several ways. The squadron visited Algiers, whose Dey inspired almost every nation in those days with a degree of terror which we find it difficult now to understand.

Hostilities appeared imminent, and Perry had an interview with the Dey. Things were, however, brought to a temporary pacific ending.

It was during this voyage that the unfortunate difficulty between Captain Heath, of the marines, and Captain Perry took place. The marine officer, doubtless in a state of partial inebriety, appeared before the captain, when Perry lost his temper and struck him. Probably no one more deeply regretted the hasty blow than did the inflicter. But the original offender became almost a martyr by the rash punishment which he had received for an indiscretion. Charges and countercharges grew out of this matter. Neither of the officers was punished. A duel subsequently grew out of it. Perry received his opponent's fire, but did not return it. So the affair closed.

Again Perry had a brief furlough for home life. But little time was given him to enjoy the tranquil pleasures of which he was very fond. Orders came from Washington that his services were required, and as usual he promptly obeyed the summons,

This time it was not with the haughty flag of England that he was to try fierce conclusions.   It was the young republics of South America that were now troubling us.   They were at war with Spain.   They had scarce any commerce, while Spain had still a large remnant of those mighty fleets that had tempted the cupidity of Raleigh, Drake, and other bold adventurers.   But not content with worrying the ships of old Spain, the State of Venezuela, it was alleged, issued letters of marque to almost any adventurer who could get possession of a hull and sails ; the flag did not so much matter.   Indeed, the thin division between piracy and privateering was invisible.   As some United States merchantmen had been captured and adjudicated as "good prizes," it was determined to send Commodore Perry as an envoy to stop this nefarious business, either by fair means or by force.

In June, Perry, on board the *John Adams*, with the schooner *Nonsuch* as a tender, sailed for the Orinoco.

On the passage they touched at Barbadoes, where the governor and other British authorities received them with due courtesy, and gave Perry some good advice as to the climate, fevers, hurricanes, and other matters.

On arriving at the mouth of the great stream it became evident that the *Adams* drew too much water to ascend, so Perry shifted his flag to the *Nonsuch*, a far lighter vessel.   He has given us a graphic account of the various annoyances experienced on this small craft : " Confined on board a small vessel.   Rise in the morning, after being exhausted by heat. The sun, as soon as it shows itself, striking almost through one ; mosquitoes, sandflies, and gnats covering you.   As the sun gets up, it becomes entirely calm, and its rays pour down a heat that is insufferable.   The fever it creates, together with the irritation caused by the insects, produce a thirst which is insatiable ; to quench which, we drink water at eighty-two degrees,

About four o'clock a rain squall, accompanied by a little wind, generally takes place. It might be supposed that this would cool the air ; but not so. The steam which rises as soon as the sun comes out makes the heat still more intolerable. At length night approaches ; the wind leaves us. We go close in shore and anchor ; myriads of mosquitoes and gnats come off to the vessel and compel us to sit over strong smokes created by burning oakum and tar, rather than endure their terrible stings. Wearied and exhausted, we go to bed to endure new torments. Shut up in the berth of a small cabin, if there is any air stirring, not a breath of it can reach us. The mosquitoes, more persevering, follow us, and annoy us the whole night by their noise and bites, until, almost mad with the heat and pain, we rise to go through the same troubles the next day.''

These annoyances were of course only experienced as they proceeded up the river.

The *Nonsuch*, after crossing the difficult bar, had over three hundred miles of rapid current to stem. We with our powerful steam-tugs cannot begin to realize what that meant. But Perry was not the man to be disheartened at such difficulties. Still, he had so long been accustomed to the free airs of the ocean on large vessels that this '' cabined, cribbed, confined '' style of living was exceedingly irksome to him.

For much of the river through which the *Nonsuch* passed the shores were destitute of human habitation, as they were for weeks little better than swamps. True, they were clothed with all that exuberant vegetation common in the tropics, where the blaze of the fierce tropical sun drew out of the rich mire mammoth trees, wreathed with every description of gigantic vegetation.

As they advanced up stream, when the wind fell they were obliged to resort to towing at times, or else they made fast to a tree, and so arranged the helm as to keep them clear of the shore.

At such times Perry would land, and, gun in hand, bring down some of those beautifully variegated tropic birds which flit amid the gorgeous blossoms, literally " gilding refined gold."

On the arrival of Perry at the capital of Venezuela he at once secured the valuable services of an American, Dr. Forsyth, long a resident of that State.

In the Hall of Congress they were received by the Vice-President. The usual formal introductions over, Perry at once opened the business in hand. He said the American President had sent him as a naval officer to informally deliver a message upon the present state of affairs between the two countries. The Vice-President said he cordially welcomed the commodore, and believed everything could be adjusted satisfactorily.

We will now quote from the note-book of the captain his account of the after progress of negotiations :

" The next day, being the 28th, I requested Mr. Forsyth to call on the Vice-President, and know when I could be received for the purpose of opening my business. He replied that, to show his disposition to avoid ceremony, and his satisfaction at the mode I had adopted, he would call at my lodgings that evening, where we could have a free, friendly, and uninter-rupted conversation, and avoid the curiosity of the people, who were much excited to learn the object of my mission. In the evening he called, as he had promised, when I explained to him fully the object of my visit to Venezuela ; recapitulating, in the first place, the good offices which the United States had exerted to procure the recognition by Spain of the independence of her former colonies. While they had considered it their duty to observe a faithful and impartial neutrality, the part which they have taken, by negotiation with the European powers, had con-tributed more to promote the cause of South America than taking part against Spain would have done. Spain had solicited the Congress of Aix-la-Chapelle to mediate between her and her colonies, they returning to their allegiance, and she granting to them certain commercial privileges heretofore withheld. The government of the United States was informed of this before the meeting of that Congress. It had been proposed that the United States should join in the mediation ; but they refused to interfere in any plan of mediation except upon the basis of the complete independence of the colonies. This occasioned dissatisfaction to France and Russia. Great Britain, aware that the mediation could not be effected without the concurrence of the United States, stipulated that there should be no resort to force against South America. France and Russia assented ; but proposed, should the accommodation be rejected, to prohibit all commercial intercourse with them, to which Great Britain objected. The last expedient proposed was, that the Duke of Wellington, in behalf of the Congress, should arrange with the cabinet of Madrid ; the duke insisting, in any event, that force should not be used. Spain wished the perfect restoration of her colonies ; but, finding it could not be obtained, declined all interposition on other terms. While our government always took occasion to manifest its good wishes, it never lost sight of the duty of neutrality, considering the war a civil one : South America wishing to gain her independence, Spain to maintain her supremacy. For the United States to have recognized either, while the war still continued, would have been to take part. Hence their motive for refusing to have communication with Mr. Clemente, claiming to be received as the representative of Venezuela, while the war continued and her independence was incomplete. I then furnished Mr. Zea with the two acts of our Congress with regard to neutrality and piracy, and demanded indemnity for various spoliations, particularly the unjust seizure of American property by the schooner *Brutus*, commanded by Nicholas Joly, under the Amelia Island flag, which property had been condemned illegally and sold within the territory of Venezuela. I also explained the views of the government with regard to privateers, and that commissions issued to them in blank were considered illegal. I asked also for an official list of those commissioned by Venezuela, that I might forward it to our government.

" The Vice-President listened attentively, and appeared much gratified with the information I gave him with regard to the exertions of the United States, in behalf of South America, with the powers of Europe. His government knew that something unfavourable to South American liberty had been agitated by the allied powers, but of what nature they had hitherto been ignorant. Respecting Mr. Clemente, he said that the government of Venezuela was more displeased with him than the President of the United States could be ; that his conduct was unauthorized, and a source of mortification to them ; that the manner in which he had been treated was such as his improper conduct deserved ; and that the note of Mr. Adams, stating the impossibility of having any communication with him, was couched in such delicate terms that even if there were any who had a disposition to be offended at it, it was impossible for them to be so with justice ; that a gentleman of talent and great prudence had been expressly selected to go to the United States, and he trusted would conduct himself in such a manner as to afford no cause of complaint. On the other points he stated his disposition to do justice to those who had suffered from the aggressions of cruisers in the service of Venezuela. He stated that Congress was then engaged on the subject of their cruisers, and that laws would be passed to place them under rigorous restrictions. As soon as possible, I should be furnished with a copy of the laws and a list of the cruisers. With regard to the acts of Congress, he said that it was the duty of every government to bring to punishment those engaged in acts of piracy ; but that, although no explanation was necessary on this subject, he received it as an act of friendship and delicacy on the part of the United States. He concluded by saying that he had no doubt I should receive entire satisfaction upon all the points I had mentioned, and that we should have the mutual pleasure of doing away the little difficulties that had existed between the two countries, when the most friendly relations, he hoped, would ensue.

" On Sunday, the 1st of August, I called on the Vice-President, and handed him the notes which I had addressed to him, and entered again into explanations with him on the relations of the two governments. In this, as in the former interview, I received assurance of a prompt and favourable issue to my business. Yet, from the indolence of these people, I am not sanguine of an early termination of my visit—a visit which affords me no pleasure further than a prospect of succeeding to the full extent of my wishes. The climate is bad, the town is extremely sickly. The creoles are also dying daily. I have nothing to do but wait patiently the time of the Vice-President, and occasionally urge him to expedite my papers."

A week later he adds · " The Vice-President assured me that, as it depended entirely on himself, an immediate and favourable answer would be given me ; that indemnity for the vessels might be expected ; and I should not be detained. Sickness taking place on board the schooner to an alarming degree, and a fever prevailing in the town of a malignant description, carrying off daily both natives and foreigners, I requested Mr. Forsyth to suggest to the Vice-President that it would be very agreeable to me to depart. He appointed the Sunday following for an interview, and said he would be ready to communicate his answers. I waited on him on Sunday. He said the papers were ready, with the exception of the answer

in relation to one of the claims ; that he would write me a note
the next morning ; and wished, if possible, that I would consent to stay until the last of the week.   I said, if there was any
public business that required me to do so, I should consider it
a duty to remain.   I afterward discovered from Mr. Forsyth
that it was only to give me a dinner ; so I thought it advisable
to write a note signifying that I must depart.

" The communications I made to the Vice-President appeared in the first instance to produce a favourable impression,
but at present he affects, as I am told, to think that the sole
object of my visit is to reclaim the property that has been
illegally captured.   He joins others in the opinion that it will
be policy to restore this property, as it will make a favourable
impression on the minds of foreign nations.   They will not
readily give up so fruitful a source of revenue as the privilege
of plundering at pleasure the peaceful commerce of all nations.

" I find a great degree of hostility exists here towards my
government and country, and, notwithstanding the frank and
friendly communications I have made to this government, no
steps have been taken to do it away.   The English are the
favourites.   This I should not mind if there had not been
attempts to cast reflections on my government on the part of the
British, and practise on the ignorant to our disadvantage.   Dis-
trusting the warmth of my temper, I keep a strict guard upon
myself ; but I am really, at this moment, through their mis-
representations, looked upon almost as an enemy, merely because I have reclaimed property captured in the most illegal
manner.

" The idea prevails generally among the people, and even
among some men of intelligence, that the government of the
United States is cold and indifferent to their fate ; that it takes
no interest in their struggle for independence.   I have replied
to this charge, that, having determined upon neutrality, what-

ever our feelings of partiality might be, we dealt fairly and honourably with both parties ; truth and justice being the basis of all our acts, it would be inconsistent with our character to profess one thing and do another. Jealousies and dissensions have already arisen, and it does not require any great foresight to believe that they will become very serious. The English in their service have to suffer every privation from want of clothing and wholesome food. However well I may wish this cause, I cannot desire to see my countrymen suffer the privations and hardships which the English in this service have done : making campaigns in this climate without tents or anything to secure them from the burning sun ; furnished regularly with neither pay nor clothing ; their only provisions miserable beef without salt, and occasionally a few plantains ; held in little estimation by the natives, who, when they first arrive, envy them their fine coats, and afterwards despise them for their inability to endure the climate. Many of the officers have returned sick from the army, with a shirt that could only endure being washed by a syringe, and a pair of pantaloons, the legs of which had retired to an alarming elevation. The troops would all desert if there were any secure refuge for them to escape to, and the officers resign if pride did not deter them.

" Having only stepped upon the threshold of the country, it scarcely becomes me to give an opinion as to its state. What little I have seen has, however, impressed me most unfavourably. What, however, would be the result, should those in power, depraved as they are, be cut off ? Who is to supply their place ? Spanish policy has aimed at the entire extinction of talent and information among the natives. The blacks are numerous, and aware of their strength ; great alarm exists in the minds of the few intelligent as to their future conduct and obedience. Should Bolivar and a few others be taken off, there will be an end to everything like government, even of a military despotism, for there are none to supply their place ; and the country must inevitably fall into the hands of brigands, who will, by their robberies and murders, desolate the land, and by their piracies at sea form a nuisance to the commerce of the world.''

It was the 11th of August before Perry obtained a reply from the government to his note claiming satisfaction. It promised almost everything asked.

Greatly against his will, he was persuaded to remain until the 14th of August, to partake of a farewell dinner very courteously pressed upon him.

Daily he paid visits to the *Nonsuch*, encouraging the sick with hopeful words, and seeing that everything was done for their comfort. The doctor, Mr. Morgan, had been sick, but was convalescent.

On the 15th of August he joined in a grand fête for the proclamation of the Constitution. After it he went on board the schooner, and she at once proceeded down the river.

On the morning of the 17th the *Nonsuch* was at anchor on the bar that makes at the mouth of the Orinoco.

While sleeping in his berth during the night, Perry got quite wet from spray that came down the necessarily open hatchway. Early in the morning he was suffering from a chill.

Luckily, Dr. Forsyth was on board as a passenger. Dr. Morgan was himself sick. Every symptom seemed to foretell that the commodore had been seized by a serious illness. Blood-letting was tried, but it was at once seen that none could be spared. Both the physicians exhausted the whole of their resources in trying to bring about a favourable result.

When asked not to feel alarmed, the patient replied · '' I feel no alarm at whatever may happen : the debt of mortality must be paid !'' At another time he observed : '' Few persons have greater inducements to make them wish to live than I ; but I

am perfectly ready to go if it pleases the Almighty to take me ;
' the debt of nature must be paid ! ' ''

Shortly after noon, on the 23d of August, when the *Nonsuch*
was but about half a dozen miles from port, Perry was seized
with vomiting, the most unfavorable symptom of the disease.

Satisfied that the supreme moment approached, Perry summoned his two lieutenants, Claxton and Salter, to his presence.
He told them that he left all his property and the care of his
children to his wife.   Later to Mr. Handy he gave in charge
all official papers and his instructions from Washington.

Soon after he was visited by his friends from the *John Adams*,
among them his deeply attached companion, Lieutenant
Turner.   Suppressing his emotions, he calmly asked after the
crew and officers of the *John Adams*.   Then he asked for a
special interview with Mr. Handy.   Perry lay on a mattress in
the little cabin of the schooner, and as he grasped the hand of
his faithful confidential secretary the emotions of both were
hardly controllable.   All efforts to prolong his valuable life
were in vain, and just at half past three he quietly expired.

Thus died Oliver Hazard Perry, at the early age of thirty-four.
It was the anniversary of his birth.   His death was as tranquil,
in spite of all the concomitant surroundings of discomfort, as
though he were sinking to slumber in a quiet chamber of his
deeply loved distant home.

The schooner lay about a mile away from the *John Adams*,
and the fall of the commodore's pennant too quickly announced
his death.

Intense regret was felt by all hands on both ships, from the
captain to the smallest boy, and all expressed a desire that his
remains should be at once conveyed home in the ship he had
so recently commanded.   Sanitary reasons, however, compelled
the surgeons to rule that the body ought to be, for the time, interred at Port Spain, from whence they could be transferred

at a later period to the land he so deeply loved and had so gloriously served.

Sir Ralph Woodford, the governor of the British island of Trinidad, was applied to for a permit allowing the commodore's body to be buried on shore.

This request was at once courteously granted, accompanied by the governor's deep regret at the loss of so great and good a man.

To account for these extraordinary demonstrations of respect at the funeral of Perry, it may be well to mention that there were at the time many officers serving in Trinidad who had been made prisoners after the capture of Barclay's squadron, and subsequent to the battle of the Thames.

So deeply touched were the officers of the American vessels that they made this expression of their feelings in the most public manner :

" The officers of the United States vessels *John Adams* and *Nonsuch* tender their grateful acknowledgments to the inhabitants of Port Spain for their kind and respectful attention to the funeral rites of their late commander, Commodore Perry. The disposition manifested by all classes was highly in unison with their feelings, and merits their warmest thanks."

The governor replied, expressing his " regret that the hopes which he had entertained of receiving Commodore Perry within that government with the consideration due to his rank and merits had been so fatally disappointed."

Every tribute of respect and admiration that the people and Congress of the United States could bestow was given to the memory of the heroic commodore, and profound and lasting was the sorrow felt for his most untimely death.

Liberal provision was made for the widow of the gallant man, as well as for each of his young children.

The personal appearance of Perry is thus given by one well

acquainted with him. He was lofty in stature, and of a most graceful contour. "He was easy and measured in his movements, and calm in his air. His brow was full, massive, and lofty, his features regular and elegant, and his eye full, dark, and lustrous. His mouth was uncommonly handsome, and his teeth large, regular, and very white. The prevailing expression of his countenance was mild, benignant, and cheerful, and a smile of amiability, irresistibly pleasing, played in conversation about his lips. His whole air was expressive of health, freshness, comfort, and contentment, bearing testimony to a life of temperance and moderation."

At the proper time a national vessel was despatched to convey the remains of Perry to Newport, where a granite monument records his acts but cannot help to eternize his fame. It will be a sad day for the Republic when his deeds find no place in the *hearts* of his countrymen.

ADMIRAL DAVID GLASCOE FARRAGUT.

A.D. 1801—1870.

THE family of David Glascoe Farragut is of Catalonian origin. Minorca, one of the Balearic Isles, was the residence of George, the father of the great admiral. In 1776 he arrived in America, and very soon he enlisted in the army of the land of his adoption.

After the war of the Revolution George Farragut married Miss Elizabeth Shine, of North Carolina. The lady was of Scotch descent. He took up land at a place called Campbell's Station, in the State of Tennessee.

David was born on the 5th of July, 1801. When yet quite a lad he was appointed a midshipman, and was to sail under Captain Porter, the famous commander of the *Essex*.

In July, 1812, young Farragut was sailing on board the *Essex* as a midshipman. It was on this cruise that David smelled powder fired in anger for the first time.

The frigate *Essex* contrived to lure the British ship *Alert* into an engagement. The latter was the first to open fire. Immediately the carronades of the *Essex* sent an answer to the Briton's guns. After the second discharge of the artillery of the *Essex* the enemy's men left their guns, and in eight minutes from the first shot " the meteor flag of England" was stuck to the Stars and Stripes.

Lieutenant Finch rowed on board to take formal possession of the prize. She proved to be the British ship *Alert.* Her armament was twenty carronades, eighteen-pounders. She was not really a match for the *Essex*, but in consequence of so much arrogant boasting, it was the opening wedge that showed what might yet be done when the *Essex* met " one of her size."

Captain Porter made an arrangement with Captain Finch of the *Alert* by which the captured frigate was sent to St. John's under a flag of truce ; this rendered her exempt from capture. In her were sent some of the English prisoners released under satisfactory arrangements.

The cruise was continued for some time longer, but the eager Porter found no enemy's vessel anxious to meet him; so, as provisions were getting short and the crew stinted, and the good ship needed overhauling, he returned to harbor for instructions.

She was accordingly safely brought to her moorings in the Delaware.

On the 28th of October, 1812, the *Essex*, thoroughly repaired, refurnished, and provisioned, set sail once more in quest of an enemy.

Her crew all told, from captain to smallest boy, numbered 319 souls.

On December 11th, just after crossing the Equator, the *Essex* signalled a brig of rather suspicious appearance. She hoisted English colors just at sundown. As the captain much liked her looks, he made up his mind not to injure the hull, if possible, thinking she would prove of value to the United States navy. The Englishman had no intention, however, of proving an easy capture, for he came under the stern of the *Essex* in order to rake her and then run off before the wind. A round of musketry from Porter's marines spoiled this plan, and she was forced to yield. The prize was called the *Nocton.*

The prisoners, some passengers, and over fifty thousand dollars in specie were transferred to the *Essex* that night.

He permitted the prisoners and passengers to sail in the prize on their pledging their word of honour to remain prisoners till properly exchanged.

After this for some time little of any special interest relating to young David occurred ; they had touched at two or three Portuguese settlements, were provided with the usual fruits, vegetables, and fowls to be found in such places, and then they started round Cape Horn, that terror to even the best captains sailing in the stanchest vessels.

The *Essex* had her share of bad weather, scanty fare, and tossing about on the crests of mighty waves or dipping into the deep intervals between. But we have no authentic details of the actions or thoughts of the boy who in after years was to give employment to the pens of poets and the pencils of painters in chronicling his doings.

After safely rounding the Cape the frigate sailed along the coast of South America, the crew viewing with feelings of awe the dismal, forbidding, rocky shores of Chili, with the mighty Andes piercing the clouds with their icy pinnacles.

No war-ship of the enemy was encountered, but on the 28th of April, 1813, the boats of the frigate captured three British whale-ships, whose united value was some five hundred thousand dollars. This streak of luck satisfied those of the sailors who were grumbling that they had come all that distance, getting neither fighting nor prize-money.

By the end of May the captain's fleet had been increased by captures till it was now quite formidable. We give a list of vessels, guns, and crews ; *Essex,* 46 guns, 245 men ; *Georgiana,*

16 guns, 42 men ; *Atlantic*, 6 guns, 12 men ; *Greenwich*, 2 guns, 10 men ; *Montezuma*, 2 guns, 10 men ; *Policy*, unarmed, 10 men—in all, 80 guns, 333 men.

So well had the men been treated that not one had deserted, although in those sunny seas it is difficult to keep sailors true to their flag.

It was about this time that the prizes increased so fast that there were not lieutenants enough "to go round" to command them ; so in many cases midshipmen were placed as captains, with reliable petty officers as the *real* sailing officers.

On the 12th of July the *Essex* captured the piratical craft the *Seringapatam.* This fine vessel was said to have been built at the order of the famous Indian ruler, Tippoo Saib. Twenty-two guns were put into her, and made her a style of ship to be avoided. A vessel which had been previously captured was rechristened the *Essex Junior*, and she did not belie the compliment.

A sad event occurred at Charles Island, whose cause is veiled in oblivion. A duel took place, and at the third fire Lieutenant John S. Cowan, of the *Essex* was killed. His age was twenty-one. An inscription intimating the regret of his shipmates was planted at his head.

From the Gallapagos Islands, which had for some time been made the rendezvous of the fleet, the *Essex* started on a long cruise among the islands of that distant sea. Of course a youth so intelligent and enterprising as young Farragut must have stored up a knowledge of men and seamanship, which doubtless proved of vast use to him in the future.

The departure of the *Essex* from one of the islands of the Pacific occurred on the 9th of December, 1812. Many of the seamen could with difficulty be brought to submit to the strict discipline imperative at sea, especially on board ships of war. The commander was called upon to check a rising mutiny.

The leader, one White, was put into a native canoe, turned adrift, and became " a man without a country."

About the same time a native of Otaheite—of a race of men, be it here said, who make capital seamen—received a blow from a savage boatswain. What did the poor fellow do? Return the blow? No ; the poor *savage* burst into a fit of weeping, and remarking no one should again disgrace him in that way, leaped overboard and was drowned.

While the *Essex* and the *Essex Junior* were in the neutral port of Valparaiso, the British frigate *Phœbe* with her consort the *Cherub* entered the roadstead. Captain Hillyar of the *Phœbe* and Captain Porter of the *Essex* had frequently met on previous occasions in friendly ports, and seemed to be good friends. But both appeared quite ready to engage in hostilities.

At last Captain Hillyar caught the *Essex* in a comparatively crippled condition, and by sheer power of numbers overcame the fine old ship. Porter, though defeated, lost no laurels. On the contrary, his defeat was more honorable than many victories have been.

It was in reporting this battle that Porter wrote, eulogizing little Farragut's conduct as a midshipman, giving as a reason for not advising his present promotion, *that he was too young.* Indeed, as an old salt remarked, " many boys haven't cut adrift from their mother's apron-strings at his age."

Porter contrived to effect his escape by means of a boat, and landed on the coast of Long Island in a way that reads more like a romance than sober reality. How he was received needs no telling.

Little Farragut reached Boston, where he soon rejoined his heroic captain.

The autumn of 1814 brought peace with it. Through the good offices of Captain Porter, David Farragut was placed in a school at the pleasant little town of Chester, Pennsylvania. He continued here for a year, making good use of his brief scholastic training.

At the end of this year Farragut was sent on board the *Washington*, of seventy-four guns, Commodore Isaac Chauncey. The Rev. Mr. Folsom, since an eminent professor, was chaplain. This worthy gentleman quickly discovered the midshipman's excellent qualities. Indeed, so much did he become attached to the lad, that when he was appointed consul to Tunis he managed that Farragut got leave of absence to go with him.

Farragut remained in Tunis about a year, deriving great advantage from the instructions and counsels of Mr. Folsom. Then he returned to the Mediterranean fleet.

On New Year's day, 1821, Farragut, then seventeen, was appointed lieutenant.

He saw service in the West Indies. But no incidents happened to bring out his latent abilities.

Three years passed away, when we find him at the Norfolk Navy-Yard. Here he remained, attending to arduous but monotonous duties, till 1832. It was early in this period that he married Miss Loyall, daughter of a highly respectable gentleman of Norfolk. Unfortunately this estimable lady was for years a suffering invalid. Farragut proved a kind and loving husband until death relieved her of her pain.

Farragut was next appointed to the *Vandalia*, cruising off the coast of Brazil. He was married to Miss Virginia Loyall, sister to his first wife, after his return to Norfolk.

One son, Loyall, was given to them. He will doubtless add fresh lustre to the grand name transmitted to him.

From 1837 to 1840 Farragut served on board the sloop-of-war *Natchez*, on the West India station, or at the Norfolk Navy-Yard. He received his full commission as commander in September, 1840. While cruising off Brazil he received the command of the *Decatur*, sloop-of-war.

When he came home to Norfolk, in February, 1843, he left the *Decatur* for a lengthened furlough.

In the spring of 1844 Farragut received command of the receiving-ship *Pennsylvania*, a task requiring not brilliant talent, but superior powers of direction and management. Here the commander did excellent service.

During 1847 he was sailing around the Leeward and Windward Islands. Doubtless their lovely shores must have recalled the boyhood hours that he spent among the smiling islands of the sunny Pacific. At the end of the year he again returned to Norfolk. After this for some time he was not on active service.

For about three years from March, of 1851, he was engaged inspecting ordnance at different places.

The discovery of gold in California made it imperative that we should look to naval matters in that, one of our latest and best acquisitions. So the ever-reliable Commodore Farragut was sent to assume direction of the Mare Island Navy-Yard, which place he reached in the autumn of 1854.

In September, 1855—not a day too soon—Farragut received his commission as captain in the United States Navy.

Hitherto David Glascoe Farragut had filled every station accorded to him by his country in a manner to satisfy the most exacting of his superiors. But the days were now dawning that were to call out all the noblest qualities of the man and the officer. Now more than ever before did the country need every man to do his duty.

Every man had to be at once morally as well as physically brave.

The fierce frenzy of the secession fever had seized the hearts and heads of many of the bravest and best men of the South. But Farragut, more in sorrow than in anger, reasoned, implored, begged his countrymen to pause ere they " shot Niagara."

But the fiat had gone forth. As well reason with the waves

dashing on Cape Horn, or argue with a typhoon sweeping the ocean.

In vain were all sorts of offers made to him to join the Confederacy. But he was made of firmer stuff. His heart was filled with that same indomitable courage that upheld the other David when he went forth to do battle against the towering Goliath.

He at once declared for that flag that he had seen blown to tatters by the shot from British cannon in the harbor of Valparaiso.

On the morning of the 18th of April, 1861, his pleasant home was deserted. Farragut left Norfolk, with his sad but firm face turned toward the north star. It was with difficulty that he managed to get through the now hostile cities on his way to New York.

While Farragut was hastening to New York, the *Pawnee* and the *Cumberland* withdrew from Norfolk, having first fired the principal buildings.

The captain secured a simple, quiet home for his family at Hastings-on-the-Hudson.

His next move was to hasten to Washington and express his willingness to do any and every thing demanded of him by the authorities of his country.

The vessels of the navy were everywhere but where they ought to have been. There was no ship available ; so for the time being he was made a member of the Naval Retiring Board. But such a quiet vocation was useless in the stirring and bloody times now approaching.

Squadron after squadron had sailed from the North and were doing good service for their country in the South, but as yet no suitable employment was found for " the noblest Roman of them all."

It was at last seen that New Orleans, in many respects one of the most important cities of the Confederacy, must be taken ; for this purpose it was necessary to have some point in its neighborhood as a rendezvous for the force intended to attack it.

Below New Orleans there are few spots of land sufficiently stable to erect fortifications upon, even if such land were in our possession. But while the river was patrolled by rebel gunboats it was clearly impossible to effect a permanent landing.

It was therefore resolved to seize Ship Island, a long sand-bar, about the size and having many of the characteristic of Coney Island, New York.

The steamship *Massachusetts* was despatched with a party of soldiers, and the island was easily taken.

A powerful army, commanded by General Butler, was soon bivouacked upon the unpromising place.

The mortar fleet arrived safely from Key West with plenty of ammunition and other requisites for the terrible work in hand.

On the 15th of April the whole available force was collected in the lower reach of the mighty Mississippi. Its commander-in-chief was David Glascoe Farragut. Here was " the right man in the right place." The commander's flag floated over the steamer *Hartford*.

The Crescent City with good reason relied upon the immense strength of the forts — Jackson and St. Philip. They were more than fifty miles below the city itself. They had been planned, built, and manned to make the best possible defence, and were deemed almost impregnable. Both of these fortresses presented immensely powerful batteries, front and rear. The river, too, at this place rushes down with fearful velocity.

These two forts are almost opposite each other, and an enormous iron chain was stretched between them, supported near midstream by floating hulks. Nearly two hundred cannon, of different bore but all immensely large, were ready to pour a deluge of shot upon anything that dared attempt the passage,

Tennyson's famous lines do not any too strongly describe the defences ready to annihilate the daring invader.

A short distance up the river were moored floating batteries, iron-clad steamers, and steam-rams ; while fire-rafts were ready to augment the horrors prepared for the Federal fleet, should it by any possibility pass the fiery barriers awaiting it lower down. The Confederates might well deem themselves secure.   And so they would have been against any common foe.   But a few hours later it seemed as though all the old Runic war-dogs had awakened from their trance of centuries and were once again upon the seas.

Well-meaning friends urged upon Farragut the utter impossibility of surmounting the terrific obstacles.   His reply was simply, " You may be right.   But I was sent here to make the attempt.   I came here to reduce and pass the forts and to take New Orleans, and I shall try it !"

Every precaution that true seamanship could prompt was taken, and in addition to the usual precautions the wooden vessels were festooned with chain-cables to resist fire and shot.

After the customary council of war, Farragut issued the following order · " The flag-officer, having heard all the opinions expressed by the different commanders, is of the opinion that whatever is to be done will have to be done quickly.   When, in the opinion of the flag-officer, the propitious time has arrived, the signal will be made to weigh and advance to the conflict.   He will make a signal for close action, and abide the result—conquer or be conquered."

Acting with the commander, like Castor with Pollux, was the son of his old captain and friend, Commodore David D. Porter, commanding the powerful flotilla of mortar boats.

Some alarm was caused by a fire-raft rushing like a flaming meteor right on the fleet, but Porter had taken measures to render them harmless,

For several days a terrific combat of shells was fought between the United States fleet and the Confederate defences, but little progress had been made in getting toward New Orleans. But on the night of the 21st two valiant officers, Crosby and Caldwell, contrived to reach the chain undiscovered, and broke it l This left a channel-way for the fleet. No sooner had the Confederates discovered this than tremendous bonfires were lit upon the shores, so that the gunners could see plainly to bring a concentric fire upon the fleet as it moved slowly against the current through this fearful channel. Some officers proposed landing sailors to put out the fires.

"No ! no ! by no means ; those fires are the lighthouses by which I mean to steam through the gap in the chain, throw a few shells or shot at them, to give the rebels an idea that we want them to put them out, and thus incite them to more strenuous exertions to keep them bright and alive."

On the 24th at 2 o'clock A. M. a preconcerted signal was given, and the attacking fleet started for death or victory. In two lines the stately ships advanced. One was to attack Fort Philip, the other Fort Jackson. Steadily, though slowly, they threw the rushing tides aside, moving on without regarding any impediment.

" It may be safely said that such a naval conflict was never witnessed on this earth before. The enemy were on the alert ; the beacon-fires soon blazed so brightly as to expose every movement of the fleet, and the whole stormy scene was illumined with a lurid glare, which added vastly to its sublimity and its almost fiendlike horror. The *Cayuga* was the first which passed the chain-boom, under a terrible fire from both of the forts, which struck her repeatedly from stem to stern. The rest of the squadron rapidly followed. They were now directly abreast of the forts, exposed to the direct action of their guns, while the river above was crowded with the fire-rafts, rams, and gunboats of the foe.

" They all came plunging down together upon the heroic fleet. First came an immense fire-raft, pushed by the ram *Manassas*, directly upon the flagship *Hartford*. In endeavouring to avoid it the ship was crowded ashore, and the flaming raft was pushed down upon its side. In a moment the majestic ship seemed enveloped in flames, half way up to her tops. Fortunately the ship was backed off from the shoal, and by immense exertions of the fire department the flames were extinguished. The thunder of over three hundred guns from the forts, the rebel gunboats, and the national fleet, joined with the distant booming of the mortars, filled the air with a continuous roar, louder than heaven's heaviest thunders.

" Shot and shell did frightful execution on ship and battlement. The whole scene was soon so enveloped in the sulphurous smoke of the battle that friends could with difficulty be distinguished from foes, and often the flash of opposing guns alone guided the fire. The rebels fought with that desperation which was to be expected of Americans, even when engaged in an infamous cause. While the national ships were yet under the fire of the forts, they were assailed by the monster rams and floating batteries which the foe held in reserve. These enormous rams, aided by the swift current, and under full headway of steam, dashed with their iron prows upon our ships, discharging at close range their heavy guns as reckless as if no harm could touch them. It is impossible to recount the exploits of the gallant men who fought beneath the Stars and Stripes, in these hours of deadly encounter.

" Every ship in the fleet signalized itself by heroism which could not be surpassed. We cannot record the deeds of all · let us allude to a few as specimens of the rest. The United States steamship *Brooklyn*, in the darkness, and while exposed to the hottest fire, became entangled in the barricading hulks and chains. In attempting to extricate the ship her bow grazed the shore. She, however, worked her way through, when the ram *Manassas* came rushing upon her from the gloom. At the distance of ten feet the ram discharged her shot, which pierced the ship, and then, with a crash, struck her side, battering in the starboard gangway. The chain armor saved the ship from destruction, and the ram slid off and disappeared in the darkness.

"Fort Jackson, in the liftings of the smoke, caught a glimpse of the majestic ship, and opened upon her a raking fire. Just then a large rebel steamer came rushing up on the port broadside. When at the distance of but sixty yards the *Brooklyn* poured into the audacious stranger one single volley of shell and red-hot shot, and the fragments of the steamer, in a mass of crackling flame, drifted down the stream.

"The *Brooklyn*, still groping its way along, lighted by the flames of an approaching fire-raft, and yet enveloped in its resinous smoke, soon found itself abreast of St. Philip, almost touching the shore. The ship chanced to be in such a position that she could bring almost every gun to bear. Tarrying for a moment, she poured into the fort such a storm of grape and canister as completely to silence the work. The men stationed in the tops of the frigate said that, by the light of their bursting shrapnels, they could see the garrison 'running like sheep for more comfortable quarters.'

"The *Brooklyn* then rushed into the nest of rebel gunboats, fighting them indiscriminately, with her broadsides striking the most terrific blows, and continuing the contest, in connection with the other vessels, for an hour and a half, until the rebel fleet was annihilated. After the action was over, Commodore Farragut took the hand of Captain Craven of the *Brooklyn* in both of his, and said, 'You and your noble ship have been the salvation of my squadron. You were in a complete blaze of fire ; so much so that I supposed your ship was burning up. I never saw such rapid and precise firing. It never was surpassed, and probably never was equalled.'

" The *Mississippi* encountered the ram *Manassas*, rushing upon her at full speed. The noble old frigate, undaunted, instead of evading the blow, turned to meet her antagonist, and, with all steam on, made a plunge at the monster. Just as the blow was to come which would decide whose head was to be broken open, the *Manassas*, taking counsel of discretion, dodged. But as she glided by, a point-blank broadside from the immense armament of the *Mississippi* swept off her smokestack, crashed through her iron sides, and set her on fire. The crew took to the shore, and the redoubtable ram drifted, a total wreck, down the stream. The nondescript monster presented a curious spectacle as she floated along, the flames bursting through the broken chinks of her mail, her shot-fractures, and her port-holes. Commodore Porter, wishing to save her as a curiosity, sent some boats to pass a hawser around the ram and secure it to the shore. Scarcely was this done when the monster uttered, as it were, an expiring groan, as the water rushed in, driving the air and the belching flames through her bowport, and then, ' like a huge animal, she gave a plunge and disappeared under the water.' The achievements of the *Varuna*, under Captain Boggs, were among the crowning glories of this eventful day. It has been well said, he ' fought a battle fully equal in desperate hardihood and resolute bravery to the famous sea-fight of John Paul Jones, which nothing human could surpass.' After taking or destroying six of the enemy's vessels, an unarmored point was pierced, and while the water rushed in, the crew jumped into the boats of the *Oneida*, sent for their rescue, as she went down with her dead, ' victorious in death,' her flag still flying, covered with glory.''

By midday after the fierce battle, word was sent to General Butler that there was no longer any obstacle to his entering New Orleans.

Considering the terrific nature of the defence and the before unheard-of means brought to bear to burn, swamp, pulverize, annihilate the Union fleet, the losses were inconsiderable. Three gunboats had been rendered unserviceable, thirty men were killed outright, and a little over one hundred men wounded.

After this great victory Commodore Farragut ordered that there should be observed a festival of thanksgiving to Almighty God for their great success.

The loss of New Orleans was a stunning blow to the Confederate cause. They were bereft of six strong forts, eighteen gunboats, and twelve hundred good fighting men ; add to which the Union flag was flying over the largest and richest city of the South—a city, indeed, whose Bourse affected the exchanges of the civilized world.

Besides, " open sesame" had been uttered, and the entrance to the mighty Mississippi was in safe hands.

The victory brought forth hearty thanks from Congress, and the President sent a highly eulogistic personal letter.

No further impediment remained to Farragut's progress up stream.

Soon after Congress enacted a law creating the grade of Rear-Admiral, which rank was first conferred on David Glascoe Farragut.

For a time the Admiral bestowed his attention on what to some might seem small game, but not so to the recently appointed Admiral. Anything in the line of duty was deserving of and received his closest attention. So he cleared the coast around the mouth of the Mississippi of lawless rangers and blockade runners.

But with the spring of 1863 a wider scope was given to the exercise of his great talents and cool courage.

General Grant's plan was to attack Vicksburg in the rear. To enable him to execute this operation it was proposed that the Admiral should get above Port Hudson. Admiral Foote, meanwhile, was to join him below Vicksburg. If by joining their forces they could overpower the guns of the great rebel stronghold, General Grant was to aid the design with the land forces.

The *Hartford*, bearing the flag of Farragut, was followed by the *Richmond*, the *Mississippi*, the *Monongahela*, the *Albatross*, *Kineo*, and *Genesee*. The six mortar-boats were to keep below the batteries and fire from that position as might be deemed advisable.

The evening of the 14th of March was quite dark, and it was hoped that the garrison of Fort Hudson might be caught napping. But no such good fortune! The Confederates had been apprised by their vigilant scouts of the coming attack upon the strong fortifications of Port Hudson. Reverting to the same tactics which they had practised during their defence of New Orleans, they luridly lit up the heights by flaring flames as if a city were burning, so that every spar, every shroud, on each vessel was lit up as if under the light of electricity. Danger, as ever before, only strengthened the leading characteristics of the gallant Admiral. Right in the vista of glistening light ploughed the Federal squadron, fully under the heavy guns of the Confederates.

" We had left the mortar-boats well astern, when a sulphurous light was seen gleaming on the shore, on our port side. Flashing up for a moment, a dull explosion followed. It was evidently an imperfect rocket. Another was essayed ; but, instead of ascending, it ran along the surface of the river close to the bank. A little farther up a third was tried, and with com-

plete success. It ascended high in the air, where it burst in the
usual manner. Instantaneously it was answered by a field-piece
from the opposite shore, aimed at the *Hartford.* The Admiral
was not slow in returning the compliment. Three or four guns
fired from the flag-ship in rapid succession testified to the alacrity
with which the wager of battle was accepted.

   " The return of the rebel fire by the *Hartford* was promptly
followed up by a hot fire from the artillery pieces of the rebels,
and quite a brisk action ensued between them. The scene as
viewed from the *Richmond* was both brilliant and spirited. The
flashes of the guns, both on shore and afloat, were incessant,
while the roar of cannon kept up a deafening and almost incessant sound. Great judgment was here necessary to prevent the *Richmond* from running into the *Hartford*, and, in fact,
to keep the war vessels generally from running into each other.

   " And now was heard a thundering roar, equal in volume to
a whole park of artillery. This was followed by a rushing
sound, accompanied by a howling noise that beggars description. Again and again was the sound repeated, till the vast
expanse of heaven rang with the awful minstrelsy. It was apparent that the mortar-boats had opened fire. Of this I was
soon convinced on casting my eyes aloft. Never shall I forget
the sight that then met my astonished vision. Shooting
upward at an angle of forty-five degrees, with the rapidity of
lightning, small globes of golden flame were seen sailing
through the pure ether—not a steady, unfading flame, but
coruscating like the fitful gleam of a fire-fly—now visible and
anon invisible. Like a flying star of the sixth magnitude, the
terrible missile—a thirteen-inch shell—nears its zenith, up and
still up—higher and higher. Its flight now becomes much
slower, till, on reaching its utmost altitude, its centrifugal force
becomes counteracted by the earth's attraction, it describes a
parabolic curve, and down, down it comes, bursting, it may be,

ere it reaches *terra firma*, but probably alighting in the rebel
works ere it explodes, where it scatters death and destruction
around. But while the mortar-boats were at work, the *Essex*
was not idle. Unmanageable as she is, especially in so strong
a current, she did not follow the rest of the fleet, but remained
at the head of the ' bummers,' doing admirable service with her
heavy guns.

" All this time the *Richmond* had to hang back, as Admiral
Farragut seemed to be so enamoured with the sport in which
he was engaged as to be in no hurry to pass by. Once or
twice, in consequence of the dense column of smoke that now
rolled over the river, our bowsprit was almost over the taffrail of
the *Hartford*, and there was an incessant call on the part of
Second Lieutenant Terry, who commanded the forward part of
the ship, to stop the engines. And here I may as well say that
this gallant young officer behaved in the most chivalrous manner throughout the entire engagement, cheering on the men,
and encouraging them, by his example, to stand to their guns
like men, though little of this they required to induce them to
perform their whole duty.

" The *Richmond* had by this time got within range of the
rebel field-batteries, which opened fire on her. I had all along
thought that we would open fire from our bow-guns, on
the top-gallant forecastle, and that, after discharging a few
broadsides from the starboard side the action would be wound
up by a parting compliment from our stern-chasers. To
my surprise, however, we opened at once from our broadside guns. The effect was startling, as the sound was unexpected ; but beyond this I really experienced no inconven-
ience from the concussion. There was nothing unpleasant
to the ear, and the jar to the ship was really quite unappre-
ciable. It may interest the uninitiated to be informed how
a broadside is fired from a vessel-of-war. I was told on

board the *Richmond* that all the guns were sometimes fired off simultaneously, though it is not a very usual course, as it strains the ship. Last night the broadsides were fired by commencing at the forward gun, and firing all the rest off in rapid succession, as fast almost as the ticking of a watch. The effect was grand and terrific, and if the guns were rightly pointed—a difficult thing in the dark, by the way—they could not fail in carrying death and destruction among the enemy.

"Of course we did not have everything our own way, for the enemy poured in his shot and shell as thick as hail. Over, ahead, astern, all around us flew the death-dealing missiles, the hissing, screaming, whistling, shrieking, and howling of which rivalled Pandemonium. It must not be supposed, however, because our broadside-guns were the tools we principally worked, that our bow and stern-chasers were idle. We soon opened with our bow eighty-pounder Dahlgren, which was followed up not long after by the guns astern, giving evidence to the fact that we had passed some of the batteries.

"While seated on the 'fish-davit,' on the top-gallant fore-castle—the *Hartford* and the *Richmond* blazing away at the time—a most fearful wail arose from the river, first on our port-bow, then on the beam. A man was evidently overboard, probably from the *Hartford* or the *Genesee*, then just ahead. The cry was, 'Help, oh! help!' 'Help, oh! help!' 'Man overboard,' called out Lieutenant Terry; 'throw him a rope.' But, poor fellow, who could assist him in such a strait? We were in action; every man was at his gun; to lower a boat would be folly; in fact, it could not be done with any hope of success. Consequently, although the man was evidently a good swimmer, to judge by his unfailing cries for help for a long time, nothing could be done to rescue him, and he floated astern of us, still sending up that wailing cry for help, but without effect. The terrible current of the Mississippi was too much for him, and he, without doubt, sank beneath the waves of the mighty river.

"Just after this fearful incident firing was heard astern of us, and it was soon ascertained that the *Monongahela*, with her consort, the *Kineo*, and the *Mississippi* were in action. The *Monongahela* carries a couple of two hundred-pounder rifled Parrott guns, besides other ticklers. At first I credited the roar of her amiable two hundred-pounders to the 'bummers,' till I was undeceived, when I recalled my experience in front of Yorktown last spring, and the opening of fire from similar guns from Wormley's Creek. All I can say is, the noise was splendid. The action now became general. The roar of cannon was incessant, and the flashes from the guns, together with the flight of the shells from the mortar-boats, made up a combination of sound and sight impossible to describe. To add to the horrors of the night, while it contributed toward the enhancement of a certain terrible beauty, dense clouds of smoke began to envelop the river, shutting out from view the several vessels, and confounding them with the batteries. It was very difficult to know how to steer to prevent running ashore, perhaps right under a rebel battery, or into a consort. Upward and upward rolled the smoke, shutting out of view the beautiful stars and obscuring the vision on every side. Then it was that the order was passed, 'Boys, don't fire till you see the flash from the enemy's guns.' That was our only guide through the 'palpable obscurity.'

"But this sole dependence on the flashes was likely to be attended with serious consequences, as the following incident will show:

"We had got nearly into the middle of the hornet's nest when an officer on the top-gallant forecastle called out, 'Ready with the port-gun.' The gun was got ready and pointed, and was about to be discharged, when Lieutenant

Terry called out, ' Hold on ; you are about to fire into the
Hartford.' And such was the fact ; for the flash of the *Hart
ford's* guns at that moment revealed the spars and rigging of
that vessel. Consequently the gun was not fired, nor was it
discharged during the engagement, the fighting being confined
entirely to the starboard side.

" Still the fight went on, and still the roar of cannon and the
screaming, howling, whistling of shot and shell continued to
make ' night hideous.' Still, too, the pure atmosphere was be-
fouled with the smell of ' villainous saltpetre' and obscured with
smoke, through the opaque mass of which the stars refused to
twinkle. Intermingled with the boom of the cannonade arose
the cries of the wounded and the shouts of their friends, suggesting that they should be taken below for treatment. So
thick was the smoke that we had to cease firing several times ;
and to add to the horrors of the night it was next to impossible
to tell whether we were running into the *Hartford* or going
ashore, and if the latter, on which bank, or whether some of
the other vessels were about to run into us or into each other.
All this time the fire was kept up on both sides incessantly. It
seems, however, that we succeeded in silencing the lower batteries of field-pieces. The men must have been driven from
their guns ; and no wonder, if they were in that terrific storm
of iron.

" While a brisk fire was kept up from the decks of the
several vessels, the howitzers in the tops were not permitted to
remain idle. Intermingled with the more sullen roar of the
larger guns, the sharp, short crack of the brass pieces was heard
from their elevated positions, adding harmony to the melody of
the terrific concert.

" The phrase is familiar to most persons who have read accounts of sea-fights that took place about fifty years ago, but it
is difficult for the uninitiated to realize all the horrors conveyed

in ' muzzle to muzzle.'   For the first time I had, last night, an
opportunity of knowing what the phrase really meant.   Let the
reader consult the map, and it will be seen that the central
battery is situated about the middle of the segment of a circle I
have already compared to a horseshoe in shape, though it may
be better understood by the term ' crescent.'   This battery
stands on a bluff so high that a vessel in passing immediately
underneath cannot elevate her guns sufficiently to reach those
on the battery ; neither can the guns on the battery be sufficiently depressed to bear on the passing ship.   In this
position the rebel batteries on the two horns of the crescent can
enfilade the passing vessel, pouring in a terrible cross-fire, which
the vessel can return, though at a great disadvantage, from her
bow and stern-chasers.

"We fully realized this last night ; for, as we got within
short-range, the enemy poured into us a terrible fire of grape
and canister, which we were not slow to return—our guns being
double-shotted, each with a stand of both grape and canister.
Every vessel in its turn was exposed to the same fiery ordeal on
nearing the centre battery, and right promptly did their gallant
tars return the compliment.   This was the hottest part of the
engagement.   We were literally muzzle to muzzle, the distance
between us and the enemy's guns being not more than twenty
yards, though to me it seemed to be only as many feet.   In
fact, the battle of Port Hudson has been pronounced by officers
and seamen who were engaged in it, and who were present at
the passage of Foit St. Philip and Fort Jackson, below New
Orleans, and had participated in the fights of Fort Donelson,
Fort Henry, Island Number Ten, Vicksburg, etc., as the
severest in the naval history of the present war.

"Shortly after this close engagement we seemed to have
passed the worst.   The enemy's shot and shell no longer swept
our decks like a hail-storm, but the fire from the batteries was

kept up in a desultory manner. The starboard bow gun could no longer be brought to bear. Consequently Lieutenant Terry ordered the men on the top-gallant forecastle to leave the guns in that part of the ship, and to descend to the main deck to help work the broadside guns. Our stern-chasers, of course, were still available, for the purpose of giving the enemy a parting blessing. I left my station on the top-gallant forecastle shortly after the men who had been working the bow-guns, and passed under where I had been sitting, taking up my station on the port side, just opposite the forward gun on the starboard side, where but a few minutes before a shell had exploded.

" I was not long in this position when there came a blinding flash through the very port I was opposite to, revealing a high bank right opposite, so close that a biscuit might have been tossed from the summit on board the *Richmond*. Simultaneously there came a loud roar, and I thought the shot had passed through the port I was opposite to. Indeed, so close were we to the battery that the flash, the report, and the arrival of the shot, crashing and tearing through our bulwarks, were instantaneous, there not being the intermission of a second between.

" It must have been about this time that Lieutenant Commander Cummings, the executive officer of the *Richmond*, was standing on the bridge that connects the starboard with the port gangway, with his speaking-trumpet in his hand, cheering the men. Near him stood Captain Alden, when a conical shot of large calibre passed through the hammocks, over the starboard gangway, taking off the left leg of the lieutenant just above the ankle, battering his speaking-trumpet (a prize) flat, and knocking Captain Alden down with the windage, and went through the smokestack. Mr. Cummings was immediately taken below, where his wound was promptly attended to by Dr. Henderson, the ship's surgeon, but not before the brave young man had lost a large quantity of blood on his way down.   On being carried below he used the following patriotic words, which are worthy of becoming historical : ' I would willingly give my other leg so that we could but pass the batteries.'

"The Rev. Dr. Bacon, the loyal rector of Christ Church, New Orleans, who was acting as chaplain on board the *Richmond*, was on the bridge when Mr. Cummings received his terrible wound. He fortunately escaped unhurt, though he had been all over the ship, in the thickest of the fight, carrving messages and exhorting and encouraging the men.

"It was no easy matter, in the midst of such a dense cloud of smoke, to know where to point our guns.   Even the flashes of the enemy's guns shone dimly through the thick gloom. Several times the order was given to cease fire, so as to allow the smoke to clear away ; but as there was scarcely a breath of wind stirring, this was a very slow process ; still the order was necessary, to prevent the several vessels from running into each other.   In this respect the rebels had a decided advantage over us ; for while they did not stand in danger of collision, neither was there any apprehension of firing into their friends.   The wide river was before them, and if they did not hit our vessel at each discharge, they could but miss at the worst.

"Matters had gone on this way for nearly an hour and a half —the first gun having been fired at about half-past eleven o'clock—when, to my astonishment, I heard some shells whistling over our port side.   Did the rebels have batteries on the right bank of the river ? was the query that naturally suggested itself to me.   To this the response was given that we had turned back. I soon discovered that it was too true.   Our return was, of course, more rapid than our passage up.   The rebels did not molest us much, and I do not believe one of their shots took effect while we were running down rapidly with the current.

" We were soon quietly at anchor, and were busy discussing the events of the fight, exchanging congratulations and comparing notes, when the lookout man in the maintop hailed the deck as follows :

" ' On deck there ! '

" ' Hallo ! '

" ' A large fire ahead ! '

" ' Where away ? '

" ' Just above the bend.'

" ' What is it like ? '

" ' Like a fire-raft.'

" On this Captain Alden, to whom the circumstance was duly repoited by the officers of the deck, sings out :

" ' Keep a good lookout.   Man the bow-guns, and stand by to slip the cable.'

" Shortly after this a small steamer came down, the master of which informed Captain Alden that the *Mississippi* was on fire.

" In the dense smoke that prevailed, excluding every object from view, the glorious old *Mississippi* went ashore right opposite the centre and worst battery.   She was soon discovered by the enemy.   Up to this time she had not sustained any serious injury.   She now became a standing target for the whole range of rebel batteries.   The rebels began to pour into her a perfect shower of shot and shell, which was promptly returned by the *Mississippi*.   This murderous work continued for half an hour. Finding it impossible to escape, Captain Smith judiciously but reluctantly gave orders to set the ship on fire to prevent her falling into the hands of the rebels.   Accordingly her after-part was fired, the rebels all the time continuing to pour in their shot and shell as fast as they could bring their guns to bear. During this part of the contest no fewer than two hundred and fifty rounds were fired from the *Mississippi*.   The artillery practice of the rebels would have been worthy of a better cause. The *Mississippi* was riddled through and through. Four men were known to have been killed ere the ship was abandoned. Among them was Acting Master Kelly, the whole of whose abdomen was shot away. Three were ascertained to have been wounded. There may have been some more casualties, but it is impossible to tell to what extent at present, though a great many exaggerated stories are afloat on the subject. Several were known to have jumped overboard soon after the ship was set on fire, and there can be no doubt that some of them were drowned.

"Soon after the vessel had been fired two shells came crashing through her, exploding and setting fire to some turpentine and oil which they upset. This caused the flames to spread, whereupon a master's mate hurried on to the gundeck and reported that the flames had reached the entrance to the magazine. The ship was then at once abandoned, and all hands on board, including the wounded men, were put ashore on the bank of the river opposite Port Hudson. This was accompanied by a deafening yell of exultation from the rebels on perceiving the blazing up of the fire. The *Mississippi* burned till she became lightened, to which the removal of nearly three hundred men contributed, when she swung off into deep water. She had grounded with her head up stream ; but on swinging off she turned completely round, presenting her head down the river, which position she retained till she blew up.

"At length it was reported on board the *Richmond* that the *Mississippi* was coming down, and we all turned out on the poop-deck to see the sight. It was a most magnificent spectacle. From the midships to the stern the noble vessel was enveloped in a sheet of flame, while fire-wreaths ran up the shrouds, played around the mainmast, twisted and writhed like fiery serpents. Onward she came, keeping near to the right

bank, still bow foremost, as regularly as if she was steered by a
pilot. It was, indeed, a wonderful sight. Captain Smith, her
recent commander, and several of her officers, who had by this
time arrived on board the *Richmond*, assembled on the poop-
deck, their emotion almost too great for words. Next to his
wife, children, or sweetheart, there is nothing that a sailor loves
more than his ship—nothing that he regrets the loss of so
much ; and in the absence of the above-mentioned domestic
ties his ship is to him wife, child, and sweetheart. The feeling
of regret at the loss of his ship is enhanced when, as in the case
of the *Mississippi*, the gallant craft has achieved historical renown. No wonder, then, that the officers of the *Mississippi*
should feel a sinking at the heart on witnessing the destruction
of their floating home, while they were powerless to save her.

" As she arrived opposite the port side of the *Richmond*, some
apprehension was entertained that her port broadsides might
give us a parting salute of not a very agreeable nature. Captain
Smith assured Captain Alden, however, that her port guns had
all been discharged. Just as she had cleared us, her starboard guns began to go off. This was accompanied by the explosion of the shells she had on deck, ready for use. These
exploded at short intervals. The flames now began to increase
in volume from amidships to the stern, and the howitzer on the
maintop was discharged with the heat. Majestically the gallant
craft—gallant even in its last moments—moved down the
stream till, turning the bend at the lower part of Prophet
Island, she was hidden from our view, and nothing more was
seen but a white glare shooting up skyward. Shell after shell
still exploded at intervals, and thus a couple of hours passed
away till the *Mississippi* was some eight or ten miles below the
Richmond. The shells now began to explode more rapidly, indicating that the fire has reached the shell-room, and cannot be
far from the powder magazine. This proves to be the fact ; for

presently a sudden glare of bright flame shoots upward toward the zenith, spreading skyward in the form of an inverted cone ; an interval of a few seconds elapses ; then comes a stunning roar, causing the *Richmond* to tremble from truck to keelson, and the gallant *Mississippi,* that so long ' has braved the battle and the breeze,' is no more ; all that remains of her is sunk in the bosom of the mighty river from which she derived her name.

" Passing through the starboard side of the *Richmond,* amidships, a conical eighty-pounder passed through a pile of cordage on the berth-deck, narrowly missing some powder-boys who were handing up ammunition. Thence it entered the machinery-room, passing through and smashing the steam-drum, and damaging both safety-valves, so as to prevent them from closing. Taking its course under the steam-chest, the shot came out on the other side, when it broke in two, and both pieces dropped below. Here I may take this opportunity of mentioning that Confederate iron in these regions is a very inferior metal. It is not half smelted, but right in the centre are large stones.

" Early this morning the decks of the *Richmond* presented a melancholy spectacle. Where the two men fell there was a great pool of clotted gore, which I saw a seaman tossing overboard with a shovel. The whitewashed decks, too, were anything but tidy ; but, hey ! presto, as if by magic, the stalwart arms of some two or three hundred men, with the aid of a plentiful supply of Mississippi water, have made everything as clean and neat as a lady's boudoir. The bodies of the two men who were killed have been removed forward, and to them has been added the body of the boatswain's mate, who lost both legs and an arm and who has since died. The three bodies have been neatly sewed up in their hammocks, and they are to be put into coffins for interment on shore. Headboards, with

their names inscribed on them, will be placed at the heads of
their graves, so that the bodies may be reclaimed at any time by
their friends or relatives.''

The indefatigable Admiral found time to take a trip to New
Orleans, and directed operations against Donaldsonville, where
as usual he was successful.

After New Orleans the large and prosperous city of Mobile
was the next place of importance in the extreme south of the
Confederacy. It was very strongly fortified. Three of the
most powerful fortifications on the southern seaboard dominated
the channel. Forts Powell, Morgan, and Gaines reflected
credit upon the engineering skill of the Confederates.

It was in the second week of July that Farragut and Generals
Granger and Canby had an interview, in which, after studying
the difficulties of the attack the affair was arranged. How well
will appear by what follows.

This was the inspiring order to the fleet ·

" U. S. FLAGSHIP HARTFORD, OFF MOBILE BAY, July 12, 1864.

" Strip your vessels and prepare for the conflict. Send down
all your superfluous spars and rigging, trice up or remove the
whiskers, put up the splinter nets on the starboard side, and
barricade the wheel and steersman with sails and hammocks.
Lay chains or sand-bags on the deck over the machinery to resist a plunging fire. Hang the sheet chains over the side, or
make any other arrangement for security that your ingenuity
may suggest. Land your starboard boats, or lower and tow
them on the port side, and lower the port boats down to the
water's edge. Place a leadsman and the pilot in the port-
quarter boat, or the one most convenient to the commander.

" The vessels will run past the forts in couples, lashed side
by side, as hereinafter designated. The flagship will lead and
steer from Sand Island N. by E. by compass, until abreast of

Fort Morgan ; then N. W. half N. until past the Middle Ground, then N. by W., and the others, as designated in the drawing, will follow in due order until ordered to anchor ; but the bow and quarter line must be preserved, to give the chase guns a fair range ; and each vessel must be kept astern of the broadside of the next ahead ; each vessel will keep a very little on the starboard quarter of his next ahead, and, when abreast of the fort, will keep directly astern, and as we pass the fort will take the same distance on the port quarter of the next ahead, to enable the stern guns to fire clear of the next vessel astern.

" It will be the object of the Admiral to get as close to the fort as possible before opening fire ; the ships, however, will open fire the moment the enemy opens upon us with their chase and other guns, as fast as they can be brought to bear. Use short fuses for the shell and shrapnel, and as soon as within three or four hundred yards give them grape. It is understood that heretofore we have fired too high ; but with grapeshot it is necessary to elevate a little above the object, as grape will dribble from the muzzle of the gun.

" If one or more of the vessels be disabled, their partners must carry them through, if possible ; but if they cannot, then the next astern must render the required assistance. But as the Admiral contemplates moving with the flood tide, it will only require sufficient power to keep the crippled vessels in the channel.

" Vessels that can must place guns upon the poop and top-gallant forecastle, and in the top on the starboard side. Should the enemy fire grape, they will remove the men from the top-gallant forecastle and poop to the guns below until out of grape range. The howitzers must keep up a constant fire from the time they can reach with shrapnel until out of its range.

" D. G. FARRAGUT, *Rear-Admiral*,"

It would be folly for us to paint a second-rate picture of this great achievement when we can give the gallant Admiral's own description. It will be seen that in his hand the pen is only a little less mighty than the sword :

"U. S. FLAGSHIP HARTFORD, MOBILE BAY, August 12, 1864.

"SIR : I had the honor to forward the Department on the evening of the 5th instant a report of my *entrée* into Mobile Bay on the morning of that day, and which, though brief, contained all the principal facts of the attack.   Notwithstanding the loss of life, particularly on this ship, and the terrible disaster to the *Tecumseh*, the result of the fight was a glorious victory ; and I have reason to feel proud of the officers, seamen, and marines of the squadron under my command, for it has never fallen to the lot of an officer to be thus situated and thus sustained. Regular discipline will bring men to any amount of endurance, but there is a natural fear of hidden dangers, particularly when so awfully destructive of human life as the torpedo, which re-quires more than discipline to overcome.

"Preliminary to a report of the action of the 5th, I desire to call the attention of the Department to the previous steps taken in consultation with Generals Canby and Granger on the 8th of July.   I had an interview with these officers on board the *Hartford*, on the subject of an attack upon Forts Morgan and Gaines, at which it was agreed that General Canby would send all the troops he could spare to coöperate with the fleet.   Cir-cumstances soon obliged General Canby to inform me that he could not despatch a sufficient number to invest both forts, and in reply I suggested that Gaines should be the first invested, engaging to have a force in the sound ready to protect the land-ing of the army on Dauphin Island in the rear of that fort, and I assigned Lieutenant-Commander De Krafft of the *Conemaugh* to that duty.

" On the 1st instant General Granger visited me again on the *Hartford*. In the mean time the *Tecumseh* had arrived at Pensacola, and Captain Graven informed me that he would be ready in four days for any service. We therefore fixed upon the 4th of August as the day for the landing of the troops and my entrance into the bay, but owing to delays mentioned in Captain Jenkins's communication to me, the *Tecumseh* was not ready. General Granger, however, to my mortification, was up to the time, and the troops actually landed on Dauphin Island.

" As subsequent events proved, the delay turned to our advantage, as the rebels were busily engaged during the 4th in throwing troops and supplies into Fort Gaines, all of which were captured a few days afterwards. The *Tecumseh* arrived on the evening of the 4th, and everything being propitious, I proceeded to the attack on the following morning. As mentioned in my previous despatch, the vessels outside the bar which were designed to participate in the engagement were all under way by forty minutes past five in the morning, in the following order, two abreast and lashed together :

" *Brooklyn*, Captain James Alden, with the *Octorara*, Lieutenant-Commander C. H. Green, on the port side.

" *Hartford*, Captain Percival Drayton, with the *Metacomet*, Lieutenant-Commander J. E. Jouett.

" *Richmond*, Captain T. A. Jenkins, with the *Port Royal*, Lieutenant-Commander B. Gherardi.

" *Lackawanna*, Captain J. B. Marchand, with the *Seminole*, Commander E. Donaldson.

" *Monongahela*, Commander J. H. Strong, with the *Kennebec*, Lieutenant-Commander W. P. McCann.

" *Ossipee*, Commander W. E. LeRoy, with the *Itasca*, Lieutenant-Commander George Brown.

" *Oneida*, Commander J. R. M. Mullany, with the *Galena*, Lieutenant-Commander C. H. Wells.

" The iron clads *Tecumseh*, Commander T. A. M. Craven, the *Manhattan*, Commander J. W. A. Nicholson, the *Winnebago*, Commander T. H. Stevens, and the *Chickasaw*, Lieutenant-Commander T. H. Perkins, were already ahead inside the bar, and had been ordered to take up their positions on the starboard side of the wooden ships, or between them and Fort Morgan, for the double purpose of keeping down the fire from the water battery and the parapet guns of the fort, as well as to attack the ram *Tennessee* as soon as the fort was passed. It was only at the urgent request of the captains and commanding officers that I yielded to the *Brooklyn* being the leading ship of the line, as she had four chase guns and an ingenious arrangement for picking up torpedoes, and because in their judgment the flagship ought not to be too much exposed. This I believe to be an error ; for apart from the fact that exposure is one of the penalties of rank in the navy, it will always be the aim of the enemy to destroy the flagship, and, as will appear in the sequel, such attempt was very persistently made, but Providence did not permit it to be successful.

" The attacking fleet steamed steadily up the main ship channel, the *Tecumseh* firing the first shot at 6.47. At six minutes past seven the fort opened upon us, and was replied to by a gun from the *Brooklyn*, and immediately after the action became general. It was soon apparent that there was some difficulty ahead. The *Brooklyn*, for some cause which I did not then clearly understand, but which has since been explained by Captain Alden in his report, arrested the advance of the whole fleet, while at the same time the guns of the fort were playing with great effect upon that vessel and the *Hartford*. A moment after I saw the *Tecumseh*, struck by a torpedo, disappear almost instantaneously beneath the waves, carrying with her her gallant commander and nearly all her crew. I determined at once, as I had originally intended, to take the lead, and after ordering the *Metacomet* to send a boat to save if possible any of the perishing crew, I dashed ahead with the *Hartford*, and the ships followed on, their officers believing that they were going to a noble death with their commander-in-chief. I steamed through between the buoys where the torpedoes were supposed to have been sunk. These buoys had been previously examined by my flag-lieutenant, J. Crittenden Watson, in several night reconnoissances. Though he had not been able to discover the sunken torpedoes, yet we had been assured by refugees, deserters, and others, of their existence ; but believing that from their having been some time in the water they were probably innocuous, I determined to take the chance of their explosion.

" From the moment I turned to the northwestward to clear the middle ground, we were enabled to keep such a broadside fire upon the batteries of Fort Morgan that their guns did us comparatively little injury. Just after we passed the fort, which was about ten minutes before eight o'clock, the ram *Tennessee* dashed out at this ship, as had been expected, and in anticipation of which I had ordered the monitors on our starboard side. I took no further notice of her than to return her fire. The rebel gunboats *Morgan*, *Gaines*, and *Selma* were ahead, and the latter particularly annoyed us with a raking fire, which our guns could not return. At two minutes after eight o'clock I ordered the *Metacomet* to cast off and go in pursuit of the *Selma*. Captain Jouett was after her in a moment, and in an hour's time he had her as a prize. She was commanded by P. N. Murphy, formerly of the United States Navy. He was wounded in the wrist ; his executive officer, Lieutenant Comstock, and eight of the crew killed, and seven or eight wounded. Lieutenant-Commander Jouett's conduct during the whole affair commands my warmest commendations. The *Morgan* and *Gaines* succeeded in escaping under the protection of the guns of Fort Morgan, which would have been prevented had the other gunboats been as prompt in their movements as the *Metacomet.* The want of pilots, however, I believe, was the principal difficulty. The *Gaines* was so injured by our fire that she had to be run ashore, where she was subsequently destroyed, but the *Morgan* escaped to Mobile during the night, though she was chased and fired upon by our cruisers.

"Having passed the forts and dispersed the enemy's gunboats, I had ordered most of the vessels to anchor, when I perceived the ram *Tennessee* standing up for this ship ; this was at forty-five minutes past eight. I was not long in comprehending his intentions to be the destruction of the flagship. The monitors and such of the wooden vessels as I thought best adapted for the purpose were immediately ordered to attack the ram, not only with their guns, but bows on at full speed. And then began one of the fiercest naval combats on record. The *Monongahela,* Commander Strong, was the first vessel that struck her, and in doing so carried away his own iron prow, together with the cutwater, without apparently doing his adversary much injury. The *Lackawanna,* Captain Marchand, was the next vessel to strike her, which she did at full speed ; but though her stern was cut and crushed to the plank ends for the distance of three feet above the water's edge to five feet below, the only perceptible effect on the ram was to give her a heavy lift. The *Hartford* was the third vessel which struck her, but as the *Tennessee* quickly shifted her helm, the blow was a glancing one, and as she rasped along our side we poured our whole broadside of 9-inch solid shot within ten feet of her casemate. The monitors worked slowly, but delivered their fire as opportunity offered. The *Chickasaw* succeeded in getting under her stern, and a 15-inch shot from the *Manhattan* broke through her iron plating and heavy wooden backing, though the missile itself did not enter the vessel.

" Immediately after the collision with the flagship I directed Captain Drayton to bear down for the ram again.   He was doing so at full speed, when, unfortunately, the *Lackawanna* ran into the *Hartford* just forward of the mizzenmast, cutting her down to within two feet of the water's edge.   We soon got clear again, however, and were fast approaching our adversary when she struck her colors and ran up the white flag.   She was at this time sore beset : the *Chickasaw* was pounding away at her stern, the *Ossipee* was approaching her at full speed, and the *Monongahela, Lackawanna*, and this ship were bearing down upon her, determined upon her destruction.   Her smokestack had been shot away, her steering-chains were gone, compelling a resort to her relieving tackles, and several of the port-shutters were jammed.   Indeed, from the time the *Hartford* struck her until her surrender, she never fired a gun.   As the *Ossipee*, Commander Le Roy, was about to strike her, she hoisted the white flag, and that vessel immediately stopped her engine, though not in time to avoid a glancing blow.   During the contest with the rebel gunboats and the ram *Tennessee*, and which terminated by her surrender at ten o'clock, we lost many more men than from the fire of the batteries of Fort Morgan. Admiral Buchanan was wounded in the leg, two or three of his men were killed, and five or six wounded.   Commander Johnston, formerly of the United States Navy, was in command of the *Tennessee*, and came on board the flagship to surrender his sword and that of Admiral Buchanan.   The surgeon, Dr. Conrad, came with him, stated the condition of the Admiral, and wished to know what was to be done with him.   Fleet-Surgeon Palmer, who was on board the *Hartford* during the action, commiserating the sufferings of the wounded, suggested that those of both sides be sent to Pensacola, where they could be properly cared for.   I therefore addressed a note to Brigadier-General R. L. Page, commanding Fort Morgan, informing him that Admiral Buchanan and others of the *Tennessee* had been wounded, and desiring to know whether he would permit one of our vessels under a flag of truce to convey them with, or without, our men wounded to Pensacola, on the understanding that the vessel would take out none but the wounded, and bring nothing back that she did not take out. This was acceded to by General Page, and the *Metacomet* proceeded on this mission of humanity.

" As I had an elevated position in the main rigging near the top, I was able to overlook not only the deck of the *Hartford*, but the other vessels of the fleet. I witnessed the terrible effects of the enemy's shot and the good conduct of the men at their guns ; and although no doubt their hearts sickened, as mine did, when their shipmates were struck down beside them, yet there was not a moment's hesitation to lay their comrades aside and spring again to their deadly work. Our little consort, the *Metacomet*, was also under my immediate eye during the whole action up to the moment I ordered her to cast off in pursuit of the *Selma*. The coolness and promptness of Lientenant-Commander Jouett throughout merit high praise ; his whole conduct was worthy of his reputation. In this connection, I must not omit to call the attention of the Department to the conduct of Acting Ensign Henry C. Nields, of the *Metacomet*, who had charge of the boat sent from that vessel when the *Tecumseh* sunk. He took her in under one of the most galling fires I ever saw, and succeeded in rescuing from death ten of her crew within 600 yards of the fort. I would respectfully recommend his advancement. The commanding officers of all the vessels who took part in the action deserve my warmest commendations, not only for the untiring zeal with which they had prepared their ships for the contest, but for their skill and daring in carrying out my orders during the engagement. With the exception of the momentary arrest of the fleet when the *Hartford* passed ahead, and to which I have already adverted, the order of battle was preserved, and the ships followed each other in close order past the batteries of Fort Morgan, and in comparative safety, too, with the exception of the *Oneida*. Her boilers were penetrated by a shot from the fort which completely disabled her, but her consort, the *Galena*, firmly fastened to her side, brought her safely through, showing clearly the wisdom of the precaution of carrying the vessels in two abreast. Commander Mullany, who had solicited eagerly to take part in the action, was severely wounded, losing his left arm. In the encounter with the ram, the commanding officers obeyed with alacrity the order to run her down, and without hesitation exposed their ships to destruction to destroy the enemy. Our iron-clads, from their slow speed and bad steering, had some difficulty in getting into and maintaining their position in line as we passed the fort, and in the subsequent encounter with the *Tennessee*, from the same causes were not so effective as could have been desired ; but I cannot give too much praise to Lieutenant-Commander Perkins, who, though he had orders from the Department to return north, volunteered to take command of the *Chickasaw*, and did his duty nobly.

" The *Winnebago* was commanded by Commander T. H. Stevens, who volunteered for that position. His vessel steers very badly, and neither of his turrets will work, which compelled him to turn his vessel every time to get a shot, so that he could not fire very often, but he did the best under the circumstances.

" The *Manhattan* appeared to work well, though she moved slowly. Commander Nicholson delivered his fire deliberately, and, as before stated, with one of his 15-inch shot broke through the armor of the *Tennessee*, with its wooden backing, though the shot itself did not enter the vessel. No other shot broke through her armor, though many of her plates were started, and several of her port-shutters jammed by the fire from the different ships.

"The *Hartford*, my flagship, was commanded by Captain Percival Drayton, who exhibited throughout that coolness and ability for which he has been long known to his brother officers. But I must speak of that officer in a double capacity. He is the fleet-captain of my squadron, and one of more determined energy, untiring devotion to duty, and zeal for the service, tempered by great calmness, I do not think adorns any navy. I desire to call your attention to this officer, though well aware that in thus speaking of his high qualities I am only communicating officially to the Department that which it knew full well before. To him, and to my staff in their respective positions, I am indebted for the detail of my fleet.

"Lieutenant J. Crittenden Watson, my flag-lieutenant, has been brought to your notice in former despatches. During the action he was on the poop attending to the signals, and performed his duties as might be expected—thoroughly. He is a scion worthy the noble stock he sprang from, and I commend him to your attention. My secretary, Mr. McKinley, and acting ensign E. H. Brownell were also on the poop, the latter taking notes of the action, a duty which he performed with coolness and accuracy.

"Two other acting ensigns of my staff (Mr. Bogart and Mr. Heginbotham) were on duty in the powder division, and, as the reports will show, exhibited zeal and ability. The latter, I regret to say, was severely wounded by a raking shot from the *Tennessee* when we collided with that vessel, and died a few hours after. Mr. Heginbotham was a young married man, and has left a widow and one child, whom I commend to the kindness of the Department.

"Lieutenant A. R. Yates of the *Augusta* acted as an additional aide to me on board the *Hartford*, and was very efficient in the transmission of orders. I have given him the command, temporarily, of the captured steamer *Selma*.

" The last of my staff, and to whom I would call the notice of the Department, is not the least in importance. I mean Pilot Martin Freeman. He has been my great reliance in all difficulties in his line of duty. During the action he was in the maintop, piloting the ships into the bay. He was cool and brave throughout, never losing his self-possession. This man was captured early in the war in a fine fishing-smack which he owned, and, though he protested that he had no interest in the war, and only asked for the privilege of fishing for the fleet, yet his services were too valuable to the captors as a pilot not to be secured. He was appointed a first-class pilot, and has served us with zeal and fidelity, and has lost his vessel, which went to pieces on Ship Island. I commend him to the Department.

" It gives me pleasure to refer to several officers who volunteered to take any situation where they might be useful, some of whom were on their way north, either by orders of the Department or condemned by medical survey. The reports of different commanders will show how they conducted themselves.

" I have already mentioned Lieutenant-Commander Perkins of the *Chickasaw* and Lieutenant Yates of the *Augusta*. Acting volunteer Lieutenant William Hamilton, late commanding officer of the *Augusta Dinsmore*, had been invalided by medical survey, but he eagerly offered his services on board the iron-clad *Chickasaw*, having had much experience in our monitors.

" Acting volunteer Lieutenant P. Giraud, another experienced officer in iron-clads, asked to go in one of these vessels, but as they were all well supplied with officers I permitted him to go on the *Ossipee*, under Commander Le Roy. After the action he was given temporary charge of the ram *Tennessee.*

" Before closing this report, there is one other officer of my squadron of whom I feel bound to speak, Captain T. A. Jenkins of the *Richmond*, who was formerly my chief of staff, not because of his having held that position, but because he never forgets to do his duty to the government, and takes now the same interest in the fleet as when he stood in that relation to me. He is also the commanding officer of the second division of my squadron, and, as such, has shown ability and the most untiring zeal. He carries out the spirit of one of Lord Collingwood's best sayings : ' Not to be afraid of doing too much ; those who are, seldom do as much as they ought.' When in Pensacola he spent days on the bar, placing the buoys in the best positions ; was always looking after the interests of the service, and keeping the vessels from being detained one moment longer in ports than was necessary. The gallant Craven told me only the night before the action in which he lost his life : ' I regret, Admiral, that I have detained you ; but had it not been for Captain Jenkins, God knows when I should have been here. When your order came, I had not received an ounce of coal ! '

" I feel that I should not be doing my duty did I not call the attention of the Department to an officer who has performed all his various duties with so much zeal and fidelity.

" Very respectfully, your obedient servant,
" D. G. FARRAGUT,
" *Rear-Admiral, Commanding W. G. Squadron.*"

Something like the same ardent feelings of joy were manifested over the engagement at Mobile as over the fall of Vicksburg or of New Orleans,

President Lincoln addressed the annexed personal letter to the heroic sailor ·

"EXECUTIVE MANSION, September 3.

"The national thanks are tendered by the President to Admiral Farragut and Major-General Canby for the skill and harmony with which the recent operations in Mobile Harbor and against Fort Powell, Fort Gaines, and Fort Morgan, were planned and carried into execution.

"Also, to Admiral Farragut and Major-General Granger, under whose immediate command they were conducted, and to the gallant commanders on sea and land, and to the sailors and soldiers engaged in the operations, for their energy and courage, which, under the blessing of Providence, have been crowned with brilliant success, and have won for them the applause and thanks of the nation.

"ABRAHAM LINCOLN."

The admiration and gratitude of the people found formal expression in Congressional resolutions.

The Admiral took a furlough for a short time, but before casting off moorings he took a feeling farewell of all the brave shipmates he was to leave behind.

On the 20th of November the *Hartford* sailed from Pensacola. She had a very stormy time of it before she dropped anchor in New York.

A committee, mainly composed of the leading citizens of New York, proceeded down the bay to offer the Admiral the hospitalities of the city and congratulate him on his magnificent achievements. It would take many pages to give a list of all who exerted themselves to give visible proof of their love and admiration of the brave sailor and excellent citizen.

As soon as the *Hartford* was within hail of the visiting committee, Admiral Farragut was descried on the after-deck. Beside him was his trusted and tried friend, Captain Drayton. Reaching the flagship the visitors were soon made at home.

After brief salutation Mr. Draper addressed the man they had united to receive, in the following words :

" ADMIRAL FARRAGUT : It becomes my pleasing duty to in-form you, on behalf of a committee which we here represent, that arrangements have been made to tender to you a reception somewhat worthy of your great services to the country ; and in order that I may perform my duty acceptably to the gentlemen who commissioned me, I have to state that they are ready to give you a cordial welcome on your arrival in the city. They fully appreciate the honours which you have bestowed on the flag and the country, which you have so often successfully defended. You hold most justly a proud place in the affections of the city. On your arrival you will be received by a meeting of the principal citizens, who will be ready to congratulate you on your visit to the city, and to show their appreciation of your great efforts in support of the nation.''

After the reading of the resolutions the Admiral briefly re-plied. He thanked the committee for their kind attentions, and ended by saying that himself and those engaged with him had merely done their duty.

As the Admiral then appeared on the historic deck of the good staunch vessel, he looked to be some years under sixty. He was evidently a powerful, wiry man, who could take good care of himself even yet in the furious onset of a " boarding scrimmage.''

As soon as the *Hartford* dropped her anchor she fired two broadsides, and the party with the hero they escorted left for the city.

The Battery and the wharves were crowded as soon as it be-came known that the gallant Admiral had arrived.

Loud cheer after cheer rent the air as David Glascoe Farragut stepped on the soil of the greatest city of the Republic his valor had so much aided in preserving.

Thousands pressed forward eagerly to touch the hands that gripped the shrouds aloft in the midst of one of the most furious fights that ever took place.

The Admiral was driven to the Custom-House, where many of the best citizens were already assembled. A brief time was passed in formalities, when, the meeting having been organized, Mr. Moses Taylor formally and most warmly extended the greeting of the citizens at large.

At the request of the Merchants' Committee the resolutions of a meeting held the previous evening were read, as follows :

" Recognizing the illustrious service, heroic bravery, and tried loyalty which have distinguished the life of Rear-Admiral D. G. Farragut in the cause of his country, especially the lofty spirit of devotion by which he has been animated during all the period of the present war, and the signal victories achieved by him over the utmost skill and effort of the Rebellion ; therefore,

" *Resolved*, That a committee of fifty citizens, to be named by the chair, with power to add to their number, be appointed to receive Admiral Farragut on his arrival, now soon expected, at this port.

" *Resolved*, That a Federal salute be fired in honour of the arrival of the flagship *Hartford* with Admiral Farragut on board.

" *Resolved*, That the city of New York, following the example of the great free cities of the world in doing honour to their illustrious countrymen, honors itself by tendering to Admiral Farragut an invitation to become a resident thereof, and that the committee be appointed to devise the best mode of carrying this resolution into effect, so that the man, his achievements, and his fame may belong to the city.

" *Resolved*, That we see with the highest satisfaction that the

President, in his annual message, and the Secretary of the Treasury, recommended the creation of a higher grade of naval rank, with the designation of Admiral Farragut as the recipient, as a national recognition of distinguished service and exalted patriotism."

Loud and long-continued cheers were given as the address ended.

Then the official speaker for the people said :

" ADMIRAL FARRAGUT AND MEMBERS OF THE COMMITTEE · Thus far we have fulfilled the duty which has been assigned to us.   The sub-committee have met the *Hartford*, and found on board her honoured commander, Admiral Farragut, and his captain.   We have performed that duty, on behalf of the committee, with feelings of pride and satisfaction ; and, as representing a generous community, have endeavoured to exhibit the gratitude of the entire nation, as expressed through this city, for the services and gallantry of the noble Admiral who is now before us.   I shall say nothing more, Admiral Farragut, than to repeat what I have said to you this morning, that all our citizens, of every age and condition, receive you with open arms and heartfelt gratitude."

To which the Admiral gave this response :

" MY FRIENDS : I can only reply to you as I did before, by saying that I receive these compliments with great thankfulness and deep emotions.   I am entirely unaccustomed to make such an address as I would desire to do upon this occasion ; but, if I do not express what I think of the honour you do me, trust me I feel it most deeply.   I don't think, however, that I particularly deserve anything from your hands.   I can merely say that I have done my duty to the best of my abilities.   I have been devoted to the service of my country since I was eight years of age, and my father was devoted to it before me. I have not specially deserved these demonstrations of your regard. I owe everything, perhaps, to chance, and to the praiseworthy exertions of my brother officers serving with me.

" That I have been fortunate is most true, and I am thankful, deeply thankful for it, for my country's sake. I return my thanks to the committee for their resolutions, especially for the one in regard to the creation of an additional rank."

The enthusiasm grew greater and greater as the people began fully to realize that the modest, unpretentious gentleman who stood in their midst was the great naval captain whom even the British writers had compared with their Drakes and Nelsons.

A stirring ode was then recited by that true Union soldier and accomplished poet, Colonel A. J. H. Duganne. It had the ring of the Runic rhymes of the ancient Scalds, and intensified, if possible, the enthusiasm of the assemblage. We have but space for the two concluding stanzas, merely remarking that the reader can no more judge of the beauty of the whole poem by these fragments, than he could estimate the beauty of the entire Parthenon by seeing a few of its *relievos* in detached parts.

> So, when, from blazing ports,
> Hurtling at Rebel forts
>   Cannon-blows thunderous,
> Down on MOBILE he led
> War-ships, like dragons red,
> While all the deep sea fled,
>   Quaking, from under us :
> Where the blue rockets flashed,
> Where the hot shell was dashed,
> Where the shot madly crashed,
>   There we saw Farragut !
> High at the mast-head lashed,
>   There was old Farragut.
> Castles once more we passed ;
> Ships on the shore we cast ;
> Lashed to our banner mast
>   Still was bold Farragut !

Messmates ! at morn we fight :
This may be our last night ;
　　Fill up the can again !
If we must bravely fall,
God keep our dear ones all !
God shield the Admiral,
　　Leading our van again !
When, o'er yon channel bars,
Stream out the rocket stars,
Then, to the signal spars,
　　Up will climb Farragut :
Listening to cannon-jars,
　　There will be Farragut !
Wrapped in his battle-cloak,
Woven from fire and smoke,
God bless his heart of oak ;
　　There we'll see FARRAGUT !

Soon after the enthusiastic applause that followed on the recitation of the poem had somewhat lulled, the meeting adjourned.

After a few days spent in discussion and exchange of ideas, the resolves of the committee, under the leadership of Mr. Moses Taylor, crystallized. The members met once again in the Custom-House, and as soon as the assemblage had come to order the chairman stated that he had been chosen to the proud position of being presenter to Vice-Admiral Farragut of a testimonial, previous to which he proceeded to read from an exquisitely engrossed sheet of parchment.

After the reading of the address Mr. Taylor took in his hands a large package, tied with ribbons of the colors which make up the Star-spangled Banner. It contained in United States government bonds fifty thousand dollars. Then he placed both the package and the parchment in the hands of Admiral Farragut.

The gallant officer appeared more "taken aback" than he had ever been by any ocean storm. Recovering his calmness, he spoke as follows :

"Gentlemen : I cannot allow this opportunity to pass without making some reply to what you so kindly say of me in making the gift, although I reserve to myself the privilege of rendering a more fitting acknowledgment at some future time. I will now respond to a few of the points in the address as I remember them.   As to the duties you speak of, that were performed by myself in command of the fleet in the South and Southwest, I have only to say, as I have repeatedly said before, that they were done in obedience to orders from the Department at Washington.   I have carried out the views of the Department in accomplishing what I promised to endeavor to do.   In opening and protecting commerce I have simply done my duty in the sphere to which I was called.

"But when it comes to personal matters, I can only say, would that I had language to express the gratitude I feel for what you have done.   From the moment, I may say, I made the entrance to this harbor, I have been the recipient of honours of every description, and it would be impossible for me, even if I were in the habit of making speeches, to express what I so heartily feel.   As to becoming a resident of New York, nothing would be more grateful to my feelings.   I came here, I can hardly say as a refugee ; but being forced out of the South, where I had resided more than forty years, came naturally to this city, as the metropolis of the country, and made my resting-place on the banks of the Hudson.   I have every reason to be grateful ; you have always extended to me and my family the kindest treatment, and it would be but natural that we should feel a desire to be with you.   But, gentlemen, you know I am a public officer, and must go just where I am ordered.

"Still it may be that, consistently with my obligations, I can be here ; and I will endeavour to make such arrangements, if it appears that at the same time I can perform my duty to my country."

As soon as Farragut could tear himself away from his enthusiastic admirers he stole away to his home at Hastings-on-the-Hudson. For he had all Washington's love of a rural home life.

But he who serves a grateful country has to pass through an almost cruel quantity of hand-shaking.

He was waited upon by committees intently determined on meeting the hero of New Orleans and Mobile.

He was treated with the highest civic honours by legislatures and corporations. Great cities and small villages were equally anxious for a visit from the universally admired sailor.

Embracing the earliest hours that were at his own disposal, Farragut went to Virginia to visit the fields in which he had worked and stroll through the woods over which he had hunted. .

In the year 1866 the grade of " Admiral " was legally established. The first to receive this honourable designation was the one who best deserved it—David Glascoe Farragut. And had the question been put to a popular vote there is no doubt the choice would have been ratified by an almost unanimous acclaim of the whole nation.

It was in this year that Admiral Farragut made a voyage nearly round the world in the United States ship *Franklin.* At every port the good ship touched attentions of every kind were shown to the modest hero.

Returning to his native land, he very soon thereafter paid California a visit. Returning, he had the misfortune to be seized with an illness which ultimately proved fatal. He died on the 14th day of August, 1870, at Portsmouth, N. H. He was in the sixty-ninth year of his age at the time of his decease,

He lies in Woodlawn, a beautiful cemetery near New York City, and on every Decoration Day, blow high or blow low, never an anniversary of that period is missed without floral offerings being plentifully strewn over the tomb of David Glascoe Farragut.

DAVID DIXON PORTER.

A.D. 1813—

DAVID DIXON PORTER was born in June, 1813, at the town of Chester, Pennsylvania. His father was the famous Commodore David Porter, who, among many other marvellous exploits, made such an heroic defence in the United States ship *Essex* against terrific odds in the harbor of Valparaiso.

It may well be surmised that so able a man as Commodore David Porter did not allow his son to lack education in all branches necessary to fit him for a naval officer. His own strong natural inclination, as well as the wish of his father, led him to adopt this as his profession. How well he has used the advice and training given him by his father and others who aided to develop his great abilities will be shown by the following interesting pages, the author of which claims no praise except that he has closely confined himself to admitted facts, often giving the narrative in the very words of unprejudiced witnesses.

Never did a hero come more honestly into possession of heroic qualities than did David Dixon Porter. For his father, Commodore David Porter, was undoubtedly one of the most skilful, brave, and persevering sailors that ever trod a deck.

To the elder Porter, in the year 1824, was intrusted the

arduous duty of sweeping away the piratical craft that made sailing among the West India Islands almost as dangerous as voyaging in the neigbourhood of the Barbary coast. This, too, in spite of the fact that the English had many national vessels cruising among these lovely tropical islands. Of course, it would be a comparatively easy matter to extirpate piracy at the present time with the aid of a few small steamers, but at the time Commodore David Porter was sent to clear the seas of them it was by no means an easy matter. Most of the vessels employed in this infamous pursuit were fast sailing vessels, heavily sparred, and carrying a monstrous cloud of canvas. They were also strongly manned, and by first-class seamen— men who could handle the cutlass and the boarding pike as well as any men-of-wars-men. But the unceasing vigilance of the old commodore drove them from the open sea into their difficult island havens, and there he either captured or destroyed their ill-omed craft. After this expedition, honest traders could sail as safely among the Leeward and Windward Islands as they could in the Delaware or the Hudson. The pirates had been furnished with a long rope by the powers who should have checked their inhuman proceedings ; but Porter brought them up with a round turn once he was put upon their track.

In the year 1826 Commodore David Porter, finding that there was no likelihood of soon seeing any active service in the United States Navy, tendered his resignation. Soon after he received his commission as Admiral of the Mexican Navy. About the same time the great English sailor Cochrane, afterward Lord Dundonald, left the English service to enter the navy of one of the South American republics.

David D. Porter entered the United States Navy as midshipman, on board the *Constellation*, in the year 1829. In that grade he served for six years ; part of the time on board the *United States,*

After satisfactorily going through his examination, he became a " passed " midshipman in 1835. For the following six years he was principally engaged on the coast survey. Here he doubtless acquired a knowledge of the harbors, lights, draught of water, and other particulars of inestimable advantage to him in the course of his professional career.

In 1841 he was commissioned a lieutenant, and served with that rank on board the *Congress* for four years. After a brief period of service at the Observatory at Washington he was placed on active duty under Commodore Tattnall in the Gulf of Mexico, and took a leading part in the naval operations of the Mexican war.

In 1849 he was allowed to take command of one of the Pacific Mail Company's steamers, and remained several years in the service of that company. While he commanded one of the California steamships—the *Crescent City*—he performed an exploit which attracted no little attention at the time. In consequence of the *Black Warrior* affair the Spanish Government had refused to permit any United States vessels to enter the port of Havana. Running under the shotted guns of Moro Castle he was ordered to halt. He promptly replied that he carried the United States flag and the United States mails, and, by the Eternal, he would go in ; and he did, the Habaneros fearing to fire upon him. He said afterward that he intended firing his six-pounder at them once, in defiance, after which he would haul down his flag.

At the beginning of the year 1861 he was under orders to join the Coast Survey on the Pacific, but, fortunately, had not left when the rebellion broke out. His name at this time stood number six on the list of lieutenants. The resignation of several officers who joined the rebels left room for his advancement, and the *Naval Register* for August 31st, 1861, places him number seventy-seven on the list of commanders. He was placed in command of the steam sloop of war *Powhatan*, a vessel of about twenty-five hundred tons, and armed with eleven guns, and was for some time actively engaged in blockade duty.

The Secretary of State made choice of Lieutenant Porter to go on a delicate service to the Island of Hayti. This mission he performed satisfactorily, returning such a report as fully proved how well fitted he was for the trust committed to his care.

When James Buchanan was President, Porter was selected by the Secretary of War to proceed to the East to bring a supply of camels to this country, it being supposed by many eminent naturalists and others that these animals could be successfully acclimated, and might prove useful and profitable in the arid stretches of sand and desert to be found in portions of our territory acquired from Mexico. His part of this business was fulfilled in a manner satisfactory to the Department.

When the war of the attempted Secession burst upon the country Porter ranked as a lieutenant, and was engaged on shore.

The United States ship *Powhatan* was despatched upon a secret mission under sealed order. The object, as it afterward appeared, was to aid in the relief of Fort Pickens.

Soon after he was made commander and intrusted with the important work of aiding Farragut in the impending attack upon the forts defending the passage of the Mississippi below New Orleans.

Steam had rapidly worked a wonderful revolution in naval warfare. These changes were emphasized by the doings of our naval forces at Port Royal and at Hatteras. If the forts below it could be safely passed New Orleans became the unresisting spoil of the victor.

In looking round for the proper men to get together the fleet and munitions, Commander Porter was one of the first chosen by Secretary of the Navy, Gideon Welles. He was deemed peculiarly fitted to take counsel with, as he had seen many of the places likely to be the scene of some of the operations in contemplation. When taken into consultation it was found that he thoroughly answered the requirements.

As this was one of the most important operations of the war, or indeed of any war, as it triumphantly proved that given good staunch ships, brave crews, skilful gunners, and fitting leaders, a fleet can pass unscathed by almost any batteries on shore, and as there has been much angry discussion as to the share of different persons in projecting and accomplishing this daring and successful enterprise, we give, in the language of one who knew all about it, the first conception and final execution of the passage of Forts Jackson and St. Philip :

" A blockade of three thousand five hundred miles in length, greater in extent than the whole coast of Europe from Cape Trafalgar to Cape North, was ordered in April ; and as we had not vessels, guns, or men for such a work, a navy had to be improvised to enforce it. Ships in the merchant service which could be made available were forthwith procured, guns were manufactured, men were enlisted, and the whole resources of the country were put in immediate requisition to meet the crisis. But although the energies and abilities of the nation were taxed and called out with wonderful and unexampled rapidity, they did not satisfy the impatience of the people, who had been taught, and were willing to believe, the rebellion could be suppressed and peace be restored in ninety days.

" Naval officers were invariably prohibited from giving information of naval movements for publication, and newspaper correspondents, always inquisitive and generally intelligent, were for this reason carefully excluded from the expeditions, and as far as possible from all knowledge in regard to naval operations. This rigid and restrictive policy of the navy was in

such marked contrast to that of the military, where correspondents were generally welcomed and often furnished with every
facility to obtain and publish army operations, was unsatis-
factory, led to much misrepresentation of the Navy Department, and sometimes to gross injustice to the navy.

" Very soon in the war the attention of the Navy Department,
previously occupied, was intently directed toward New Orleans,
the most important place in every point of view in the insurrec-
tionary region, and the most difficult to effectually blockade.
The whole country, and especially the great Northwest, was interested in the free and uninterrupted navigation of the Mississippi, the ocean outlet of the immense central valley which
contains within its slopes one half the States and territory and
is the very heart of the Union. New Orleans is the great depot
for its products, and Forts Jackson and St. Philip, which protected it, were the gates that barred ocean communication with
the city. To gain possession of the river and of the city was
one of the first objects which addressed itself to the administration after the war opened, and was imperatively demanded by
the great States which were especially interested.

" The difficulty of guarding and closing the passes of the
Mississippi, and all water communication with New Orleans,
which was as difficult as the blockade of Wilmington at a later
period, the escape of the *Sumter*, the disaster to the naval vessels commanded by Captain Pope and others, the knowledge
that formidable iron-clad vessels were being rapidly constructed
at New Orleans, the low alluvial banks of the river, on which
the army was disinclined to attempt to plant and erect batteries
and garrison them in that sickly swamp, were facts keenly
felt ; and it seemed that a vigorous blow at the centre by the
capture of New Orleans itself would be less difficult, less
expensive, less exhausting, would be attended with less loss of
life and be a more fatal blow to the rebels, than the most ex-

tensive, stringent, and protracted blockade that could possibly be established.

"Outside of President Lincoln, the Secretary of the Navy, and General McClellan, but half a dozen people knew anything about the contemplated enterprise. . . .

"It had long been realized that to have an effective blockade of all the passes at the mouth of the Mississippi was utterly impossible by naval vessels alone. One or more batteries above the delta was deemed the best, and perhaps the only effectual method of preventing communication. In the mean time the rebels had in July taken possession of and repaired the fortifications at Ship Island, ten or twelve miles off the coast, and some sixty miles from New Orleans, about equidistant from Mobile, and one hundred miles from the mouth of the Mississippi.

"The chief engineer officer of the Army of the Potomac, who had been employed on Forts Jackson and St. Philip, and knew their strength, was, by advice of General McClellan, consulted. This officer fully appreciated the magnitude of the movement and its immense importance to the country. He also approved ascending the river to capture the city, but considered it all-important that the forts should be reduced before any attempt was made to go above them. This he recommended should be a combined army and navy movement with iron clads and mortars.

"The *Powhatan*, having steamed over ten thousand miles with her condemned machinery, was now obliged to return to the United States, where she was laid up at about the time of the Du Pont expedition to Port Royal, and Lieutenant Porter was detached. He immediately sought other active service, and the capture of New Orleans being proposed by him, he was put in communication with General McClellan, and General Barnard of the Engineers, to talk the matter over. They were unanimous in their opinion that the city could be taken, and preparations were accordingly made to attempt the capture of the forts at or near the mouth of the Mississippi River. Admiral Farragut was ordered to command the naval forces, and Lieutenant Porter, having recommended a large force of mortar vessels, was directed to equip them without delay.

"Commander Porter was informed that the Navy Department intended to send an expedition to capture New Orleans two months earlier than General Butler. He did, when let into the confidence of the Department, and made aware of its programme, ' recommend a large force of mortar vessels,' and he is entitled to the credit of having proposed that appendage to the squadron. It was not a part of the original programme of the Navy Department. He and General Barnard should have the credit of appending the mortar flotilla to the original programme of the Navy Department. The historian must have little practical knowledge, and must have made only superficial investigation, who could come to the conclusion that such an expedition could have been instituted and completed within the time specified by themselves. The history of the world may be searched in vain for such an achievement. The navy programme for the expedition moved on favorably, though delayed beyond expectation, chiefly by the preparation of the bomb fleet of mortar vessels for Commander Porter, who was never wanting in energy, and who, as well as others, was actively employed after the 18th of November in preparations for the enterprise.

"After studying over the question as to the commanding officer of this expedition for a long time, it was finally resolved to give the supreme power into the hands of David Glascoe Farragut, a man who had as yet never had a fleet under his control. But he had done his whole duty so ably and loyally on all occasions in which he had been tried, that it was felt that he was just the man who had nearly all the qualities needed to execute so immense an enterprise.

"But to make assurance doubly sure, Mr. Fox, of the Navy Department, was directed to obtain Commander Porter's opinion of Captain Farragut. There had been an intimacy between the families of Farragut and Porter, dating back to the administration of Mr. Jefferson, when the father of Admiral Farragut had conferred essential favors on the elder Porter, who had reciprocated those favors by assisting young Glascoe Farragut, then a boy nine or ten years of age, to obtain a midshipman's warrant. He adopted him as a protégé, and made him virtually one of his family. In gratitude and affection young Farragut soon after took the name of David, and was so baptized in the Episcopal Church at Newport. As Commander Porter had been let into the secret of the expedition, and the relations between him and Farragut were such as here stated, there was propriety in getting his opinions preliminary to inquiries of Farragut himself. The inquiries resulted in showing that all persons well acquainted with naval affairs and people selected Farragut as the man just suited to command such an expedition. It now became important to ascertain the ideas, feelings, and views of Captain Farragut himself, and this, if possible, before informing him of the expedition, or committing the Department in any respect. Nothing, as has been stated, was put on paper which related to the actual destination of the expedition, and every movement was made so obscure that the real place to be attacked could not possibly be learned. When the whole plan of procedure had been explained to Farragut he signified his belief as to the practicability of the scheme.

"The proposal of Commander Porter for a bomb flotilla met his decided approval. He deemed such a battery absolutely essential to success.

"So large a squadron as that which composed the expedition could not be prepared and fitted without time. Most of the immense mortars and shells were to be cast ; some of the naval vessels were on the stocks when the enterprise was first ordered, and even the *Hartford*, which became the flagship of Admiral Farragut, had not been refitted after her return from the East Indies, when Commander Porter was sent off to prepare the mortar fleet. The whole energy and power of the Navy Department had been thrown into the work, and it is questionable if so large a force under similar circumstances was ever so speedily called out, prepared, and organized by any government.

"After all the vessels had cleared the land, their commanders were at liberty to open their sealed orders. For it must be borne in mind that only Farragut, Porter, and one or two others knew where they were bound.

"They then learned that they were to capture the great Southern capital of commerce and fashion, believed to be almost impregnably fortified, and being able to boast that the best soldiers of Britain had been foiled in attempting its capture."

The operations preceding the actual attack and the great combat itself we give in the words of an impartial historian, merely premising that it is impossible to dissever the acts of Commander Porter from those of Farragut and other leading officers. Suffice it to say that wherever courage and skill were specially needed, there David D. Porter was to be found engaged.

"Ship Island, between the mouth of the Mississippi and the Bay of Mobile, about sixty-five miles from New Orleans, was occupied in December, 1861, by General Phelps, with a part of a force of volunteers raised by General B. F. Butler in New England for confidential service. Phelps then issued an earnest but untimely proclamation, declaring the aim of the government to be the overthrow of slavery. On March 25th, 1862, after a severe and hazardous passage, General Butler arrived at Ship Island with the remainder of his forces, which now numbered 13,700 men, and which were destined to aid the naval forces under Commodore Farragut in the capture of New Orleans.

" Ship Island is situated in longitude 89° and a little north of latitude 30°, and is the property of the State of Mississippi. It is about sixty miles from New Orleans, nearly the same distance from the Northeast Pass, at the mouth of the Mississippi River, forty miles from Mobile, and ninety from Fort Pickens. It lies between Horn Island on the east and Cat Island on the west, and is distant about five miles from each. Some ten or twelve miles to the north, on the main land of Mississippi, are the towns of Balexi, Pascagoula, and Mississippi City. These towns are favorite summer resorts for the wealthy planters and merchants of the Gulf States, and, in consequence of a bar off their shore, were now the places of refuge for rebel gun-boats.

" Ship Island is somewhat undulating, and extends in a slight curve about seven miles east-northeast and west-south-west. At West Point (the western end), where the fort is located, the island is little more than an eighth of a mile wide, and is a mere sand-spit, utterly barren of grass or foliage of any kind. This eastern end, or East Point, is about three quarters of a mile in width, and is well wooded with pine, cedar, and live oak.

" The whole island contains a fraction less than two square miles of territory. Excellent water can be obtained in un-limited supply by sinking a barrel anywhere on the place. The great advantage of this is too palpable to require com-ment.

" The island possesses a very superior harbor, into which nineteen feet can be carried at ordinarily low water. It is situated north of the west end of the island. The anchorage, with water equal to the depth on the bar, is five miles long, and averages three and a quarter miles in width. The harbor is safe for the most dangerous storms in the Gulf—those from the east-ward, southward and eastward, and southward—and might be easily entered during these storms without a pilot, if good light-houses were placed in proper positions. The rise and fall of the tide is only from twelve to fourteen inches.

" This fort, which is situated on the sand-spit at the extreme western end of the island, is nearly circular in shape, somewhat resembling a pear in form. Its construction was commenced by the Federal Government, and when in a state of considerable progress was burned by the rebels, who afterward rebuilt and then abandoned it. It is of brick, and rendered bomb-proof by sand-bags placed five or six feet deep in front of the walls.

" The rebels built eleven casemates, and our forces have built two more since they have occupied the fort. The casemates are bomb-proof. The fort is at present but one tier high. It is provided with Dahlgren's 9-inch shell guns of very heavy cali-bre and in perfect order, and they are hourly expecting sixteen more very heavy guns from Pensacola. Besides this, Captain Manning's battery landed five of their steel rifled cannon, with the Sawyer projectile. There were six of these guns on board the *Constitution*, but unfortunately one of them was lost over-board in removing them from the transport.

The subjoined account of the attack upon the batteries below New Orleans and the subsequent capture of the city itself, is taken from the graphic descriptions of correspondents who ac-companied the fleet, in different vessels. We give these descriptions in the writers' own animated phraseology, and these passages will be found not only more forceful but far more accurate than many of the so-called historical accounts, penned by men who " never saw a *squadron on the seas*."

The fleet started to attack Forts St. Philip and Jackson on the 16th of April, 1862. On the 17th the rebels began to send down fire-rafts,

"I have just come from the deck, having witnessed one of the finest sights it has ever been my lot to see. The rebels sent down a scow, about one hundred feet long, filled with pine knots, and well saturated with tar. The breeze was fresh from the southward, and it burned upward finely, looking very much like a prairie fire. Signal was made for boats to tow the raft away from the shipping, and about forty boats were manned and sent away, each provided with grapnels and fire-buckets. The picket boats *Kineo* and *Kathadin* worked around it, and fired one or two shells in it, but the *Westfield* went up and ran her bow into it, and then played a powerful stream of water on it. Now the boats found an opportunity, and went alongside and boarded the fire-raft, and commenced bailing water into it, and in twenty minutes they put the fire out. They then towed it ashore near where one that came down in the morning was moored. While this was going on the rebels had small row-boats out watching the progress of their skill, and saw probably with regret their inglorious results and our high enjoyment. No amusement they could possibly get up could be more acceptable to our men. The mortar fleet sailors were in ecstasies, and they extinguished the flames in short order, and received the hearty cheers of the vessels as they passed along. With their two fire-rafts the rebels have accomplished nothing, except to learn us how to handle them."

"Then began the terrific and unceasing bombardment. Probably the heaviest and longest continued that ever took place. It was on the 18th that the first bomb was discharged, and it was six days after before there was the least cessation. The mortar vessels had covered their mast-heads and rigging with green tree branches, so that, while lying under the friendly shelter of the trees near the forts, their masts appeared as trees over the tops of the genuine ones. The vessels which lay on the other side of the river covered their sides with tree branches, and if it were not for their masts one could not tell there were any vessels there.

" On the 19th our mortar vessels were working well, and I learn they fire on an average eighty shells per day. According to that estimate they must have thrown already about about four thousand shells up to noon to-day. It is becoming very tedious to hear nothing but bang, bang, bang, all day and all night, without having a knowledge of the effect of our efforts.

" The work is terribly shattered, and the casemates are nearly broken in many places. The gun-boats yesterday entirely destroyed one. Only a few men have been killed as yet. We have nearly silenced the water-battery, disabled a 10-inch columbiad, and knocked the carriage of another to pieces. Our fire is represented as being terrific, and the least damage causes so much consternation that it requires the utmost efforts on the part of the officers to quiet the men. Our shells, when they fall, bury themselves from twelve to fourteen feet in the earth close to the fort, then explode, and make the whole fort fairly tremble with the shock. Occasionally one bursts in the fort ; but those which burst outside do the most execution. There are about 1500 men in both forts, mostly foreigners, but commanded by Southerners.

On the 24th Commodore Farragut determined to run past the forts. Forming the fleet in three divisions it started, steaming up the stream.

" At precisely twenty minutes of four o'clock the enemy opened fire from Fort St. Philip. At that moment the largest Star-spangled Banner in the fleet was hoisted at the peak, while the fore and main also sported the national ensigns. Full speed was given to the ship, the engineers did their duty nobly, and on we went, as it were, into the jaws of death. At the time the enemy opened fire the mortar vessels went to work, and the rapidity with which they threw shells at the rebels was truly wonderful.

"At five minutes of four oclock our bow gun belched forth fire and smoke, and a messenger, in the shape of a 9-inch shell, was sent to Fort Jackson—the work, by the way, which we were to attend to. In a few minutes more the broadside firing was commenced. Both forts were replying as fast as they could. Broadside after broadside was being delivered to them in rapid succession, while the mortar vessels were adding to the dreadful noise.

"Shot, shell, grape, and canister filled the air with deadly missiles. It was like the breaking up of a thousand worlds—crash—tear—whiz! Such another scene was never witnessed by mortal man. Steadily we steamed on, giving them shell, the forts firing rifle-shot and shell, 10-inch Columbiads, 42, 32, and 24 pounder balls; and, to add to this state of affairs, 13 steamers and the floating battery *Louisiana*, of the enemy, were pouring into and around us a hail-storm of iron perfectly indescribable. Not satisfied with their firing, fire-raft after fire-raft was lit and set adrift to do their work of burning. The ram was busy at work trying to shove them under the bows of our vessel.

"As we drew near abeam of the forts we intermingled grape with shell, which had the effect to silence in a measure the barbette guns. The shot from the enemy, which for some time had gone over us, now began to cut us through.

"While in the port mizzen rigging the flag-officer narrowly escaped being hit with a rifle shell. A shell burst on deck, and the concussion stunned Lieutenant George Heisler, of our Marine Corps, so that for a time his life was despaired of. It was a time of terror. Our guns were firing as rapidly as possible, and the howitzers in the tops were doing excellent execution.

" The rebel steamers were crowded with troops, who fired volleys of rifle-balls at us, most of which did us no harm. One of them came near us, and I think I am safe in saying she contained two hundred men. Our howitzers opened on them, and Captain Broome, of the Marine Corps, opened into her with two 9-inch guns.

" An explosion, terrific yells, a career, and that fellow was done for. Their steamers were bold and fearless, but no sooner did they come in sight of our gunners than they were sunk. The *Varuna* sunk six of them one after another.

" In the midst of this awful scene down came a tremendous fire-raft, and the ram shoved her under our port quarter. The flames caught our rigging and side, and for a moment it seemed we must fall a prey to the ravages of fire. A fire was also burning on the berth-deck. The fire hose was on hand, and we soon subdued the flames and gave the ram a dose of rifle shell. She, however, came up for us again, but some other vessel tackled her and she hauled off. During this stage of affairs we *grounded*, and our fate seemed sealed ; but our men worked like beavers, and the engineers soon got the ship astern and afloat. It defies the powers of my brain to describe the scene at this time. The river and its banks were one sheet of flame, and the messengers of death were moving with lightning swiftness in all directions. Steadily we plied shell and grape, interspersed with shrapnel.

" The boats were fast being riddled by well-directed broadsides, and they who were able made for the shore to run them on, so that they could save their lives. Some were on fire and others were sinking. Our boys were cheering with a hearty good-will, and well they might, for we had almost won the day, and we were nearly past the forts. Our ship had been on fire three times, and she was riddled from stem to stern.

" After being under a terrific fire for one hour and twenty minutes we were past the forts, badly cut up ; a shot hole through mainmast, two in stern, and several through us. Words cannot express any adequate idea of the engagement. Wrapped in smoke, firing and being fired at, shot and shell whistling like locomotive demons around, above, before, and in the rear of you ; flames from fire-rafts encircling you, splinters flying in all directions, and shells bursting overhead !

" We steamed up to Quarantine, when lo ! the ram made his appearance and saucily fired at the *Richmond.* The *Mississippi* being near at hand, about ship for the black devil, and at him she went with the idea of running him down. The ram ran, but finding the *Mississippi* gaining on him, he run his nose into the bank of the river, and immediately about thirty men came up out of the hatch and run on shore. The *Mississippi* fired two or three broadsides into her and boarded her, but finding she was of no earthly account again fired into her, and she drifted down the river, sinking very fast."

Captain Porter himself thus describes her last end :

" Before the fleet got out of sight it was reported to me that the celebrated ram *Manassas* was coming out to attack us, and, sure enough, there she was, apparently steaming along shore, ready to pounce upon the apparently defenceless mortar vessels. Two of our steamers and some of the mortar vessels opened fire on her, but I soon discovered that the *Manassas* could harm no one again, and ordered the vessels to save their shot. She was beginning to emit smoke from her ports, or holes, and was discovered to be on fire and sinking. Her pipes were all twisted and riddled with shot, and her hull was also well cut up. She had evidently been used up by the squadron as they passed along. I tried to save her as a curiosity, by getting a hawser around her and securing her to the bank, but just after doing so she faintly exploded. Her only gun went off, and emitting flames through her bow port, like some huge animal she gave a plunge and disappeared under the water.''

The gallant old *Cumberland*, sunk by the rebel iron-clad was fairly matched by the *Varuna*. Captain Boggs of that steamer finding that a steamer (name unknown) was about to run into him, put the vessel in such position that in being damaged he could repay it with interest. On came a large steamer all clad with iron about the bow, and hit the *Varuna* in the port-waist, cutting and crushing in her side. She dropped alongside and cleared out to butt again. She hit the *Varuna* a second time, and while in a sinking condition the *Varuna* poured the 8-inch shells into him so fast that the rebel vessel was set on fire and driven on shore.

The brave Captain Boggs narrates this encounter as follows : '' I have the honour to report that after passing the batteries, with the steamer *Varuna* under my command, on the morning of the 24th, finding my vessel amid a nest of rebel steamers, I started ahead, delivering her fire both starboard and port at every one that she passed. The first on her starboard beam that received her fire appeared to be loaded with troops. Her boiler was exploded and she drifted to the shore. In like manner three other vessels, one of them a gunboat, were driven on shore in flames, and afterwards blew up. At six A.M. the *Varuna* was attacked by the *Morgan*, iron-clad about the bow, commanded by Beverly Kennon, an ex-naval officer. This vessel raked us along the port gangway, killing four and wounding nine of the crew. Butting the *Varuna* on the quarter and again on the starboard side, I managed to get three 8-inch shells into her abaft her armour, as also several shot from the after rifled gun, when she dropped out of action, partially disabled. While still engaged with her another rebel steamer, iron-clad, and with a prow under water, struck us in the port gangway, doing considerable damage. Our shot glancing from her bow, she backed off for another blow, and struck again in the same place, crushing in the side ; but by going ahead fast the concussion drew her bow around, and I was able, with the port-guns, to give her, while close alongside, five 8-inch shell abaft her armour. This settled her and drove her ashore in flames. Finding the *Varuna* sinking, I ran her into the bank, let go the anchors, and tied her up to the trees. During all this time the guns were actively at work crippling the *Morgan*, she making feeble efforts to get up steam. This fire was kept up until the water was over the gun-trucks, when I turned my attention to getting the wounded and crew out of the vessel. The *Oneida*, Captain Lee, seeing the condition of the *Varuna*, had rushed to her assistance, but I waved her on, and the *Morgan* surrendered to her, the vessel in flames. I have since learned that over fifty of his crew were killed and wounded, and she was set on fire by her commander, who burned his wounded with his vessel. I cannot award too much praise to the officers and crew of the *Varuna* for the noble manner in which they supported me, and their coolness under such exciting circumstances, particularly when extinguishing fire, having been set on fire twice during the action by shell.

" In fifteen minutes from the time the *Varuna* was struck she was on the bottom, with only her top-gallant forecastle out of water.

" The officers and crew lost everything they possessed, no one thinking of leaving his station until driven thence by the water."

The Chalmette batteries were discovered on each side of the river at a quarter to eleven. They mounted ten guns each. The signal was made to prepare for battle.

" No flag was flying on either work, nor did they hoist one at any time. At eleven o'clock both batteries opened fire on the *Cayuga*. Owing to the very swift current we were unable to go ahead very fast, and it was five minutes after they opened fire before we could fire a bow gun. The enemy cracked away at us, and the shot flew around us very rapidly, most of their shot raking along our deck and striking on or near the poop. For twenty minutes we stood the fire without being able to return a broadside, which we knew would soon silence them. In the mean time the other vessels were working with their bow guns on both works.

"At the end of the twenty minutes we were within about fifty yards of the battery of ten guns, one being a mortar. Then we let drive a broadside. Its effect was terrible, and nearly silenced the work. Another broadside of grape, five second shell, and a sprinking of shrapnel finished that work ; but as the rebels did not hoist a white flag, as they should do, we gave them another touch up, three cheers, and then left them to run as fast as they chose. The other battery was soon silenced, this ship throwing in a broadside to aid in the good work. The enemy fired at us with infantry, and an artillery company was coming to their support, when they found it was of no use. I think the enemy lost quite a number in the engagement. We lost one man, Thomas, captain of the fore-castle and of a rifle Parrott. It is supposed he was blown overboard by the wind of a passing ball, and reached the shore in safety. I heard of one man being blown overboard from the *Brooklyn.*

"As we steamed along we found five large ships on fire with full cargoes of cotton, and they were nearly consumed.

"The people of the city afterwards told our sailors that on Thursday night the panic broke out in the city, and all the cotton was brought out and set on fire, and that the mob could be scarcely restrained from firing the public buildings and then the private dwellings. It was a night not equalled by anything even in the French revolutions.

" A band of desperadoes had charge of affairs, and they were backed by Lovell, who, however, denies it; but he is accountable for the destruction of property, as he set the example by firing his own cotton first. A ram lay alongside of the levee, partially sunk, and her woodwork was on fire. Another ram affair was sunk on the Algiers side of the river. I am unable to obtain the details of the loss by fire to shipping and cotton. It will be weeks before it can be ascertained, and I have a right to suppose that we never will be able to give the full particulars of the wanton destruction of property which has occurred in and around this city during the last two days.

" The river was filled with ships on fire, and all along the levee were burning vessels, no less than eighteen being on fire at one time, and the enemy were firing others as fast as they could apply the torch. The atmosphere was thick with smoke and the air hot with flames. It was a grand but sad sight. Hundreds of thousands of dollars' worth of property was being wantonly destroyed. At the levee, just by the Custom-House, lay a burning ram (the *Anglo-Norman*).

" The view from our decks was one such as will never, in all human probability, be witnessed again. A large city lay at our mercy. Its levee was crowded by an excited mob. The smoke of the ruins of millions' worth of cotton and shipping at times half concealed the people. While men were hastening up the levee, firing ships and river craft as fast as possible, the people were rushing to and fro. Some of them cheered for the Union, when they were fired upon by the crowd. Men, women, and children were armed with pistols, knives, and all manner of weapons. Some cheered for Jeff Davis, Beauregard, etc., and used the most vile language toward us and the good old flag. Pandemonium was here a living picture. Order was to them a thing past and forgotten, and the air was rent with yells of defiance.

"At two o'clock Captain Bailey went on shore, flying a flag of truce, to communicate with the authorities.

"It was with the greatest difficulty that the naval officers reached the City Hall, where the City Council, the Mayor, and Major-General Lovell were awaiting the arrival of our communications.

"Flag-officer Farragut sent word to the authorities that he demanded the surrender of the city of New Orleans, and assured them of the protection of the ' old flag.' The city being under martial law, the civil authorities of course could do nothing ; but Major-General Lovell said, ' Sir, I will never surrender the city.' He was politely informed that the city was in our power, and as much as we regretted the wanton destruction of property, we would not disturb them, provided they made no demonstration against us. After some talk Lovell agreed to evacuate the city with his troops (from eight to fifteen thousand), and turn the city over to the civil authorities, and that they might do as they pleased. The interview was carried on with despatch, and Captain Bailey and Lieutenant Perkins (his aide) took a carriage and returned to their boat. On the route they were insulted, pistols pointed in their faces, and all manner of indignities offered to them. The officer in charge of the boats—Acting Master Morton—was the recipient of all manner of insults, but suffered no bodily harm.

"After dark I went on deck to see New Orleans by gaslight. How changed the scene ! A little over twelve months ago miles of shipping lined the levee ; the buildings hid behind the forests of masts and rigging of vessels bearing the banners of all nations of the world. None were here now. The busy hum of workmen and the cheery song of the sons of Africa, who worked at night, were not to be heard. No hissing puff of steamers going and coming to and from the cities on the banks of this great river. No ships, no signs of life were present now. A few gaslights were burning along the levee, and the dull embers and heavy smoke gave proof of a reign of anarchy and terror. The buildings were wrapped in a sombre light, and we felt that it was a city clothed in sackcloth and ashes.''

The batteries above New Orleans next received attention.

" At three o'clock the four heavy vessels—*Hartford, Brooklyn, Richmond,* and *Pensacola*—got under way and proceeded up the river, with a view of silencing two batteries located just above Carrollton. As we passed along the levee in the upper part of the city *considerable Union feeling* was manifested by all classes.

" At Jefferson City we saw the ways from which the ram *Mississippi* was launched a week ago. The enemy were building ways for the construction of another ; but now the place was deserted by all workmen, and quite a crowd of quiet spectators filled their places.

" On arriving at Carrollton we began to look out for the batteries ; but it was not until we had passed some three miles above that place that we found them, deserted, and fires burning along the line of earthworks.

" The ship dropped slowly alongside, and Lieutenant Kautz, Engineer Purdy, and myself went on shore to reconnoitre and spike the guns. On landing, quite a crowd of people gathered around us, but made little or no demonstrations of joy or sorrow. We were told that the work was called Fort John Morgan, and that it was constructed to prevent an approach to New Orleans by the river from the northward.

" It was an extended field-work, reaching from the river-bank to Lake Pontchartrain. The work was well constructed, and we travelled along its line for about two miles. In the work near the river were nine 42-pounders and two 32-pounders ; along the line, nine 24-pounder carronades and four 18-pounders.

" Five guns were dismounted, and platforms and circles for thirteen guns, not mounted, were found. The mounted guns were all spiked, with the exception of fifteen, which Mr. Purdy spiked. A fire had been kindled under each gun-carriage, and they were nearly destroyed at the time we visited it.

" The magazine was empty, of course. A good hot shot furnace was undisturbed, and about one thousand round of 32-pounder shot lay around, intermingled with broken stands of grape. Marks of a hasty retreat were plainly visible, and we were informed that when we attacked the Chalmette batteries, below the city, the troops which were located in Fort John Morgan were transferred to the former place, and after their defeat they came up here and carried away their remaining stores, took the Jackson Railroad, and left.

" Of the battery on the other side of the river a boat from the *Oneida* went there and spiked the guns, and then left. Dark coming on we dropped down the river opposite Carrollton and anchored for the night.

" Meanwhile General Butler had pushed his men through a bayou and landed them above Forts St. Philip and Jackson. The commanders of those forts wished to resist still ; but the men would not fight, and even trained the barbette guns on their officers. They surrendered accordingly. But the commander having subsequently blown up the *Louisiana*, Captain Porter put him in double irons.

" During the siege of Vicksburg, owing to .heavy rains and the rapid rise of the river above and opposite, the head of the great canal, which had been laboriously constructed, gave way, and the water poured in at a tremendous rate. The force of the current, however, did not break the dam near the mouth of the canal, but caused a crevasse on the western side, through which the water flowed in such profusion as to inundate the lower part of the peninsula to the depth of four or five feet. When the fracture occurred a number of soldiers were on the levee, and were thrown into the torrent. Some swam and scrambled out ; but several of them would have been drowned but for the heroic exertions of John C. Keller, one of the officers of the transport *Swallow,* who succeeded at great personal risk in placing them once more upon *terra firma,* much wetter if not wiser men."

Another eye-witness says

" Night before last the dam at this end of the canal gave way under a pressure of ten feet of Mississippi, and in a few minutes thereafter there was a torrent roaring and boiling through in a manner that would do honour to a first-class maelstrom. Unfortunately the water above the dam that came pouring through did not come along the projected channel of the canal, but from a direction much below, the consequence of which promises to be that, before this can be corrected, another channel will be scooped out, of which we can make no use. The dredging machines are hard at work night and day, and may possibly be able to correct the difficulty. Two or three days will decide the matter, and then we shall know whether the much-talked-of and long-worked at canal will prove a failure or a success."

Two days thereafter it was written :

" The water has been rushing through the cut with great force, threatening to inundate the entire lower part of the peninsula. On this account McClernand's Thirteenth Army Corps has been ordered to Milliken's Bend, fifteen miles above, where the ground is higher ; but his command has as yet made only a beginning of moving.

" Those familiar with the country hereabout say the land above the canal will not be flooded, though the portion below the city, in the direction of Vicksburg, is already four feet under water. The dam at or near the mouth of Farragut's Ditch stands firm, but a crevasse has been made in the embankment on the west side, and through this the river is pouring at a rapid rate.

" The water, it is supposed, will run along inside of the levees constructed opposite Warrenton, and thence into the swamps, which are lower than where our troops are, without interfering for some days with the encampment.

" The canal itself is not likely to be injured by the destruction of its head, but will rather be benefited thereby—being deepened and widened by the rush of the current. The cut is 60 feet broad and $2\frac{1}{2}$ feet below the surface of the soil inside of the levee, but about 7 feet below the level of the river."

On the 26th of December, 1862, Porter opened fire with the gunboats under his command, upon the batteries placed upon the bluff at Vicksburg. This appeared to offer a chance to the armies to press forward to the attack. But after several attempts it was found, by the useless loss, that all attempts to capture the rebel stronghold from that side were entirely visionary.

As General McClernand, who had been substituted for General Sherman in command, had adopted a new plan of defence, he summoned Porter to his assistance with those ubiquitous gunboats of his, that appeared to be gifted with some innate qualities for sailing in shoaler water and navigating more crooked streams than any other craft. The boats proceeded up White River, and thence found their way to the Arkansas, approaching Fort Hindman or Arkansas Post. This place was the key to the country from the Mississippi to Little Rock, and it had for some months been decided that it would be expedient to take possession of it.

Accordingly on the 10th of January, 1863, General McClernand and Commodore Porter, with the gunboat flotilla under command of the latter, ascended the Arkansas.

During the night the gunboats discharged a few shots, and the next morning, the troops having been properly posted for an assault, the work at once began.

"It was five minutes past one when the gunboats *Baron De Kalb, Cincinnati,* and *Louisville,* all iron-clads, steamed up to within about three hundred yards of the fort and opened fire upon it. Just so soon as the gunboats hove in sight, and before they fired a shot, the fort opened on them. On a sort of sandy beach, by the bend in the river, the rebels had erected several targets, which were to assist them in aiming at the gunboats. Barricades had also been placed in the river opposite the fort ; but the high-water had washed part of them away and left the channel open. The bombardment increased in rapidity as other vessels of the squadron came into position. It took some time to get good range of the casemated guns and the barbette gun on the fort. The *Baron De Kalb* had orders from the Admiral to fire at the right-hand casemate, the *Louisville* at the middle one, and the *Cincinnati* at the great 9-inch Dahlgren gun *en barbette.* In half an hour after the bombardment commenced the casemates were struck by the shell from the gunboats. When the range was obtained the shells from the gunboats struck the guns in the fort almost every shot, until every one was silenced and smashed. The *Cincinnati* fired shrapnel at first and cleared the crew away from the 9 inch Dahlgren gun on the parapet, when the *Baron De Kalb* broke off the muzzle with a 10-inch shot. The *Lexington,* light draught, Lieutenant-Commander James W. Shirk, moved up at two o'clock, and with her rifled guns replied to the Parrott rifled guns in the fort, while the *Rattler,* Lieutenant-Commander Walter Smith, and the *Gilde,* Lieutenant-Commander Woodworth, threw in shrapnel, and in company with the ram *Monarch,* Colonel Charles E. Ellet, of the army, commanding, pushed up close to the fort. Each of the gunboats silenced the gun it was instructed to fire at about the same time. At twenty minutes past two all the heavy smooth-bore and rifled guns in the fort were most effectually silenced. The *Black Hawk,*

Lieutenant-Commander K. R. Breese, the Admiral's flagship, steamed up and took part in the fight. The Admiral himself, with his secretary, Dr. Heap, was in the little tug which was all the time screaming and dancing about among the gunboats, directing and superintending the fight.

"The troops were ordered to advance at the firing of the signal gun. They pushed forward, but were met by a very fierce fire from the rebel works.

"The troops in front were now sharply engaging the rebels in their works, while our artillery, and their field-pieces behind the breastwork near the fort, were blazing away at each other with great rapidity. In one instance the rebels galloped the horses up to the parapet with a gun, and when the horses wheeled with it, in order that it might be placed in position, our infantry fire killed all the horses in the traces, and the artillerists scampered off in an instant and left their gun. At a shot from one of our Parrott guns, which knocked one of the timbers from the breastwork, at least a hundred rebels ran away from behind the intrenchment into the bastioned fort. Our caissons were now coming from the front for ammunition. At ten minutes past three most of Morgan's men were in line, and the remainder were forming in columns in the rear. In five minutes more they were advancing with vigour. Sharp musketry and artillery firing was kept up all the time. At twenty minutes past three a heavy column of Morgan's men was seen moving up to the left of the line, near the river bank. It was at first supposed that it might be a storming column rushing on the works at a double-quick, for it is well known that when Morgan moves he moves with vigour ; but the next we knew the advancing column, enveloped in clouds of smoke, had halted. It was not a storming column. It was a body that was moving quickly to the front to extend the advancing line.

"The time now was fifteen minutes past three. The fight

was quite severe on both sides. Although the heavy guns in
the fort were silenced, the field-pieces and the infantry behind
the parapet with great determination continued to resist our
vigorous advance. Our line extended from the river on the left
round in front of the fort, and to the bayou on the right. The
engagement was general along its whole extent. Morgan sent
word that his left was advancing steadily, and as the gunboats
commanded the river he had sent for Lindsay's brigade to return from the other side.

"It was now nearly four o'clock. The Admiral's flagship
was coming close to the bank, and with the other gunboats
was pouring shot into the fort ; Lindsay's brigade, across the
river, was also firing into the works, while Morgan's and Sherman's men were advancing fast in front. The white flag was
seen in several places on the parapet ; enthusiastic cheers arose
from our troops in front ; the firing ceased ; the rebels rose from
behind the breastwork ; our troops rushed wildly forward, with
flags flying, and many could not resist the rush behind, which
pushed them into and over the intrenchments. The fort had
surrendered.

"The moment the lieutenant in the tree had reported the
cheering along the line and had concluded with 'I believe the
fort has surrendered,' General McClernand and staff dashed off
and were soon in the enemy's intrenchments, surrounded by
thousands of the men. When the flag was shown on the river-
side the jolly jack tars had jumped ashore and were soon in
the fort, followed by Admiral Porter and a number of his
officers. Colonel Dunnington, commander of the fort, surrendered his sword to the Admiral in person. General Churchill,
commander of the forces, soon appeared with his staff, and surrendered himself and his troops to General McClernand. 'I
am sorry to meet you under such circumstances,' said General
McClernand ; 'but your men fought bravely to-day in defend-

ing the fort.' General Churchill replied, that for himself he had not intended to surrender ; that there was treachery somewhere on his lines ; that he had ridden to the left with his staff, and on hearing the cheering supposed it was the cheering of his men, but on riding back into the fort had found our troops just taking possession. He said that in the morning he had issued orders to the troops that they must die in the ditches in preference to surrendering the Post. It is certain that the enemy could no longer successfully resist, and also that white flags were shown on the parapets in several places at the same time. Some of the soldiers told me that General Churchill had ordered the surrender. General Churchill told me that he did not ; but, on the contrary, that the place was surrendered by traitors on his lines. It may be that the soldiers, seeing that further resistance was useless, concluded to abandon the defence. One thing is certain, there was great unanimity among the rebels in the surrender.

"Post of Arkansas is the oldest settlement in the State. Nearly two centuries ago there was a Spanish town in the immediate vicinity, and I believe a small Spanish fort. It is situated on the right bank as you ascend the Arkansas River, about fifty miles from its mouth, and 117 miles from Little Rock, the capital of the State. It was settled in 1685 by the Acadian French, and was the trading-post for furs from the surrounding country. From the high point on which the fort is constructed down to the Mississippi River the land along the course of the Arkansas overflows during the winter and the spring. There is now no town at Post of Arkansas, only a few stores, and then at intervals for a dozen miles along the river bank an occasional house."

"The fort is a regular, square-bastioned work, one hundred yards exterior side, with a deep ditch some fifteen feet wide and a parapet eighteen feet high. A number of killed and wounded were lying in the ditches when we entered, and many sick soldiers in the hospital. All the heavy guns were broken by our shot, and were lying about in fragments on the ground. Ammunition captured by the rebels in the steamboat *Blue Wing*, a large amount of war materials and supplies of various kinds, and about five thousand prisoners have fallen into our hands by this brilliant achievement of our arms."

On the 18th of May, 1863, Porter ran past the batteries at Vicksburg and captured the rebel batteries at Grand Gulf.

Nearly at this time two Union rams, the *Indianola* and the *Queen of the West*, had been taken by the rebels. But Commodore Porter, always fruitful in expedients, improvised a big scare, by way of a Roland for their Oliver. He fixed up a large flat-boat in the similitude of a barge ram ; her smoke-stacks were of pork barrels, her furnaces of mud. She was started on her way down the river from above Vicksburg. As she drew near the rebel vessels a panic appeared to seize them, and they steamed the *Queen* up Red River while they blew up the *Indianola*.

Soon after General Grant took command of the army. After making two ineffectual attempts on other methods he determined on a third attempt. In this way he intended to flank the defences of Vicksburg by a very circuitous route so as to enter the Mississippi from the Yazoo. Five thousand of his forces were on board transports under General Ross, while seven gunboats accompanied them. They encountered snags and fallen trees, making less way than quarter of a mile an hour. Batteries had been erected by the Confederates, and it was found impossible to pass them. Grant essayed several other projects for passing the batteries, but all were futile.

On the Mississippi the rebel batteries extended for about eight miles. It was determined to run the fleet past them. The army meanwhile was to pass inland so as to reach New

Carthage below Vicksburg. It was on the night of the 16th of April that Commodore Porter arranged that his eight gunboats should go down the river in single file. The city batteries fired viciously at them as they went down. The Unionists sharply replied, but little damage was thus far done on either side. Of three transports that followed closely in the wake of the gunboats, one only escaped, two being destroyed by the fire of the batteries.

A few nights thereafter six more transports passed the batteries unharmed.

On the 19th of May the army had drawn closely around Vicksburg, while on the river was Porter's fleet of gunboats, ready for any service.

By breaching and mining the Union army drew nearer and nearer to the heart of Vicksburg. On the 3d of July a mine was sprung that disabled one of the rebel forts. This was opposite the centre of the besieging force. Instantly a rush was made for the breach. A terrible hand-to-hand fight followed. Vicksburg was won. General Pemberton had conducted the defence with much skill, and his troops fought well. But how valiantly the Unionists had fought is shown by the fact that 27,000 soldiers remained to be paroled. The capture of Vicksburg was hastened by the incessant shelling of its defences by Commodore Porter's mortar fleet.

Previous to the 8th of May Porter's fleet had taken Alexandria, a very strongly fortified place. By May 25th it was calculated that Commodore Porter had destroyed $10,000,000 worth of property on the Yazoo.

For his arduous duties in the taking of Vicksburg in conjunction with the army, Porter received the thanks of Congress and also received his commission as Rear-Admiral. This promotion dated from the day of the capture of Vicksburg.

Admiral Porter did not allow his new honours to grow rusty ;

on the contrary, each promotion incited him to deeds of greater daring, if possible.

The latter part of 1863 was spent by him in patrolling the Mississippi with his vessels, preventing the rebels fortifying the bluffs or otherwise interrupting the free navigation of the Mississippi. During the spring months of the next year Admiral Porter was in command of the North Atlantic Blockading Squadron. This lengthy line of blockade extended from Wilmington to Cape Fear River.

It having been determined to try to silence the forts at the entrance to Cape Fear River, Admiral Porter set about the difficult task of subduing them. His squadron consisted of thirty-five vessels, holding nineteen more in reserve. After a fierce bombardment of little more than one hour he completely ruined them.

He and his fleet lent very effectual assistance to the army in the capture of Fort Fisher.

For his valuable services on this occasion Congress once more voted him thanks, this making four times that he had been publicly and officially thanked for his services by the representatives of his countrymen.

In July, 1866, Porter received his promotion to the rank of Vice-Admiral. At the same time he was also appointed head of the United States Naval Academy.

Soon after the election of General Grant to be President of the United States, Vice-Admiral Porter was given control of the Navy Department under the Secretary.

In August, 1870, David Dixon Porter reached the lofty rank of Admiral.

Admiral Porter has on more than one occasion actually commanded in service the largest fleets ever under the flag of any one of our officers.

Admiral David Dixon Porter is a little above average height, and of exceedingly powerful frame and wiry muscles. He was esteemed in his prime to be the strongest man in the navy.

Some years ago the Admiral was married to a daughter of Captain C. P. Paterson. He is the father of several children.

No less than four officers of the name of Porter participated in the late war, all relatives of the Admiral.

CPSIA information can be obtained at www.ICGtesting.com
Printed in the USA
BVOW06s0912091215

429838BV00029B/540/P